The Discourse of Police Interviews

The Discourse of Police Interviews

EDITED BY MARIANNE MASON
AND FRANCES ROCK

THE UNIVERSITY OF CHICAGO PRESS CHICAGO AND LONDON

The University of Chicago Press, Chicago 60637
The University of Chicago Press, Ltd., London

Published 2020
Printed in the United States of America

29 28 27 26 25 24 23 22 21 20   1 2 3 4 5

ISBN-13: 978-0-226-64765-4 (cloth)
ISBN-13: 978-0-226-64779-1 (paper)
ISBN-13: 978-0-226-64782-1 (e-book)
DOI: https://doi.org/10.7208/chicago/9780226647821.001.0001

Library of Congress Cataloging-in-Publication Data

Names: Mason, Marianne, editor. | Rock, Frances, 1974– editor.
Title: The discourse of police interviews / edited by Marianne Mason and Frances Rock.
Description: Chicago : The University of Chicago Press, 2020. | Includes index.
Identifiers: LCCN 2019018462 | ISBN 9780226647654 (cloth : alk. paper) | ISBN 9780226647791 (pbk. : alk. paper) | ISBN 9780226647821 (e-book)
Subjects: LCSH: Police questioning. | Reid technique. | Interviewing in law enforcement. | Criminal investigation—Language. | Forensic linguistics.
Classification: LCC HV8073.3.D57 2019 | DDC 363.25/4—dc23
LC record available at https://lccn.loc.gov/2019018462

♾ This paper meets the requirements of ANSI/NISO Z39.48–1992 (Permanence of Paper).

Contents

List of Conventions ix

CHAPTER 1. Introduction 1
Marianne Mason

SECTION I. The Discourse of Reid and PEACE

CHAPTER 2. When Police Interview Victims of Sexual Assault: Comparing Written Guidance to Interactional Practice 21
Elizabeth Stokoe, Charles Antaki, Emma Richardson, and Sara Willott

CHAPTER 3. Obtaining Valid Discourse from Suspects PEACE-fully: What Role for Rapport and Empathy? 42
Ray Bull and Bianca Baker

CHAPTER 4. The Guilt-Presumptive Nature of Custodial Interrogations in the United States: The Use of Confrontation, Appeals to Self-Interest, and Sympathy/Minimization in the Reid Technique 65
Marianne Mason

CHAPTER 5. The Discourse Structure of Blame Mitigation in a Police Interrogation 85
Philip Gaines

SECTION II. **Police Interview Dynamics and Negotiation**

CHAPTER 6. Now the Rest of the Story: The Collaborative Production of Confession Narratives in Police Interrogations 113
Gary C. David and James Trainum

CHAPTER 7. Patterns of Cooperation between Police Interviewers with Suspected Sex Offenders 136
Tatiana Tkacukova and Gavin E. Oxburgh

CHAPTER 8. Supporting Competing Narratives: A Membership Categorization Analysis of Identity Work in Police-Detainee Talk 156
David Yoong and Ayeshah Syed

SECTION III. **Discursive Transformations in Bilingual Police Interviews**

CHAPTER 9. Narrative Construction in Interpreted Police Interviews 179
Ikuko Nakane

CHAPTER 10. Interactional Management in a Simulated Police Interview: Interpreters' Strategies 200
Sandra Hale, Jane Goodman-Delahunty, and Natalie Martschuk

CHAPTER 11. Non-Native Speakers, Miranda Rights, and Custodial Interrogation 227
Bethany K. Dumas

SECTION IV. **The Discursive Journey and Institutional Applications of Police Interviews**

CHAPTER 12. "Tell Me in Your Own Words . . .": Reconciling Institutional Salience and Witness-Compatible Language in Police Interviews with Women Reporting Rape 249
Nicci MacLeod

CHAPTER 13. "Are You Saying You Were Stabbed . . . ?": Multimodality, Embodied Action, and Dramatized Formulations in "Fixing" the Facts in Police Interviews with Suspects 268
Alison Johnson

CHAPTER 14. Functions of Transmodal Metalanguage for Collaborative Writing in Police-Witness Interviews 299
Frances Rock

CHAPTER 15. Reconstructing Suspects' Stories in Various Police Record Styles 329
Tessa (T. C.) van Charldorp

CHAPTER 16. Police Records in Court: The Narrative Fore- and Backgrounding of Information by Judges in Inquisitorial Criminal Court 349
Fleur van der Houwen

Index 367

Conventions

Figures and tables are numbered according to chapter number and therein sequentially (e.g., fig. 13.1). Data excerpts and examples are numbered in the chapters, following the chapter number and beginning at "1" for each chapter (e.g., 1.1, 2.1, etc.).

Because transcription approaches for conversational data differ, the excerpts in some of the chapters of the volume vary from narrow to broad.

The following abbreviations for participants in data excerpts are used in the majority of the chapters:

Abbreviation	**Participant(s)**
D	Detective
F/M	Female/male interviewee
I/D	Indirect/direct speech
I	Interpreter
IE/Int	Interviewee (naive/lay)
Int#	Interview number
J	Judge
O	Officer
P	Police
PI/IR	Police interviewer

RS	Reported speech
SOL	Solicitor
S/Sus	Suspect
W	Witness

The following transcription conventions have been used (adapted from Jefferson 2004):

Symbol	**Description**
(.)	Micropause—a pause of no significant length
(0.7)	Timed pause—long enough to indicate a time
[ ]	Square brackets showing where speech overlaps
> <	Arrows showing that the pace of speech has quickened
< >	Arrows showing that the pace of the speech has slowed
( )	Unclear section
(( ))	Entry requiring comment but without a symbol to explain it
Underlining	Rise in volume or emphasis
↑	Rise in intonation
↓	Drop in intonation
,	Slightly rising intonation
?	Rising intonation
word?	Question mark shows emphatic upward intonation
word¿	Inverted question mark shows unemphatic upward intonation
word,	Comma shows continuing intonation
word.	Period shows terminal intonation
CAPITALS	Louder or shouted words

(h)	Laughter in the conversation/speech
=	Will be at the end of one sentence and the start of the next, indicating that there was no pause between them.
: : :	Colons indicating a stretched sound
-	Hyphen after a word or part of a word indicating a cut-off or self-interruption
£	"Smiley" voice
x	Sound of typing
°word°	Spoken more softly
Hhh	Exhalation or laughter
hh	Inhalation or laughter
Hah, heh, etc.	Laughter
→	Entered by the analyst to show a sentence of particular interest not usually added by the transcriber
((word))	Transcriber's note
(), (word)	Transcriber unable to hear or uncertain
— ‖	Reading/quoting tone
(guess)	Unclear fragment, best guess
(?)	Unintelligible fragment
{ }	Nonverbal feature
"Speech marks"	Words being read back from the statement
SMALL CAPITALS	Words being proposed
italics	Writing aloud
{. . . Italics . . .}	Writing aloud and its duration
boldface	Items of interest and for discussion

CHAPTER ONE

Introduction

Marianne Mason

> Wisdom is not acquired save as the result of investigation.
> —Sara Teasdale

The Discourse of Police Interviews

Language and the law/forensic linguistics (FL) is a growing field with an established research presence. To date, books on language and the law have predominantly ranged from those designed to introduce the field (e.g., Levi and Walker 1990; Gibbons 1994; Cotterill 2002; Olsson 2004; Kredens and Goźdź-Roszkowski 2007; Gibbons and Turell 2008); those aimed at summarizing (to a greater or lesser extent) the breadth, and applications, of the study of language and the law (e.g., Conley and O'Barr 1998; Tiersma 1999; Gibbons 2003; Coulthard and Johnson 2010); and those focused on one part or aspect of the legal system in greater detail (e.g., Conley and O'Barr 1990; Solan 1993; Komter 1998; Shuy 1998, 2005, 2014, 2017; Ehrlich 2001; Heydon 2005; Solan and Tiersma 2005; Maryns 2006; Rock 2007; Berk-Seligson 2009; Heffer, Rock, and Conley 2013; Ehrlich, Eades, and Ainsworth, 2016). *The Discourse of Police Interviews* aims to further the discussion by focusing exclusively on how police interviews are discursively constructed and institutionally used to investigate and prosecute crimes.

This volume examines leading debates, approaches, and topics in contemporary police interview research. Furthermore, the volume aims to promote dialogue not only between scholars who specialize in language and the law, but also among scholars in cognate disciplines, such as linguistic anthropology, criminology, law, and sociology, to name a few. To this end, the volume explores themes including the sociolegal, psychological, and discursive framework of popular police interview methods, such as PEACE and Reid, the role of the discursive practices of institutional representatives (e.g., police officers, interpreters) in bringing about (or not) linguistic transformations, and the impact that these transformations can have on the construction and evidential quality and value of linguistic evidence.[1]

Framing the Police Interview

The police interview is an essential component of "the construction of proof" (Baldwin 1993) in the investigation (and prosecution) of a crime. The process of "constructing proof" discursively has been examined through a myriad of research perspectives, ranging from institutional, psychological, ethnolinguistic, and metalinguistic. For the benefit of the reader, this section will frame the key concepts that are particularly relevant to, and addressed in, the chapters of this volume.

The Language of Institutions

Institutional talk is task related and involves at least one participant who represents a formal organization. As Drew and Heritage (1992) note this type of discourse is not determined by context alone but rather created through the interaction itself. A feature of creating institutional talk is the role of asymmetries of knowledge in interaction, such as those between professional and lay actors. Drew (1991) suggests that unequal distribution of knowledge is a source of asymmetry in institutional talk, or what Linell and Luckmann (1991) describe as "inequivalences" of knowledge between interactants. Linell and Luckmann put forth conditions for dialogue that may give rise to asymmetries, such as differences in rights to develop topics and differences between interactants regarding their knowledge of each other and their level of access to knowledge (1991: 5–6). In institutional settings, such as legal ones, these inequivalences may hinge on both individual and sociocultural factors:

> patterns of asymmetry or dominance are generated in actual social intercourse. Some of these patterns may be dependent on properties of individuals. . . , and some on roles tied to the professions, organizations, social strata, etc. It is important to emphasize that whether asymmetries or symmetries are actually found, these are not merely expression of individual intentions or motives. There are also social structures and traditions "speaking through actors." (Linell and Luckmann 1991: 9)

Asymmetries in discourse may also represent an interactant's dominance in an exchange (which mirrors society's institutional structures) and may include interactants' strive for mutuality in understanding. As Maynard eloquently notes, discourse asymmetry "may have an institutional mooring, but also an interactional bedrock, and the latter needs sociological appreciation as much as the former" (1991: 486).

Finding a suitable definition for institutional discourse that includes both interactional and (socio) institutional features, however, has been challenging. More contemporary approaches have focused on the relationship between the interactants in an attempt to put forth a definition that accurately describes the exchange. Thornborrow (2002), for example, argues that institutional discourse is perhaps best defined as a local phenomenon in which the relationship between a participant's current institutional role and his/her current discursive role "shapes the organisation and trajectory of the talk" (2002: 5). This definition of institutional discourse is also cautiously endorsed by Haworth (2006), who examined dynamics of asymmetries and power in police interviews.

Haworth argues that a working definition (and description) of institutional discourse needs to include "the interplay between the discursive and institutional roles of participants" (2006: 741), as well as their institutional identity and status. The latter also includes procedural and cognitive frameworks shared by institutional actors. This distinction is important since knowledge of legal principles and professional training/experience are traditionally within the domain of institutional, rather than lay actors. In custodial settings, as those examined in this volume, lay knowledge of institutional procedures is often not sufficient for lay persons to navigate successfully the procedural frameworks that may be applied to them.

Ethnolinguistics and Discursive Psychology

In addition to the social and institutional moorings of police interviews, ethnolinguistic and psychological factors also play a role in shaping the dynamics (and possible legal outcomes) of these types of exchanges. Research on police interviews that include non–native speakers of English, for example, has shown that interpreters (even professionally trained ones) make changes that may affect power negotiations between police and suspects (Berk-Seligson 2009; Nakane 2014). These changes, as Berk-Seligson (2009) finds, may also cross an ethical and legal line when police officers conduct interviews without using a professional interpreter; instead opting to act as both interpreters and interviewers. Other research in the field has shown that interpreters who possess professional and/or linguistic competency, but not a cultural understanding of the community for which they are interpreting may also have an impact on how the members of a community are treated in the justice system (Eades 1995). More recently, a group of researchers proposed a set of guidelines for the reading of the waiver/caution to non–native speakers of English (see Communication of Rights Group 2016). These guidelines state that to ensure the protection of individual rights and the integrity of an investigation factors such as, level of education, cognitive abilities, context, and wording used to invoke individual rights must be considered when questioning both native and, particularly, a special type of vulnerable population: non-native speakers of English.

Psychology as a discipline has also investigated extensively the police interview. This field has traditionally focused on practitioner-oriented analysis (Clarke and Milne 2001; Bull and Milne 2004), detection of deceit (Vrij, Mann, Kristen, and Fisher 2007), and confessions (Gudjonsson 2003). Much of the work in this field has been methodological and quantitative. The behavior of the interviewer and interviewee, rather than the interaction between the two, is the focus of most psychology based research on police interviews. Yet, research in discursive psychology has provided a more integrated approach in which "psychological themes such as motive and intent, agency and involvement, are managed as part of talk's business" (Edwards 2005: 262). The focus of this type of analysis is to examine how emotions, attitudes, and ideas are constructed in social interaction observed in talk (Billig 1999).

In police interviews, a discursive psychological approach may provide insights into how perceptions of blame or responsibility are manifested in police-layperson exchanges. A number of chapters in this volume examine popular interview methods, such as PEACE and Reid, that use (to different extents) psychological principles such as empathy, minimization, and/or coercion (e.g., Mason 2013, 2016) to establish rapport with, and obtain information from, the interviewee.

Reported Speech, the Police Report, and Its Institutional Applications

Reported speech (RS) is the practice of "reporting. . . the words of other people" (Stokoe and Edwards 2007: 338). In police interviews, interviewers may employ RS to reorient interviewees to earlier topics that the interviewer wishes to probe further. Some common strategies include interviewer's presenting alternatives to an interviewee's version of events, reformulating an interviewee's narrative in a more institutionally valuable way (Johnson 2008), and altering the interviewee's words to slightly, but significantly, change his or her narrative of events (Haworth 2015). With this process of reorientation, the interviewee's accounts may incur changes and transformations that potentially result in a skewed portrayal of events.

The reporting, or repeating/paraphrasing, of some verbiage which replays the prior interaction (Clift and Holt 2007) may also include multimodal cues (Matoesian and Gilbert 2018). Although emotions are widely studied in several disciplines, the interplay of different multimodal cues with linguistic cues is yet to be fully understood in actual conversation. Research on multimodality provides insights on the coordinated use of verbal expressions, prosodic cues, and embodied actions in everyday interactions. In police interviews, multimodal analysis has focused on how actions of settling on agreed evidential facts (such as blame allocation and moral evaluation) are accomplished through the coordination of the reported talk with bodily interaction such as posture, gesture, gaze, and the manipulation of objects. Gestures that accompany the reformulation of narrative facts in police interviews, for example, may dramatize the evidence and/or challenge the suspect's narrative.

The police interview may also undergo transformations in the journey from oral to textual production. The police report is a written rendition of an interviewee's story and an important institutional outcome of police interviews (e.g., Jönsson and Linell 1991; Haworth 2010). Research in the field has focused primarily on examining the transformations that occur in the writing of the police report, including the role of metalanguage, and the institutional applications of this type of discourse. With regard to discursive transformations, the police report may be written up as a summarized version of the talk in the record. The text may also become more formal and exclude side talk and other context of the interaction, such as how the police interview was interactionally negotiated and constructed. The police report, hence, is not simply the police officer's verbatim account of the interviewee's narrative during police questioning, but rather a type of negotiated, police-directed "storytelling."

The role of metalanguage in the rendition of a police report is also key to understanding the complexity of this type of discourse. Metalanguage examines how individual's "talk about talk" or what Maschler (1994) describes as the action of "metalanguaging." As Maschler notes, "at the same time that the speaker is languaging about the world, he/she is also communicating information about how the utterance is intended; i.e., the speaker is metalanguaging—using language to communicate information about languaging" (330). Maschler adds that metalanguaging involves contextual constraints, such as linguistic structure, interpersonal relations, and medium of interaction. The function of metalanguage is also a strategic one, in which speakers orient addressees to their explanations of the speakers' linguistic structures and intent. This process of directing and negotiating talk may result in linguistic transformations.

Olson (1991) notes that the analysis of oral metalanguage may be extended to writing. In police interviews, the textual transformations that occur between talk and text can be made explicit by metalanguage. The police officers' use of metalanguage, for example, can express their decisions about what to write when they produce a report for witnesses, victims, or suspects of a crime. Metalanguage, and meaning making, in the writing of the police report produces (and reproduces) power asymmetries between the police interviewer and interviewee. Furthermore, the interviewee's answers may be made to "fit" the police officer's written construction of events to conform to the institutional demands of the text, such as its evidentiary uses in court. The interview, hence, may be reproduced and recontextualized from the interview room to the courtroom: a type of discursive "travel." This is the case in countries such as the Netherlands where interviewees are normally not heard in court (e.g., van der Houwen and Sneijder 2014). The statements interviewees provide police officers (and the transformations that occur in the construction from talk to police report), as chapters in this volume explore, may be used instead as testimonial evidence to arrest and detain, prosecute, and, ultimately, obtain a conviction.

Overview of this Volume

The Discourse of Police Interviews is designed to provide the reader with a backstage view, if you will, of the discursive features and institutional applications of police interviews in various jurisdictions, such as in Australia, Belgium, the Netherlands, United Kingdom, and the United States. Throughout the volume, the authors who are leading researchers in the field, both established and up-and-coming, consider the discursive features of cases in which police officers conduct interviews. The chapters include a variety of examples and/or case studies that enable the reader to see police interviews in action.

The fifteen chapters of the volume (in addition to the introduction) are organized in four major sections that reflect the main themes of the volume:

Section I: The Discourse of Reid and PEACE

Section II: Police Interview Dynamics and Negotiation

Section III: Discursive Transformations in Bilingual Police Interviews

Section IV: The Discursive Journey and Institutional Applications of Police Interviews

Each section is composed of small collections of three to five chapters. These chapters are arranged according to broad topics that are, in turn, connected to the broader theme of police interview discourse. The main focus of each section is: the sociolegal, psychological, and discursive framework of police interview methods, specifically Reid and PEACE (section I), the role of interview dynamics, negotiation, and cooperation in (English) monolingual (section II) and bilingual (section III) settings, and the construction and evidential quality and value of linguistic evidence (section IV). The selection of topics within sections is for the benefit of the reader who may be searching for a particular area of research within the broader theme of the volume.

Section I: The Discourse of Reid and PEACE

The first section initiates the discussion by introducing the reader to the sociostructural framework of police interviews. This section explores the institutional and interactional bedrock of police interview methods commonly used in the United States and United Kingdom: Reid and PEACE. Stokoe, Antaki, Richardson, and Willott's chapter starts the discussion on PEACE. They examine the challenges of reconciling recommended PEACE guidelines, particularly the effectiveness of rapport building, with social and contextual challenges that may arise in interviews with lay persons who are potentially vulnerable, such as minors, victims of sexual assault, and those who suffer from a mental disability or disorder. Bull and Baker's chapter also discusses PEACE but takes on a more psychological approach. They focus on the relationship between the development and maintenance of rapport (an essential component of PEACE) and effective noncoercive interviews. They discuss the role of rapport building in reducing the interviewee's anxiety, anger, or distress, while increasing the likelihood of obtaining more complete and reliable information during a police interview.

The Reid technique (Inbau, Reid, Buckley, and Jayne 2005), which is the dominant police interview method in the United States, is the focus of Mason's and Gaines's chapters. In Reid, the main goal of the police interview is to determine the suspect's guilt or innocence, focusing on the suspect's (presumed) possibility of guilt. This particular aspect of Reid is explored in Mason's chapter. She examines how the Reid technique is used in police-suspect exchanges, looking primarily at three key aspects of the interview: the sympathetic detective/minimization strategy, confronting the suspect with evidence of guilt, and appealing to the suspect's self-interest. Mason shows how these three (common) strategies further Reid's "guilt-presumptive" goals, since they may be used, with varying degrees of effectiveness, to take a suspect's "innocence off the table."

Gaines's chapter also examines the use of the Reid technique, yet he focuses on the psychodiscursive framework of the method. He looks at two key discursive and psychological components of Reid: blame maximization and, in particular, blame mitigation. Gaines notes that the techniques of maximization and minimization are complementary approaches that lead the suspect to a psychological state in which confessing is seen as the only means to end a coercive interrogation. Gaines demonstrates the value of a discourse analytic approach to understanding how police interviewers in the United States perform the work of admission extraction using the Reid technique.

Section II: Police Interview Dynamics and Negotiation

The second section of the volume focuses on the use of discursive categorization to analyze the dynamics and cooperation patterns of police interviews. The chapters in this section examine the institutional and discursive practices of police interviews and the potential social and legal connotations of negotiation and cooperation in this type of discourse. The authors in this section also provide further insights into possible solutions (or remedies) to minimize outcomes, such as coercive or unempathic interviewing practices in interviews featuring suspects, (vulnerable) victims, and witnesses of a crime.

David and Trainum's chapter starts the section by examining police officers' and suspect's coconstruction of the suspect's narrative accounts of a crime during police interviewing. They discuss how police officers may use their position as interviewers to provide prompts and feedback that help shape the story being communicated by the accused. The resulting confession, although might be ascribed to a suspect, is shown to be the product of a discursive collaboration between the suspect and police. Tkacukova and Oxburgh's chapter also looks at police-layperson discursive dynamics but with interactions that feature two interviewers. Tkacukova and Oxburgh note that in the United Kingdom the official guidelines on cooperation between the interviewers are vague, and it is up to individual officers how to manage the interview and each officer's level (and type) of cooperation during the interview. This may result in lack of preparation and/or critical thinking, which may compromise the police interview.

Interview dynamics in police-suspect exchanges is also examined in Yoong and Syed's chapter. This chapter provides a unique perspective because the interaction involves a dispute between a police officer and a detainee whose professional identity as a politician carries considerable power. The authors show how in these types of interactions both the interviewer and detainee create, use, and interpret cultural and societal categories with the goal of organizing "social orders" and actions through talk.

Section III: Discursive Transformations in Bilingual Police Interviews

The third section of the volume, as the previous one, examines the interview dynamics of cooperation and negotiation within the institutional construction of police-suspect exchanges, but with the added caveat that the interactants are not proficient in each other's native languages. In these types of exchanges, the suspect is not proficient in, for example, English and the police officer is not proficient in the suspect's first language. These scenarios which have become increasingly more common have added two possible elements to the police interview: the ("bilingual") police officer acting as interviewer and interpreter and the use of a legal interpreter to linguistically mediate the exchange.

The analysis of this type of discourse parts from the connection between ethnography and language use in legal settings. To this aim, the chapters in this section look at (and propose recommendations for) three sociocultural and interactional features of bilingual police-layperson exchanges: narrative construction in police interviews, non–native speakers' invocation of Miranda during police interviews, and interactional management in police interviews.

Nakane's chapter opens the discussion by examining the impact of interpreter mediation on the construction of narratives in police interviews. She focuses her analysis on turn taking, questioning strategies and resistance strategies in triadic interaction, and the importance of maintaining pragmatic equivalence of force and quality. Nakane stresses the need for police investigators to be made aware of the challenges that may arise in interpreter mediated police interviews, specifically the interpreter's effect on turn-taking, resolution of repair sequences (interruptions), control of the exchanges, and accurate delivery of meaning and intent.

Hale, Goodman-Delahunty, and Martschuk's chapter also explores interpreter mediated police interviews, yet they apply an empirical approach to the analysis of simulated police interviews to study the performance of trained versus untrained interpreters. The authors stress that most past empirical studies have focused on trained and untrained interpreters' accuracy of propositional content. They argue that little is known about the relative skill of these two groups regarding two key performance tasks: the management and coordination of turn-taking and their compliance with ethical protocols.

The final chapter of the section looks at a different challenge in bilingual police encounters: non–native speakers of English and the invocation of Miranda rights. Dumas's chapter examines three cases in which the police officers served as interpreters (when needed) in order to ascertain whether the suspects' English proficiency was sufficient for them to understand the entirety of their Miranda rights, including the right to counsel. Dumas discusses how suspects, who police officers deem to have adequate comprehension of Miranda, may experience misunderstanding and confusion about the meaning and intent of the waiver, which in turn may affect the type and quality of information provided during police questioning.

Section IV: The Discursive Journey and Institutional Applications of Police Interviews

Section IV examines the discursive journey of police interviews and the institutional uses of this type of discourse. The section opens with Macleod's chapter. She describes how interviewers' reporting of an interviewee's speech can be used for audience design and to fix meaning and establish institutional salience with "significant witnesses." As Macleod discusses, these types of witnesses include the victims themselves, those who have an immediate relationship with the event in question, and those who have a relationship with the victim. Macleod's chapter explores how formulation, reflexivity, and reported speech are sites in which interviewers may draw upon to accomplish institutional goals.

The role of reported speech in police interviews is also examined in Johnson's chapter. She discusses how police interviewers engage suspects in forensic questioning with the objective to transform the "facts" or events of a criminal case from unsettled to settled. Johnson focuses on police interviewers' use of questions such as "Are you saying X?" which she argues challenge suspects to accept a summarized police version of events. In her chapter, Johnson also addresses how actions of settling on agreed evidential facts are accomplished through the coordination of the reported talk with bodily interaction that may challenge, contest and undermine the suspect's narrative.

The next three chapters of section IV examine the construction and institutional uses of the police record. Rock's chapter starts the discussion by examining the relationships between talk and text which develop in police interviews. The chapter shows how in police interviews the textual transformation process involved can be made explicit by metalanguage. The chapter looks at the use of metalanguage in a case study with multiple interviews in which a police officer's literacy practices in interviewing were somewhat distinctive in consistently making text production processes explicit to witnesses.

Van Charldorp's and van der Houwen's chapters also explore the discursive features of reported speech, such as the construction of the police record, in addition to its evidentiary uses in court. Van Charldrop's chapter examines the transformations that take place when an interview is written into the police record. She provides an overview of the three different police record styles (the monologue, recontextualized, and question-answer) that are often found in police records in the Netherlands and Belgium. In her chapter, she reflects on how the suspects' spoken stories are transformed within these particular styles. She notes that the styles in which the police records are written up contribute to how accurate, formal, and institutionalized the suspect's story becomes.

The findings of van Charldrop's analysis are particularly significant because of the institutional role the police record plays in the litigation of a case. In the Netherlands, for example, a police record can be one of two pieces of evidence needed to convict a suspect of a crime. The officer's construction of the suspect's narrative, if it does not reflect closely the suspect's own words, may affect how readers of a document, such as judges, and its audience evaluate a suspect's statements to police. How police interviews are reproduced and recontextualized in the courtroom is further explored in van der Houwen's chapter.

In the Netherlands, judges have the task to "find the truth" and investigate the legal validity of the prosecutor's claims. Van der Houwen focuses her discussion on the type of information on the record judges report in the courtroom. For van der Houwen, the manner in which information is reported or summarized from the case file has implications for what is designated as more or less "important" (or fore- or backgrounded information). How judges report a suspect's story to the court, hence, may implicate the suspect to a greater (or lesser) extent, which may affect his or her legal fate.

Concluding Remarks

The Discourse of Police Interviews will be part of a continuum of study of legal discourse and, in particular, policing discourse. This volume situates the police interview as part of a complex, and multistage, criminal justice process. One of its main contributions is to show how the police interview is shaped and constructed discursively. The findings of the chapters in this volume, hence, should be of interest to academics and practitioners in a variety of fields in which discursive practices reflect socioinstitutional understandings and knowledge. The volume is also designed to serve a wider purpose in showing the possible real-world applications of forensic linguistic research.

Furthermore, the volume highlights the need for more collaborative research in police interview analysis not only among established fields (e.g., criminology, psychology, law, and linguistics) but also across jurisdictions. To this aim, the chapters of this volume present suggestions for future research including, but not limited to (1) understanding the role and uses of Reid and PEACE in our times; (2) examining the discursive practices, and legal implications, of police interviews with vulnerable persons; (3) exploring the areas in which psychology and policing discourse intersect; (4) delving further into the role of metalanguage, reflexivity and bodily actions in the negotiation of linguistic footing in police interviews; and (5) analyzing the construction and evidentiary uses of the police record. Moreover, as this volume puts forth, the complexity of this type of discourse, the legal system's reliance on written interview records (often a summary) over audio or audiovisual recordings, and the legal applications (and implications for laypersons) of police interviews also require an in-depth discussion of the need for (across-the-board) video recording of police interviews. This volume, hence, hopes to inspire future investigation into what makes police interviews such an important linguistic, legal, and sociocultural concern.

Note

1. PEACE stands for:

    Planning and Preparation
    Engage and Explain
    Account, Clarification, and Challenge
    Closure
    Evaluation

References

Baldwin, John. 1993. "Police Interview Techniques: Establishing Truth or Proof?" *British Journal of Criminology* 33(3): 325–352.

Berk-Seligson, Susan. 2009. *Coerced Confessions: The Discourse of Bilingual Police Interrogations*. Berlin: Mouton de Gruyter.

Billig, Michael. 1999. *Freudian Repression: Conversation Creating the Unconscious*. Cambridge: Cambridge University Press.

Bull, Ray, and Rebecca Milne. 2004. "Attempts to Improve the Police Interviewing of Suspects." In *Interrogations, Confessions, and Entrapment*, edited by G. Daniel Lassiter, 181–196. New York: Plenum.

Clarke, Colin, and Rebecca Milne. 2001. *National Evaluation of the PEACE Investigative Interviewing Course*. Police Research Award Scheme. London: Home Office.

Clift, Rebecca, and Elizabeth J. Holt, eds. 2007. *Reporting Talk. Reported Speech in Interaction*. Studies in Interactional Sociolinguistics 24. Cambridge: Cambridge University Press.

Communication of Rights Group. 2016. Guidelines for Communicating Rights to Non-Native Speakers of English in Australia, England and Wales, and the USA. http://www.aaal.org/?page=CommunicationRights.

Conley, John M., and William M. O'Barr. 1990. *Rules versus Relationships: The Ethnography of Legal Discourse*. Chicago: University of Chicago Press.

Conley, John M., and William M. O'Barr. 1998. *Just Words: Law, Language and Power*. Chicago: University of Chicago Press.

Cotterill, Janet, ed. 2002. *Language in the Legal Process*. Basingstoke: Palgrave Macmillan.

Coulthard, Malcolm, and Alison Johnson, eds. 2010. *The Routledge Handbook of Forensic Linguistics*. Oxford: Routledge.

Drew, Paul. 1991. "Asymmetries of Knowledge in Conversational Interactions." In *Asymmetries in Dialogue*, edited by Ivana Markova and Klaus Foppa, 21–48. Hemel Hempstead: Harvester Wheatsheaf.

Drew, Paul, and John Heritage. 1992. "Analysing Talk at Work." In *Talk at Work: Interaction in Institutional Settings*, edited by Paul Drew and John Heritage, 3–65. Cambridge: Cambridge University Press.

Eades, Diana. 1995. *Language in Evidence: Issues Confronting Aboriginal and Multicultural Australia*. Sydney: University of New South Wales Press.

Edwards, Derek. 2005. "Discursive Psychology." In *Handbook of Language and Social Interaction*, edited by Kristine L. Fitch and Robert E. Sanders, 257–273. Mahwah, NJ: Lawrence Erlbaum Associates.

Ehrlich, Susan. 2001. *Representing Rape: Language and Sexual Consent*. London and New York: Routledge.

Ehrlich, Susan, Diana Eades, and Janet Ainsworth, eds. 2016. *Discursive Constructions of Consent in the Legal Process*. Oxford: Oxford University Press.

Gibbons, John, ed. 1994. *Language and the Law*. London: Longman.

Gibbons, John. 2003. *Forensic Linguistics: An Introduction to Language in the Justice System*. Malden, MA: Blackwell.

Gibbons, John, and M. Teresa Turell, eds. 2008. *Dimensions of Forensic Linguistics*. Amsterdam: John Benjamins.

Gudjonsson, Gisli H. 2003. *The Psychology of Interrogations and Confessions*. New York: John Wiley.

Haworth, Kate. 2006. "The Dynamics of Power and Resistance in Police Interview Discourse." *Discourse and Society* 17(6): 739–759.

Haworth, Kate. 2010. "Police Interviews in the Judicial Process: Police Interviews as Evidence." In *Routledge Handbook of Forensic Linguistics*, edited by Malcolm Coulthard and Alison Johnson, 169–94. Abingdon: Routledge.

Haworth, Kate. 2015. "The Discursive Construction of Evidence in Police Interviews: Case Study of a Rape Suspect." *Applied Linguistics* 38(2): 194–214.

Heffer, Chris, Frances Rock, and John Conley, eds. 2013. *Legal-Lay Communication: Textual Travels in the Law*. Oxford: Oxford University Press.

Heydon, Georgina. 2005. *The Language of Police Interviewing: A Critical Analysis*. Basingstoke: Palgrave Macmillan.

Inbau, Fred E., John E. Reid, Joseph P. Buckley, and Brian C. Jayne. 2005. *Criminal Interrogation and Confessions: Essentials of the Reid Technique*. 1st ed. Sudbury, MA: Jones & Bartlett.

Johnson, Alison. 2008. "From Where We're Sat . . .": Negotiating Narrative Transformation through Interaction in Police Interviews with Suspects." In "Narrative Analysis in the Shift from Texts to Practices," edited by Anna De Fina and Alexandra Georgakopoulou. Special issue, *Text and Talk* 28(3): 327–349.

Jönsson, Linda, and Per Linell. 1991. "Story Generations: From Dialogical Interviews to Written Reports in Police Interrogations." *Text* 11(3), 419–440.

Komter, Martha. 1998. *Dilemmas in the Courtroom: A Study of Trials of Violent Crime in the Netherlands*. Mahwah, NJ: Lawrence Erlbaum Associates.

Kredens, Krzysztof, and Stanisław Goźdź-Roszkowski. 2007. *Language and the Law: International Outlooks*. Frankfurt am Main: Peter Lang.

Levi, Judith N., and Anne G. Walker, eds. 1990. *Language in the Judicial Process*. New York: Plenum Press.

Linell, Per, and Thomas Luckmann. 1991. "Asymmetries in Dialogue: Some Conceptual Preliminaries." In *Asymmetries in Dialogue*, edited by Ivana Marková and Klaus Foppa, 1–20. New York: Harvester Wheatsheaf.

Maryns, Katrijn. 2006. *The Asylum Speaker: Language in the Belgian Asylum Procedure*. Manchester: St Jerome.

Maschler, Yael. 1994. "Metalanguaging and Discourse Markers in Bilingual Conversation." *Language in Society* 23(3): 325–366.

Mason, Marianne. 2013. "Can I Get a Lawyer? A Suspect's Use of Indirect Requests in a Custodial Setting." *International Journal of Speech, Language, and the Law* 20(2): 203–227.

Mason, Marianne. 2016. "The 'Preparatory' and 'Argumentation' Stages of Police Interrogation: A Linguistic Analysis of a Criminal Investigation." *Language & Communication* 48: 79–87.

Matoesian, Gregory, and Kristin Enola Gilbert. 2018. *Multimodal Conduct in the Law: Language, Gesture and Materiality in Legal Interaction.* Cambridge: Cambridge University Press.

Maynard, Douglas. 1991. "Interaction and Asymmetry in Clinical Discourse." *American Journal of Sociology* 97(2): 448–495.

Nakane, Ikuko. 2014. *Interpreter-Mediated Police Interviews: A Discourse-Pragmatic Approach.* London: Palgrave Macmillan.

Olson, David. 1991. "Literacy as Metalinguistics." In *Literacy and Orality*, edited by David Olson and Nancy Torrance, 251–270. Cambridge: Cambridge University Press.

Olsson, John. 2004. *Forensic Linguistics: An Introduction to Language, Crime and the Law.* London: Continuum.

Rock, Frances. 2007. *Communicating Rights: The Language of Arrest and Detention.* Basingstoke and New York: Palgrave Macmillan.

Shuy, Roger W. 1998. *The Language of Confession, Interrogation, and Deception.* Thousand Oaks, CA: Sage.

Shuy, Roger W. 2005. *Creating Language Crimes: How Law Enforcement Uses (and Misuses) Language.* Oxford: Oxford University Press.

Shuy, Roger W. 2014. *The Language of Murder Cases: Intentionality, Predisposition, and Voluntariness.* Oxford: Oxford University Press.

Shuy, Roger W. 2017. *Deceptive Ambiguity by Police and Prosecutor.* Oxford: Oxford University Press.

Solan, Lawrence M. 1993. *The Language of Judges.* Chicago: University of Chicago Press.

Solan, Lawrence M., and Peter M. Tiersma. 2005. *Speaking of Crime: The Language of Criminal Justice.* Chicago: University of Chicago Press.

Stokoe, Elizabeth, and Derek Edwards. 2007. "'Black This, Black That': Racial Insults and Reported Speech in Neighbour Complaints and Police Interrogations." *Discourse & Society* 18(3): 337–372.

Thornborrow, Joanna. 2002. *Power Talk: Language and Interaction in Institutional Discourse.* Harlow: Longman.

Tiersma, Peter M. 1999. *Legal Language.* Chicago: University of Chicago Press.

van der Houwen, Fleur, and Petra Sneijder. 2014. "From Text to Talk in Criminal Court: Prosecuting, Defending, and Examining the Evidence." In "Quoting from the Case File: Intertextuality in Judicial Settings," edited by Sigurd D'Hondt and Fleur van der Houwen. Special issue, *Language & Communication* 6: 37–52.

Vrij, Aldert, Samantha Mann, Susanne Kristen, and Ronald P. Fisher. 2007. "Cues to Deception and Ability to Detect Lies as a Function of Police Interview Styles." *Law and Human Behavior* 31(5): 499–518.

SECTION I

The Discourse of Reid and PEACE

CHAPTER TWO

When Police Interview Victims of Sexual Assault

Comparing Written Guidance to Interactional Practice

Elizabeth Stokoe, Charles Antaki, Emma Richardson, and Sara Willott

Introduction

When police officers formally interview suspects, witnesses and victims, their conduct comes under a legal framework designed to ensure two things: forensic usefulness in detecting a crime, and legal acceptability of the evidence produced in court. The former is meant to make the interview questions helpful in determining whether a crime has been committed, and to identify the offender. The latter is meant to ensure that the information obtained at interview be solicited in a matter that abides by relevant legislation (in the UK, the Police and Criminal Evidence act 1984; and at a more general level, the Equality Act, 2010, and the Human Rights Act, 1998). It needs also to be of sufficient quality to persuade the competent authority (in the UK, the Crown Prosecution Service) to charge a suspect, and, if the case gets there, to stand up in court.

Since the introduction in the UK of the Police and Criminal Evidence Act (usually referred to by its initials as PACE), various local and national efforts have been made to help turn the formal language of the Act and its Codes (secondary legislation for the Act's provisions) into practical recommendations that officers can follow. Of these, the most widely authoritative are the Ministry of Justice's UK-wide guidelines, *Achieving Best Evidence in Criminal Proceedings: Guidance on Interviewing Victims and Witnesses, and Guidance on Using Special Measures* (UK Ministry of Justice 2011), and the College of Policing's documentation of authorized professional practices (College of Policing n.d.), which sets standards of practical police work in England and Wales. Those documents give extensive guidelines and detailed recommendations on interviewing that expand on the drier legal statute.

Such guidelines feed into the training that police officers receive. Like other professionals, police are trained to communicate with the people they encounter as part of their working lives. Much police training focuses on how to interview suspects, witnesses, and victims, and there is a long tradition of research that underpins interview techniques. Less attention is paid to whether or not police align with this training. Research shows that training fails, but very often all the work is based on post hoc evidence, so we don't know what actually happens in police interviews as they are carried out in real time. This is especially true of what happens in police interviews with people with intellectual disabilities (ID), for which there is a marked paucity of evidence comparing guidelines with actual practice.

It might be argued that such research is especially urgent given that people with intellectual disabilities are more likely to be sexually abused (McEachern 2012) and sexually assaulted (Petersilia 2001) than people without such disabilities. They are likely in consequence to suffer "marked increases in the frequency and severity of emotional, physiological and behavioural symptoms of psychological distress" (Rowsell, Clare, and Murphy 2013: 257). For those few who bring a complaint (Brown et al. 1995, for example, estimate that this is only 6 percent of those actually abused), the legal process can cause them emotional and psychological distress as they relive the incident. By definition (either via the *Diagnostic and Statistical Manual of Mental Disorders* [*DSM*] or the more global *International Classification of Diseases* [*ICD*]), a person with intellectual disabilities is deficient in mental capacity in terms of language, memory, and comprehension, and impaired in their ability to make social judgments, empathize, and understand others' points of view. So in an interview, the person with ID will face problems of comprehension and expression over and above those faced by people with typical mental capacity. That makes it still more important for interviewers to follow guidelines that seek to minimize the difficulties for the interviewee.

The aim of this chapter, then, is to consider the formalized communication guidance for interviewing victims, particularly vulnerable adult victims, and compare this guidance to what actually happens in live, unfolding interviews between these victims and police officers. It will be important to note that the police interviewers will be conscious of a potential conflict between some of the guidelines on rapport and questioning and the overriding forensic objectives of this interview: to provide evidence that a crime has taken place, to make sure that the perpetrator is identifiable, and to determine that the witness's account will stand up in court.

Legal and Institutional Codes of Practice

Achieving Best Evidence in Criminal Proceedings (UK Ministry of Justice 2011; hereafter referred to as *ABE*), is the document that provides formal guidance on interviewing victims and witnesses, including guidance for child victims and vulnerable adults ("those who have a mental disorder, learning disability or physical disorder/disability that is likely to have an impact on the quality of their evidence"). Its terms are further elaborated in the College of Policing's documentation of authorized professional practices (hereafter referred to as *APP*). Both sets of guidelines contain much legal and procedural detail (e.g., issues of consent, the duration and location of the interview, how it is to be recorded, etc.), but our focus is particularly on the guidance given for the conduct of the interview as a communicative exchange. The key issue we shall be considering is the way in which the police officers manage the difficulties that emerge from following one of the basic principles of the process: establishing an environment of trust, confidence, and rapport, as indicated by this foundational principle in *ABE*:

> The lead interviewer should be a person who has established or is likely to be able to establish rapport with the witness, who understands how to communicate effectively with witnesses who might become distressed, and who has a proper grasp of the rules of evidence and criminal offences. (54).

This is echoed in the College of Policing principles:

> Investigators must act fairly when questioning victims, witnesses or suspects. They must ensure that they comply with all the provisions and duties under the Equality Act 2010 and the Human Rights Act 1998.
>
> Acting fairly means that the investigator must not approach any interview with prejudice. The interviewer should be prepared to believe the account that they are being given. . . .
>
> People with clear or perceived vulnerabilities should be treated with particular care, and extra safeguards should be put in place. (Principle 2)

In this chapter, we shall distill evidence from our empirical research (see Antaki et al. 2015a, 2015b, and 2015c) to examine how officers actually employ the *ABE* and the College of Policing's *APP* guidelines as they establish rapport while at the same time realizing the forensic objectives that are their prime institutional targets.

Data and Method

Access to such sensitive data as interviews between police officers and complainants alleging sexual assault is (quite properly) not easily given, so we are very grateful to a certain police force in England, which will remain anonymous. Local force personnel selected 20 videotapes of interviews from archived cases (that is, cases that were no longer under investigation) involving complainants with intellectual disabilities. Interviews lasting between 21 minutes and just over two hours were recorded between 2010 and 2013 by trained officers. In order for us to use the tapes for research, police had them visually and aurally anonymized before they left the station. We excluded from analysis one tape that was incomplete. Of the 19 cases remaining, ten dealt with alleged rape and the rest with sexual assault. Internal evidence from the tapes showed that two of the complainants were children under 16 (a boy and a girl); 14 were young women; one was a mature woman; and two were men (one young and one in early middle age). All had some kind of what the police called "learning disability," but the case files were very variable in specifying the interviewee's specific diagnosis. Three of the cases led to a court case, and two of these resulted in a guilty verdict; the other 17 led to no further action. These proportions are in line with figures on charges and convictions of sexual assault in the UK nationally.

Description of the Environment of the Interview

The general procedure followed by the police in this force (and nationally) is that once a case is brought to their attention, basic details of the alleged offense are recorded, an officer is assigned to the case, and the alleged victim is invited for interview. Before this interview, the officer may or may not investigate the matter further. If the complainant is thought to have an intellectual disability, steps may be taken to identify its nature (for example, by consultation with educational, medical, or social work authorities). In the cases to which we were allowed access, such information was recorded and appeared on the cover of the case file only in sketchy form (for example, a complainant might be recorded as having "learning disabilities," with no further details).

On the day of the interview, at the station, the complainant (and, as mandated by PACE, any accompanying "appropriate adult," who may be a friend or relative, caregiver, social worker, or other professional) is met by the assigned officer. Before the interview proper there will be a short, neutral preliminary conversation which normally serves as an opportunity for the officer to inform the interviewee that the upcoming discussion is an official one that will be recorded for use in court, should the matter proceed. The complainant and the accompanying adult are then shown the layout of the interview room and the observation room, and the cameras are pointed out and explained. The companion may remain present in the interview room but will take no part in the conversation.

The interview then proceeds along the PEACE model, which, in the UK, although not mandatory, is generally taken to be the ideal format of the interview process. The name is an acronym of *P*lanning and preparation; *E*ngage and explain; *A*ccount clarification and challenge; *C*losure; and *E*valuation. Figure 2.1 illustrates the chronology of these phases.

Our concern in the analysis reported in this chapter was to capture the exact interchange between interviewer and interviewee in the "take and develop account" sequence within the Account Clarification and Challenge stage of PEACE. It is in the details that we shall see the kind of behavior that neither role playing nor retrospective interviewing can bring

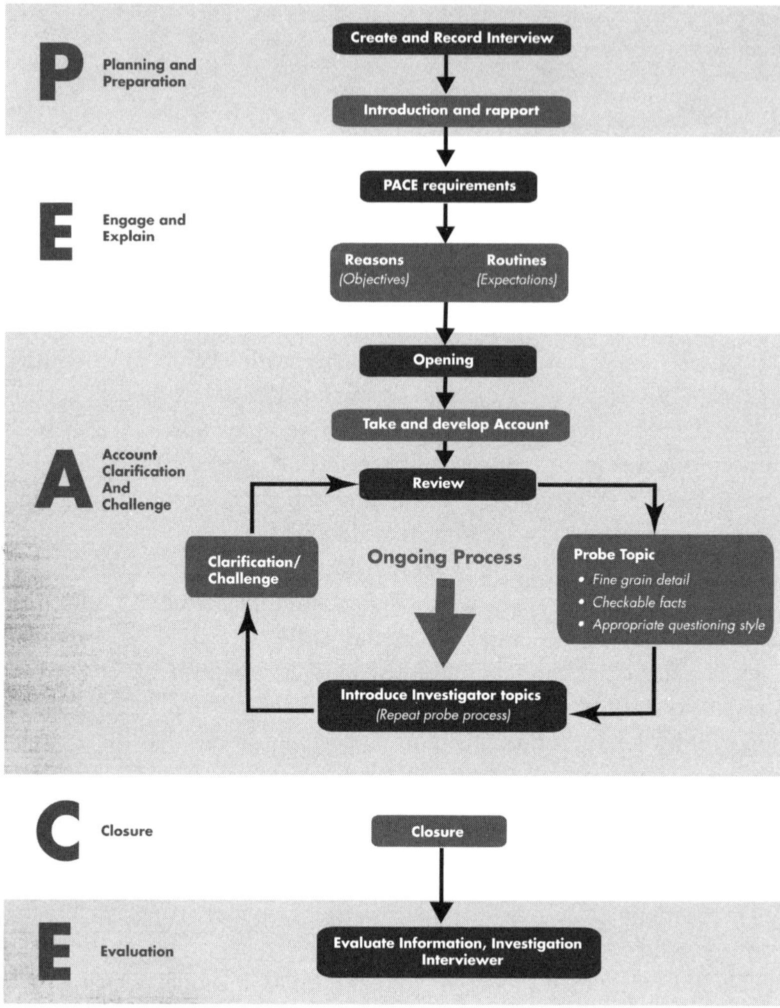

FIGURE 2.1. The PEACE model of police interviewing

to light (for a general discussion of this issue see Stokoe 2013). The particular methodology that we shall use is conversation analysis (CA) (for a comprehensive overview, see Sidnell and Stivers 2012), which, building on a base established in ordinary conversation, has been used extensively in research on how practitioners deliver their services in a wide variety of environments (for an overview of applied conversation analysis, see Antaki 2011). This particular data set is comparatively unusual in that the practitioner (the police officer) has a specific, legally oriented set of interview mandates and recommendations to refer to as a guide to their conduct. More typically, interviewers (for example, welfare benefit officers [Toerien et al. 2013] or help-line call takers [Hepburn and Potter 2011; Butler et al. 2010]) either do not have official interview practice guidelines or only have local recommendations for establishing good relations with the interviewee. Police officers have more formally mandated and, as we shall see, potentially overriding objectives.

Analysis

Our analysis will concentrate on the fundamental dilemma in what the police interviewer must achieve in his or her interview, which is deeply embedded in the twin objectives of *ABE* and the national police *APP* guidelines. On the one hand, the interviewer must build rapport with the complainant; on the other, they must subject what the interviewee says to impartial forensic testing. In the sections below we report separately on the design of empathic responses (and their absence) and the design of probing, challenging questions that hint at contradictions—or worse—in the interviewees' account.

Building Rapport versus Being Impartial

For the successful outcome of the interview, it is thought important by *ABE* and in the *APP* guidelines that rapport be established with the interviewee—indeed, the ABE guidelines mandate that this be done "to communicate empathy." This excerpt from the guidelines gives a clear instruction:

> H.2.2.6: A guiding principle for developing rapport is to communicate empathy. Here the interviewer needs to demonstrate a willingness to try to understand the situation from the witness's perspective. Some witnesses may be unhappy or feel shame or resentment about being questioned, especially on personal matters. In the rapport phase, and throughout the interview, the interviewer should convey to the witness that they have respect and sympathy for how the witness feels. (*ABE*, Appendix H)

And in the *APP*:

> Witness Interviews. Interviews are a means by which an investigator can both obtain and impart information. Many witnesses fear the consequences of providing information. They, therefore, need to be confident that the investigator will deal with the information they provide appropriately. (Section 3)

The building of rapport and the communication of empathy is not merely for its own sake, but rather to aid in the production of usable evidence:

> 3.1 The basic goal of an interview with a witness is to obtain an accurate and reliable account in a way which is fair, is in the witness's interests and is acceptable to the court. (*ABE*, 68)

and

> If the investigator establishes trust with the interviewee beforehand, they are more likely to give a full and accurate account. (*APP*, Section 3)

The other horn of the dilemma for the interviewer is that the evidence be "acceptable to the court." *ABE* mandates the interviewer to ensure that it has been gathered fairly and impartially, without prejudice and in "in the witnesses' interest": it ought to be free of any taint that it was acquired under any interviewer influence. The acceptability of evidence to the court will be one of the key principles in deciding whether a case is brought against a suspect, should matters proceed that far.

Let us consider a case where the interviewer has a choice to make between, on the one hand, giving an empathic response, and, on the other hand, withholding it in order not to seem to be, as it were, siding with the interviewee's perspective on what allegedly happened. Consider the excerpt below.

Excerpt 2.1: Interview 9, line 157 ("Scared")

P: How many other times did he touch your boo:bs.
(0.8)
F: That's the only time he's done it.
P: °'kay °. (.) <which was about three years ago.
F: yeah.

(0.7)
P: How did that make you fee:l¿ (name).
(1.5)
F: Scared.
(1.0)
P: °'kay:[h°,
F: [I din't say anything to anybody¿
P: Right.
(1.0)
P: And when was the first time you told anybody
about it.

What is notable is that at line 9 the interviewee describes herself as having been "scared"—a state that would, in everyday interaction, usually require some sort of acknowledgment by the listener of the distress and negativity implied; as conversation analysis has consistently shown, such announcements project news receipts that display the hearer's understanding. However, the interviewer treats it clinically, with a very unemphatic, abbreviated "okay." This is quite different to the kind of emphatic response one might see in everyday situations among peers, where the premium is not only on a clear empathic assessment of the others' emotions, but on its being provided as soon as it is recognizable, even before it has been explicitly articulated.

Compare the excerpt above with, for example, this exchange from Hepburn and Potter (2012).

Excerpt 2.2 (From Hepburn and Potter 2012: 201–202, notation slightly simplified; note that the # sign in line 6 indicates "creaky voice")

Ker: Bit of a loose and?=Did you have a lot've
time off=or:
(2.0)
Jil: N::uh.
(1.4)
→Ker: #O:aw::,=a'y'hev'n a hard ti:me,

Kerry indicates a high degree of monitoring of her friend's state of mind by diagnosing Jill's "nuh" (spoken with creaky voice) as being an unhappy one and offers what comes across as a warmly sympathetic encouragement to Jill to expand on her troubles. This kind of early, emotion-laden empathic response was wholly lacking in our data. The closest that anything comes to it is a businesslike receipt moderated by some effort at rapport maintenance, as is seen in the next excerpt.

Excerpt 2.3: Interview 3 ("Pinned me up against the wall")

F: I went into the bathroom to go to the toilet
and that's when he followed me in.
(0.6)
P: Okay. An' what happened when he's followed
you in.
(0.4)
F: (he pih-) ((*gulps and sobs*))
P: I know it's really difficult, [I know-
F: [((*wails*))
P: I know you're struggling to [talk about it.]
F: [*gulps*]
F: ((*sobs*))
(1.3)
F: ~He pinned me up the wall and ra:ped me~.
((*wails for 2 secs*))
P: °Okay°.
(3.5)

At lines 8 and 10, the police interviewer does orient to the emotional tone of the interviewee's account (she is gulping and sobbing as she recounts the exact moment that she was raped)—but note that she does so not by sympathizing but by empathizing. The difference is that the latter need only show that one has understood the other person's state of mind, rather than being committed to supporting it, commiserating with it, or otherwise affiliating with it (Potter and Hepburn 2003). And indeed, notice that what the interviewer understands is not that the interviewee is distressed, or that the events that she experienced were distressing (or worse), but that she has difficulty in expressing them—a markedly more neutral element of the interviewee's state of mind (compare, for example, "this must be awful for you," or "be brave, this must be horrible"—possible formulations in everyday conversations, but wholly absent from these interviews). This gearing-down of sympathy to empathy (for the limited aspect of the respondents' difficulty in expressing themselves) was common throughout the interviews.

The "empathy" in the *ABE* guidelines, then is realized in these interviews as "understanding" the difficulties that the interviewee is experiencing. What seems to be restraining the interviewers is the overarching mandate to collect evidence—that is, to solicit an account that would be usable in court and not be accused of being tainted by arguably overfriendly encouragement. As we shall return to in the discussion, interviewers are aware that should the tape be played in court, counsel for the alleged assailant's defense would be alive to any possibilities of casting doubt on the impartiality of the interview, including being "sympathetic" to the complainant.

Empathic versus Forensic Questioning

ABE lays out the full range of issues involved in managing interviews with suspects and witnesses. The major difficulties it foresees with witnesses' accounts is inconsistency and omission (sections 2.161–2.167) caused by anxiety, memory problems, comprehension difficulties, inappropriate questioning, or other innocent reasons. Its recommendations for probing are couched in terms of understanding or clarifying what witnesses say. The excerpt from the *ABE* guidelines below is quite clear:

> 3.68 Where there are significant inconsistencies in the witness's account interviewers should explore them after they have probed their basic account. *Witnesses should only be challenged directly over an inconsistency in exceptional circumstances and even then only when it is essential to do so. Rather, such inconsistencies should be presented in the context of puzzlement by the interviewer and the need to be quite clear what the witness has said.* On no account should the interviewer voice their suspicions to the witness or label a witness as a liar: there may be a perfectly innocuous explanation for any inconsistency. (*ABE*, section 3.68; emphasis added)

Inevitably, as has been noted, guidelines such as *ABE* only offer general principles, not specific scripts, so it is left to the discretion of the interviewer to embody the principle in practice. In our data, such questions came in the "Account Clarification and Challenge" phase of the PEACE format, and we found that interviewers were generally careful to couch probing and follow-up questions in the recommended way, as matters of their own difficulties in understanding. Here is an example.

Excerpt 2.4: Interview 3 ("Pulled that dress up")

P: So he's pulled that dress up.
(0.7)
P: He's then- he's put his cock inside you.
F: Yeah.
P: Okay .hhh I just need to understand exactly how.=I've got
to try and visualise it to make sure I understand exactly
what you're saying. .hhh You're saying to [me that he's] got
F: [<hhhhh>]
P: your arms,
F: Yeah.

Just before this excerpt, the complainant said that the assailant had pulled her dress up and held her hands up above her head, but did not say anything about her underwear. The interviewer is attempting to clarify how the rapist managed to insert his penis into the complainant's vagina. She does so by appealing to her (the interviewer's) own need to "understand exactly how" and her "try[ing to] . . . visualise it to make sure I understand exactly what you're saying" (lines 05–07). This is consistent with the *ABE* recommendation that "inconsistencies should be presented in the context of puzzlement by the interviewer and the need to be quite clear [as to] what the witness has said." In all of the interviews, this recommendation was adhered to in most of the questions. However, there were also significant departures from the recommendations. In most interviews, interviewers departed from the guidelines on at least one occasion.

We found two kinds of departure from neutral understanding checks. In an apparent breach of the injunction to respect and empathize with the interviewee, both implied, to some degree, a fault and failing in the account. First, the interviewers implied *implausibility*, by probing physical details, chronology, and so on, in a manner that implied not that the interviewee's account was correctable, but that it was paradoxical or implausible. Second, interviewers implied *imprudence*, by probing the complainant's behavior, choices, or decisions in a way that that implied that he or she had done something questionable (inappropriate, ill-advised, poorly judged, and so on), or more frequently, failed to do something sensible in the circumstances (appropriate, expectable, responsible, prudent, and so on).

Excerpt 2.5 below is an example of the interviewer challenging an apparent inconsistency in the interviewee's account in a manner that implies that the account is internally implausible.

Excerpt 2.5: Interview 6 ("Trousers")

P: uh- (.) when you first (0.3) see (anon)
doing this, what can you see, where
where was his penis before he's (0.3) putting
thee: uh (1.5) you said that he's put his
hand down his trousers and got it out, (0.5)
has he done anything to his trousers.
(0.3)
F: No.
(1.0)
P: He jus' ( ) (.) got it out.
(0.3)
P: Okay:, and where is he, (0.3) where's his
trousers and where's his penis.
(1.5)
F: ( ), (0.5) (what he) he put his hand
(down 'is trousers an' (.) >pulled it out<)
(0.7)
→ P: So where-. (0.5) because ob- if he's got
→ his trousers on, (0.5) how has his penis come
→ out from his trousers, where is it.
(0.3)
F: He's ( ) it.
(0.7)
P: °'kay°, so he's put his hand down, down his
trousers, (0.5) has he undone his trousers,
or has he took his trousers off?

In the excerpt above, the interviewer has established that the alleged perpetrator's penis was visible. But when she asks "has he done anything to his trousers," the interviewee says "no" (line 08). This seems to be an inconsistency, which she checks neutrally (lines 12–13) by asking *where's his trousers and where's his penis*, making it plain that there is some problem in the interviewee's account of the relationship between the one and the other. The interviewee's reply (lines 20–21) seems to be that the assailant pulled his penis out of his trousers. This apparently does not satisfy the interviewer, who makes a marked contrast between the state of the trousers and the appearance of the penis. Her use of an if-then construction (*if he's got his trousers on, how has his penis come out*, lines 18–20) strongly implies that the two elements of the description are incompatible—that it would be physically implausible, if not impossible, for the penis to come out if the man had done nothing to the trousers (e.g., pulled them off, opened the flies, undone the zip, etc.). It is this kind of inconsistency or contradiction that *ABE* has in mind when it warns that "occasions may arise where the witness is motivated to either fabricate or exaggerate their account of an event" (*ABE* section 2.162).

The next excerpts illustrate probing questions—again, asked in the "account clarification and challenge" phase of the PEACE format—in which interviewers imply that that the interviewee had been somehow at fault in her or his conduct. In the first excerpt below, a young interviewee is describing walking along a path at school with another pupil, before he stopped her an assaulted her.

Excerpt 2.6: Interview 6 ("Stopped at that point")

P: W- where are you, (0.3) where are you both
standing, when you get to this wall.
(0.5)
F: Jus' against the wall.
P: Who's standing against the wall.
(1.5)
F: Me.
(1.0)
P: °So° tell me about that.
(0.3)
P: How are you,
(0.3)
F: Wuz jus'=standin against the °wall°,
[(°my back to the wall, sort of like that°)
P: [So your back-.
P: >'kay so you're<–what's made you stop.
(2.5)
F: What made you stop.

19 P: °.h Yeah°. ’cause you’re walking, you’re
20 looking for (anon), why did you (0.5)
21 stop there (.) to lean against the wall.
22 (3.0)
23 F: then that’s the bit when he’s got his penis out.
24 P: °I know°.=what- (1.5) I understand that,
25 but what made you: stop. you know, why–
26 how come (.) you stopped at that point,
27 and didn’t, didn’t carry on (0.3)
28 [following (him).
29 F: [we, we, we- b’cause I thought he was (.)
30 looking for (anon), but ( ) (not so
31 important or something) ( ).
32 (0.3)
33 P: °Right°. (0.3) so you’ve stopped.

The interviewer has established that the interviewee has stopped walking and now has “her back to the wall” before being assaulted. For evidential purposes, the interview needs the interviewee to state explicitly how it was that she came to a halt, and took up a position against a wall. There are many ways in which this could have been probed, but the interviewer opts for the formulation “how come you stopped at that point and didn’t carry on.” The agency here is the interviewee’s, and the implication is that it was in her powers to carry on waling (and therefore avoid the assailant). To be sure, the interviewer does use the mandated expression of puzzlement (in the repaired line 24), but this is only a preface to something tendentious. She uses the formulation “how come you did X and not Y,” which, pragmatically, implies very strongly that Y was the more reasonable or expectable (in this case, more prudent and safer) course of action (see, e.g., Collins 1991; Fitzpatrick 2005).

In the excerpt below, again the interviewee’s decision making is called into question. Here the interviewee has recounted being raped on a canal towpath, then leaving with her assailant before separating from him. At some point thereafter she calls into a shop.

Excerpt 2.7: Interview 14 (“All you’d been through”)

01 P: .h (.) when you wen’ in: to: the shop,
02 (0.8)
03 P: Were there people inside shop?

(0.3)
F: Yeah.
P: There were. (.) did you think about telling
anyone inside the shop?
F: No.
(0.5)
P: °Why°.
(1.7)
F: I dunno, I just (.) (dunno).
(0.2)
P: You didn't want to.
(1.0)
P: How come you didn't want to,
(0.7)
F: I don't know hh.
(0.7)
P: °.hh° I'm just trying to understand that i- if
you know, if there's any reason that you
did:n't (0.3) speak to the people in the shop
after, you know, what you'd just been through.
(0.4)
F: I wouldn't tell anyone.

The interviewer has established that the complainant went into a shop, and goes out of her way to get the interviewee to say whether there were "there were people inside" (a redundant question, but one that puts the availability of interlocutors firmly in view). On this basis she asks whether the complainant told anyone (that is, any of the people the interviewee has just stated were present in the shop); when the answer is no, she asks baldly *why* (line 10). To be asked one's motivation for something one did not do is, pragmatically, to imply that one ought to have done it, or that doing it would have been normal in the circumstances; it casts the nonaction as not normatively expectable (at least, from the point of view of the questioner). For an interviewee with an intellectual disability, such complexity would be hard to process. Then the interviewer uses the "how come format"—the strongest form one could use as a presumptive query (here, of what the complainant did not do). Finally the interviewer makes clear her judgment—albeit again prefaced by the "trying to understand" phrasing recommended by *ABE*—that the complainant's actions required explanation "after what you had been through."

Below is the final excerpt we will use to illustrate the interviewer challenging the interviewee's decision making. Here the interviewee has recounted the graphic details of the rape, which the interviewer glosses (in line 4) as "all this has been going on." The interviewer asks, "Have you said anything to him," which the interviewee finds a difficult formulation to reply to—presumably because her account of the rape made clear that "saying something to him" would be a description inconsistent with the panic, distress and violence of the scene. The interviewer then specifies three alternatives: "fought," "shouted," and "screamed." When the interviewee says she did none of these, the interviewer would have a number of ways of probing the reason (for example, "tell me about that," or "can you take me through that," and so on). The format she chooses is "why didn't you do that."

Excerpt 2.8: Interview 3 ("Have you screamed"; #=creaky voice)

01 P: °Right okay°, (0.5) so- (0.8) you don't know why he's
02 finished, you haven't said anything to him, (0.5)
03 during, (0.5) have you done anything at all, (0.3)
04 whilst this has been going on.
05 F: What d'ju mean?
06 P: Well- have you tried to–have you fought him in any way,
07 have you shouted?=have you screa:med,
08 F: no,
09 P: Okay, why didn't you do that.
10 (0.8)
11 F: #dunno,#
12 P: °Okay°, that's fine, it's just I need to know (.)
13 exactly what was [happening.
14 F: [.hhh

Two things are noticeable about the formulation "why didn't you do that." One is that the "that" treats all the options as effectively adding up to one thing (presumably "fight him off" or "make some protest"), although by using the indexical pronoun saves the interviewer from being so explicit. The other thing to notice is that the format "why didn't you" strongly implies that there was a more expectable, perhaps better, more reasonable, more "normal," course of action that was not followed. At its extreme, this could be construed as an implication that the interviewee's choice of not fighting back or making a protest damages her claim that the sex was nonconsensual. Such an implication would be pursued in court by defense counsel seeking to exonerate their client. To raise it in the police interview, unempathic as it may sound, would be justified locally as being in the interests of testing the complainant's case before such hostile courtroom cross-examination.

Conclusions

In this chapter we have examined how police interviewers depart from standard guidelines when dealing with intellectually disabled complainants alleging sexual assault. The sample of 19 interviews we obtained included people with Down syndrome, autism, and with unspecified "learning disabilities," and who were sometimes challenged by other difficulties such as deafness or physical disability. People with such limited intellectual and social capacities may find the challenges of talking about sexually explicit events especially difficult. We know that, by definition, people with intellectual impairments cannot process information efficiently, and cannot express themselves fluently. In terms of their emotional reactions, we also know that such vulnerable victims of sexual crime are likely to suffer marked psychological distress (Rowsell, Clare, and Murphy 2012: 257). These two elements of their difficulties prompted us to pay close attention to police guidelines on questioning and rapport, as expressed in the UK Ministry of Justice's publication *Achieving Best Evidence*, and the College of Policing's authorized professional practice standards of police work. These guidelines are quite clear that vulnerable witnesses need special care, and that building rapport is important; and that questions ought not presume bad faith or other fault.

Much of the interviewers' questioning is indeed in line with the guidelines. But the unpredictable contingencies of interaction sometimes mean that official mandates cannot be strictly adhered to, or that one objective overrides another (see, e.g., Antaki and Rapley 1996 on administering "quality-of-life" questionnaires to people with intellectual disabilities). In these interviews we found that police officers sometimes had difficulties reconciling a dilemma at the heart of the official guidelines: the need, on the one hand, to offer rapport and empathy to the interviewee (who, if their account is true, will have suffered a potentially traumatizing experience) but, on the other hand, to conduct the interview without potential accusation of bias, and in the interests of maximizing the quality and quantity of evidence they can obtain.

We found that although the guidelines require rapport building and explicitly warn against questions which imply blame, we found that interviewers used very constrained versions of the former, and, on occasion, tendentious versions of the latter. That is to say, they would offer only very minimal expressions of empathy when the interviewees reported (as they all did) events which were at last upsetting (an unwanted kiss at a bus stop) or potentially traumatizing (sexual molestation by a parent). Even when the interviewee broke down, the interviewer would restrict their responses to concerns that the interviewee was all right and could carry on. In terms of probing and challenging questions, officers would on occasion step over the bounds of neutral interviewing and questions which implied some degree of fault, imprudence or even complicity on the part of the interviewee (for example, asking "how come" she had carried on walking along with her assailant even after he had indicated he wanted sex).

The question that arises is why discrepancies emerge between the idealizations of the official guidelines and what happens in actual practice. In large part, we believe that they are the result of the greater institutional force of one driving principle in the guidelines at the expense of the other. The objective of getting the maximum forensically useful evidence room from the interview seems, at least occasionally, to outweigh the need to establish rapport with the interviewee. Given the constraints of the police officer's job, and the pressure to make the most efficient use of the interview with a view to identifying a crime, locating the perpetrator and brining a conviction, it is perhaps understandable that empathy is sometimes withheld, and that questions are on occasion seemingly unsympathetic or even hostile. This combination may emerge in local police culture as the one most likely to yield information unbiased by sympathy, and most likely to be robust against the kind of questioning that would be expected from the defense counsel in cross-examination. One way or another, however, what our research reveals is that the generalized recommendations in formal guidelines (still less the terms used in the underpinning legal statute) are insufficient in themselves to specify how, exactly, the police interviewer just operate in the unpredictable contingencies of any specific interview. And perhaps more fundamentally, the formal guidelines embody a dilemma that the officers themselves on occasion have to solve, but choosing between establishing rapport and meeting their forensic objectives.

References

Antaki, Charles, ed. 2011. *Applied Conversation Analysis: Intervention and Change in Institutional Talk*. Basingstoke: Palgrave Macmillan.

Antaki, Charles, and Mark Rapley. 1996. "Questions and Answers to Psychological Assessment Schedules: Hidden Troubles in 'Quality of Life' Interviews." *Journal of Intellectual Disability Research* 40(5): 421–437.

Antaki, Charles, Emma Richardson, Elizabeth Stokoe, and Sara Willott. 2015a. "Dealing with the Distress of People with Intellectual Disabilities Reporting Sexual Assault and Rape." *Discourse Studies* 17: 1–18.

Antaki, Charles, Emma Richardson, Elizabeth Stokoe, and Sara Willott. 2015b. "Police Interviews with Vulnerable People Alleging Sexual Assault: Probing Inconsistency and Questioning Conduct." *Journal of Sociolinguistics* 19 (3): 328–350.

Antaki, Charles, Emma Richardson, Elizabeth Stokoe, and Sara Willott. 2015c. "Can People with Intellectual Disability Resist Implications of Fault when Police Question Their Allegations of Sexual Assault and Rape?" *Intellectual and Developmental Disabilities* 53 (5): 346–357.

Butler, Carly W., Jonathan Potter, Susan Danby, Michael Emmison, and Alexa Hepburn. 2010. "Advice-Implicative Interrogatives: Building 'Client-Centered' Support in a Children's Helpline." *Social Psychology Quarterly* 73(3): 265–287.

Collins, Chris. 1991. "Why and How Come." In *More Papers on Wh- Movement*, edited by Lisa Lai Shen Cheng and Hamida Demirdash, 31–45. MIT Working Papers in Linguistics 15.

College of Policing. n.d. *Authorised Professional Practice: Investigative Interviewing*. Accessed 12 May 2016. https://www.app.college.police.uk/app-content/investigations/investigative-interviewing/#.

Fitzpatrick, Justin.2005. "The Whys and How Comes of Presupposition and NPI Licensing in Questions." In *Proceedings of the 24th West Coast Conference on Formal Linguistics*, 138–145. Somerville, MA: Cascadilla Press, 2005.

Hepburn, Alexa, and Jonathan Potter. 2011. "Designing the Recipient Managing Advice Resistance in Institutional Settings." *Social Psychology Quarterly* 74(2): 216–241.

Hepburn, Alexa, and Jonathan Potter. 2012. "Crying and Crying Responses." In *Emotion in Interaction*, edited by Anssi Peräkylä and Marja-Leena Sorjonen, 194–210. Oxford: Oxford University Press.

McEachern, Adriana G. 2012. "Sexual Abuse of Individuals with Disabilities: Prevention Strategies for Clinical Practice." *Journal of Child Sexual Abuse* 21(4): 386–398.

Petersilia, Joan R. 2001. "Crime Victims with Developmental Disabilities: A Review Essay." *Criminal Justice and Behavior* 28(6): 655–694.

Potter, Jonathan, and Alexa Hepburn. 2003. "'I'm a Bit Concerned'—Early Actions and Psychological Constructions in a Child Protection Helpline." *Research on Language and Social Interaction* 36(3): 197–240.

Rowsell, A. C., Isabel C. H. Clare, and Glynis H. Murphy. 2013. "The Psychological Impact of Abuse on Men and Women with Severe Intellectual Disabilities." *Journal of Applied Research in Intellectual Disabilities* 26(4): 257–270.

Sidnell, Jack, and Tanya Stivers, eds. 2012. *The Handbook of Conversation Analysis*. Chichester: Wiley-Blackwell.

Stokoe, Elizabeth. 2013. "The (In)authenticity of Simulated Talk: Comparing Role-Played and Actual Interaction and the Implications for Communication Training." *Research on Language and Social Interaction* 46(2): 165–185.

Toerien, Merran, Roy Sainsbury, Paul Drew, and Annie Irvine. 2013. "Putting Personalisation into Practice: Work-Focused Interviews in Jobcentre Plus." *Journal of Social Policy* 42(2): 309–327.

UK Ministry of Justice. 2011. *Achieving Best Evidence in Criminal Proceedings: Guidance on Interviewing Victims and Witnesses, and Guidance on Using Special Measures*. London: HMSO. Accessed June 2014. http://www.justice.gov.uk/downloads/victims-and-witnesses/vulnerable-witnesses/achieving-best-evidence-criminal-proceedings.pdf.

CHAPTER THREE

Obtaining Valid Discourse from Suspects PEACE-fully

What Role for Rapport and Empathy?

Ray Bull and Bianca Baker

Introduction

The major aims of this chapter are (1) to explain why the "PEACE" approach to interviewing suspected persons was developed in England and Wales some 25 years ago in order to gain relevant information rather than merely confessions, (2) to describe the psychological research underlying this approach which is fast growing in popularity around the world, (3) to articulate that some of the key elements of this approach (such as using rapport) are hard to define, and (4) to overview some of the psychological research on the actual effectiveness of the "PEACE" approach. Given that this approach does indeed seem to gather relevant discourse from suspects, it is thus highly likely that it will be of interest to those whose work involves discourse analysis of police interviews and interrogations.

Coercive Interrogations

Many publicized miscarriages of justice around the world have been found to be (entirely or partly) due to coercive/oppressive interrogating that has often resulted in confessions that have not been provided voluntarily (Leo 2008; Bull, Valentine, and Williamson 2009). Indeed, those whose role it is to obtain useful information/discourse from people suspected of having been involved or planning wrongdoing have in many countries received training in oppressive interrogation techniques. However, as the winner of the 2016 Nobel Prize for Literature, Bob Dylan, once said, "The times they are a-changin'"—as we will see later in this chapter. So why have thousands of investigators around the world believed that in order to obtain useful information from wrongdoers they have had to resort to oppressive procedures, given that many may well have chosen to become investigators in order to help humanity? In his 2008 book Leo outlined the commonsense notion/belief that wrongdoers will not of their own volition choose to offer valid, incriminating information. However, recent research questions such a belief (see below).

In the majority of countries there has typically taken place little dialogue between researchers and investigative organizations about how best to obtain discourse from suspected persons. Thus, training (often offered by commercial, for-profit companies) had not been built upon published, peer-reviewed research, because so little of this has been available until recently.

In the 1990s Tom Williamson, a senior police officer in London, made clear his view that "unethical behaviour by interrogators has undermined public confidence and left the police service with a serious skills deficit in its ability to obtain evidence through questioning." He further noted that "it does not take much skill to beat a confession out of a suspect detained in police custody," nor "much skill to fabricate a confession and allege that it was made during police questioning" (1993: 107).

A few years ago Alison et al. contended that "there is compelling evidence that coercion . . . and the attempted debasement and humiliation of suspects creates significant long term disadvantages and elevates future threats, without securing any significant life-saving intelligence" (2013: 412). They examined electronically recorded interviews with suspected (and later convicted) terrorists and found that a form of interviewing was related to obtaining of more (relevant) discourse/information. This they described as "motivational interviewing" and they noted its similarity to our much earlier work in that "Bull and Cherryman identified the presence of the following qualities in 'skilful' police interviews: . . . communication skills, empathy, flexibility, open-mindedness, clear structure, and open questions" (1996: 413).

In order to validly determine if an interviewee is providing a truthful or false account psychological research is making it ever clearer that the best clues to rely on are within the content of what people say. For example, Johnston et al. correctly summarized the relevant literature when stating that "recently, techniques based on the evaluation of the actual words of a person, literally the verbal content of their statements, has emerged as the most reliable method of differentiating between true and false statements" (2016: 340; see also Johnston et al. 2014).

The pervasive notion that those planning or having been involved in wrongdoing will not willingly provide verbal information/discourse has actually not benefitted from relevant research, partly because such research had not been conducted until fairly recently. However, such research is making it ever clearer that only a minority enter an interview/interrogation with their mind actually set on denial. For example, in Australia Kebbell, Hurren, and Mazerolle (2006) found that only half of the convicted sex offenders with whom they held a research interview said that they had entered the police interview having already decided whether to deny or confess. In fact, less than 20 percent had planned to deny, and around 30 percent had planned to confess. The other 50 percent entered the police interview not yet having decided whether to deny or confess.

Kebbell, Hurren, and Mazerolle (2006) noted that some wrongdoers who may actually be considering (prior to and/or at the beginning of the interview) whether to confess may subsequently decide not to do so simply because of the coercive way in which they have been interrogated. This "psychological reactance" in interrogations was briefly mentioned by Gudjonsson (2003) and by Holmberg and Christianson (2002), but as yet there is limited available research on it in such settings (though it has been more fully researched in other settings such as sales and marketing; see, e.g., Lessne and Venkatesan 1989).

Whether denial or admission actually occurred was related by Holmberg and Christianson (2002) to the type of interrogation experienced by serious offenders. They found a relationship between the interviewees' reactions and their denial or admission in that those who reported being frightened, stressed, or insulted were less likely to have admitted to the crime. These Swedish researchers concluded that a dominant interviewing style was associated with suspects denying crime.

Moving Away from Coercion

In England and Wales in the mid-1980s in light of

1. various decisions by the (national) Court of Appeal to quash previous convictions based on confessions that were subsequently deemed to be "unreliable" (e.g., because of police behavior) and
2. media and public concern about police interviewing

the government brought in the Police and Criminal Evidence Act, which (among other things, such as seeking to reduce oppressive investigator behavior) mandated that beginning in 1986 all interrogations with suspects would be recorded (e.g., on audiotape). Such electronic recordings for the very first time allowed those given access to them thorough examination of what actually took place, including the discourse.

In the years immediately following (i.e., the later 1980s), a few studies were conducted based on such recordings and were later published. For example, in 1992 the Home Office (part of the government in England and Wales) published the pioneering research by Baldwin that it had commissioned (summarized in Baldwin 1993). Prior to this, very little research had been published on what actually goes on in police interviews. Baldwin found in his analysis of interviews recorded soon after 1986 that in only 20 of the 600 interviews he examined did suspects change their story during the course of an interview. In only nine cases did the change of heart seem attributable to the skills of the interviewer, and only three involved serious offenses. The great majority of suspects stuck to their starting position (admission, denial, or something in between) regardless of how the interviews were conducted. (Pearse and Gudjonsson 1997 shared similar findings regarding interviews conducted in the late 1980s in England.)

Other studies carried out on interviews conducted in the late 1980s also concluded that although these mandated, nationwide tape recordings revealed few signs of oppressive interrogating, there was evidently a widespread skills deficit.

A Major Change in Interviewer Behavior

The studies that we have so far mentioned (and a small number of others—see Milne and Bull 1999 for a comprehensive review) all concerned interviews conducted before a major change in police interviewer training occurred in England and Wales. Indeed, such studies brought about the change. This change involved a number of highly experienced police investigators forming a working party (in 1990) to develop up-to-date training on interviewing and interrogating. In light of their deliberations they recommended what they called the PEACE model or approach. This change, which began in 1992, it involved guidance documents and training courses that all police interviewers had to attend and that contained much research-based cognitive and social psychology (Milne and Bull 1999).

In 1990 draft reports of the early research studies mentioned above (conducted soon after the recording of interviews with suspects became mandatory in 1986) led Tom Williamson to convene a small working party of detectives and psychologists (including Eric Shepherd, Stephen Moston, and this chapter's first author) that in 1991 produced an (unpublished) comprehensive overview of aspects of psychology that might be useful to the improvement of interviewing and interrogating. This overview was made available to the national team of detectives that was developing PEACE. Once that team of detectives had written their guidance documents, they sent drafts to the first author of the current chapter asking whether they had "got the psychology correct?"—They indeed had.

What Is the PEACE Approach?

The PEACE approach is based on a number of basic principles that were chosen by the police. These include:

1. the purpose of investigative interviewing is to obtain accurate and reliable information from suspects, witnesses, or victims in order to discover the truth about matters under investigation;
2. interviews should be approached with an open mind. Information obtained from the person who is being interviewed should always be tested against what the investigator already knows or what can reasonably be established.

Thus, the main aim of this PEACE approach is to obtain discourse. This approach emphasizes that investigative interviews should always consist of five phases:

Firstly, **P** = Planning and Preparation (prior to interviewing)

Secondly, **E** = Engage and Explain (including establishing rapport)

Thirdly, **A** = Account (free narrative followed by different question types)

Fourthly, **C** = Closure (including summarizing)

Finally, **E** = Evaluation (e.g., using the recording)

This (then) novel approach to the interrogating (now called interviewing) of suspected wrongdoers emphasized that such interviews should not be rushed into but should be well prepared for, including gathering prior to the interview as much knowledge as possible about each suspect in order to ***p***lan effectively (Scott et al. 2015), especially for the second phase of ***e***ngaging meaningfully with each suspect (i.e., seeking to establish rapport with every suspect; we will return to the topic of rapport later in this chapter).

In 1990, around the time the PEACE model/approach was being developed, the first author of the current chapter, together with a law professor, was commissioned to draft for the government in England the official *Memorandum of Good Practice on Video Recorded Interviews with Child Witnesses for Criminal Proceedings* (the first type of witness interviews to regularly be video-recorded in England). Producing this required reading of all the then-available relevant literature (which was not, so many years ago, as substantial as it is now). It was clear that the interviewing of young persons should follow the "phased" procedure of

1. establishing rapport
2. trying to obtain a "free narrative" account
3. only then asking questions (of various types in an appropriate order)
4. closure.

With regard to the first, rapport phase, this 1992 government document stated the current first author's view: "Never start without it" (22).

Some Studies of PEACE

Experienced Detectives' Beliefs

In the mid-1990s this chapter's first author was asked by the Home Office to identify any skills gaps in "specialist" police interviews (e.g., of suspects in serious cases and/or adolescent suspects and/or suspects with a "low IQ") conducted by PEACE-trained, experienced investigators. With the assistance of Julie Cherryman, we first asked experienced detectives what they believed the most important skills were, and from their responses as well as the relevant professional and academic literature a questionnaire was compiled (Bull and Cherryman 1996). Then a much larger sample of police detectives and interviewers was asked how necessary each of the skills listed in the questionnaire was. The skills deemed most necessary were (in order of importance):

- listening
- preparation
- questioning
- knowledge of subject
- flexibility
- open-mindedness
- rapport
- compassion or empathy.

Bull and Cherryman (1996) then obtained recordings of specialist interviews with suspects. Each of four experts on investigative interviewing independently rated these for the 28 skills (plus for "overall skill level") identified in our prior work (e.g., the questionnaires I've just mentioned). The skills that differentiated between interviews judged as skilled and those they judged as not skilled were:

- communication skills
- empathy or compassion
- flexibility
- keeping the interviewee to relevant topics
- responding to what the interviewee says
- open-mindedness
- use of closed questions

- providing a structure for the interview
- use of open questions
- appropriate use of pauses and silences.

Even in the more skilled interviews, some skills were often absent:

- appropriate use of pauses and silences
- avoidance of closed questions
- flexibility
- empathy or compassion (for more on empathy, see below).

Is the PEACE Approach Effective?

In our study of 142 interviews with people who may have been involved in benefit fraud, we examined whether interviewing in a way that is compatible with the PEACE approach bore any relationship to the actual outcomes of these interviews (Walsh and Bull 2010). Overall we found that better PEACE interviewing was associated with securing a greater number of comprehensive accounts (available for discourse analysis), both exculpatory ones and admissions.

For the account phase, several significant positive associations between interview skills and interview outcomes were found, including "encourages suspect to give an account," "develops topics," "uses appropriate questions," "explores received information," being "open-minded," "active listening," and "cognitive interviewing."

Overall, 63 percent of those interviews rated as satisfactory or above for the PEACE account phase obtained a comprehensive account or a full confession (available for discourse analysis), whereas only 12 percent of those rated as "needs further training" did so.

Is Rapport Effective in PEACE Interviews?

Walsh and Bull (2012a) studied rapport in these benefit-fraud interviews and found that opportunities to build rapport were often missed in the initial stages. Also, even where some rapport had initially been built, it was not always maintained, partly because some of the tasks undertaken later in the interview (which may well have assisted rapport maintenance) were often conducted poorly. In terms of the effects of rapport, we found that some of the interviewers they assessed as "at or above PEACE standard" when building rapport in the opening engage-and-explain phase regressed in the gaining-of-an-account phase.

In fact, 40 percent of those who were rated regarding rapport development as "satisfactory" in the engage-and-explain phase fell below the minimum acceptable PEACE standard regarding rapport maintenance in the subsequent account phase. Moreover, all of those rated as skilled at rapport building in the engage-and-explain phase failed to maintain this standard of performance, with half of them being rated as no more than satisfactory and the other half unsatisfactory at sustaining rapport in the account phase.

When examining the relationships between the building or maintenance of rapport and subsequent interview outcomes, those interviewers who were rated at or above the PEACE standard of performance in their rapport-maintenance skills in the account phase were, regardless of the quality of rapport-building performance in the opening engage-and-explain phase, three times as likely to achieve either a comprehensive account from the interviewees than those who were assessed as below minimum acceptable standards. Interviewers rated as at or above the PEACE standard in *both* their rapport-building and rapport-maintenance skills were over five times more likely to obtain satisfactory outcomes. In 2016 Watkins suggested that maintaining rapport throughout the entire interview can be particularly important when interviewing Aboriginal people, who place a high value on personal relationships and interpersonal respect.

Overcoming Denials and Noncooperation PEACE-fully

Walsh and Bull (2012b) also examined how the interviewers attempted to overcome suspects' initial denials of knowing about wrongdoing by assessing 85 interviews with individuals suspected of benefit fraud not only for interviewer tactics and skills, along with other attributes, but also for interviewee movement or "shift" to providing relevant information. It was found that shifting from denying to providing relevant, incriminating information indicating guilt, admissions, and/or confessions occurred more often when certain tactics and skills or other attributes were present (many of which are recommended by PEACE).

Of the 22 skills/tactics examined, 13 were found to differentiate significantly between interviews in which suspects shifted versus did not shift, these being disclosure of evidence, emphasizing contradictions, encouraging the account, gentle prods open questions, probing questions, repetitive questioning, persistence, positive confrontation, providing appropriate structure, regular summarizing, silence, and showing concern (see our later section on empathy). Those tactics found not to be effective in our study of overcoming denials were maximization, minimization, intimidation, challenging the account, interruptions, leading questions, suggesting a scenario, and situational futility. Some of these traditionally have been part of training in the United States and other countries (e.g., Inbau, Reid, Buckley, and Jayne 2001).

A Good or Effective Interviewer

In a review of what may contribute to being a good or effective interviewer this chapter's first author presented a comprehensive overview of the published literature on (1) what is believed and (2) what is actually known about the characteristics that may contribute to someone's being good or effective investigative interviewers (Bull 2013).

Beliefs

One of the points included in this overview of the available information was that in their review of what constitutes best practice when interviewing people who may possess "incriminating" information (yet may sometimes be unwilling to divulge this), Read et al. (2009) noted that when Powell asked officers who were perceived as being particularly good at engaging members of threatened and marginalized communities (e.g., Australian aboriginals), they perceived courtesy, respect, patience, and honesty to be their most valued professional assets.

Similarly, in their survey of the views of interviewers (from a variety of countries) working on criminal investigations or on "intelligence" issues, Sivasubramaniam and Goodman-Delahunty (2013) reported that being patient; showing kindness, respect, and concern; and appealing to cooperation were rated highly (as were confronting the accused with evidence of guilt and identifying contradictions in his or her story). Various forms of "mild" coercion were not rated at all highly. Additionally, in their survey of interviewers' views on the question "What qualities make a good interrogator?" Russano and Narchet (2013) found "interpersonal skills" to be most frequently mentioned, followed by "patience," "flexible/adaptable, "ability to empathize," "good communicator," and "good listener." Among Russano and Narchet's participants were some with experience of interviewing high-value targets, and these were unanimous in their observations that rapport building is the most effective approach. Recently, Cleary and Warner (2016) found that over 80 percent of a large sample of experienced police officers in the United States reported having received training on building rapport. Thus, experienced interrogators and interviewers nowadays believe such skills as rapport and empathy to be important. But what is the actual relationship?

The Actual Relationship

The actual relationship between interviewer characteristics and interview outcome and/or information gain was studied in Japan by Otsuka et al. (2011). Police officers (n=274) who interviewed adult suspects (who denied having committed a crime when arrested but later confessed during or after being interviewed) filled in a questionnaire that included their level of "empathic understanding." For most types of crime studied (murder, rape, and robbery), a significant positive association was found between officers' (self-reported) "level of empathic understanding" and "full confessions."

Another country where relevant research is now being carried out is South Korea. There the senior police officer Roon Yi (unpublished) recently found that domineering interview tactics had a negative influence on obtaining confessions and/or providing relevant information; however, respect, as perceived by the interviewees, was significantly associated with the obtaining of confessions.

Another of our studies (Leahy-Harland and Bull 2017) focused exclusively on real-life taped interviews with people suspected of serious crimes. We found a number of significant associations between interviewer strategies and suspect responses. Rapport/empathy and open-type questions were associated with an increased likelihood of suspects' admitting the offense, whilst "describing trauma" and "negative questions" were associated with a decreased likelihood of suspect admissions. We also found that the interviewers of these suspected murderers and rapists did not demonstrate a "dominating approach" in these lengthy interviews. We also examined which strategies were associated with these interviewees continuing to respond relevantly and found positive associations for "rapport/empathy," "presentation of evidence," and "requests attention," but negative associations for "explicitly asks for account/tell truth," "emphasises seriousness of offence," and "situational futility."

In a study of people detained and interviewed on suspicion of having knowledge relating to terrorism (e.g., in Sri Lanka or in Indonesia), Goodman-Delahunty, Martschuk, and Dhami (2014) found that detainees were more likely to disclose meaningful information in response to social strategies, and that disclosures were more complete in response to noncoercive strategies, especially rapport building.

But What Is "Rapport" and What Is "Empathy"?

Several of the studies described above have mentioned rapport and/or empathy, but what do these two words actually mean? In the *Oxford English Dictionary*, *rapport* is defined as "a close and harmonious relationship in which people understand each other's feelings or ideas and communicate well," and *empathy* as "the ability to understand and share the feelings of another." But in terms of interviewer (or interrogator) behavior, how well do such definitions help us to (1) determine whether rapport or empathy is being demonstrated, (2) get a handle on whether empathy and/or rapport is indeed experienced by the interviewee, and (3) train interviewers to demonstrate rapport and/or empathy?

A major life challenge that faces us all (and especially psychologists, with their emphasis on methodological rigor) is the paradox that the things in life that are easier to define, and thus to measure and operationalize, are typically not that important, but the things that are difficult to define, quantify, and thus conduct research on are very often extremely important. As Albert Einstein supposedly once observed, "Not everything that counts can be counted, and not everything that can be counted counts."

So, What Is Rapport?

Like other important concepts such as love (Lehrer 2016), rapport has been described, defined, and assessed somewhat differently depending on the researcher(s). For example, in 2013 the national College of Policing (for England and Wales) stated that "establishing rapport means being genuinely open, interested and approachable, as well as being interested in the interviewees' feelings or welfare" (2013: 2). However, as pointed out by Alison, Giles, and McGuire (2015) and by Vallano and Schreiber Compo (2015), there is a dearth of valid measurement tools to describe rapport. Driskell, Blickensderfer, and Salas (2013) described rapport as a connection or relationship between two parties. Like several other researchers, they mention Tickle-Degnen and Rosenthal's (1990) description of rapport as involving the three components of mutual attentiveness, positivity and coordination. Each of these components is somewhat open to operationalization or assessment; however, Driskell, Blickensderfer, and Salas (2013) noted that rapport is reflected in both feelings and behavior. Thus, whereas behavior can in principle be observed and assessed, feelings are internal, and therefore not really available to objectivity required of researchers. Yet it is how the interviewees *feel*, rather than the behavior of the interviewers or interrogators, that is likely to have a direct influence on the amount of discourse they provide.

In 2013 Abbe and Brandon published a review of the role of rapport in investigative interviewing. In addition to providing descriptions of Tickle-Degnen and Rosenthal's (1990) three components, they noted that whereas "mutual respect" may well be important in the interrogation setting, that "pseudo-rapport" may be damaging. Furthermore, they articulated that "operational accord," wherein interviewer and interviewee have a shared view of at least some of the goals of the interview, may be important, as it seems to be in therapeutic settings, where it can be thought of as a component of a working alliance. (See below for a discussion of Vanderhallen, Vervaeke, and Holmberg's 2011 study of the role of the working alliance in investigative interviews.) Abbe and Brandon suggested three forms of social influence as the components of rapport: (1) interest based, wherein the interviewee perceives that there is something to be gained by compliance; (2) relationship based, wherein the interviewee is invested in building or maintaining a relationship with the interviewer; and (3) identity based, wherein the interviewer appeals to the interviewee's self-concept, values, or beliefs. However, their thoughtful review offers limited guidance on how to operationalize these notions and components.

If the discipline of psychology wishes to lay claim to being a science, it must grapple with the issue of how to quantify the notions and factors it deems important. Abbe and Brandon pointed out that research on the social and interpersonal dynamics of law-enforcement interviewing has proceeded in a largely atheoretical fashion, and that research on investigative interviewing tends to be descriptive in nature. But if theories are to be developed and advanced, they need to be in a form that allows them to be tested. To date, limited progress has been made in this regard for the notion of rapport.

The operationalization of the working alliance in Vanderhallen and Vervaeke (2014) seems to be among the most comprehensive to date. In their analyses of real-life police interviews, they used a variety of measures for interviewees to complete after their interview: (1) an inventory to assess investigator empathy, (2) ten items relating to investigator interview style (humanitarian or domineering), (3) a hostility subscale of the "Symptom Checklist," (4) the "Working Alliance Inventory," and (5) how clearly the interviewer explained things (see also Vanderhallen, Vervaeke, and Holmberg 2011). Of these five measures, only "hostility" failed to be significantly associated with the interviewees' satisfaction (assessed using a 12-item questionnaire). Vanderhallen and Vervaeke did not set out to assess rapport directly. Nevertheless, they noted that the varying definitions of rapport impede the general understanding of what interviewers should do to establish it.

The work of Vanderhallen and Vervaeke provides a step forward, yet we should ask whether work on rapport needs to attempt to mimic the hard sciences, which have developed theories that can actually and repeatedly be tested with unfailing accuracy. Perhaps people are too varied, too complex, to ever allow this kind of prediction. As the highly respected research psychologist James Deese concluded in 1969, "The model of experimenting taken from the physical sciences is useful as an aid in psychological research, but I have reached the conclusion that it no longer belongs in the center of psychology" (cited in Bull 1982: 522).

What Is Empathy?

Recent research suggests that to obtain comprehensive discourse from suspects, interviewers should display empathy. Displays of empathy have been known for decades to enhance human relationships, whether privately, professionally in corporations, or in therapeutic settings. However, a variety of descriptions and definitions of empathy exists that may limit the extent to which it can be applied productively. Here we offer our evolving conceptualization of empathy, which we feel will allow for a deeper understanding of the term and how and why it may be employed in police interviews.

We wish to describe the various types, aspects, and levels of empathy as being on a continuum. (Here we have been informed by the work of Dan Zahavi, among others.) Toward one end of such a continuum is what can be described as "rational" or "cognitive" empathy, and toward the other end, "affective" or "emotional" empathy (see fig. 3.1).

Rational or cognitive empathy relates to the displaying of empathy toward or for another person's situation while not internally experiencing the relevant emotion or affect—for example, displaying an understanding of a person's sad plight but not feeling sad. This can be seen as an ability to construct a working model of others' emotional states (Reniers et al. 2011). More simply, it is the rational side of empathy, where an individual may be able to imagine how another person is feeling.

Affective empathy (or emotional empathy) is placed toward the other end of the continuum and can be seen (Reniers et al. 2011) as an ability to be sensitive to and vicariously experience the feelings of others. This is the emotional aspect of empathy, where in its fullest extent one individual is experiencing the same emotional state as the other, also known as *empathic contagion*, or literally catching the contagious emotions of another individual.

Between these two forms of empathy, and often important in therapeutic settings, is "affect sharing" (Herzog 2016), which is a mirroring of

1. Openness
2. Listening
3. Non-judgment/unbiased
4. Understanding (e.g. current situation)

passive (1-4)

5. Working together
6. Changing perspectives
7. Building rapport
8. Understanding Actions
9. Appreciating emotions/distress

active (5-9)

FIGURE 3.1. Empathy continuum, taken from Baker, Bull, and Walsh (in submission)

the clients' affects by the therapist, but this may not require the therapist actually to experience the emotions as the client is experiencing them.

The empathy-altruism hypothesis states that when one person empathizes with another, he or she is more likely to help the other (Batson 2011). According to Batson, such empathy can dissolve the boundaries between two individuals. Applying affective empathy may thus dissolve boundaries between two individuals, reaching a point of no longer experiencing one's own emotions because one is preoccupied with being enthralled in the emotions of the other. However, empathy at the affective end of the continuum may produce problems in some professional settings. During police interviews, experiencing the emotions as the suspect may interfere with the professionalism of the investigator, given that it is the role of the investigator to remain skeptical and objective during their interviews, which among other things may better enable them to decide whether what the suspect is saying is truthful (Bull 2013). Therefore, it could be argued that professional empathy, such as investigative empathy, should lie somewhere in the middle of this empathy continuum. Furthermore, genuinely experiencing the emotions being experienced by suspects could unduly influence interviewers' and investigators' well-being. However, feigning empathy could be detected by suspects, who may then react negatively to this, resulting in no or limited discourse.

In the United Kingdom, strict confidentiality is rightly imposed on and required of researchers and expert witnesses who are given access to police interviews. Therefore, we are not able to provide excerpts from the privileged access granted to us. However, we have been given special permission to quote from one case we worked on that in our opinion demonstrates to some extent the use of empathy and rapport in each of the police interviewer's three utterances. In this case the man being interviewed was suspected of having physically and sexually abused children. During the interview he admitted to the physical abuse but not to the sexual abuse. He was going to be interviewed again at a later date about the alleged sexual abuse. Toward the end of the interview the police interviewer (PI) said to the suspect (S):

PI: Just before we conclude this interview I want to give you some information for yourself. It's information about support lines in case you want to speak to anybody because of the serious nature of the allegations.

S: To make sure I don't jump from a bridge.

PI: . . . we understand that it's an upsetting and confusing time for you . . . we just need to make sure you're safe.

A few seconds later:

S: . . . I want to say to you that I'm sorry if I was rude to you—I was saying stupid things. . . .

PI: . . . we said that you've been arrested on suspicion, we haven't said that you've actually done any of these things . . . it's for us to ask you questions to try to ascertain what has gone on. . . .

In Baker, Walsh, and Bull's (2016) study of police interviewers' perceptions and employment of empathy, it was found that investigators in several countries (with differing legal systems and cultural/historical/political backgrounds) defined empathy somewhat similarly. The investigators were also asked to report their use of empathy during investigative interviews and it was found that the countries differed with regard to self-reports on the use of empathy and of coercive methods. For example, English investigators reported using empathy when interviewing suspects (to demonstrate an understanding of the situation a suspect is in) and not using any coercive methods (as also found in the analyses of English police interrogations/interviews by Bull and Soukara 2010, among others). Slovenian investigators claimed to employ empathy, but also problematic methods, such as minimization and maximization.

The *Oxford English Dictionary* makes the important point that "people often confuse the words empathy and sympathy . . . sympathy means 'feelings of pity and sorrow for someone else's misfortune.'" Thus, in order to obtain discourse police interviews, it may be best to display a degree of empathy that involves active perception and understanding of the suspect's situation. Indeed, Alison et al. defined empathy as the "extent to which the interviewer understands the suspect's perspective" (2013: 417). However, the use of rationalizations (offering reasons to explain away criminal behavior, as advocated in much interrogator training by some U.S. organizations) may be counterproductive (and unethical) if these are not actually relevant to a particular suspect's situation (i.e., to his or her reasons for committing the offense being investigated). Among other aims, the designers of the PEACE approach wanted to develop a model that would be ethical.

PEACE in Our Time?

In light of the research, a growing number of countries and organizations have decided to adopt the PEACE model of investigative interviewing, which is based largely on psychology. However, adopting a new and different approach away from interrogating for the purpose of obtaining confessions toward interviewing for the purpose of engaging in discourse and obtaining information may be a challenge for some investigators and investigative organizations, especially if they are not provided with adequate descriptions of the essential components of investigative interviewing such as rapport and empathy. Adopting a new method can easily be taken to imply that the traditional (old?) approach was not appropriate, leading those who have for years been using the traditional approach, understandably, to feel threatened by the proposed changes. For example, in their 2007 survey of the views on interrogation of top administrators of the largest American municipal police departments, Zalman and Smith noted that their data suggest that proposed changes are likely to face resistance from police officials, interrogating officers, and perhaps also from the police training industry.

The challenge facing those who conduct relevant research is to successfully convey what a new approach involves and its effectiveness. This is very much in line with what George Miller called for in his 1969 presidential address at the annual conference of the American Psychological Association when he stated that psychologists should give psychology away to the world in a meaningful manner. Indeed, a few years ago a new national initiative commenced in the United States that was designed largely by psychologists to obtain information effectively yet ethically from people suspected of planning or having been involved in crimes such as terrorism. This substantive development is known as human information gathering (HIG), and close to its commencement the first author of the current chapter was invited to attend two meetings (months apart) in Washington, D.C., to give presentations on what the PEACE approach involves, why and how it was developed, and how interviewers are trained in it in England. HIG has importantly funded a series of research studies selected by a committee involving Chris Meissner, who (with Dan Lassiter) said in 2010 in the conclusion of their edited volume that "one alternative . . . [to] psychologically coercive interrogative methods . . . [is] the PEACE approach to investigative interviewing . . . used in Great Britain" (Lassiter and Meissner 2010: 229). More recently, in their overview of research on rapport building, Valano and Schreiber Compo (2015) concluded by advocating that law enforcement in the United States adopt the information-gathering method.

Furthermore, in 2016 the United Nations' Special Rapporteur on Torture and other Cruel, Inhuman or Degrading Treatment or Punishment, Juan E. Méndez, submitted his report, which was then transmitted by the U.N. Secretary-General to the U.N. General Assembly. In this report its summary stated:

> The Special Rapporteur . . . advocates the development of a universal protocol identifying a set of standards for non-coercive interviewing methods and procedural safeguards that ought, as a matter of law and policy, to be applied at a minimum to all interviews by law enforcement officials, military and intelligence personnel and other bodies with investigative mandates.

In mentioning this universal protocol, the U.N. Special Rapporteur noted that "encouragingly, some States have moved away from accusatorial, manipulative and confession-driven interviewing models with a view to increasing accurate and reliable information and minimizing the risks of unreliable information and miscarriages of justice." He added that "the essence of an alternative information-gathering model was first captured by the PEACE model of interviewing adopted in 1992 in England and Wales . . . investigative interviewing can provide positive guidance for the protocol."

In addition, the Special Rapporteur stated that

> investigative interviewing . . . comprises a number of essential elements that are key to the prevention of mistreatment and coercion and help to guarantee effectiveness. Interviewers must, in particular, seek to obtain accurate and reliable information in the pursuit of truth; gather all available evidence pertinent to a case before beginning interviews; prepare and plan interviews based on that evidence; maintain a professional, fair and respectful attitude during questioning; establish and maintain a rapport with the interviewee; allow the interviewee to give his or her free and uninterrupted account of the events; use open-ended questions and active listening; scrutinize the interviewee's account and analyse the information obtained against previously

available information or evidence; and evaluate each interview with a view to learning and developing additional skills.

In particular, the Special Rapporteur emphasized that "the development and maintenance of rapport is also a crucial determinant of effective non-coercive interviews. Rapport can help to reduce the interviewee's anxiety, anger or distress, while increasing the likelihood of obtaining more complete and reliable information."

In our opinion, the Special Rapporteur has recommended to the United Nations a model of interviewing (replacing interrogation) that is firmly based on the available research evidence largely derived from modern psychological work on enhancing interviewing practices.

References

Abbe, Allison, and Susan Brandon. 2013. "The Role of Rapport in Investigative Interviewing: A Review." *Journal of Investigative Psychology and Offender Profiling* 10: 237–249.

Alison, Laurence, Emily Alison, Geraldine Noone, Stamatis Elntib, and Paul Christiansen. 2013. "Why Tough Tactics Fail and Rapport Gets Results." *Psychology, Public Policy, and Law* 19: 411–431.

Alison, Laurence, Susan Giles, and Grace McGuire. 2015. "Blood from a Stone: Why Rapport Works and Torture Doesn't in 'Enhanced' Interrogations." *Investigative Interviewing: Research and Practice* 6: 5–23.

Baker, Bianca, Ray Bull, and Dave Walsh. (In submission). "Police Interviewers' Definitions and Use of Empathy in Several European Countries."

Baker, Bianca, Dave Walsh, and Ray Bull. 2016. "An International Comparison of Investigative Interviewing with Suspected Sex Offenders: Is There Room for Empathy?" Paper presented at the Annual Conference of the European Association of Psychology and Law, Toulouse, France, 5–8 July.

Baldwin, John. 1993. "Police Interview Techniques: Establishing Truth or Proof?" *British Journal of Criminology* 33: 325–352.

Batson, C. Daniel. 2011. *Altruism in Humans*. Oxford Scholarship Online. https://doi.org/10.1093/acprof:oso/9780195341065.001.0001.

Bull, Ray. 1982. "Can Experimental Psychology Be Applied Psychology?" In *Psychology in Practice*, edited by Sandra Canter and David Canter, 335–345. Chichester: Wiley.

Bull, Ray. 2013. "What Is 'Believed' or Actually 'Known' about Characteristics That May Contribute to Being a Good/Effective Interviewer?" *Investigative Interviewing: Research and Practice* 5: 128–143.

Bull, Ray, and Julie Cherryman. 1996. *Helping to Identify Skills Gaps in Specialist Investigative Interviewing: Enhancement of Professional Skills.* London: Home Office, Police Department.

Bull, Ray, and Stavroula Soukara. 2010. "A Set of Studies of What Really Happens in Police Interviews with Suspects." In *Police Interrogations and False Confessions: Current Research, Practice, and Policy Recommendations*, edited by G. Daniel Lassiter and Christian Meissner, 81–96. Washington, DC: American Psychological Association.

Bull, Ray, Tim Valentine, and Tom Williamson, eds. 2009. *Handbook of Psychology of Investigative Interviewing: Current Developments and Future Directions.* Chichester: Wiley-Blackwell.

Cleary, Hayley, and Todd Warner. 2016. "Police Training in Interviewing and Interrogation Method." *Law and Human Behavior* 40: 270–284.

College of Policing. 2013. *Investigation: Investigative Interviewing.* https://www.app.college.police.uk/app-content/investigations/investigative-interviewing/.

Deese, James. 1969. "Behavior and Fact." *American Psychologist* 24: 515–522.

Driskell, Tripp, Elizabeth Blickensderfer, and Eduardo Salas. 2013. "Is Three a Crowd? Examining Rapport in Investigative Interviews." *Group Dynamics: Theory, Research and Practice* 17: 1–13.

Goodman-Delahunty, Jane, Natalie Martschuk, and Mandeep K. Dhami. 2014. "Interviewing High Value Detainees: Securing Cooperation and Disclosures." *Applied Cognitive Psychology* 28: 883–897.

Gudjonsson, Gisli. 2003. *The Psychology of Interrogations and Confessions: A Handbook.* Chichester: Wiley.

Herzog, Bruce. 2016. "Establishing the Therapeutic Impact of Empathy through 'Affect Sharing.'" *International Journal of Psychoanalytic Self Psychology* 11: 152–168.

Holmberg, Ulf, and Sven-Åke Christianson. 2002. "Murderers' and Sexual Offenders' Experiences of Police Interviews and Their Inclination to Admit or Deny Crimes." *Behavioral Sciences & the Law* 20: 31–45.

Inbau, Fred E., John E. Reid, Joseph P. Buckley, and Bruce C. Jayne. 2001. *Criminal Interrogation and Confessions.* 4th ed. Gaithersberg, MD: Aspen.

Johnston, Shawn, Alexis Chandelier, Dana Powers-Green, and Syeda Rahmani. 2014. "Attributes of Truthful versus Deceitful Statements in the Evaluation of Accused Child Molesters." *SAGE Open* (July–September): 1–10.

Johnston, Shawn, Alexis Chandelier, Dana Powers-Green, and Gabriel Johnston. 2016. "Attributes of True and Deceptive Statements Made in Criminal Investigations." *Journal of Forensic Psychology Practice* 16: 347–373.

Kebbell, Mark, Emily Hurren, and Paul Mazerolle. 2006. "Sex Offenders' Perceptions of How They Were Interviewed." *Canadian Journal of Police and Security Services* 4: 67–75.

Lassiter, G. Daniel, and Christian A. Meissner, eds. 2010. *Police Interrogations and False Confessions: Current Research, Practice, and Policy Recommendations.* Washington, DC: American Psychological Association.

Leahy-Harland, Samantha, and Ray Bull. 2017. "Police Strategies and Suspect Responses in Real-Life Serious Crime Interviews." *Journal of Police and Criminal Psychology* 32: 138–151.

Lehrer, Jonah. 2016. *A Book about Love.* New York: Simon & Schuster.

Leo, Richard A. 2008. *Police Interrogation and American Justice.* Cambridge, MA: Harvard University Press.

Lessne, Greg, and M. Venkatesan. 1989. "Reactance Theory in Consumer Research: The Past, Present and Future." *Advances in Consumer Research* 16: 76–78.

Lin, Tsan-chang, and Chih-hung Shih. 2013. "A Study of Police Interrogation Practice in Taiwan." Paper presented at the Asian Conference of Criminal and Operations Psychology, Singapore, 20–23 May.

Milne, Becky, and Ray Bull. 1999. *Investigative Interviewing: Psychology and Practice.* Chichester: Wiley.

Otsuka, Yasuke, Taeko Wachi, Kazumi Watanabe, Kaeko Yokota, and Hiroki Kuraishi. 2011. "Factors that Determine the Level of Confession in Denying Suspects." Poster presented at the Annual Conference of the American Psychology–Law Society, Miami, FL, 2–6 March.

Pearse, John, and Gisli Gudjonsson. 1997. "Police Interviewing Techniques at Two South London Police Stations." *Psychology, Crime & Law* 3: 63–74.

Read, Julianne, Martine Powell, Mark Kebbell, and Becky Milne. 2009. "Investigative Interviewing of Suspected Sex Offenders." *International Journal of Police Science and Administration* 11: 442–459.

Reniers, Renate, Rhiannon Corcoran, Richard Drake, Nick Shryane, and Birgit Völlm. 2011. "The QCAE: A Questionnaire of Cognitive and Affective Empathy." *Journal of Personality Assessment* 93: 84–95.

Russano, Melissa, and Fadia Narchet. 2013. "Interrogation Practices and Beliefs: Does High-Value Target Experience Matter?" Paper presented at the Annual Conference of the American Psychology–Law Society, Portland, OR, 7–9 March.

Scott, Adrian, Jane Tudor-Owen, Paul Pedretti, and Ray Bull. 2015. "How Intuitive Is PEACE? Newly Recruited Police Officers' Plans, Interviews, and Self-Evaluations." *Psychiatry, Psychology and Law* 22: 355–367.

Sivasubramaniam, Diane, and Jane Goodman-Delahunty. 2013. "An International Survey of Intelligence Interviewing Practices and Beliefs." Paper presented at the Annual Conference of the American Psychology–Law Society, Portland, OR, 7–9 March.

Tickle-Degnen, Linda, and Robert Rosenthal. 1990. "The Nature of Rapport and Its Nonverbal Correlates." *Psychological Inquiry* 1: 285–293.

Valano, Jonathan P., and Nadja Schreiber Compo. 2015. "Rapport Building with

Cooperative Witnesses and Criminal Suspects: A Theoretical and Empirical Review." *Psychology, Public Policy, and Law* 21: 85–99.

Vanderhallen, Miet, and Geert Vervaeke. 2014. "Between Investigator and Suspect: The Role of the Working Alliance in Investigative Interviewing." In *Investigative Interviewing*, edited by Ray Bull, 63–90. New York: Springer.

Vanderhallen, Miet, Geert Vervaeke, and Ulf Holmberg. 2011. "Witness and Suspect Perceptions of Working Alliance and Interviewing Style." *Journal of Investigative Psychology and Offender Profiling* 8: 110–130.

Walsh, Dave, and Ray Bull. 2010. "What Really is Effective in Interviews with Suspects?" *Legal and Criminological Psychology* 15: 305–321.

Walsh, Dave, and Ray Bull. 2012a. "Examining Rapport in Investigative Interviews with Suspects: Does [*sic*] Its Building and Maintenance Work?" *Journal of Police and Criminal Psychology* 27: 73–84.

Walsh, Dave, and Ray Bull. 2012b. "How Do Interviewers Attempt to Overcome Suspects' Denials?" *Psychiatry, Psychology and Law* 19: 151–168.

Watkins, Kerry. 2016. "The Vulnerability of Aboriginal Suspects When Questioned by Police." *Criminal Law Quarterly* 63: 474–503.

Williamson, Tom. 1993. "From Interrogation to Investigative Interviewing; Strategic Trends in Police Questioning." *Journal of Community and Applied Social Psychology* 3: 89–99.

Zalman, Marvin, and Brad Smith. 2007. "The Attitudes of Police Executives toward Miranda and Interrogation Policies." *Journal of Criminal Law and Criminology* 97: 873–942.

CHAPTER FOUR

The Guilt-Presumptive Nature of Custodial Interrogations in the United States

The Use of Confrontation, Appeals to Self-Interest, and Sympathy/Minimization in the Reid Technique

Marianne Mason

"There's absolutely no doubt that this happened," you say. "Now let's move forward and see what we can do."

—quoted in Douglas Starr, "The Interview: Do Police Interrogation Techniques Produce False Confessions?" *New Yorker*, 9 December 2013

Introduction

In custodial settings in the United States, suspects who are under arrest are often subjected to routine booking questions (Skelton and Connell 2004; Mason 2013) and, subsequently, police questioning. As Gudjonsson notes, "Investigative interviewing forms a crucial part of most police investigations" (2003: 627). The type of police questioning that may further the interests of justice has been fairly debated and includes examining various police questioning techniques, such as PEACE (see Milne and Bull 1999) and Reid (Inbau, Reid, Buckley, and Jayne 2005).

In the United Kingdom, PEACE came about in response to a number of high-profile wrongful convictions based on false confessions (Leo 2008). After PEACE was instituted in 1986, police questioning in the United Kingdom shifted from a confrontational model aimed at eliciting incriminating statements and confessions to a model of investigative interviewing. The latter is more conversational and is designed to obtain information rather than confessions. In the United States, which is the focus of this chapter, the dominant interrogation model is the Reid technique (Inbau, Reid, Buckley, and Jayne 2005). Reid originated from law enforcement's need to find alternatives to the violent questioning of suspects, also known as the "third degree," which was endemic in early 19th-century policing.

In the Reid technique psychological, rather than physical, pressure is placed on the suspect to facilitate confession. The police officer is trained to use the Reid technique in order to detect, through informal interviews with the suspect and/or accusers and witnesses, the suspect's possible guilt or innocence. Once the police officer determines the suspect's guilt in the preliminary investigation stage, coupled with observing his or her body language (Dixon 2010), he or she proceeds to interrogate the suspect—the "argumentation stage" (Walton 2003) of police interrogation. Police interrogation in the United States is often based on the assumption that the suspect is guilty (Kassin and Gudjonsson 2004; Leo 2008). For many police officers, this assumption allows for a great deal of latitude in the interrogation techniques used to question suspects and obtain a confession.

This chapter will examine the discursive features of three of the interrogation strategies most commonly used within the Reid interrogation spectrum: the sympathetic-detective/minimization strategy, confronting the suspect with evidence of guilt, and appealing to the suspect's self-interest (see Davis, Leo, and Follette 2010). To accomplish this task, the researcher will examine the police interrogations of two suspects who were charged with murder and rape respectively. The analysis will show how the police officers in each case dismissed the invocations of the right to counsel of both suspects and proceeded to use the three aforementioned strategies to direct the suspects to provide a confession, while taking "innocence off the table" (Kassin, Leo, Meissner, Richman, Colwell, Leach, and LaFon 2007; Davis, Leo, and Follette 2010; Mason 2016) and ignoring the suspects' frequent denials (Shuy 2005). Removing the option of a suspect's innocence, particularly if it leads to a suspect's providing information or a confession, may substantiate (partially or fully) the police officers' construction of a suspect's alleged guilt (Shuy 1998; Leo 2008).

Background of the Cases

This chapter examines the police interrogation of two male suspects: one who would be tried for rape and the other on three counts of murder. In the former case, the police interrogation of the suspect, Jones,[1] and of his female accuser occurred at the police station in a rural county in the southeastern United States. The accuser, who was 16 years of age at the time of the incident, stated that she was sexually assaulted by a male truck driver in the back of his truck. The suspect, who was in his mid-30s, was arrested and charged with rape and aggravated sexual battery. After Jones's arrest, two police officers, Detective Martin (a male officer) and Officer Stewart (a female officer), interrogated the suspect. The police interrogation of the suspect was audio-recorded, as is customary in the police station in which the interrogation took place. Officer Stewart took notes for the police record, and Detective Martin asked most of the questions (94 percent) using a variety of strategies. The interrogation also includes routine booking questions and the reading of the suspect's Miranda rights. This part of the exchange between the police and the suspect exchanges lasts approximately 20 minutes. The argumentation stage of the interrogation follows the police officers' reading of the Miranda warning and lasts approximately 70 minutes. This portion of the data comprises 78 police-initiated turns of talk and 75 responses from the suspect. On three occasions the suspect did not respond to the officers' questions.

In the second case, the police interrogation of the suspect, Smith, occurred at a police station in a large metropolitan area in the southeastern United States. The suspect, who was in his mid-20s at the time of the incident, was charged with three counts of murder. According to the police, Smith violated his temporary protective order (TPO) of no contact (owing to "domestic violence") when he visited his former girlfriend's residence. Smith shot and murdered his former girlfriend's mother and two male friends. After Smith's arrest, Detective Miller and Detective Peterson (both male) interrogated Smith. The police officers shared interrogating duties, but they specialized: Detective Peterson was often confrontational with the suspect, whereas Detective Miller often appealed to the suspect's self-interest. The police officers took turns managing topics, which appears to be consistent with the Reid technique (Kassin, Leo, Meissner, Richman, Colwell, Leach, and LaFon 2007). The police interrogation was audio-recorded, and Detective Peterson took notes for the police record. The interrogation includes routine booking questions and the reading of Smith's Miranda rights. This part of the police-suspect exchanges lasts approximately 15 minutes. The argumentation stage of the suspect's interrogation follows the police officers' reading of Miranda and lasts approximately 110 minutes. This portion of the data comprises 126 police-initiated turns of talk and 118 verbal responses from the suspect. On eight occasions the suspect was emotional (cried) and did not respond verbally to the officers' questions.

The excerpts included in this chapter are the author's transcription of the audio-recorded police interrogations of the suspects Jones and Smith. The suspects' defense attorneys provided the researcher with the audio-recorded police interrogations of their clients. The suspects had jury trials and were found guilty of most of the charges against them. Jones was sentenced to eight years in prison, and Smith was given a life sentence without the possibility of parole. Both cases are under appeal.

Examining the Blueprint of a Police Interrogation

Suspects who are in police custody in the United States may interact discursively with police officers during the booking stage of the police interrogation. During the booking process, the sequences of talk are often aimed at completing "paperwork" and obtaining personal information from the suspects (Mason 2013), such as their home address, telephone number, employment information, date of birth, place of residence, and so on. After the paperwork is completed, police officers may read suspects their Miranda rights. If the suspect invokes his or her Miranda rights before the caution is read, it is considered a prewaiver invocation for counsel. Excerpt 4.1 is Jones's prewaiver invocation.

Excerpt 4.1

JONES: I've been charged with some rape and I ain't rape nobody.

DETECTIVE MARTIN: OK. Before I- before I talk to you, I'm gonna, um, gotta read you your rights.

JONES: Can I get a lawyer?

DETECTIVE MARTIN: Listen, that's what she's fixing [JONES: I] to explain to you.

JONES: I need somebody, 'cause, I ain't rape nobody.

OFFICER STEWART: Listen, she's fixing to explain you something.

An invocation for counsel may also occur after "paperwork" is completed and the suspect has been read his or her Miranda rights (post-waiver), as illustrated in excerpt 4.2, Smith's invocation for counsel.

Excerpt 4.2

DETECTIVE MILLER: Understanding these rights listed above, do you wish to speak with us, (.) today? And there is a section where you need to initial "yes" or "no." I need for you to say whether or not you want to speak for-you want to speak with us, though.

SMITH: Can I get an attorney?

DETECTIVE PETERSON: Huh?

SMITH: I want to get an attorney. Like.

DETECTIVE PETERSON: Here's the way it works, dude. If you get an attorney we are gonna wait for him to show up, we're not gonna call one for you. You're gonna go straight to the jail. OK. This is your chance to tell us what happened. So, if you got anything that you wanna tell us, now is the time to do it.

SMITH: OK.

DETECTIVE PETERSON: So, sign your name here and print your name next to it.

In both excerpts 4.1 and 4.2, the police officers dismiss the suspects' invocations for counsel on the grounds that they were formulated indirectly and thus were equivocal. This perception is founded on legal rulings such as *Davis v. United States* (1994), which narrowed the scope in which a suspect can reasonably invoke counsel (see Ainsworth 1993, 2008, 2012; Kaiser and Lufkin 2005; Mason 2013). Following *Davis*, invocations for counsel must be performed in a manner that a reasonable police officer deems unequivocal before they are given any legal effect. This ruling, however, does not define what a reasonable police officer would understand as an unequivocal invocation for counsel. Research (Ainsworth 1993, 2008) shows that traditionally police officers and the courts have expressed a preference for invocations for counsel that are formulated as direct speech acts (e.g., "I want an attorney" or "Get me an attorney") and that do not require conversational implicature (Grice 1975) for their understanding.

The interpretation of indirect invocations for counsel as equivocal lies in their alleged potential ambiguity. In this view, indirect invocations (e.g., "Can I get an attorney?"), unlike direct ones (e.g., "Get me an attorney"), may have a literal (e.g., "Am I able to get one?" or "I may want an attorney") or implied meaning (e.g., "I want to talk to an attorney"). This potential duality in meaning and function may render the request inherently equivocal, since it is possible that the suspect's indirect request for counsel is being used with a, primary, literal function. Research in pragmatic theory, however, does not support this legal argument. On the contrary, it provides an explanation for the interviewee's cognitive processing and context-based uses.

Indirect requests for counsel, such as "Can I get a lawyer?," are types of on-record negative politeness that differ in their grammatical realization (from direct requests) but not in their pragmatic function (Brown and Levinson 1987; Holtgraves 1994, 2002, 2005; Holtgraves and Ashley 2001; Arundale 2006). In custodial settings, this type of indirect request strategy, although it deviates from maximum communication efficiency (Grice 1975), performs a relatively clear speech act: a request for counsel. This act is presumed to occur without inference and is grounded in English-speakers' apparent aversion to directness, coupled with a desire to save addressees' face (Goffman 1959, 1967; Brown and Levinson 1987; Terkourafi 2011, 2012).

Historically, the Court's stance on Miranda invocations has facilitated police officers' treatment of indirect invocations for counsel as equivocal (Ainsworth 1993, 2008, 2012; Leo 2001; Mosteller 2008; Weisselberg 2008; Mason 2013). In practice, the upholding of a suspect's right not to self-incriminate seems to reflect a disconnect between legal precedence, the goals of police interrogation, and respondents' linguistic choices in coercive settings. The reading of Miranda and police officers' treatment of a suspect's invocation for counsel thus may mark the onset of coercive police interrogations. Modern interrogation techniques, such as the Reid technique, which include dismissing the suspect's Miranda invocations, "may be thought of as an extended 'anti-Miranda' warning" (Davis, Leo, and Follette 2010: 442).

The Reid technique consists of nine steps, albeit not all applied in any given interrogation, that are organized sequentially to persuade the suspect, who may not be inclined to cooperate, to speak to the police (Ofshe and Leo 1997). The nine-step technique aims to disarm the suspect through a confrontational tone, prevent the suspect from denying his or her guilt, and suggest various "themes" (for each crime) that "explain" the suspect's behavior. The latter often includes police officers' minimizing of the suspect's actions and/or sympathizing with the suspect and his or her predicament ("I know you love your kids and didn't mean to hurt them"), as well as appealing to the suspect's self-interests with time-limited offers ("Look, stop wasting our time and tell us what happened right now").

From a conversational-analysis perspective (Sacks, Schegloff, and Jefferson 1974; Schegloff 1992, 2006), the turns of talk that make up sequences of actions ("topics") in the Reid technique of interrogation follow socially organized procedures. In police interrogations, what is said (topics) and when it is said (sequences) are often predetermined by clearly defined procedures and strategies aimed at eliciting a suspect's confession. This chapter focuses on the sequences of turns of talk that mark the onset of the argumentation stage of the Reid technique of police interrogation. This stage is divided into three main topic units (or actions) based on the occasion of interaction in the suspect's police interrogation: "confrontation," "appeals to self-interest," and "sympathy/minimization." The purpose of this analysis is to shed light on the role the Reid technique plays in shaping police officers' management of topics in exchanges between police and suspects.

Confronting the Suspect

In the Reid technique of interrogation, police officers often confront suspects with evidence that supports the officers' claims and corrodes the suspects' denials. Of note, some of the police officers' alleged evidence may be gathered during the investigative interview of witnesses and/or victims of crime, also known as the "preparatory stage" of police interrogation (Walton 2003; Mason 2016). The questioner formulates questions to ask the suspect, such as those that confront the suspect with evidence of guilt. Police officers may also use false-evidence ploys to extract a confession (Leo 2008). In the data, confrontation is the most common (45 percent) discursive action initiated by the police officers and has distinct face-threatening discursive components, as illustrated in excerpt 4.3.

Excerpt 4.3

DETECTIVE PETERSON: The only thing you are thinking about is yourself. You don't give a fuck about your kids. You don't give a fuck about any of the people you shot.

SMITH: Man. It's not like that. I'm not- I'm not that kind of person.

DETECTIVE PETERSON: You are this kind of person. There's a stack of reports on you already, prior to this. (.) We, I mean we quit printing out copies of incident reports when we got to number seven. We were like there's not even need to keep on printing these things out. You're already in trouble with- she's already got a TPO on you. That ain't no fucking joke. Already that's two strikes against you.

SMITH: That's a lie.

DETECTIVE PETERSON: You know you're not even supposed to be there. But you went over anyway. You don't care.

In excerpt 4.3, Detective Peterson is using confrontation ("The only thing you are thinking about is yourself") to threaten the suspect's face or public persona. In this excerpt, Detective Peterson is attempting to frame Smith's character in an unflattering light, that is, as a selfish and uncaring person.

From a linguistic perspective, interactants may use face strategically to accomplish what Arundale (2006) describes as "connectedness" and/or "separateness." He defines connectedness as "a complex of meanings and actions that may be apparent as unity, interdependence, solidarity, association, congruence, and more, between the relational partners." (204). He notes that separateness, on the other hand, is "meanings and actions that may be voiced as differentiation, independence, autonomy, dissociation, divergence, and so on" (205). In police interrogations such as Smith's, separateness is used often, particularly during confrontation, to establish a disconnect between the suspect's alleged actions (e.g., murder) and the actions of a law-abiding and upstanding individual: "You know you're not even supposed to be there."

Other representative examples of police officers' use of confrontation include their use of evidence gathered at the scene of the crime and/or through interviewing witnesses or accusers. Excerpts 4.4 and 4.5 illustrate this type of police-initiated exchange.

Excerpt 4.4

DETECTIVE PETERSON: When you went into the apartment- When you went into that apartment Karen was hiding and you pointed a gun at your fucking son. And you also shot three other fucking people, so stop lying.

SMITH: I didn't shoot nobody.

DETECTIVE PETERSON: The only person that I have knowledge about that has a gun is you. And you say you own a .40 caliber.

SMITH: Yes, I do.

DETECTIVE PETERSON: Guess which fucking shell casings were all over the scene. Ha, .40 caliber. How about that? (.)

SMITH: I- I didn't shoot.

DETECTIVE PETERSON: Then why is there a fucking bullet hole right on the door? (.) You're making this worse by lying.

SMITH: I ain't lying.

Excerpt 4.5

DETECTIVE PETERSON: From the very beginning this man told you don't insult our intelligence [SMITH: I'm not in-] How many times you think we've done this fucking thing before?

DETECTIVE PETERSON: Cause the things- first off, the things you are saying don't add up and they don't fall in line with what other people are telling us. Pretty much everything you said up to this point is bullshit.

SMITH: It's not- It's not bull. I'm telling you the truth.

DETECTIVE PETERSON: Here's what's gonna happen, dude, when this goes to court. You'll go in there and they're gonna say, what did he say? He gave this fucking bullshit story. (.)

SMITH: I'm not fucking lying.

DETECTIVE MILLER: Look, you need to talk to us and tell us what happened. This is your last opportunity to tell us the truth. It will be better for you if you tell us the truth.

During the confrontation stage of police interrogation, most of the police-initiated exchanges are formulated as statements of fact, followed by a short pause that prompts the suspect to respond. In except 4.4 Detective Peterson connects evidence gathered at the scene of the crime, specifically the type of gun used to shoot the victims and the weapon Smith acknowledges owning: a .40 caliber. Yet, the police officers' attempt at confronting the suspect with evidence (even when provided by the suspect) does not result in Smith's confessing or providing additional information about the shootings. In this excerpt, as in others in the data, the suspects' responses during this type of discursive action often (in 96 percent of cases) consist of denials and forms of negation, such as "I didn't shoot."

Excerpt 4.5 also shows how police officers use confrontation to break down the suspect's possible perception that the police officers do not have a strong case against him (and/or will not continue to pursue the case). As Detective Peterson states, "The things you are saying don't add up." Furthermore, this excerpt illustrates how police officers may switch topics and/or lead the questioning officer during interrogation. In excerpt 4.5, Detective Peterson leads the confrontation of the witness, a confrontation that is met with frequent denials. These types of responses are contrary to the prescribed (main) function of the confrontation strategy: to get the suspect to provide information or, ideally, a confession. To manage the suspect's denials, Detective Miller takes over Smith's interrogation. He introduces another strategy frequently used in the Reid technique of interrogation: "appeals to self-interest" with a time-limited offer ("This is your last opportunity to tell us the truth").

Appeals to Self-Interest with and without a Time-Limited Offer

In the Reid technique of police interrogation, police officers may attempt to persuade suspects that they are trapped and powerless (Kassin, Leo, Meissner, Richman, Colwell, Leach, and LaFon 2007). The police officers then seemingly offer suspects a way to minimize their punishment if they provide a statement: "the suspect's admission is, in effect, his *quid pro quo* for an end to the interrogation and avoidance of worst case scenario." (Leo 2008: 133). The appeals-to-self-interest strategy is often realized linguistically using two face-management strategies, separateness and connectedness (Arundale 2006). On the one hand, police officers assert their power over suspects by emphasizing the gravity of their alleged crime; on the other, they express solidarity with the suspects by providing seemingly beneficial alternatives that minimize or avoid a worst-case scenario. Excerpt 4.6 illustrates this type of interrogation strategy, which is observed 37 percent of the time in the data.

Excerpt 4.6

DETECTIVE MILLER: All right. I need you to understand me. I need you to look at me. From one man to another man. This is serious as it can be and based on how things go here, this morning in talking with one another, can dictate what happens to you the remainder of your life. If you care anything about yourself and what could happen to you, you'll cooperate.

SMITH: I didn't kill nobody.

DETECTIVE MILLER: If you don't divulge to us or tell us anything then you leave it to other people to interpret exactly what happened. Because the way it is sounding right now, this particular point in time makes it- it's bad. But you leave it up to other people to interpret it, they're gonna think you're an animal. And when they think you're an animal, guess what happens?

SMITH: [Crying] I'm an animal.

DETECTIVE MILLER: Correct. Now, be a man and tell us what happened.

SMITH: I didn't kill nobody.

DETECTIVE PETERSON: Stop fucking lying. We know what happened.

In excerpt 4.6 the police officer is establishing, at the onset of this discourse move, the seriousness of the charges and the best option for the suspect: cooperate with the police officers. Detective Miller drives this point by noting that what happens during the interrogation "can dictate what happens to you the remainder of your life." Detective Miller's appeals to Smith's self-interest are aimed at establishing a connection between the suspect's compliance and the police officer's apparent ability to assist the suspect with the perceptions others form of his actions. This attempt at solidarity and connectedness, although it briefly appears to solidify understanding with the suspect ("I'm an animal"), does not result in cooperation. This is the norm in the data. In excerpt 4.6, Smith denies the accusations of murder ("I didn't kill nobody"), which prompts Detective Peterson to take over the interrogation and switch to a previous topic, confrontation: "Stop fucking lying. We know what happened."

The discursive action of appeals to self-interest may also include a time-limited offer. In the data, 27 percent of the police-suspect self-interest exchanges include this type of offer, which often consists of a series of statements in which the police officer expresses the contingency of helping the suspect if he tells the truth. Excerpt 4.7 shows Detective Martin's use of appeals to self-interest with a time-limited offer during Jones's police interrogation.

Excerpt 4.7

DETECTIVE MARTIN: This is your opportunity to be a man and to tell the truth on everything that happened, Jones. Right now is when you have to step up and tell us the truth. No more lies. What happened in the truck?

JONES: I didn't do nothing to that girl. Nothing.

DETECTIVE MARTIN: This is your time to step up. 'Cause you're not gonna have many more times other than today to tell us the truth. Listen to me. If you kissed her, touched that girl, this is the time to fess up (.).

JONES: I didn't touch that girl. We were just talking.

DETECTIVE MARTIN: We know what happened in that truck. No more fucking lies. Did you touch that girl?

JONES: No.

Excerpt 4.7 shows how Detective Martin uses time-limited constraints to put pressure on the suspect and heighten his sense of urgency to cooperate with the police: "Right now is when you have to step up and tell us the truth." The use of a time-limited constraint indicates to the suspect that the police officer has a small window of time to "assist" him. Excerpt 4.7, like other police-initiated exchanges in the case studies, also includes multiple statements that often were a variation on a theme ("this is your opportunity," "right now"). This type of repetitive, police-initiated, time-limited constraint is consistent with the cumulative and goal-directed process of police interrogation, particularly of the Reid technique. Despite the police officer's frequent use of time limits, the suspect responds with denials. This prompts Detective Martin to switch topics and return to the discourse topic of confrontation: "We know what happened in that truck."

The suspects' responses to appeals to self-interest with and without time-limited offers are similar to those provided during confrontation. The suspects respond mostly with denials (94 percent). The lack of a full confession, coupled with the suspects' frequent denials, leads the police officers to close the interrogations of both suspects using appeals to self-interest. In the data, the final or "closing" (Walton 2003) stage of the suspects' interrogations is marked by the police officers' expressions of anger and disappointment toward the suspects. The police officers' final statements thus may be described as a last effort to get the suspects to confess, as illustrated in excerpts 4.8 and 4.9.

Excerpt 4.8

DETECTIVE MILLER: Mr. Smith, you need to help us explain your story. This is your last time to do so. No more lying. People are dead because you violated the TPO. That's a felony. That means you committed felony murder.

SMITH: I am not lying. I didn't kill nobody.

DETECTIVE MILLER: That's the story you're sticking to?

SMITH: Man ().

DETECTIVE PETERSON: It's just as well because I don't want anybody to feel sorry for you. I hope that you remember that you had a chance to turn things around and be an example to your kids. But, you couldn't do that because you are too worried about your own fucking skin and then your kids end up growing up to be a couple of thugs like you. You coward. You fucking coward.

Excerpt 4.9

DETECTIVE MARTIN: If there is anything else you need to tell us, you need to do it right now. Right now is your chance. (.) OK Jones. So this is between you and me. 'Cause I'm done and I'm getting out of here. It's the last time I see you, and what are you gonna stick with? You don't even accept an opportunity, do you? (.) All right, Jones. Listen, don't say Martin didn't try, all right? All right?

JONES: OK. OK.

In excerpts 4.8 and 4.9, the police officers are communicating to both suspects the urgency of cooperating with them ("This is your last time to do so") and their implied intent to "help" them explain their "story." This part of the appeals-to-self-interest strategy relies in part on connectedness in order to reach the suspects and get them to cooperate. This strategy, however, is ineffective in obtaining a response that does not consist in denials. The police officers therefore switch back to confrontation. This discursive action (or topic) marks separateness between the suspects, who the police officers suggest are selfish and common thugs rather than decent, law-abiding individuals, since the latter would cooperate with the police. As the excerpts show, the suspects do not provide a confession and opt to maintain their innocence.

The Sympathetic Detective: The Use of Sympathy and Minimization in Police Interrogations

The sympathetic-detective strategy is "designed to instill hope of minimizing the consequences of guilt, thereby paving the way for the interrogator to suggest *how* one might be able to do so" (Davis, Leo, and Follette 2010: 442). This technique often follows the confrontation stage of police interrogation and may be "recycled" if the suspect denies involvement in the crime of which she or he is accused. Common questions and statements used in the sympathetic-detective strategy include flattering the suspect, showing empathy (an affective response) toward the suspect, and optimizing legal outcomes contingent on the suspect's admitting guilt. In the data, police officers often introduce the sympathetic-detective discourse strategy in a two-part topic sequence: sympathy and minimization. The use of sympathy, for example, appears to assist police officers in convincing suspects that they sympathize with their predicament and that confessing is in their best interest (i.e., leniency is on the table).

Convincing suspects that confessing is in their best interest is further facilitated by minimization. This strategy involves suggesting scenarios that downplay the seriousness of the crime—for instance, a police officer suggesting self-defense rather than premeditated murder to explain a fatal shooting involving a suspect. In the data, police officers use sympathy and/or minimization 18 percent of the time to interrogate the suspects. These strategies, however, are observed more often (41 percent of the time) in Smith's case. It is possible that in Smith's case the police officers were more amenable to using sympathy to explain his criminal charges (murder) than to explain Jones's charge of sexual assault. Excerpt 4.10 illustrates the police officer's use of "sympathy" and "minimization."

Excerpt 4.10

DETECTIVE MILLER: Mr. Smith, I didn't say you did it intentionally. I didn't say your intent was to go over there and kill these people, to shoot anybody. I think you got upset. I think this woman was saying something to you that pissed you off. I understand you being upset, because someone told you, you wouldn't be able to see your kids anymore. There's no doubt in my mind that you care about your kids, hands down. You don't care about nobody else. I know you care about your kids. And for someone to tell you, you would never see your kids again. I would be upset. I know you got upset. I can un- that makes sense to me. Getting upset when someone tells me, I will never see my kids again. Tell me when I can see my kids, and when I can't see my kids. I'd be upset.

SMITH: [Crying] I- I- man.

DETECTIVE MILLER: Things got outta hand, man. Things got out of hand, dude. Dude, things got out of hand. Some words were said, and you know when people get upset they say things they don't necessarily mean. When people get upset they do things they don't necessarily mean. That's understandable. That makes sense to me. (.) If you don't do anything right this very moment, you need to do this for the kids. 'Cause 'em kids love that woman and you know that. You owe them. You owe them the truth.

SMITH: [Crying] We weren't arguing. I just wanted to see my kids. I just wanted to talk.

DETECTIVE PETERSON: Stop lying. You went there when you know you weren't supposed to. You killed those people.

SMITH: I didn't kill no one.

As illustrated in excerpt 4.10, Detective Miller's discursive actions of sympathy ("I understand you being upset . . .") and minimization ("I didn't say you did it intentionally"), which were often repeated in the same turn of talk, prompt a reaction from Smith. In this excerpt, Detective Miller introduces sympathy in his interrogation as a face-saving device aimed at connectedness. This strategy facilitates solidarity with Smith ("for someone to tell you, you would never see your kids again. I would be upset") and seemed to be partially effective. Smith cried and remained silent often; he appeared broken. Smith did not show anger or engage in frequent denials, as was observed often with other types of strategies, in particular confrontation. Smith also provided more information about his whereabouts, specifically that he was at the scene of the crime because he wanted to see his children, who were with their mother at the time of the incident ("I just wanted to see my kids. I just wanted to talk"). Smith had a protective order against him, which he also acknowledged, and was not supposed to visit his ex-girlfriend or children. This strategy, however, is not employed for many turns of talk, making it difficult to determine whether in the long run it would have been effective at eliciting a confession. At the end of excerpt 4.10, Detective Peterson takes the lead in changing the topic back to confrontation and accusing Smith of lying. Smith, in turn, reverted to his preferred response type: denying the police officers' accusations.

In the case studies, the use of sympathy and minimization (combined), albeit not employed often, appears to be more effective than either confrontation or appeals to self-interest in obtaining information from the suspects. When the focus is solely (or predominantly) on sympathy, this strategy appears to be particularly effective. Excerpt 4.11 illustrates the police officer's use of "sympathy."

Excerpt 4.11

OFFICER STEWART: No one is hanging you. You're not a bad person. These things happen. Let us help. Was that girl naked in your truck?

JONES: It wasn't like that. Nothing like that. We were just talking. We were

> watching a movie. She was talking about a lot of stuff about her boyfriend. She was talking about sex stuff. (.) Her pants may have been short. They were low. She wasn't naked.
>
> OFFICER STEWART: So her pants were low? Stop lying and tell the truth.
>
> JONES: I didn't do nothing to that girl.
>
> DETECTIVE MARTIN: Stop lying. We know what happened.

Officer Stewart's use of sympathy prompts Jones to cooperate (to some extent) with the police. Jones provides details about his exchanges with the accuser. Despite Jones's cooperation and lack of denials, Officer Stewart confronts Jones with one of his statements ("So her pants were low? Stop lying and tell the truth"). Jones responds to this shift in topic with a denial ("I didn't do nothing to that girl"). The suspect's denials, in turn, appear to prompt Detective Martin to take over the interrogation and continue the confrontation of the suspect. This switch in topic (and police officer) informs the suspect that anything but an admission of guilt will be considered a lie. In the Reid technique denials are deemed unacceptable responses, since obtaining a confession is the primary goal of this type of interrogation.

Revisiting excerpts 4.10 and 4.11 shows that the suspects' responses to the police officers' use of sympathy and minimization (combined) or primarily sympathy were often (in 76 percent of cases) emotional and included (in 47 percent of cases) information about the criminal act of which they were accused. The sympathetic-detective strategy thus seems to have affected the suspects in a manner unlike other Reid-based techniques. The use of sympathy and minimization, in particular, appears to have facilitated the police officers' connecting with the suspects, possibly because this discursive action establishes common ground between the police officers and the suspects at a more personal and affective level (e.g., "we all make mistakes").

Despite the apparent potential effectiveness of a discursive action that emphasizes sympathy and minimization, this interrogation strategy is not commonly used in contemporary policing (Kassin, Leo, Meissner, Richman, Colwell, Leach, and LaFon 2007). According to a survey on police interrogation practices in the United States, "The typical interrogation often, but not always, includes confronting the suspect with evidence of his or her guilt and appealing to his or her self-interests. Somewhat less frequently, interrogation sometimes includes offering the suspect sympathy, moral justifications and excuses" (Kassin, Leo, Meissner, Richman, Colwell, Leach, and LaFon 2007: 389). The findings of this chapter further the notion that police officers favor face-work strategies that emphasize separateness or distance between the suspect and the police and are consistent with the adversarial nature of interrogation.

Conclusion

In this chapter we examined the linguistic features of three of the discursive strategies most commonly used in the Reid technique of interrogation: sympathy and/or minimization, confrontation, and appeals to self-interest. A conversation-analytic approach was used to examine the topic structure and linguistic goals of this type of discourse. The results of the analysis show that police officers engaged in guilt-presumptive strategies aimed at "taking innocence off the table" and ignoring the suspects' frequent denials. This process commences with the suspects' invocations for counsel, before or after their Miranda warning, and progresses to the police officers' use of Reid based strategies during the "argumentation stage" of police interrogation.

In the case studies, the suspects' invocations for counsel were dismissed as equivocal on the grounds that they were formulated indirectly and, hence, ambiguously. The invocation of Miranda initiates the argumentation stage of interrogation and sets the tone for subsequent police-suspect exchanges, presumably a guilt-presumptive one. The police officers' topic selection during interrogation is consistent with the goals of the Reid technique. The two most frequently used discourse topics in the data are confrontation and appeals to self-interest. These topics, however, were frequently ineffective in gathering information from the suspects, possibly due to their emphasis on separateness. The suspects often responded to confrontation and appeals to self-interest (with or without a time-limited offer) with denials. Very little evidentiary or incriminating information is provided. The use of sympathy and minimization, on the other hand, appear to have been the most effective discourse topics in both suspects' interrogations.

These two topic sequences, which are part of the sympathetic-detective strategy, were used less often in the data but appeared to prompt responses other than denials. Sympathy seems to have been the most effective strategy for gathering information from the suspects, although not a confession. This strategy's effectiveness may be linked to its emphasis on connectedness and empathy, a finding shared by prior research on noncoercive interviewing (e.g., Alison, Alison, Noone, Elntib, and Christiansen 2013). Still, the police officers' use of sympathy in the data was very limited. In essence, sympathy was not given enough time (as measured in turns of talk) before the police officers switched back to confrontation and/or appeals to self-interest. Future studies, hence, are needed to examine the role of affective and/or emotive factors, in particular sympathy, in shaping suspects' responses during police interviews. This type of study, for example, may take the form of a collaboration between researchers of PEACE and Reid and result in common recommendations for police interview practices in the United States and the United Kingdom.

Note

1. The author provided expert testimony in the criminal cases. The cases are on appeal, and at the attorneys' request the names of all parties (e.g., case names), including the defendant/suspect, police officers, and locations, have been changed.

References

Ainsworth, Janet E. 1993. "In a Different Register: The Pragmatics of Powerlessness in Police Interrogation." *Yale Law Journal* 103(2): 259–322.

Ainsworth, Janet E. 2008. "You Have the Right to Remain Silent, but Only If You Ask for It Just So: The Role of Linguistic Ideology in American Police Interrogation Law." *International Journal of Speech, Language and the Law* 15(1): 1–21.

Ainsworth, Janet E. 2012. "The Meaning of Silence in the Right to Remain Silent." In *The Oxford Handbook of Forensic Linguistics*, edited by Larry Solan and Peter Tiersma, 287–298. Oxford: Oxford University Press.

Alison, Laurence J., Emily Alison, Geraldine Noone, Stamatis Elntib, and Paul Christiansen. 2013. "Why Tough Tactics Fail and Rapport Gets Results." *Psychology, Public Policy, and Law* 19: 411–431.

Arundale, Robert B. 2006. "Face as Relational and Interactional: A Communication Framework for Research in Face, Facework, and Politeness." *Journal of Politeness Research* 2: 193–216.

Brown, Penelope, and Stephen C. Levinson. 1987. *Politeness: Some Universals in Language Usage*. Cambridge: Cambridge University Press.

Davis v. United States. 1994. 512 U.S. 452.

Davis, Deborah, Richard A. Leo, and William C. Follette. 2010. "Selling Confession: Setting the Stage with the 'Sympathetic Detective with a Time-Limited Offer.'" *Journal of Contemporary Criminal Justice* 26(4): 441–457.

Dixon, David. 2010. "Questioning Suspects: A Comparative Perspective." *Journal of Contemporary Criminal Justice* 26(4): 426–440.

Goffman, Erving. 1959. *The Presentation of Self in Everyday Life.* New York: Doubleday.

Goffman, Erving. 1967. *Interaction Ritual: Essays on Face-to-Face Behavior.* New York: Random House.

Gudjonsson, Gisli H. 2003. *The Psychology of Interrogations and Confessions.* New York: John Wiley.

Holtgraves, Thomas M. 1994. "Communication in Context: The Effects of Speaker Status on the Comprehension of Indirect Requests." *Journal of Experimental Psychology: Learning, Memory and Cognition* 20: 1205–1218.

Holtgraves, Thomas M. 2002. *Language as Social Action: Social Psychology and Language Use.* Mahwah, NJ: Erlbaum.

Holtgraves, Thomas M. 2005. "Comprehending Conversational Indirectness in a Social Context." In *Social and Cultural Factors Involved in Figurative Language Processing*, edited by Albert N. Katz and Herbert L. Colston, 73–98. Mahwah, NJ: Erlbaum.

Holtgraves, Thomas M., and Aaron Ashley. 2001. "Comprehending Illocutionary Force." *Memory & Cognition* 29: 83–90.

Inbau, Fred E., John E. Reid, Joseph P. Buckley, and Brian C. Jayne. 2005. *Criminal Interrogation and Confessions: Essentials of the Reid Technique.* 1st ed. Sudbury, MA: Jones & Bartlett.

Kaiser, David A., and Paul Lufkin. 2005. "Deconstructing *Davis v. United States*: Intention and Meaning in Ambiguous Requests for Counsel." *Hastings Constitutional Law Quarterly* 32(3): 737–767.

Kassin, Saul M., and Gisli H. Gudjonsson. 2004. "The Psychology of Confessions: A Review of the Literature and Issues." *Psychological Sciences in the Public Interest* 5(2): 33–67.

Kassin, Saul M., Richard A. Leo, Christian A. Meissner, Kimberly D. Richman, Lori H. Colwell, Amy-May Leach, and Dana LaFon. 2007. "Police Interviewing and Interrogation: A Self-Report Survey of Police Practices and Beliefs." *Law and Human Behavior* 31(4): 381–400.

Leo, Richard A. 2001. "Questioning the Relevance of Miranda in the Twentieth-first Century." *Michigan Law Review* 99(5): 1000–1029.

Leo, Richard A. 2008. *Police Interrogation and Criminal Justice.* Cambridge, MA: Harvard University Press.

Mason, Marianne. 2013. "Can I Get a Lawyer? A Suspect's Use of Indirect Requests in a Custodial Setting." *International Journal of Speech, Language and the Law* 20(2): 203–227.

Mason, Marianne. 2016. "The 'Preparatory' and 'Argumentation' Stages of Police Interrogation: A Linguistic Analysis of a Criminal Investigation." *Language and Communication* 48: 79–87.

Milne, Rebecca, and Ray Bull. 1999. *Investigative Interviewing: Psychology and Practice*. Chichester: Wiley.

Mosteller, Robert P. 2008. "Police Deception before Miranda Warnings: The Case for Per Se Exclusion of an Entirely Unjustified Practice at a Particularly Sensitive Moment." *Duke Law School Faculty Scholarship Series* 130: 1239–1272.

Ofshe, Richard J., and Richard A. Leo. 1997. "The Social Psychology of Police Interrogation: The Theory and Classification of True and False Confessions." *Studies in Law, Politics, and Society* 16: 189–251.

Sacks, Harvey, Emanuel A. Schegloff, and Gail Jefferson. 1974. "A Simplest Systematics for the Organization of Turn-Taking for Conversation." *Language* 50(4): 696–735.

Schegloff, Emanuel A. 1992. "On Talk and Its Institutional Occasions." In *Talk at Work: Interaction in Institutional Settings*, edited by Paul Drew and John Heritage, 101–134. Cambridge: Cambridge University Press.

Schegloff, Emanuel A. 2006. "Interaction: The Infrastructure for Social Institutions, the Natural Ecological Niche for Language, and the Arena in which Culture Is Enacted." In *Roots of Human Sociality: Culture, Cognition and Interaction*, edited by Nick Enfield and Stephen C. Levinson, 70–96. London: Berg.

Shuy, Roger W. 1998. *The Language of Confession, Interrogation, and Deception*. Thousand Oaks, CA: Sage.

Shuy, Roger W. 2005. *Creating Language Crimes: How Law Enforcement Uses (and Misuses) Language*. Oxford: Oxford University Press.

Skelton, Meghan S., and James G. Connell III. 2004. "The Routine Booking Question Exception to Miranda." *University of Baltimore Law Review* 34: 78–94.

Terkourafi, Marina. 2011. "The Puzzle of Indirect Speech." *Journal of Pragmatics* 43: 2861–2865.

Terkourafi, Marina. 2012. "Politeness and Pragmatics." In *The Cambridge Handbook of Pragmatics*, edited by Katarzyna Jaszczolt and Keith Allan, 617–637. Cambridge: Cambridge University Press.

U.S. Supreme Court. 1966. *Miranda v. Arizona*. 384 U.S. 436.

Walton, Douglas. 2003. "The Interrogation as a Type of Dialogue." *Journal of Pragmatics* 35: 1771–1802.

Weisselberg, Charles D. 2008. "Mourning Miranda." *California Law Review* 96(6): 1521–1601.

CHAPTER FIVE

The Discourse Structure of Blame Mitigation in a Police Interrogation

Philip Gaines

Introduction: Maximization and Minimization in the Behavioral Sciences Literature

One of the most striking developments in the modern history of criminal justice in the United States has been the rapidly increasing number of DNA-based exonerations of persons convicted of serious crimes, some of whom had been incarcerated for decades. As of this writing, the Innocence Project reports a total of 356 such exonerations, the scientifically unarguable proof of which—thanks to increasingly sophisticated and accurate DNA testing—makes it undeniable that these were wrongful convictions. To add to this disturbing state of affairs is the fact that the major contributing factor in such cases was a confession by the suspect to a crime that he or she did not commit. In a recent update to its statistics on DNA exonerations in the United States, the Innocence Project reports that 29 percent of such cases involved false confessions.[1]

Although it is difficult for most of us to imagine someone falsely confessing to a serious crime, extensive research has demonstrated that through coercive interrogation tactics by police interviewers, a suspect will admit to a crime of which he or she is innocent and will even participate in the composition of a detailed written confession. In a summary of the basic elements of coercive questioning and their powerful effects, Richard Leo—a pioneering researcher of false confessions in police interrogation—concludes that "the question of how it can be that innocent suspects give false confessions has been answered: The methods of maximization and minimization generate them" (Davis and Leo 2010: 191). *Maximization* and *minimization* here refer to the two overarching interrogation procedures identified by Saul Kassin as constituting the essence of the nine-step Reid technique—"overwhelmingly the most widely-used interrogation method in the US" (Meyer and Reppucci 2007: 760–61; Kassin 2014: 114; Kassin, Kukucka, Lawson, and DeCarlo 2014: 74; Horgan, Russano, Meissner, and Evans 2012: 76)—which is based on Inbau, Reid, Buckley, and Jayne's *Criminal Interrogation and Confessions* (now in its fifth edition), called by Kassin and McNall "the most popular of . . . several manuals . . . available to advise law enforcement officials on how to get recalcitrant suspects to confess" (1991: 234).

The techniques of maximization and minimization are complementary approaches to bringing a suspect to a psychological state in which the decision to confess is seen as the only means of escape not only from the stress of a coercive interrogation, but also from what is perceived as the inevitable and dire consequences of continued denial—most likely including certain conviction and imprisonment. According to Kassin and McNall, maximization is a

> "hard-sell" technique in which the interrogator tries to scare and intimidate the suspect into confessing by making false claims about evidence (e.g., staging an eyewitness identification or a fraudulent lie-detector test) and exaggerating the seriousness of the offense and the magnitude of the charges.

The other side of the interrogation coin is minimization, the

> "soft-sell" technique in which the police interrogator tries to lull the suspect into a false sense of security by offering sympathy, tolerance, face-saving excuses, and even moral justification, by blaming a victim or accomplice, by citing extenuating circumstances, or by playing down the seriousness of the charges. (Kassin and McNall 1991: 234–235)

Once the interrogator has intimated the risks associated with not confessing and then mitigated the significance of the offense and the risks of confession, the last step is to offer the suspect a "deal" (Russano, Meissner, Narchet, and Kassin 2005), in which implied promises of leniency are made in exchange for a confession. Russano and colleagues conclude from their experimental research results that "offering deals to suspects in the real world may lead innocent persons to confess simply because they believe that they are better off accepting the known consequences of the deal than taking their chances of winning at trial" (Russano, Meissner, Narchet, and Kassin 2005: 485). The psychological research on maximization and minimization (see below) is extensive, and its findings are compelling in their implications for understanding how so many police interrogations have—owing to their coercive nature—resulted in false confessions. However, linguistic- and discourse-analytic work on police interrogation has rarely treated the American model of interrogation, focusing instead on jurisdictions in the United Kingdom and elsewhere, which since 1984 have been characterized by methods that expressly avoid overtly coercive techniques. Research on police interrogation in the United States is critically needed, particularly in view of the accelerating pace of DNA-based exonerations of wrongly convicted prisoners. This chapter represents an initial foray into a discourse-analytic examination of certain elements of maximization and minimization as enacted in an actual interrogation—with particular attention paid to what I call *blame mitigation*. The text is a transcript of the police interview of 16-year-old Nga Truong, which resulted in her false confession of having smothered her child. The transcript was prepared by the author after comparing the official version produced by the Worcester (Massachusetts) Police Department with the complete audiovisual recording of the interrogation. Numerous corrections were made to the departmental transcript in light of obvious conflicts with the recorded material.[2] This study will show that a focus on blame mitigation can be an effective strategy of minimization leading to a false confession.

The Interrogation of Nga Truong

As part of a 2007 investigation into the sudden crib death in Worcester, Massachusetts, of three-year-old Khyle Truong, his mother, Nga Truong, was interrogated by two detectives of the Worcester Police Department. The officers use classic Reid techniques in the interrogation, beginning with the behavior-analysis phase, in which the interviewer asks a series of questions not necessarily related to the crime and attends to the answers with an eye toward behaviors that suggest evasion, contradiction, and deception. Once the officer is convinced that ample reason has been given to assume that the suspect is not being truthful, the interview shifts to the guilt-presumptive interrogation phase, in which the discourse is exclusively oriented toward securing an admission of guilt.

In the Truong interrogation, the interviewing officers employ nearly all of the standard maximization techniques (as identified in prior psychological research—see, e.g., Kassin and McNall 1991; Kassin and Kiechel 1996; Kassin 1997; Ofshe and Leo 1997a, 1997b; Meissner and Russano 2003; Drizin and Leo 2004; Kassin and Gudjonsson 2004; Russano, Meissner, Narchet, and Kassin 2005; Kassin 2005, 2006; Blair 2007; Meissner, Horgan, and Albrechtsen 2009; Davis, Leo, and Follette 2010; Evans, Meissner, Brandon, Russano, and Kleinman 2010; Kassin, Drizin, Grisso, Gudjonsson, Leo, and Redlich 2010):

- Emphasizing the seriousness of the situation and the charges
- Presenting an unfriendly demeanor
- Scaring or intimidating the suspect
- Presenting an unforgiving portrayal of the crime
- Confronting the suspect with false evidence
- Accusing the suspect of being guilty
- Refusing to accept denials or claims of innocence
- Communicating certainty of the suspect's guilt
- Noting contradictions in the suspect's story
- Intimating the costs and consequences of continued denial, including suggesting that if the suspect continues to deny guilt, her actions will be portrayed in their worst possible light
- Appealing to accountability to God or religion
- Appealing to the suspect's conscience.

The interviewing officers' use of minimization techniques is much narrower in scope, focusing on:

- Citing mitigating or extenuating circumstances
- Minimizing the oral, psychological, moral, and legal consequences of confessing
- Shifting the blame.

This final minimization technique, shifting the blame, lies at the heart of my analysis. The rest of both the maximization and minimization techniques are referenced here since they appear and reappear regularly in the course of the development of the officers' discourse of blame mitigation. Utterances enacting all of these techniques can be noted in the co-texts and contexts of the transcript extracts, which focus on blame mitigation.

The Discourse Structure of Blame Mitigation

As mentioned, one of the canonical elements of minimization is mitigation of the suspect's blame or responsibility for the crime. Research has shown (see, e.g., Meissner and Russano 2003: 58; Drizin and Leo 2004: 14; Kassin and Gudjonsson 2004: 55, 60) that mitigating culpability can be accomplished in a number of ways—by suggesting that the suspect's actions were spontaneous, accidental, provoked, rationalizable, done in self-defense, pressured, drug-induced, or otherwise justifiable by external factors. This critical component of minimization is often enacted through what is referred to in the psychological literature as *theme development*: "Interrogators are trained to minimize the crime through 'theme development'—a process of providing moral justification or face-saving excuses" (Kassin 2015: 35). Kassin outlines the process of developing and using themes: "The interrogator offers sympathy and understanding, minimizes the crime, and offers the suspect motivation 'themes'—for example, suggesting that a murder was spontaneous, provoked, peer-pressured, or accidental rather than the work of a cold-blooded murderer" (2014: 114). As with all techniques of minimization, the purpose of blame mitigation through theme development is not simply to alleviate a sense of guilt or make the suspect feel better about what he or she has done. Rather, the point is to cause suspects to believe they will be dealt with less harshly since their actions were not so bad after all: "Research shows that . . . by design, minimization tactics lead people to infer that they will be treated with leniency if they confess" (Kassin and McNall 1991).

As this analysis will show, the themes developed by the interviewing officers in the Nga Truong case are that (1) her actions were *provoked* (viz. by her mother), (2) her actions were *spontaneous* and out of her control, and (3) her actions arose from *psychological dysfunction*—the resolution of which becomes her responsibility. Topics informing each of these themes appear both recursively and discontinuously throughout the interview, often being interrupted and then rejoined multiple times. However, an overarching format for the development of the themes—what I will call *accumulative construction*—suffuses the officers' discourse. This format effectively elicits the suspect's assent, along the way, to noninculpatory propositions, but it also progressively and ultimately leads to an admission of guilt for the crime.

The Accumulative Construction of Provocation

Typically provocation is presented by interrogators as coming from the victim him- or herself. Inbau, Reid, Buckley, and Jayne note that "the interrogation technique of condemning the victim can . . . be used advantageously in . . . sex crimes" (2013: 257). The authors suggest the following approach to mitigating an alleged rapist's culpability—one that focuses on the idea that the perpetrator was provoked by the behavior of the victim:

> Joe, no woman should ever be on the street at night looking as sexy as she did . . . It's too much of a temptation for any normal man. If she hadn't gone around dressed like that, you wouldn't be in this room now.

> There's a limit to the teasing and excitement men can take; then something's got to give . . . if she's not willing to go all the way, she ought to stop way short of what this gal allowed you to do.

Here the hypothetical victim is presented as having provoked the alleged rapist by dressing provocatively and encouraging him through allowing intimate physical contact. Thus, blame for the crime is assigned to the provoking victim.

In the Truong case, the victim was a very young child—not a likely candidate for provocation (although see below). Instead, the detectives (D1 and D2) posit the suspect's (S) mother as the one bringing about the provocation. The interrogators develop the theme of "provoked actions" by focusing on two progressively related elements:

1. S had historically been burdened unfairly with her mother's responsibilities.
2. S had been made resentful and angry by her mother's selfishness.

Establishing the Burden of Responsibility for Child Care

Early in the interrogation,[3] D1 establishes that S has had a history of having to babysit for her mother (line 267):

151[4]	D1:	Have you had to take care of your- your brothers all along?
152		Have you done a lot of, you know, [babysitting ( )]?
153	S:	[I take care of them sometimes.]

257	D1:	Where was your mother, your mother is Van, where was she?
258	S:	She was in her room.
259	D1:	How come?
260	S:	Because she's been sick.
261	D1:	She's been sick. What does she have?
262	S:	I think a cold.
263	D1:	Just a cold?
264		So you were, um, in charge of the children?
265	S:	Yes.
266	D1:	Again?
267		You take care of your brothers a lot?
268	S:	Sometimes.
269	D1:	Yeah.

Note that D1's questions contain subtle presuppositions about the conditions of S's babysitting. Taking care of her brothers has been something she has "had to" do (line 151), suggesting some level of compulsion or duress. Moreover, it has been "a lot" of babysitting (line 152) and caregiving (line 267). Note that these are presuppositions that S in fact resists (lines 153 and 268). On the day of Khyle's death (line 257), D1 hints at S's mother's avoidance of responsibility by suggesting that her having "just a cold" was inadequate reason for her to stay in her room and leave the care of the children to S (lines 263–264). "Again?" (line 266) indicates D1's commiseration with S over the frequency with which her mother leaves her "in charge" of the children—a level of responsibility suggested to be inappropriate for a sixteen-year-old. In summary, D1 here frames S's babysitting responsibilities as unavoidable, continual, and onerous.

In D1's formulation, exacerbating the burden of S's unfair babysitting responsibilities is the fact that her mother not only does not insist on a bedtime for the children but has not even provided them with beds:

320 D1: Do these kids have a bedtime?
321 S: N[o.
322 D1: [I realize one of them is fourteen, fifteen.
323 No specific bedtime?
324 As a matter of fact they don't even have beds, do they?
325 No, they sleep on the couch?
326 S: Yes.

The implication here is that S is kept up inordinately late with child care and has to deal with the children's constant presence in the evenings. In the following series of interactions, D2 focuses on more negative effects of S's having to assume her mother's child-care responsibilities:

733 D2: Is your mom sick a lot?
734 S: Not really. She gets sick sometimes.
735 D2: Yeah, but you have to get up in the morning on school days
736 and get Khyle ready and get him to school with you, right?
737 And then what happens on the weekends?
738 Does your mother expect you to take care of Johnny?
739 S: (inaudible)
740 All the kids just run around.
741 D2: Uh, does your mom stay in bed late and you get up with the kids?
742 S: Mm-hm.

S is shown to have her own child-care responsibilities in addition to those imposed by her mother (lines 735–736). She isn't even allowed to have free time on weekends because she has to take care of her brother (lines 737–738)—all because her mother leaves the chaotic [(line 740) morning child-care responsibilities to S (lines 741–742).

Examining S's Reaction to Unfair Treatment

Having established that S has been overburdened with and pressured into taking on responsibilities that should have been her mother's, D2 begins to question S about how she feels and what she thinks about it:

741 D2: Uh, does your mom stay in bed late and you get up with the kids?

742 S: Mm-hm.
743 D2: How does that make you feel?
744 S: Tired sometimes.
745 D2: Yeah, I'll bet.
746 That ain't right, is it?
747 S: I'm used to it, you know.
748 D2: Yeah, but it does get trying, doesn't it,
749 especially for a girl of your age.
750 I mean it is bad enough you are expected to take care of Khyle . . .

D2 chooses a specific situation that exemplifies S's mother's irresponsibility and then queries her on how it makes her feel (lines 741–743). This is an important framing step, for it starts to move the discourse from an essentially monologic rehearsal of S's mother's poor behavior and its damaging effects on S to a dialogic construction of S's internal emotional experience. D2's first attempt to get S to participate in this coconstruction of her negative feelings toward her mother fails: S says only that she has had a physical response of getting "tired sometimes" (line 744). However, D2 then prompts her to reveal a critical attitude toward her mother's injustice, employing a tag question to invite her participation (line 746). This attempt also fails (line 747). D2 tries again, using another tag question, to elicit from S a negative feeling toward her mother's unreasonable expectations and their being "trying" on her (lines 748–750)—to which he receives no reply.

Following a series of turns in which D1 goes over with S the sequence of events leading up to Khyle's death and D2 refers to the legal options before her, D2 continues his evaluation of S's mother's unfair expectations, framing them as putting "pressure" on S:

797 D2: and what I've seen of your mother,
798 it seems like a lot of pressure's put on you
799 to take care of not only your own child
800 but the children of your mother.
801 I mean, she's only, what, fourteen years older than you, right?
802 And I think she puts a lot of pressure on you to take care of the kids,
803 and that's, uh, that's a pretty big responsibility at your age.

First, through the use of the agentless passive voice, the pressure is presented as being "put on" S (line 798). D1 then moves to the active voice to make it salient that her mother is the one doing the pressuring (line 802).

Another series of turns has D2 and then D1 revisiting the supposed evidence of S's guilt—evidence which both officers posit as irrefutable. Then, having previously broached the matter of S's feelings about her mother's treatment of her, attempted to elicit S's agreement to its unfairness, and offered a critique of the pressure her mother has put on her, D2 asks a pivotal question:

868 D2: Do you get angry at your mom when she's laying in bed telling you
869 to change her baby's diaper?
870 Hmm?
871 S: Sometimes.
872 D2: Yeah.

D2 raises the specter of anger (line 868) as a factor in the unfolding of events surrounding Khyle's death and, in a watershed moment, acquires S's concession that she *has* been angry—albeit only "sometimes" (line 871). D1 then picks up the discourse and weighs in with his evaluative judgment of S's mother:

873 D1: 'Cause your mother keeps havin' babies,
874 and you have to take care of 'em, right?
875 That's not fair to you.
876 That's not fair to you.
877 You're a kid; you should be able to be a kid, right? (9.0)
878 Is it too much pressure for you to take care of that baby? (3.5)
879 I would think it would be, right? (5.0)
880 You've been taking care of them babies for a long time, haven't you?
881 Because your mother had kids
882 that you had to take care of (2.0) every day. (3.0)
883 Not your kids. Hers. Right?

With "That's not fair to you"—repeated for emphasis [lines 875–876)—D1 shows solidarity with D2's indignation (line 746) at S's mother's mistreatment of her. Additionally, the evaluative modal "should" (line 877) implies that S's mother has wrongfully deprived S of being "able to be a kid." D1 then follows D2's lead on the invocation of anger:

884	D1:	Why should you take care of her kids?
885		Does that—that make you angry?
886	S:	Sometimes.
887	D1:	Sometimes. (3.0)
888		Now you have one, and that's way too much to bear, isn't it? (5.5)
889	D2:	That would make anybody angry.

Again, D1 is only able to obtain an affirmation that S is "sometimes" (line 886) made angry by her mother—a qualification judged by D1 as suspicious, as evidenced by a loaded repetition of her answer (line 887). D2 then takes the significant step of naturalizing S's anger (line 889), presenting it as a common, understandable experience and removing the stigma of her being a lone bad actor in civilized society. D2 and D1 then follow up with a harangue directed at S's mother:

890	D2:	You're mother's layin' in bed tellin' you to go get a diaper
891		and put a diaper on HER kid
892	D1:	Do this, do that, feed 'em, take care of 'em. (24.0)
893	D2:	Do you and Edwin ever get to go off by yourselves? (5.0)
894		Does you mom ever volunteer to take care of Khyle? (2.5) No. (3.0)
895		So that, it's a one-way street, huh?
896		You're doin' all the work, and she's lyin' in bed.

Here D2 and D1 seek to justify and commiserate with S's anger by developing a vivid scenario of a mother giving orders to a harried daughter as the former lounges in bed (lines 890–892)—complete with an imagined script line (line 892) personalizing S's mother's thoughtless demands.

Assembling the Accumulated Provoking Factors Leading to the Victim's Death

At line 963 D1 returns to pressing S to admit her culpability in her baby's death and crucially begins to make the case for provocation as the underlying factor:

963 D1: That baby didn't suffocate on the—on the—on the mattress. (3.0)
964 The only two people in that room
965 according to you AND your mother were you and Edwin.
966 But if you didn't do it, Edwin did it. (7.0)
967 I'm leaning toward you, you know why? (7.0)
968 Do you know why?
969 S: Why? (2.5)
970 D1: Think about it. (8.0)
971 D1: You're pissed at your mother.
972 You have to keep taking care of all these kids. (16.0)

Here, for the first time, D1 posits causation for S smothering Khyle, linking her actions to her anger (lines 967–972). As D1's story goes, S is so angry at her mother ("pissed," line 971) that she kills Khyle.

Following a brief excursus exploring the circumstances of her brother Hein's death a few years before while she was babysitting him—a death legally determined to have been caused by SIDS—D1 returns to the theme of her mother's provocation of S's anger as the impetus for S killing Khyle:

1034 D1: 'Cause we know you're pissed
1035 because you have to keep taking care of your mother's kids.
1036 And all these other little kids.
1037 And you don't get to be a kid.
1038 That's what the problem is.
1039 And that's why you smothered Khyle, didn't you?
1040 S: I did not.
1041 D1: That's why you smothered him, didn't you?
1042 S: I would never kill him.

Notable here is the claim by D1 that the officers "know" (line 1034) that she was angry at her mother and the burden placed on her—a knowing flimsily based on their receipt of S's hesitant and partial agreements to the proposition in prior questioning. In line 1038, D1 asserts that he knows "what the problem is"—ostensibly, the problem that underlies S's anger, but, more important, the problem that eventuated in S's smothering Khyle (lines 1038–1040).

Following more close questioning and cajoling, D1 returns to the theme of S's anger at her mother as the reason for killing Khyle:

1113 D1: If you were angry, sick, tired; sick and tired of being sick and tired;
1114 pissed off at your mother
1115 and you did something stupid,
1116 get help. (6.0)
1117 I dare say your mother's more to blame than you are. (2.5)
1118 You had zero chance of being a kid. (7.0)

In yet another critical transition, D1 explicitly assigns the lion's share of the culpability for Khyle's death to S's mother (line 1117)—a striking example of the shifting and, hence, mitigating of the suspect's blame. The chain of reasoning, however, is not yet complete, having been left by D1 in the form of an enthymeme. In D1's construction, it has been established that S was provoked by her mother, which caused her to smother Khyle; but a crucial premise has not been explicitly stated: how exactly would such provocation bring about such a heinous act?

The Accumulative Construction of Spontaneity

ESTABLISHING INEVITABILITY AND ACCIDENT

Having assigned to her mother the greater share of the blame for provoking Khyle's death at the hands of his own mother, D2 proceeds to explain how S's anger led inexorably to her smothering her son:

1147 D2: First of all, I think that you were under a lot of stress from your mother,
1148 probably not easy having a lazy mother.
1149 S: But I would not ( ) [kill my son
1150 D2: [But how would you—
1151 I know, but how would you, uh, characterize your mother?
1152 Lazy? Energetic? (3.0)
1153 I mean, even when she's not sick,
1154 she looks like the type who just lays around in bed all day.
1155 Right? Is that true?
1156 Expects you to take care of the kids, right?

1157		'Cause the diapers are in your room, which I thought was kinda weird
1158		All the diapers for all the babies are in your room
1159		Which leads me to believe that you change most of the, uh, diapers
1160		For Johnny and for Khyle, right?
1161		Would that be true?
1162		Right. And that day you were probably tired
1163		'cause you were up late with a, uh, sick baby (4.0) right? (5.0)
1164		'Cause I've had kids, and I know how that is. (3.5)
1165		And then you get up at eight and give your baby a bottle, right?
1166		Khyle's goin' back to sleep, and you're pretty excited about that,
1167		you get some time for yourself on MySpace
1168		or maybe to go back to sleep, right?
1169		You don't get a lot of that, right? (3.0)
1170		Then what happens?
1171		Your mom calls you to change HER kid's diaper (3.0)
1172	S:	I went in the room to get a diaper and I saw Khyle there
1173	D1:	Holding his breath (5.0) right? (3.0)
1174	D2:	That wasn't exactly the ending I had, but (3.0)
1175	D1:	But it's the one you've practiced,
1176		so it's the one you're gonna keep spittin' out (10.0).

Here, D2 sets up the scene: S is already "under a lot of stress from [her] mother" (line 1147), tired because she was up late the night before (lines 1162–1163), and "excited" about the prospect of having a little time for herself (lines 1166–1167) or getting some much-needed sleep (lines 1168–1169). D2 concludes with the crisis-precipitating event: "Then what happens? Your mother calls you to change her kid's diaper" (line 1171). S attempts to pre-empt the narrative trajectory that would have her smothering Khyle (line 1172)—an attempt that is met with sarcasm and derision from D1 (lines 1173–1176). D2 continues:

1177	D2:	My guess would have been that when you went in the room
1178		Khyle was either getting up or he woke up when you went in the room
1179		and there went your free time to either go back to bed or to watch MySpace
1180		and that just set you off. (8.0)

1181 D1: Nga, it happens. This unit investigates this all the time.
1182 People shake their babies and kill them.
1183 They don't mean to do it. They get frustrated.
1184 It's too much. It's too much to handle.
1185 And they can't believe it happened when it's done, but it happens. (2.5)
1186 Now it's happened to you twice.

D2 "guess[es]" (line 1177) what happens next, unfolding an inexorable chain of events: When S goes into Khyle's room to get a diaper for her brother, Khyle is awake, presenting an obligation and responsibility requiring S's immediate attention (line 1178). With Khyle now awake, S is faced with yet one more frustrating disappointment: D2 posits that her mother's selfish demand results in the loss of her dearly hoped-for free time, and—as though in a moment of mindless, irrational reaction—this disappointment "just set [her] off" (line 1180), and she smothers Khyle.

Consider the implications for how this scenario is constructed discursively: First of all, in a striking change of focus on agency, D2 posits Khyle *himself* as the proximate cause of S's being "set off" (lines 1178–1180). What is in view now is not her mother's demand to change her brother's diaper or the annoying task of having to do so, but rather the fact that Khyle has woken up and ruined her evening (line 1179). Such is the missing thematic premise of D2's enthymeme—the factor that links her mother's provocation to the killing of her child: persons who have been provoked over and over by others and their unfair treatment are at risk of being "set off" and taking out their rage at an innocent who happens to be in the line of fire of their anger. D1 then calls upon his professional experience to explain how such a thing can happen: people kill their children without meaning to (lines 1182–1183), they become overwhelmed by their frustration (lines 1183–1184), and they "can't believe it happened" (line 1185). In applying this principle directly to S (line 1186), D1 presents another significant blame-mitigating shift of agency: Smothering Khyle is not something that S does, but rather something that "happens" to her (line 1186)—and, of course, she "didn't mean for it to happen" (line 1197):

1195 D1: Maybe you meant to just quiet him down so he'd fall back to sleep.
1196 Maybe you thought he fell asleep. (5.0)

1197 Either way, you probably didn't mean for it to happen.
1198 But it did. (50.0)

D1 then proceeds to extend the explanation, framing the killing as an accident:

1238 D1: Tell us it was an accident.
1239 D1: Tell us you didn't mean to do it.
. . .
1242 D1: If it was an accident, tell us it was an accident. (19.0)

Here, D1 urges S to accept and proffer this explanation for her spontaneous and unlooked-for action, providing yet another blame-mitigating factor.

POSITING LOSS OF CONTROL AS CAUSE FOR THE ACCIDENT

Following another rehearsal of the evidence supporting the officers' theory, D2 revisits S's spontaneous action, referencing the commonplace of the "perfect storm":

1268 D2: Nga, it's understandable–
1269 Did you ever see the movie *The Perfect Storm*?
1270 Just when everything collides at once.
1271 Okay, when three systems collide at once, it makes for a vicious storm.
1272 Sometimes we use that to say, when people lose control,
1273 they—it was just the perfect storm.
1274 It was the baby, it was your mother, it was your life, okay?
1275 Maybe that just collided all at once and you lost it. (2.5)

For D2, the "colliding systems" were Khyle, her mother, and her intolerable life situation (line 1274). In D2's account, that is where the blame lies; S's only failing is that she "lost it" (line 1275)—the "control" (line 1272) of her emotions/ and faculties. Later, D2 offers S a script line for her confession that includes the notion of "losing it":

1280 D2: "I'm a sixteen-year-old girl, I lost it, this is what happened,"

In D1 and D2's formulation, S is a victim of her mother's inculpating behavior—a person who couldn't take it anymore and snapped. Her actions were an uncontrollable, spontaneous reaction to a mentally, emotionally, and physically intolerable life situation brought on by her mother. In fact, the whole thing was just plain stupid—

1113 D1: If you were angry, sick, tired; sick and tired of being sick and tired;
1114 pissed off at your mother
1115 and you did something stupid,
1116 get help. (6.0)

—the ultimate mitigation of blame and minimization of responsibility.

The Accumulative Construction of Responsibility

PROPOSING A DYSFUNCTIONAL MOTHER-DAUGHTER RELATIONSHIP

The final technique of blame mitigation enacted by the officers is the imputation to S of psychological dysfunction as the root cause of her actions. It had already been established that S had suffered unfair treatment by her mother and that the frustration and anger resulting from such treatment caused her to lose control in the heat of the moment and take out her emotions on her son by smothering him. For D1 and D2, however, S's violent reaction was not an isolated or anomalous incident; instead, it was a manifestation of deep-seated and ongoing psychological issues. One such issue is a dysfunctional relationship with her mother:

1077 D2: You have some real issues with your mother,
1078 and I don't blame you after talking with her.

Note that D2 posits S's "real issues" (line 1077) with her mother as current and continuing. Later, D1 suggests that S's issues have resulted, at least in part, from child abuse:

1518 D1: I will say to you that I am not fully versed
1519 on the kinds of help I—that they can get you.
1520 But these ladies out here, these women that work with children like you
1521 and people that are abused and have issues at home,
1522 they have a lot of resources. (6.5)

Although the conjunction "and" (line 1521) appears to be additive, allowing for the interpretation that "children like you" and "people that are abused and have issues at home" are separate categories, this is not likely the case. The larger context of S's experiences of mistreatment at the hands of her mother certainly qualifies as abusive, which would support an interpretation in which "and" serves here as an alternative to a verbal colon or em dash—making the second phrase an extension of the first.

PROPOSING A DYSFUNCTIONAL HOMELIFE

S's issues with her mother are presented as part of a larger problem of domestic dysfunction of which S has been a victim:

1503 D1: You're not happy at home.
1504 You have a dysfunctional family

The same situation obtains with regard to anger:

1502 You've got anger issues, you've run away.

It is not clear whether S's "anger issues" are separate from her running away or are the cause of it; in any case, the latter action reflects a positing of S being alienated from her home context. In summary, S is presented as having domestic dysfunction issues, issues with her mother, child abuse issues, and anger issues. The use of "issues"—an informal, quasi psychological term for personal problems—by both officers suggests that S is not psychologically sound or healthy. S's current need, according to D2, is to get those issues resolved:

1214 D2: . . . It's gonna probably happen again
1215 Until you resolve whatever issues you have.
1216 You're sixteen years old.
1217 Now's the time to resolve it.
1218 Don't let it keep going. (2.0)

Referring to the death of Khyle and the earlier death of her brother Hein, D2 suggests that S is another murder waiting to happen, owing to her unresolved psychological problems. Hence, the blame for the smothering of Khyle is rooted in personal issues that need resolution. Further, such resolution is not something that S can arrive at by herself. She will need help:

1501 D1: You'll need some psychological help. (10.0)

In addition, she will need actual treatment to help heal her psychological problems—another indication that the blame for Khyle's death lies at the door of a mental condition rather than an intentional heinous act:

1567 D2: We have to know what exactly happened (3.0) Nga,
1568 and then try to figure out why it happened,
1569 and then that's how the—the courts decide on what treatment,
1570 how to proceed with the treatment
1571 and what exactly should happen, okay?

The specter is then raised of S's being plagued by an ongoing obsessive mental picture of her having smothered her son (lines 1493–1494)—

1493 D1: You keep seein' it, don't you?
1494 Keep seein' it in your mind what happened.
1495 You're never going to stop seeing it either, 'til you make it right. (8.0)
1496 S: What kind of help can I get? (4.0)
1497 D1: Whatever you need, we'll look for it.
1498 D2: That's not for us to decide
1499 Once you get put into the system, they'll find help—
1500 Psychological [help

—an obsession that will not go away (line 1495) until she gets psychological help (line 1500).

SECURING A PROGRESSIVE ADMISSION OF RESPONSIBILITY

Since the purpose of the interrogation phase is to secure an admission, it is critical for the officers to push for it. However, this discursive work is accomplished in an unexpected way. Early in the interrogation, D2 first broaches with S the matter of admitting "the truth":

817 D2: The truth is sometimes hard to admit
818 especially when we hurt somebody that we love. (9.0)

D2 grants that this will be something "hard" (line 817) to do, a concession also made by D1 shortly thereafter (line 907):

906 D1: I need you to tell me so we can get you some help.
907 I know it's not easy, but once- once you let it go (3.5)
908 You'll be fine. (3.5)

Here, D1 also reformulates "admitting" as "let[ting] it go" (line 907), a quasi-self-therapeutic step for S that will bring her relief (line 908). Rather than pushing immediately for an admission to the killing of Khyle, however, D1 makes a key blame-mitigation move by insisting that S admit merely that she has "a problem" (line 1102):

1099 D1: Detective Doherty told you, you're still a juvenile.
1100 We can help you.
1101 We can get you help.
1102 Your- First thing you have to do is admit you have a problem.

The "problem," as presented here, is not that of having killed her son, being under investigation and interrogation, and facing a potential murder prosecution, but rather an underlying psychological condition requiring professional help (lines 1100–1101). D1's use of the present tense "have" (line 1102) makes clear that the problem S must admit to is a current, ongoing one.

To be sure, both D2 and D1 soon put a fine point on exactly what they expect in terms of an admission from S:

1228 D2: It's a tough thing to admit
1229 To yourself, to your family, to your friends, okay? (3.0)
1230 But in the end, if it comes out (6.0)
1231 That your son was smothered by you
1232 Then how's it look after you've lied to everybody, right?
1233 How's that gonna look? (6.0)
1234 The best thing for everyone involved right now
1235 is for you to come clean
1236 tell us what happened to Khyle
1433 D1: Nga, you know, you know what you did,
1434 and we know what you did. (3.0)

1435 Based on all the evidence, there's no doubt what happened in there.
1436 All everyone's waiting for today is for you to admit to what you did
1437 so that we can start the process of getting you some help,

D2 does emphasize that S will eventually have to "come clean" (line 1235) by "admit[ting]" (line 1228) that "[her] son was smothered by [her]" (line 1231). D1 also insists that it is S's responsibility to the police and an unspecified group of observers to "admit . . . what [she] did" (line 1436)—that is, smothered Khyle. Critical at this juncture, incidentally, is D1's first move connecting getting help for S to her admission—a standard deal-making move in the Reid technique. D1 echoes D2's offer of help as contingent upon her admission (lines 1503–1506):

1503 D1: You're not happy at home.
1504 You have a dysfunctional family
1505 You can start at the beginning. (12.0)
1506 But it starts by admitting
1507 how overwhelmed you were with what was going on. (8.0)

However, in what is arguably the most strategically significant blame-mitigation move in the entire interrogation, D1 ultimately calls on S to admit not to having killed Khyle or even to having underlying psychological problems that led to her actions, but—very specifically—to having been completely "overwhelmed . . . with what was going on" (line 1507) prior to Khyle's death. The persuasive power of this ultimatum is striking: the interrogators have already elicited from S acknowledgments that her mother's unreasonable demands and expectations have been taxing her, thus providing undeniable evidence for her having been overwhelmed. Now S is being asked to "admit" to—to confess to or to take responsibility for—being overwhelmed, an experience that focuses on a subjective reaction to (usually) external stressors and one that the interrogators have already affirmed as not being her fault. Getting S to "admit" this allows for the next series of discursive steps, each building on the prior one:

1562 If as a juvenile, you admit to your frustration, your anger,
1563 what occurred, what happened, why it happened. (7.0)

1564 I can't imagine anything more difficult than that.
1565 But once you do it, you'll be on the right path. (7.0)
1566 Then maybe, just maybe, something good will come out of all this. (23)

S is now called upon to confess to "frustration" (line 1562), a condition more volitionally salient than being "overwhelmed"; "anger" (line 1562), a distinctly negative, if not censurable, mental state; and finally "what occurred, what happened, why it happened" (line 1563)—an informal chain of entailment that carries the theme of "admitting" forward through blameless feelings of victimization to a more blameworthy state of anger and, finally, to the apex of blame: the committing of murder.

Conclusion

As we have seen, for D1 and D2, the preferred approach to extracting an admission of guilt for the murder of S's son is to minimize the significance of and culpability for her actions through mitigating the blame. The discursive structure of this blame mitigation is what I have called the accumulative construction of themes, wherein the officers incrementally establish and then build on components of the themes of provocation, spontaneity, and dysfunction—ultimately to guide S to an admission of guilt. Having mitigated the blame for S's alleged actions through positing that what she did was provoked, spontaneous, and accidental, and the result of psychological dysfunction, the officers urge S's admission of the problems that led to her actions, the response of frustration and anger to those problems, and—finally—guilt for the crime itself.

A striking characteristic of this interrogation is how infrequently S actively resists either the content or the direction of the detectives' developing narrative. This is explainable, perhaps even in large part, by the fact that the interrogators begin their account with indisputable facts about S's difficult domestic situation, apply those facts to a reasonable-sounding scenario in which a person in S's position would be provoked to an ongoing state of resentment and anger, and finally link that psychological state to spontaneous violence in a last-straw moment. It is an account with all the marks of plausibility, particularly when based on a real-life situation that the suspect had been living through. To be sure, S does occasionally interject claims of innocence, but the fact that the account is essentially a monologic rhetorical argument rather than a question-and-answer, information-seeking dialogue is consistent with the Reid technique's strategy of overpowering the will of the suspect in an effort to extract an admission.

An important meta-purpose of this analysis has been to demonstrate the value of a discourse-analytic approach to understanding the procedures undertaken by American police interrogators in performing the work of admission extraction. Although the study has been limited to only one element of minimization—the mitigation of blame—there remains a vast field of analysis for the many components of both minimization and maximization that are routinely employed in police interrogation rooms throughout the United States. The discourse of coercive police interrogation in the United States—notably an intentional enactment of the guilt-presumptive Reid technique—is a new area of study. With the exception of Roger Shuy's case study–based overview, *The Language of Confession, Interrogation, and Deception*, linguistic- and discourse-analytic approaches to understanding coercive interrogation in American enforcement jurisdictions are virtually nonexistent. This chapter is an early foray into this important area of study. There is no doubt that valuable insights will be gained by the scholarly application of such methods as conversation analysis, speech-act theory, critical discourse analysis, and more.

It should be obvious that the findings of such analyses will be of more significant value than merely as an academic exercise. Consider, for example, the outcome of the Nga Truong case. After the appeals court judge read the transcript of the interrogation, she suppressed S's admission, citing evidence that it was conducted in a coercive manner. It goes without saying that determining whether an interrogation is coercive or not is largely a judgment call, akin to the perspective offered in 1964 by U.S. Supreme Court Justice Potter Stewart, who, in explaining how he was able to determine whether a particular film was pornographic, famously said, "I know it when I see it." "Seeing" coercion in a police interrogation requires not only close reading of a kind that a conscientious judge might do, but also the principled application of analytical tools to the actual in situ language and discourse of the interrogation room. If every suspect were guilty, the use of coercive techniques might offend society's sensibilities less, but the disturbingly high percentage of false confessions elicited from innocent suspects makes it clear that "seeing" coercive tactics and procedures by means of discourse analysis and linguistics is an essential process for assisting in what is clearly an important step in criminal-justice reform.

Notes

1. https://www.innocenceproject.org/dna-exonerations-in-the-united-states/.

2. The author wishes to express his profound appreciation to David Boeri of the public radio station WBUR in Boston, whose interest in this 2008 case led him to pursue and—after a lengthy but ultimately successful legal battle—gain access to the two-hour recorded interrogation. In December of 2011 WBUR aired a series featuring Boeri's critical analysis of the interview, making the interrogation and the names of the detectives part of the public record. Through Boeri's work I became interested in the case and contacted him in the hope that he might advise me how to acquire a copy of the recorded interrogation. To my surprise and delight, he offered to send me a DVD of the entire interrogation, complete with the official police transcript. My analysis could never have been undertaken without David Boeri's generous assistance.

3. The transcription seen here does not attempt to employ the detailed apparatus developed by the Conversation Analysis school. As will be seen, this interrogation is not a conversation in the traditional sense, with discrete turn-taking mechanisms, etc. Instead, it is a hybrid form of an essentially monologic process on the parts of the interviewing officers, and the responses of the suspect are almost exclusively very brief and often nonverbal. It was determined that a CA-type transcription, usually essential in working with the intricacies of genuinely interactional discourse, would not be necessary or even particularly useful in identifying and analyzing the discursive tokens relevant to this study and their realization in speech. Instead, the general approach is a form of topic analysis focusing on the patterning of discursive realizations of a range of blame-mitigation topics.

4. Line numbers are from my corrected and reformatted transcript and do not map to numbers from the official police version.

References

Blair, J. P. 2007. "The Roles of Interrogation, Perception, and Individual Differences in Producing Compliant False Confessions." *Psychology, Crime & Law* 13(2): 173–186.

Davis, Deborah, and Richard A. Leo. 2010. "Commentary: Overcoming Judicial Preferences for Person- Versus Situation-Based Analyses of Interrogation-Induced Confessions." *Journal of the American Academy of Psychiatry and the Law* 38(2): 187–194.

Davis, Deborah, Richard A. Leo, and William C. Follette. 2010. "Selling Confession: Setting the Stage with the 'Sympathetic Detective with a Time-Limited Offer.'" *Journal of Contemporary Criminal Justice* 26(4): 441–457.

Drizin, Steven, and Richard A. Leo. 2004. "The Problem of False Confessions in the Post-DNA World." *North Carolina Law Review*, 82(3): 891–1007.

Evans, Jacqueline R., Christian A. Meissner, Susan E. Brandon, Melissa B. Russano, and Steve M. Kleinman. 2010. "Criminal versus HUMINT Interrogations: The Importance of Psychological Science to Improving Interrogative Practice." *Journal of Psychiatry & Law* 38: 215–249.

Horgan, Allyson J., Melissa B. Russano, Christian A. Meissner, and Jaqueline R. Evans. 2012. "Minimization and Maximization Techniques: Assessing the Perceived Consequences of Confessing and Confession Diagnosticity." *Psychology, Crime & Law* 18(1): 65–78.

Inbau, Fred E., John E. Reid, Joseph P. Buckley, and Brian C. Jayne. 2013. *Criminal Interrogation and Confessions*. 5th ed. Burlington, MA: Jones & Bartlett Learning.

Kassin, Saul M. 1997. "The Psychology of Confession Evidence." *American Psychologist* 52(3): 221–233.

Kassin, Saul M. 2005. "On the Psychology of Confessions: Does Innocence Put Innocents at Risk?" *American Psychologist* 60(3): 215–228.

Kassin, Saul M. 2006. "A Critical Appraisal of Modern Police Interrogations." In *Investigative Interviewing: Rights, Research, Regulation*, edited by Tom Williamson, 207–228. London: Willan.

Kassin, Saul M. 2014. "False Confessions: Causes, Consequences, and Implications for Reform." *Policy Insights from the Behavioral and Brain Sciences* 1(1): 112–121.

Kassin, Saul M. 2015. "The Social Psychology of False Confessions." *Social Issues and Policy Review* 9(1): 25–51.

Kassin, Saul M., Steven A. Drizin, Thomas Grisso, Gisli H. Gudjonsson, Richard A. Leo, and Allison D. Redlich. 2010. "Police-Induced Confessions: Risk Factors and Recommendations." *Law and Human Behavior* 34: 3–38.

Kassin, Saul M., and Gisli H. Gudjonsson. 2004. "The Psychology of Confessions: A Review of the Literature and Issues." *Psychological Science in the Public Interest* 5(2): 33–67.

Kassin, Saul M., and Katherine L. Kiechel. 1996. "The Social Psychology of False Confessions: Compliance, Internalization, and Confabulation." *Psychological Science* 7(3): 125–128.

Kassin, Saul, Jeff Kukucka, Victoria Z. Lawson, and John DeCarlo. 2014. "Does Video Recording Alter the Behavior of Police during Interrogation? A Mock Crime-and-Investigation Study." *Law and Human Behavior* 38(1): 73–83.

Kassin, Saul M., and Karlyn McNall. 1991. "Police Interrogations and Confessions: Communicating Promises and Threats by Pragmatic Implication." *Law and Human Behavior* 15(3): 233–251.

Meissner, Christian A., Allyson J. Horgan, and Justin S. Albrechtsen. 2009. "False Confessions." In *Applied Criminal Psychology: A Guide to Forensic Behavioral Sciences*, edited by Richard N. Kocsis, 191–212. Springfield, IL: Charles C. Thomas.

Meissner, Christian A., and Melissa B. Russano. 2003. "The Psychology of Interrogations and False Confessions: Research and Recommendations." *Canadian Journal of Police & Security Services* 1(1): 53–64.

Meyer, Jessica R., and N. Dickon Reppucci. 2007. "Police Practices and Perceptions Regarding Juvenile Interrogation and Interrogative Suggestibility." *Behavioral Sciences & the Law* 25: 757–780.

Ofshe, Richard J., and Richard A. Leo. 1997a. "The Social Psychology of Police Interrogation: The Theory and Classification of True and False Confessions. *Studies in Law, Politics, and Society* 16: 189–251.

Ofshe, Richard J., and Richard A. Leo. 1997b. "The Decision to Confess Falsely: Rational Choice and Irrational Action." *Denver University Law Review* 74(4): 797–1122.

Russano, Melissa B., Christian A. Meissner, Fadia M. Narchet, and Saul M. Kassin. 2005. "Investigating True and False Confessions within a Novel Experimental Paradigm." *Psychological Science* 16(6): 481–486.

SECTION II

Police Interview Dynamics and Negotiation

CHAPTER SIX

Now the Rest of the Story

The Collaborative Production of Confession Narratives in Police Interrogations

Gary C. David and James Trainum

Introduction

Stories are a primary mechanism for communicating and sharing information. According to Bruner, "We organize our experience and our memory of human happening mainly in the form of narrative" (1991: 4). Narratives are so important that "people are regularly monitoring scenes for their storyable possibilities" (Sacks 1992: 218), continuously scanning for events worth telling. Stories connect us with others, bringing them into a place where they may not have been, but which can visit through our words.

A confession is a certain type of storytelling. In simple terms, a confession is an admission of guilt regarding the commission of some act, as well as the details regarding how an act was committed. As a kind of storytelling, however, confessions are unique in that the listeners (i.e., law enforcement) typically have a sense of what the story is supposed to include, and thus of whether or not the story is being told "correctly." Like children listening to a fairy tale that they have heard before, when the confession narrative does not conform to what is (believed to be) known, the listeners can challenge the teller's story. Although law enforcement may not know the whole story, they believe they know enough to know what happened.

This chapter will examine how law-enforcement agents try to elicit confession narratives, as well as the conversational mechanisms used to shape those narratives. Law enforcement is not functioning as a passive audience during the storytelling. Police officers use their position as interrogators to provide prompts and feedback that help shape the story being communicated by the accused. Confessions are typically not provided by a suspect as an uninterrupted recounting of events. Although a confession might be ascribed to a suspect (e.g., the confession of John Doe), they are the product of a conversational collaboration between the suspect and police. Additionally, they in many ways can be attributed more to the police than to the suspect in their form and content. We explore how this joint production occurs in the interrogation encounter.

Narratives and Story Telling

A complete examination of all the work done in the area of narrative, storytelling, folklore, and the like is beyond the scope of this chapter. A key point in storytelling is the temporal ordering of events that ties them together as related to one another (Franzosi 1998). Despite narrative's primacy as a routine feature of everyday life, it's perceived lack of precision means that social scientists historically have eschewed it as a topic of analysis. Despite this early narrative avoidance, "stories, not statutes or statistics, have become the subject matter of much sociolegal scholarship" (Ewick and Silbey 1995: 198). As Richardson (1990: 118) notes, "Narrative is both a mode of reasoning *and* a mode of representation." We speak of the world in narrative, and we seek to understand it through narrative. More specifically, narratives can functions as accounts, or "'story-like' interpretations or explanations" of events in people's lives, especially those that can be seen are marginal or deviant actions (Orbuch 1997: 455).

We adopt Labov's definition of narrative as "one method of recapitulating past experience by matching a verbal sequence of clauses to the sequence of events which (it is inferred) actually occurred" (1972: 360). The word "recapitulate" is an appropriate one: it simply means "to restate briefly" or "to give a brief summary." However, "capitulate" can mean "to surrender." Taken together, recapitulation can be the process of "resurrendering" details of a story that has been previously told. In this sense, confessing is a literal and figurative surrendering, in which the person surrenders details about him- or herself to the authorities.

Storytelling was originally viewed as a type of soliloquy in which listeners were passive recipients of what was being told them. Starting with the work of Sacks (1972), increasing research has been conducted to examine the interactional elements of storytelling, exploring how such occasions are locally occasioned (i.e., within a particular context) and sequentially implicative (i.e., with a turn-by-turn structure) (Jefferson 1978). This has demonstrated how the storyteller *and* story recipients shape the story as it is told. In other words, even though one person might be telling the story, storytelling itself is often at least a two-person job. Stories even can be challenged or sidetracked through byplays, crossplays, and sideplays (Goffman 1981; Goodwin 1997); "storytellings, like many other social actions, can thus be viewed as having preferred and dispreferred response types" (Stivers 2008: 33). This can include an evaluation of the facts, the performance of the telling, and the relevance of the telling to the overall context of the encounter.

In storytelling, hearers "use the speaker's talk as a point of departure for interpretive possibilities and participation frameworks of their own making" (Goodwin 1997: 100), meaning that recipients can interject in various ways, including challenging the story itself. This invokes Goffman's (1981) concepts of "footing" and "participation framework" in interaction. Footing is the stance of individuals with respect to one another during the course of an encounter. Participation framework refers to the status of interactants throughout the course of the encounter. The course of the interaction involves a fluid and changing dynamic, during which time the relationship of the persons involved can shift and move gradually and/or rapidly. People can switch from speaker to hearer and back again. They can create alignment or disagreement.

Storytelling is central to the law. Henderson observes, "Story is crucial to legal decision making because the primary task of the judge or jury is to make a plausible and coherent narrative out of the chaotic particulars of a case" (2015: 89). A confession functions in precisely this way. In the landmark case *Miranda v. Arizona* (1966), Chief Justice Earl Warren noted the narrative nature of confessions, writing that the protection of a suspect's rights will "enable the defendant under otherwise compelling circumstances to tell his story without fear" (384 U.S. 436, 466). Peter Brooks, in his book *Troubling Confessions* (2000), comments extensively on this decision, noting the fundamentally narrative nature of confessions in contemporary law as well as classic and ancient literature. In fact, it is often the case that law enforcement invites the suspect to "tell your side of the story" or "tell us what happened." Inherent in this request is an invitation to provide a narrative version of events. Because confessions at some point need to be told in a narrative structure, applying a narrative analysis to their production becomes an important element in understanding how confessions are elicited, constructed, and told.

Police Interrogation and Confession Narratives

The interrogation often is depicted as the pivotal scene in television shows and movies, building to the moment when the suspect "comes clean" about the crime he or she has committed. Confession stands as the ultimate proof of guilt, even to the point that it is given prominence over other forensic material that actually indicates innocence (see Leo and Ofshe 1998; Kassin, Drizin, Grisso, Gudjonsson, Leo, and Redlich 2010). The deference given to a confession lies in the belief that no one who was not being tortured or given the third degree, would admit guilt for a crime he or she did not commit (see Ofshe and Leo 1997). Once you confess, for all intents and purposes, you are guilty.

Ideally, a suspect would simply tell a complete story on his or her own, with minimal or no prompting and details fitting forensic evidence or eyewitness accounts. However, to be seen as a reliable confession, a suspect needs to go beyond simply saying, "I did it." The confession narrative must make sense by stating how, where, when, and why the crime was committed. The suspect should give information that the police do not provide, meaning that only a person who was there would know these details. Leo (2009) describes the "post-admission phase," in which the suspect must provide such a description. During this conversation, all the various evidentiary elements and speculation must be tied together, filling the gaps and securing the foundation of the suspect's confession. The prosecution needs a confession that is admissible as evidence, meaning that it adheres to legal requirements of being noncoercive and not in violation of any rights. This includes the giving (and waiving) of Miranda; the absence of physical violence, sleep deprivation, or threats; and the provision of food, water, and bathroom breaks. It is not uncommon to hear detectives ask a suspect at the end of an interrogation how he or she was treated and whether food or water was provided; sometimes they even videotape the person eating.

Police interrogations can be considered to be invitations for storytelling, ultimately producing a *confession narrative*. Rather than yelling and threatening, which might risk a confession's being thrown out, "the investigator needs to draw the suspect into the conversation to develop a full confession" (Inbau, Reid, Buckley, and Jayne 2005: 213). As Gubrium and Holstein observe, "Stories are assembled and told to someone, somewhere, at some time, for different purposes, and with a variety of consequences" (2009: 10). When a detective asks a suspect to "tell me what happened," the suspect is being asked to tell a story. This also can be as simple as asking for a general account of a final event (e.g., "How did she die?") or asking a set of specific questions aimed at uncovering a chain of events (e.g., "Let's go over what happened that night"). Although the approach can vary, the desired outcome is the same: to capture a suspect's account of events such that the story provides what happened in a way that comports with what is believed to be known. More specifically, the desired outcome is to get a confessional narrative that establishes the suspect's guilt and can be used for the purpose of prosecution.

Even though the suspect might initially be asked to provide an account of events related to a crime, the role of speaker and hearer can shift quickly as the police begin to offer their own version or account. This means that the ownership of the story and its details are constantly in flux, as versions can be offered and rejected through its course: "Stories told in conversation have been shown to be at least in part products of systematic interactional practices involving both storyteller and story recipients" (Lerner 1992: 247). Such a view can be directly applied to interrogations and confessions. A document that reads "Statement of John Doe" across the top thus does not only belong to Mr. Doe. Rather, it is the product of collaboration between the suspect and the interrogators, who are essentially ghostwriters. The confession is said to be possessed solely by the suspect. When an interrogation is not examined as a collaborative effort, what gets lost is the contribution made by the police toward its construction.

Kassin (2004) notes, "A confession produced by a trained interrogator is like a Hollywood drama: Scripted by his or her theory of the case, rehearsed during hours of interrogation, and enacted on camera by the suspect." Invitations to "tell me what happened" can be met with rebuttals of "Now let me tell you what happened" when the resulting story does not match what is expected or believed to have taken place. In a police interrogation, the ultimate measure of truthfulness is whether the suspect's story matches the police's theory of the case. The confession can be tantamount to a final performance, given after lines have been learned and rehearsed, with instructions provided by a director who has a vision of how the drama is meant to be enacted.

Despite the significance of the confession narrative, "very little empirical exploration of (the confession) exists, and there are only a handful of studies that examine the interactional construction of the turns prior to a confession on a conversation analytical level" (Carter 2013: 107). With increased videotaping of interrogations, researchers can give more attention to the interactional elements of police interrogation (Watson 1983, 1990; Komter 2003; Stokoe and Edwards 2007, 2008; Haworth 2013). In the following analysis, we will examine how these confessions and statements are the result of a collaborative effort and joint production. We also will look at how, despite the obvious way in which this occurs, the ownership of the statement narrative is placed firmly in the possession of the suspect, removing all traces of the role that the police played in its development.

Methodology

Materials for this project came from two primary sources. First, one of the authors is a former police and cold-case detective with over 20 years of experience who now works as a criminal case consultant. Through his work we had access to past case files of interrogations, confessions, and statements (in some instances with audio and video of the interrogations). The other author has attended police interrogation training programs relating to the Reid technique and PEACE method, a non-accusatory method used by law enforcement in the United Kingdom and Canada. Both authors have worked together on numerous cases, using a variety of linguistic-analytic approaches (e.g., conversation analysis and content analysis) to conduct case reviews primarily for defense attorneys. Permission was given to use these materials for the purposes of teaching and publishing provided there was sufficient anonymizing of the persons and jurisdictions involved. The other source of materials was the Innocence Project, which has materials available related to early cases that involved exonerations of previously convicted individuals. In particular, Brandon Garrett has maintained a "Convicting the Innocent" database with materials related to cases covered in his book by the same name.

A total of eighteen cases were examined for this chapter involving crimes that included murder, sexual assault, arson, and drug dealing. All but two suspects were male. Cases originated from twelve different states. Only eight of the cases included audio and/or video recordings of the interrogations, which allowed for verification of the transcripts provided. In the other instances, the transcripts were not evaluated for accuracy. Although transcripts can be accepted as being generally accurate, errors do occur (Shuy 1998). At present, no research has been conducted to evaluate the accuracy of interrogational transcriptions, and in general no formal quality-control processes are in place for these types of transcripts (as opposed, for instance, to medical transcription; see David, Chand, and Sankaranarayanan 2014). Therefore, the reliability of transcripts in the absence of video or audio cannot be established. Despite this limitation, sufficient data were available to examine how storytelling occurs in the context of police interrogations. Furthermore, there is no indication that the accuracy of the transcripts was challenged by the prosecution or defense or thrown out by the court.

Analysis

Interrogations can be viewed as distinctly different from interviews. Shuy notes that in an interrogation: "Interrogators make ample use of their power. They challenge, warn, accuse, deny, and complain. They are more direct. They demand and they dominate. Open-ended questions are infrequent, and problem questions tend to be challenges that often indicate disbelief in what the suspect has said" (1998: 13).In fact, the training approaches of police in interrogations (such as the Reid technique) can actively encourage challenges, forceful denials, intentional deceptions, and other interactional (and psychological) approaches in an attempt to get a confession. Under the guise of learning the truth, interrogators are encouraged to be "accusatory" and use "active persuasion" (Inbau, Reid, Buckley, and Jayne 2005: 5). Gordon and Fleischer suggest that "the 'interrogator' . . . must project to the suspect that there is absolutely no doubt in his mind as to the suspect's guilt." Furthermore, they assert that the only purpose of an interrogator is "to obtain a confession from a guilty individual" (2011: 27, 28).

As a result, the development of a confession narrative (beginning as an oral delivery but often transformed into a final written statement) has numerous unique qualities that make it distinct from other kinds of narratives. In a more everyday storytelling, the speaker (who "owns" the story) has primary control over the manner of its telling and the story's features. This is not the case in an interrogation, and in fact there are numerous differences. First, there is the question of *topic choice*. In an interrogation, the suspect (as teller of the story) often does not select the topics to be included in the story, or even what story is to be told (a feature of asymmetrical exchanges). The police typically fill this role. Secondly, the suspect has limited opportunity in terms of *speaker selection*, or who gets to speak and when. This is related to *floor control*, through which the speaker can determine who can speak next and whether an interruption can be allowed to shape the telling of the story. Thirdly, the suspect does not necessarily *own the details* of the story. Despite being asked for an account of "what happened," it is not assumed that the suspect will in fact divulge this information. Thus, the police can play a more active role in narrative construction, especially if the initial phases of the telling are out of step with what is known and believed to have happened. Fourthly, the suspect has less control over the point of *narrative termination*, or when the storytelling is complete. This relates to the last point of *verifiability*. As Bruner observes about everyday narratives, "We seem to be able to take competing version of a story with a perspectival grain of salt" (1991: 17). This is clearly not the case in an interrogation, where the point of the narrative is not just to tell a story but rather to have a story that is institutionally usable as a confession. This means that detectives need the narrative to satisfy the needs of law enforcement and prosecution.

We examine the sequences that generally are enacted in order to procure the confession narrative. These sequences are: (1) Tell us what happened; (2) Now let me tell you what happened; and (3) Tell me again what happened."

Tell Us What Happened

There is no single way in which a story begins to be told. In some instances, story "prefaces" such as "You have to hear what happened to me today!" might do the work of securing the attention of an audience (see Sacks 1992). At other times, "the overall flow of a conversation may itself be an activating mechanism" for storytelling (Gubrium and Holstein 2009: 50). A story can be invited through requests for its telling as well. Even though certain contexts might make one of the above activation mechanisms more likely than others, all will serve the purpose of initiating the process of storytelling.

Likewise, no interrogation follows a strict formula. In fact, it might be difficult to discern exactly when the interrogation begins. Although there are likely to be standard elements (such as Miranda), the order and manner in which these elements occur depend on the dynamics within the room. Differences can include the particular style of the interrogator, whether the interrogation is custodial or noncustodial, whether the investigator is afraid the suspect will invoke his or her right to silence, and the particulars of the crime itself. One could say that the interrogation begins the moment the talk starts, given that the small talk and basic questions and answers when filling out paperwork help to establish rapport building, as well as who may ask questions and who is responsible for answering. Interrogations can be thought of as beginning when the encounter between police and suspect starts. This is because everything that happens from that point forward is for the purpose of getting a confession. These moments can be important to prime the suspect to confess.

In the context of an interrogation, police officers have the interactional discretion to determine when the storytelling begins and which themes will be discussed. It is up to the suspect to relate the details by telling what he or she knows. Below are some general examples of how this may work.

Excerpt 6.1: Case 1

D: . . . . Let's talk about what happened today, why you're here? Explain what you know about why you're here.

Excerpt 6.2: Case 2

D: What we're going to do is go back over what you explained to us yesterday about how you knew these girls and where you met them, you know, just so that we understand it better.

Excerpt 6.3: Case 3

D: Tell me a little bit, what was going on with Marilyn back then, as far as her development in terms of talking, walking behaviors?

These examples demonstrate a relatively straightforward request for information and instructing the suspect on what the topic is going to be. In the first two, the detective highlights the collaborative nature of the encounter through the collective instruction "Let's talk about what happened today" or "What we're going to do." In the third example, the detective instructs the suspect to "[t]ell me a little bit, what was going on with Marilyn back then." With the additional topic parameters of "her development," the invitation is formulated to create the conversational space for a reply that is more extensive than what would be provided with closed-ended or more focused questions.

In everyday conversation, it is often the person who wants to tell a story who has to request the conversational space to do so. Storytelling can require an extended turn space in which the teller can describe what happened. In an interrogation, it is often up to the police officers to request a story. This kind of narrative request also can happen in mundane encounters. For instance, one partner might ask another partner, "How was your day?," or, more pointedly, "Anything interesting happen today?" However, in both instances, it is rarely the case that the asker knows that there is a story to be told. It is merely an invitation for the teller to provide a story if in fact there is one to be told. The person can decide whether anything happened that would warrant the other person's listening to a story.

Occasionally one person might have information that something *did* in fact happen that day. The question "Anything interesting happen today?" can be asked because the speaker knows precisely that *something interesting did in fact happen*. The question is an opportunity for the other person to relate what happened, to be honest, to "come clean." In the event that the person does not provide the story that is being requested by the asker, the conversational tables turn, and the requestor becomes the storyteller. This is what frequently happens in police interrogations.

Now Let Me Tell You What Happened

Epistemic status refers to whether a person is in a position to know something (see Heritage and Raymond 2005; Heritage 2012; Mondada 2013). In some situations a speaker might find his or her narrative being challenged by the audience: "During storytellings, tellers and recipients navigate whether and to what extent they see eye-to-eye on the events the teller is describing" (Stivers 2008: 53). This happens when an audience member can either claim direct knowledge of the story (e.g., "That's not how it happened") or simply display a lack of belief in the narrative that is being told (e.g., "I don't believe that's what happened"). These are quite different objections. The former often is based on a claim of what Pomerantz (1980) called a Type 1 knowable, in which a person can know something from firsthand experience. Police generally claim knowledge through reports, hearsay, inference, or some other indirect means (what Pomerantz 1980 refers to as "Type 2 knowables"). Interrogation becomes the mechanism through which police officers attempt to elicit the *rest* of the story (see David and Trainum 2016) in the form of a firsthand confession, one that fits what they believe to have happened.

Police raise both kinds of objections to suspect's stories. The police will also tell the suspect what they believe happened, citing both actual and nonexistent evidence. However, police cannot simply recite what happened and get the suspect to agree. Such a confession can be challenged on the grounds that it is not given in the suspect's words. This is especially problematic for police if the interrogation is recorded. There needs to be a joint construction of details and events so that a level of certainty regarding the story's accuracy can be achieved. In what follows, we examine how this takes place through the course of actual interrogations.

At numerous times in an interrogation, the statuses of hearer and teller can be very fluid. The suspect's story, in the form of a confession and/or statement, is the ultimate goal. But there may be times where police officers lose their footing (Goffman 1981) as audience and become storytellers. This is predicated on some knowledge about the event in question, which is presented as proof that the story being told does not match what happened.

Excerpt 6.4: Case 4

D: I know you didn't plan this because I've talked to several people that know you. All right. I know you didn't plan this. I think somebody put you up to this, that's who I want. . . . (You're) just along for the ride, I know that because I've done my homework.

In this excerpt, the detective formulates a particular epistemic stance where Type 2 knowables are provided as a counter to the suspect's claims. If narratives are viewed as a kind of news-delivery system, then one of their purposes is to deliver information to those who lack such information. The request to "tell me what happened" can be heard as indicating a less knowledgeable position (or K-, in epistemic-stance terms) by the police. However, subsequent challenges to suspect claims indicate that the police believe themselves to be operating from a more knowledgeable position (K+ in epistemic-stance terms).

To police claims of what they "know" or "think" happened, the suspect responded with the following statements.

- "I don't know nothing about it, sir."
- "I'm not lying to you, sir."
- "I'm being straight up with you."
- "Sir, sir. I don't know."

Even though the suspect is the person who is believed to have firsthand knowledge of events, suspects can lie in order to protect themselves or others. The police will then challenge those statements that depart from their sense of what the story should be in order to bring the suspect closer to that version.

In retrospect, this means that the initial request for a narrative is not done for information-seeking purposes, but rather for confirmation purposes. This radically shifts the nature of the interaction in terms of who is thought to have primary ownership over the narrative details. Coupled with the institutionally recognizable power differential between the police and a suspect, it could be said that the narrative ball is ultimately in the police's court. This can be manifested directly through an explicit indication that the detective knows what happened, as shown below.

Excerpt 6.5: Case 5

D: Listen to me. What I do care about is, when you come in here and you start telling me this story- now, I've already talked to- I've already talked to everybody there. Okay? So you know who was there and I know who was there. Right?

S: Exactly.

D: Okay. So . . .

S: Well, you guys didn't tell me anything, so I'm just trying to tell you . . .

D: Well, I'm not—- I don't need to tell you . . .

S: And I'm not lying.

D: . . . anything. I need you to tell me, to help me to understand.

In this excerpt, detective and suspect are contesting the story of what happened regarding a criminal complaint. The suspect's version of events is not matching what the police believe to have occurred. The exact language used is indicative of the derision felt by the detective regarding what is being told. It is interesting to see how the suspect being brought into the police station handcuffed by police becomes "when you come in here." When the suspect's response does not fit what the detective is looking for, his response is characterized as "telling me this story." These points are important to consider, as they place agency solely in the hands of the suspect. He is the one who is telling "this story" after he "[came] in here." The use of the modifier "this" can also be heard as indicating that the story is not acceptable or worthy of consideration. Taken together, the story being told is clearly not the story being sought.

This is followed up by the claims that "I've already talked to everybody there" and "you know who was there and I know who was there. Right?" The first part provides a foundation for the preceding claim that the suspect was not truthful when reciting "this story." It is not just the detective's opinion; rather, the claim is positioned as the result of his having "talked to everybody there." The second part creates the opportunity for the suspect to align with the detective's claims by formulating that they both know who was there, and that the suspect's version is not what they both know. The word "Right?" is situated as a tag question, which embeds the preferred answer in the asking of the question. Additionally, it functions as a *negative interrogative* in a hostile questioning environment (Heritage 2002). It is not just an invitation for agreement with the detective's claim; it also provides the opportunity for the suspect to change his story to *match* the detective's claim. Here, then, we see the "interrogative 'machinery'" that compels people "to confess a truth which is contrary to their own interests" (Lynch and Bogen 1996: 127).

For the suspect's part, he continues to distance himself from the detective's claims, despite an initial appearance of alignment by saying "Exactly." He follows this up with the contrast marker "Well" and the point that the detectives have not provided any information. This can be heard as referencing an earlier premise by the detective to tell him what was going on once he demonstrated an understanding of his Miranda rights. The detective says, "I don't need to tell you anything." Again, going back to typical storytelling situations, the listener and speaker can cooperate in the building of the details. There is a type of reciprocity that can be implied, such that I tell you something and you tell me something. Here, the detective refers to the power asymmetry in the interaction. She reasserts that the suspect has to "help me understand." This in essence means that the suspect needs to tell a story that matches what the detective believes took place.

In another example involving a suspected case of sexual abuse of an elderly person, a detective specifically tells the suspect that he knows what happened and that the story the suspect is telling him portrays him in a negative light. Only by shifting the narrative can this be resolved.

Excerpt 6.6: Case 1

D: There was no other time that this happened?

S: No.

D: Okay. It was just one time, in the bathroom just this one time.

S: If that's what they saw -

D: No, no, no, no, no. no. Come on now, come on. You're straying from the issue. You know what happened. Okay, you were there. You did- don't tell me you don't remember cause you remember everything else. Okay, if you're gonna tell me it just happened and you don't remember it happening, that's gonna tell me that you're probably a sexual deviant. That if it happens many other times that you're gonna say you don't remember.

The last turn of talk in excerpt 6.6 shows where the interrogation seems to be coming to an end, where the suspect is seemingly agreeing to the claims made by the detective. The detective is now trying to finalize the details of the suspect's confession. Part of this process involves determining whether the crime he is being accused of happened once or more than once.

Trouble in the storytelling arises when the suspect provides the qualification "If that's what they saw," which references claims made by two witnesses. It should be noted that the witnesses claim to have seen something unusual but could not provide concrete details of the alleged act. In the absence of forensic evidence, a confession is needed. The confession narrative needs to establish that the confession is not just based on two uncertain claims but is actually made in the suspect's own words. The detective closes off the avenue of the suspect's not remembering what happened. He needs the suspect to remember, and do so in terms that fit the police narrative. The suspect is told that if he does not remember, it must mean he is a sexual deviant. Such an extreme case comparison is taught in the Reid technique as providing an *alternative question*: Did you do this once, or do you do this all the time? It locks the suspect into two options, both of which establish guilt. The difference lies in being able to admit to something happening just once versus its happening repeatedly.

Again, the suspect has been asked to provide a story to the detective regarding a situation that is said to have occurred. When his responses do not match what the police believe happened, his story is refused. The detective raises the rhetorical stakes by saying that if the suspect maintains his current version of the story, it means that he's "probably a sexual deviant." This is not an idle accusation leveled at the suspect. Claims of deviancy made by members of law enforcement can have direct consequences. Police are in the deviancy-assessment business (Sacks 1972). If a police officer, in the context of an interrogation, places such an assessment on a person, it has potential consequences. The detective provides an out for the suspect: agree with the version of events that is being provided by the officer and be saved the negative assessment of "sexual deviant." In the end, the suspect agrees to the detective's story and abandons his own.

Thus, here we have a reformulation of the roles of listener and teller. The police, upon hearing a version of events that does not match what they believe to be true, have instructed the teller to reconsider his story. In terms of Labov's definition of narrative, there is the opportunity to "recapitulate" what was originally said in response to questions asked. The police are displaying that they in fact know what happened, and any storytelling that does not fit with this belief will not be accepted. The police can be so firm in their asserted knowledge that the suspect may wonder why he or she needs to provide additional information.

Excerpt 6.7: Case 5

D: Okay. And what kind of- you guys had an interaction that should stand out in your mind. So, tell me about the interaction that you had with Lori?

S: Well, why- why don't you refresh my memory, because I don't know what you're talkin' about.

D: Well . . .

S: You seem like you know.

D: I know exactly. I- I do.

S: All right. I . . .

D: Like I said, I've talked to everybody.

S: Like, clue me in . . .

Originally, it was the suspect's story to be told. Now, however, he is asking the police to "refresh my memory" and "clue me in." He tells the police that "[y]ou seem like you know," raising the point that no further information is needed if they already know what happened. This would be a fair point if this were just storytelling. If the hearer knows the story, there is no reason for the teller to recite it. The goal here is not just to tell a story, but to establish ownership of the story. The teller must own the details of the narrative, details that may have been provided and insisted upon by the police. The ultimate audience for the story is not the police who are in the room. It is the larger legal institution that must make use of the confession. This can result in repeated invitations to tell the story.

Tell Me Again What Happened

Beyond offering a confession that fits with the forensics of a crime, the suspect must also *own* the confession narrative. By this we mean that traces of the collaboration between police and suspect through the interrogation must be erased. If the interaction between the suspect and the detectives is the scaffolding that was used to support the building of the narrative, this support structure has to be removed so that the ownership of the narrative structure can be transferred to the suspect.

This is accomplished through the suspect's ability to retell the negotiated story in his or her "own words." However, these are not only the suspect's words; they are the product of the interrogation, born out of the collaboration that has taken place between accuser and accused. In a court of law, shared ownership of the confession will not do. The details of the confession need to be solely associated with the suspect. What has been built in the interrogation must now be delivered as a confession solely attributable to the suspect. This can be done with specific wording offered by the police, as in excerpt 6.8, when a suspect is asked if he "made a mistake."

Excerpt 6.8: Case 5

D: So, I guess, ultimately, you know, like I—I feel—I don't know. I would feel better if—I guess I'm just asking you, you know, are you willing to take ownership of this incident? You know what I'm sayin'? Like, are you willing to say that you made a mistake?

S: I did- I made a mistake.

D: Okay. Um . . .

S: Truthful and honest with ya.

It is easier to admit to making a mistake than to committing a crime. The wording offered by the detective eases entry into story ownership. Such euphemistic phrasing is a tactic in which police officers can be trained, and it is one they employ to great effect.

Even if the police believe they know what happened, the suspect still must tell them what happened. This is often phrased as necessary for the suspect to feel better, to get peace, to have closure, and so on. Ultimately, giving the confession narrative is positioned as the best way for the suspect to help him- or herself, as shown in the following excerpt.

Excerpt 6.9: Case 6

D: It's good. It's Okay, David. It's Okay. But you've got to tell us what's goin' on. I think we already know, but we just- but you need- you need to embrace it now, Okay?

S: [Nods head yes]

Excerpt 6.10: Case 7

D1: . . . what do you want the courts to know? What- what do you want? When they read the report, and the jurors are listening to it, what do you want them to know about [you]?

S: (4.0)

D1: Do you want them to know that you're reaching out for help, or do you want them to know you don't think there was anything wrong with what you done?

S: (8.0)

D1: I mean, you tell me.

S: (17.0)

D2: This is a give and take conversation.

S: I understand that.

D2: It's not one side.

S: I understand.

D2: We're giving you an opportunity to do what's right and do what you need to get done.

Notably, the suspect is admonished that "[t]his is a give-and-take conversation" and that "[i]t's not one side." This comes after the suspect has been silent, which is his right. His silence is met with a warning: "We're giving you an opportunity to do what's right." This means that *not* talking and adopting a stance of silence is wrong. In these instances, it is incumbent on the suspect to "embrace" the story and take ownership of the incident. In the final turn of talk, the suspect is encouraged to "reach out for help," which can be accomplished through accepting the claims of the detectives. One could look at the inverse of this proposition as well: if the suspect does not confess, then the suspect must not want help. In this construction of false equivalency, confessing is equal to helping yourself, and not confessing is equal to refusing to help yourself.

Additionally, the suspect might be asked to write down what happened in his or her own words (or the words that have been developed through the interrogation). It is also possible that the words will be prepared for the suspect in the form of an official statement, which the suspect will read and sign. In one interrogation, the detective said to the suspect, "I'll take you over to the interview room, over there, and I'll sit you down and give you some statements, and if you want to, write down your side of it to send to the D.A.'s office." It is unclear whether the detective's offer to "give [the suspect] some statements" was a slip. What transpired in the other room was not recorded and is therefore not known.

A recent exoneration case demonstrates how police can guide a suspect toward a confession narrative that is false. Davontae Sanford was released in June 2016 after serving nine years for a quadruple murder to which he had confessed. One of the authors worked on this case in conjunction with Sanford's legal team. During Sanford's interactions with the police and courts, he gave four statements regarding the quadruple murders in which he incriminated himself. Several matters regarding the information included in those statements stood out: (1) the large number of details that were incorrect (indicating that Sanford did not know the details of the crimes); (2) the almost complete absence of any details that could be independently corroborated; and (3) how the details changed over time to match the police investigation. This final part is not uncommon. A similar pattern emerged in the Norfolk Four case, in which the suspects who pled guilty were repeatedly interviewed because their confession narratives did not match the forensic evidence, requiring the police to lead them to develop new narratives.

If interrogations can be thought of as writer's workshops where the lines of the play are crafted, the confession narrative is the performance. The detectives can play the role of directors, calling out the need for more emotion, empathy, or lines that are forgotten or needed to fill out the story being enacted through the statement. The confession as storytelling is the thing that is long remembered, and often the only thing that is recorded. It is treated as complete when it suffices as a mechanism to do the legal work that is required. Heritage (1984: 150–151), again referencing the work of Garfinkel, notes that all descriptions are inherently limited: "No descriptions, however detailed or extensive, can exhaust the state of affairs it describes." Thus all accounts are necessarily incomplete. The questions become what is put in or left out, how those elements are put together, and what the motives are for doing so. These are important questions to ask when examining the rest of the story as it is constructed through the interrogation.

Conclusion

Conducting an interrogation is by no means an easy task. The police are faced with the challenge of determining whether or not a person is giving truthful responses and is guilty of the crime in question. It would be helpful if enough evidence were gathered that would point toward the suspect's definitive guilt. But cases are not always that straightforward. Facts can be interpreted multiple ways that fit different scenarios. The more a confession is needed to close a case, the more a detective might feel pressure to get a confession.

Ideally, a suspect would provide all of the details of a crime without any prompting. In such a situation, one could truly say that the confession is completely owned by the suspect. Short of this, it is possible for the police to provide varying levels of assistance and instruction in developing the confession narrative. When the police only seek a suspect's confirmation of details, rather than having the suspect provide them on his or her own, it becomes important to untangle whose confession it is, and to what extent the police and suspect have contributed to it separately. Thus the police can contaminate the interrogation and destroy the reliability of a confession.

The point of this analysis is not to determine guilt or innocence of any of the cases examined, nor to say that the development of a collaborative confessional narrative is always indicative of coercion. It is possible that in the interrogations we have examined, suspects confessed because they were guilty. Of course, a confession does not equal guilt, just as lack of a confession does not equate to innocence. Generally speaking, investigators seek confessions because they perceive the suspect to be guilty. Such beliefs can lead investigators to conduct interrogations in which they play a larger role than they should, which in the end can cloud the issue of guilt versus innocence. The larger point is that, because of the ways in which details can be introduced and embedded, it becomes very difficult to tell the suspect's narrative from that of the detectives.

Arriving at a common understanding is much more complex than two people merely providing their own version of things and seeing if they match or are "overlapping sets" (Garfinkel 1967). Rather, as we have seen here, the understanding is worked out through the interrogation process. Although everybody might be entitled to his or her opinion, in an interrogation everybody is not entitled to his or her story. Of course, there can be moments where someone might state, "That's my story and I'm sticking to it." At the same time, in an institutional context one version typically is privileged over another. There needs to be an official version of events which is recorded and documented in such a way that it is seen as legitimate.

Since all storytelling in interrogation is a collaborative enterprise, police need to be especially mindful of how this can lead to contamination of a confession (Shuy 1998; Garrett 2011; Trainum 2014). This extends from the interrogation phase to the postadmission phase, where police can try to "influence, shape, and sometimes even script the suspect's narrative" (Leo and Drizin 2010: 20). This chapter thus is important for understanding the origins of stories and details as they emerge in police encounters, especially in relation to claims of false confession and conversationally planting crime details for the purpose of recounting during the recorded interview.

References

Brooks, Peter. 2000. *Troubling Confessions: Speaking Guilt in Law and Literature*. Chicago: University of Chicago Press.

Bruner, Jerome. 1991. "The Narrative Construction of Reality." *Critical Inquiry* 18: 1–21.

Carter, Elisabeth. 2013. *Analysing Police Interviews: Laughter, Confessions and the Tape*. London: Bloomsbury Academic.

David, Gary C., Donald Chand, and Balaji Sankaranarayanan. 2014. "Error Rates in Physician Dictation: Quality Assurance and Medical Record Production." *International Journal of Health Care Quality Assurance* 27: 99–110. https://doi.org/10.1108/IJHCQA-06-2012-0056.

David, Gary C., and Jim Trainum. 2016. "I Know What Happened: Establishing Epistemic Stance and Status in Police Interrogations." Paper presented at the Annual Meeting of the Law and Society Association, New Orleans, 2–5 June.

Ewick, Patricia, and Susan S. Sibley. 1995. "Subversive Stories and Hegemonic Tales: Toward a Sociology of Narrative." *Law and Society Review* 29: 197–226. http://www.jstor.org/stable/3054010.

Franzosi, Roberto. 1998. "Narrative Analysis—Or Why (and How) Sociologists Should Be Interested in Narrative." *Annual Review of Sociology* 24: 517–554. http://www.jstor.org/stable/223492.

Garfinkel, Harold. 1967. *Studies in Ethnomethodology*. Englewood Cliffs, NJ: Prentice-Hall.

Garrett, Brandon L. 2011. *Convicting the Innocent: Where Criminal Prosecutions Go Wrong*. Cambridge, MA: Harvard University Press.

Goffman, Erving. 1981. *Forms of Talk*. Philadelphia: University of Pennsylvania Press.

Goodwin, Marjorie H. 1997. "Byplay: Negotiating Evaluation in Storytelling." In *Towards a Social Science of Language: Papers in Honor of William Labov*, edited by Gregory R. Guy, Crawford Feagin, Deborah Schiffrin, and John Baugh, 78–102. Amsterdam: John Benjamins.

Gordon, Nathan J., and William L. Fleisher. 2011. *Effective Interviewing and Interrogation Techniques*. Burlington, MA: Elsevier.

Gubrium, Jaber F., and James A. Holstein. 2009. *Analyzing Narrative Reality*. Los Angeles: Sage.

Henderson, Greg. 2015. *Creating Legal Worlds: Story and Style in a Culture of Argument*. Toronto: University of Toronto Press.

Haworth, Kate. 2013. "Audience Design in the Police Interview: The Interactional and Judicial Consequences of Audience Orientation." *Language in Society* 42: 45–69. https://doi.org/10.1017/S0047404512000899.

Heritage, John. 1984. *Garfinkel and Ethnomethodology*. Cambridge: Polity Press.

Heritage, John. 2002. "The Limits of Questioning: Negative Interrogatives and Hostile Question Content." *Journal of Pragmatics* 34: 1427–1446. https://doi.org/10.1016/S0378-2166(02)00072-3.

Heritage, John. 2012. "The Epistemic Engine: Sequence Organization and Territories of Knowledge." *Research on Language and Social Interaction* 45: 30–52. https://doi.org/10.1080/08351813.2012.646685.

Heritage, John, and Geoff Raymond. 2005. "The Terms of Agreement: Indexing Epistemic Authority and Subordination in Talk-in-Interaction." *Social Psychology Quarterly* 68: 15–38. https://doi.org/10.1177/019027250506800103.

Inbau, Fred E., John E. Reid, Joseph P. Buckley, and Brian C. Jayne. 2005. *Criminal Interrogation and Confessions: Essentials of the Reid Technique.* 1st ed. Sudbury, MA: Jones & Bartlett.

Jefferson, Gail. 1978. "Sequential Aspects of Storytelling in Conversation." In *Studies in the Organization of Conversational Interaction*, edited by Jim Schenkein, 219–248. New York: Academic Press.

Kassin, Saul. 2004. "Videotape Police Interrogations." *Boston Globe*, 26 April. http://archive.boston.com/news/globe/editorial_opinion/oped/articles/2004/04/26/videotape_police_interrogations/.

Kassin, Saul M., Steven A. Drizin, Thomas Grisso, Gisli Hannes Gudjonsson, Richard A. Leo, and Allison D. Redlich. 2010. "Police-Induced Confessions: Risk Factors and Recommendations." *Law and Human Behavior* 34: 3–38. https://doi.org/10.1007/s10979–010–9217–5.

Komter, Martha L. 2003. "The Interactional Dynamics of Eliciting a Confession in a Dutch Police Interrogation." *Research on Language and Social Interaction* 36: 201–228.

Labov, William. 1972. *Language in the Inner City: Studies in the Black Vernacular English.* Philadelphia: University of Pennsylvania Press.

Leo, Richard A. 2009. *Police Interrogation and American Justice.* Cambridge, MA: Harvard University Press.

Leo, Richard A., and Steven Drizin. 2010. "The Three Errors: Pathways to False Confession and Wrongful Conviction." In *Police Interrogations and False Confessions: Current Research, Practice, and Policy Recommendation*, edited by G. Daniel Lassiter and Christian Meissner, 9–30. Washington, DC: American Psychological Association.

Leo, Richard A., and Richard J. Ofshe. 1998. "The Consequences of False Confessions: Deprivations of Liberty and Miscarriages of Justice in the Age of Psychological Interrogation." *Journal of Criminal Law and Criminology* 88: 429–496.

Lerner, Gene H. 1992. "Assisted Storytelling: Deploying Shared Knowledge as a Practical Matter." *Qualitative Sociology* 15: 247–271. https://doi.org/10.1007/BF00990328.

Lynch, Michael, and David Bogen. 1996. *The Spectacle of History: Speech, Text, and Memoir at the Iran-Contra Hearings.* Durham, NC: Duke University Press.

Mondada, Lorenza. 2013. "Displaying, Contesting and Negotiating Epistemic Authority in Social Interaction: Descriptions and Questions in Guided Visits." *Discourse Studies* 15:597–626. https://doi.org/10.1177/1461445613501577.

Miranda v. Arizona. 1966. 384 U.S. 436.

Ofshe, Richard J., and Richard A. Leo. 1997. "The Decision to Confess Falsely: Rational Choice and Irrational Action." *Denver University Law Review* 74: 979–1222. https://ssrn.com/abstract=1134046.

Orbuch, Terri L. 1997. "People's Account Count: The Sociology of Accounts." *Annual Review of Sociology* 23: 455–478. http://www.jstor.org/stable/2952560.

Pomerantz, Anita. 1980. "Telling My Side: Limited Access as a 'Fishing' Device." *Sociological Inquiry* 50: 186–198. https://doi.org/10.1111/j.1475-682X.1980.tb00020.x.

Richardson, Laurel. 1990. "Narrative and Sociology." *Journal of Contemporary Ethnography*. 19: 116–135. https://doi.org/10.1177/089124190019001006.

Sacks, Harvey.1972. "Notes on Police Assessment of Moral Character." In *Studies in Social Interaction*, edited by David Sudnow, 280–293. New York: Free Press.

Sacks, Harvey. 1992. *Lectures in Conversation*. Volume 2. Oxford: Blackwell.

Stivers, Tanya. 2008. "Stance, Alignment, and Affiliation during Storytelling: When Nodding Is a Token of Affiliation." *Research on Language and Social Interaction* 41: 31–57. https://doi.org/10.1080/08351810701691123.

Stokoe, Elizabeth, and Derek Edwards. 2007. "'Black This, Black That': Racial Insults and Reported Speech in Neighbour Complaints and Police Interrogations." *Discourse & Society* 18:337–372. https://doi.org/10.1177/0957926507075477.

Stokoe, Elizabeth, and Derek Edwards. 2008. "'Did You Have Permission to Smash Your Neighbour's Door'? Silly Questions and Their Answers in Police-Suspect Interrogations." *Discourse Studies* 10(1):89–111. https://doi.org/10.1177/1461445607085592.

Trainum, James L. 2014. "'I Did It'—Confession, Contamination and Evaluation." *Police Chief* 81. http://www.policechiefmagazine.org/magazine/index.cfm?fuseaction=print_display&article_id=3368&issue_id=62014.

Watson, D. Rodney. 1983. "The Presentation of Victim and Motive in Discourse: The Case of Police Interrogations and Interviews." *Victimology* 8: 31–51.

Watson, D. Rodney. 1990. "Some Features of the Elicitation of Confessions in Murder Interrogations." In *Interaction Competence*, edited by G. Psathas, 263–295. Washington, DC: University Press of America.

CHAPTER SEVEN

Patterns of Cooperation between Police Interviewers with Suspected Sex Offenders

Tatiana Tkacukova and Gavin E. Oxburgh

Introduction

The ethos of fair investigative interviewing, which has been developing in the United Kingdom for over 30 years, views the interviewer as a neutral participant fulfilling an "inquisitorial role rather than the traditional prosecutor one" (Williamson 1994, qtd. in Milne and Bull 1999: 158). The move from a confession-seeking objective of police interviewing to a more balanced information-elicitation and search-for-the truth approach of investigative interviewing has given rise to the need to unify interview-management techniques and the subsequent development of the PEACE framework in the early 1990s. PEACE is the mnemonic acronym for the five stages of the interview process: *P*lanning and preparation; *E*ngage and explain; *A*ccount, clarify, and challenge; *C*losure; and *E*valuation. The PEACE model of interviewing recognizes the fact that conversation and, by extension, interviewing are complex activities involving several interlocutors (Milne and Bull 1999: 55). Since structuring and managing underlying conversational complexities is not a straightforward process, training materials for interviewing (e.g., Centrex 2004) provide detailed guidance on such aspects as interview phases, planning and preparation, establishing rapport, engaging with the interviewee, managing first impressions, and other important factors. What is often disregarded, however, is that in complex cases or cases with serious allegations, there are generally two interviewers in the police interview, and, irrespective of which role they assume, the presence of two police officers can interfere with an interview's dynamics. This chapter discusses the implications of tandem interviewing on interview dynamics and illustrates the advantages and disadvantages of different cooperation patterns.

Where two police officers share the interviewing process, their roles need to be preplanned during the planning and preparation phase (Ord, Shaw, and Green 2011: 53). That said, clear guidance on the preferred cooperation process is nonetheless missing from training materials (e.g., Centrex 2004; Ministry of Justice 2011). Similarly, previous research on psychological and linguistic aspects of investigative interviewing (e.g., Oxburgh, Myklebust, and Grant 2010; Grant, Taylor, Oxburgh, and Myklebust 2015) has generally focused on the questioning process as a whole, disregarding the degree of contribution of each interviewer or patterns of cooperation between them. This chapter aims to fill the void in research by analyzing the frequency, occurrence, and function of second interviewers' turns in 20 interviews with suspected sex offenders.

In general, there are several options for the involvement of the second interviewer, as well as several potential pitfalls resulting from inappropriate interjections during and interruptions of the interviewing process. Prior agreement during the planning and preparation stage on the respective roles of interviewers is essential for the success of the proceedings (see Ord, Shaw, and Green 2011: 53). The main function of the second interviewer lies in critical active listening, monitoring the interviewing process, and taking notes, thus minimizing any distractions for the lead interviewer (ibid.). Depending on the nature of the case and the prior agreement between the interviewers, the lead interviewer could either conduct the interview on his or her own and allow the second interviewer an opportunity to ask clarifying questions only in the final stage of the proceedings or stop at regular intervals (e.g., at the end of each topic or stage) to allow the second interviewer to inquire about any additional details before moving to the following topic or stage (Ord, Shaw, and Green 2011: 53–54). The success of cooperation between all participants in an interview and the smooth running of the proceedings will naturally depend on how effectively the interviewers manage to pass agendas and topics on to each other, collectively build the rapport with the interviewee, and retain a coherent information-elicitation process, including adhering to the questioning strategy and topic management.

Some potential pitfalls may include situations in which interviewers compete for the floor or ask repetitive questions, or in which the second interviewer digresses to a new topic or stage or does not recognize that the lead interviewer may need to change the strategy in the middle of questioning to postpone some unexplored topics to a more advanced stage of the interview (Ord, Shaw, and Green 2011: 54). Despite the significance of the real impact the second interviewer has on the proceedings, together with the seriousness of potential difficulties a lack of coordination may cause, the second interviewer's role has not been given as much direction or research prominence as it deserves. By discussing cooperation strategies employed in practice in the analyzed dataset, we aim in this chapter to start the debate on how best to accommodate any potential challenges.

There are many reasons for researchers and practitioners to focus on cooperation patterns and the number and type of contributions made by the two interviewers. It is usually for more serious crimes and for the interviewing of high-interest suspects (i.e., murderers and sex offenders) that two interviewers are required, so the impact of research could therefore be significant. From the perspective of psychology-oriented research, the mere fact of the physical presence of two interviewers influences the way rapport could be established (compare with, e.g., Holmberg 2009; Shepherd and Griffiths 2013: chap. 6), the basics of conversation and nonverbal communication managed (Shepherd and Griffiths 2013: chap. 3), note-taking and active-listening strategies planned (Shepherd and Griffiths 2013: chap. 7), empathy used (Dando and Oxburgh 2016), psychological well-being retained and comprehensibility and meaningfulness established (Holmberg 2009), and professional development training courses conducted (Ord, Shaw, and Green 2011: chap. 8). The cooperation between the two interviewers could also potentially influence strategies for the detection of deception (e.g., Vrij, Fisher, Mann, and Leal 2009; Dando and Bull 2011; Gamson, Gottesman, Milan, and Weerasuriya 2012) and research on the psychological aspects of (false) confessions (Gudjonsson 2003: chap. 8). Linguistically oriented research would also benefit from investigations of the impact of two interviewers' voices had on the macrolinguistic level of narrativization and genre specification (Gibbons 2003: 142), intertextuality (Rock 2013), and power relations (Haworth 2006; Newbury and Johnson 2007), as well as the micro level of turn-taking management (Carter 2009) and questioning strategies (Grant, Taylor, Oxburgh, and Myklebust 2015). This chapter will analyze the most significant aspects, which form a starting point for further research.

Data

The dataset consists of 20 audio-recorded interviews with suspects of sexual offenses, including nine with suspects accused of possessing and/or making child pornography images; six with suspects accused of the sexual abuse of minors; and five with suspects of adult rape and sexual assault. The wide range of sexual offenses illustrates a sample of naturally occurring data. For the purposes of this study, the part with police cautioning was disregarded because the primary aim is to investigate the dynamics between two police interviewers during the interviewing process itself (the main body of the interview). The overall duration of all the interviews analyzed is approximately 33 hours (see table 7.1 for the mean length of the interviews), which presents a representative dataset for a pilot study. The advantage of this medium-sized dataset is that it permits a combination of quantitative approach and detailed qualitative analysis.

The interviews were first transcribed using a verbatim orthographic transcription (e.g., includes false starts) and then fully anonymized, ensuring that any identifiable information (including names, locations, addresses, and dates) was removed. The parts of the interviews that were relevant to cooperation between the interviewers (i.e., turn-taking between the two interviewers during their discussions or handing over of questions) were additionally transcribed following the conversation-analysis (CA) approach, which enables a detailed transcription of turn-by-turn unfolding of utterances, using specific signs to mark, for instance, pauses, overlaps, hesitations, and intonation (see the next section, "Methodology," for a more detailed account of the CA approach).

Methodology

Given that cooperation patterns and dynamics between interviewers have not been previously researched, our study is largely exploratory. The initial investigation of the topic aims to define the variables for further, large-scale research. The study integrates quantitative and qualitative research methods by including three stages of the analysis: (1) qualitative categorization of individual interviews according to the PEACE model; (2) quantitative analysis of interviewers' participation in different interview phases; and (3) qualitative analysis of cooperation patterns.

Theoretical Framework and Data Analysis

The underlying theoretical framework of this study is based on conversation analysis (CA), which provides a linguistic model for analyzing conversations in a wide range of settings, putting special emphasis on patterns of interaction, the role of speakers, function of turns, and turn-taking mechanisms, as well as the construction and reinterpretation of meaning through the sequential unfolding. Because of its suitability for examining naturally occurring data organized sequentially, CA is well established in the linguistic strand of research on police interviewing (Heydon 2005; Haworth 2006; Carter 2009; Grant, Taylor, Oxburgh, and Myklebust 2015). The CA approach is nonetheless often combined with critical-discourse analysis and pragmatics, since a mixed-method approach allows a more detailed analysis of power relations, control, and resistance in institutional settings (e.g., Haworth 2006). Given that the aim of this chapter is to follow patterns of cooperation, the CA analysis alone provides a substantial framework for investigating police-interview dynamics, including turn-taking management, cooperation strategies, and turn-by-turn unfolding of meaning.

The first stage of the qualitative analysis involved dividing the interviews into three parts according to the PEACE model. The interview itself involves three main phases (engage and explain; account, clarify, and challenge; and closure) and accordingly the analyzed data are divided into those parts. As previously mentioned, the police caution stage was excluded from the analysis because it was not deemed relevant to the main focus of our study.

To ensure the objectivity and reliability of the initial qualitative analysis, the identification of the three interview phases was conducted by three researchers who independently coded the same interviews. The percentage of agreement method was then used to code for inter-rater reliability (85 percent) and any disagreements were resolved by discussing differences. To minimize the risk of misidentification and to help ensure that the interviews were coded in a consistent way, a strict set of criteria was established for all researchers to follow. The engage-and-explain phase was identified as immediately following the caution (unless it was a follow-up interview). The beginning of the account, clarification, and challenge phase was defined as the point when interviewers first challenged the suspect's account by introducing additional evidence or victims' and witnesses' accounts, or by contesting evidence elicited from the suspect. The closure phase was identified according to discourse features of summing up and offering a final opportunity for the suspect to add anything he or she wished. Although the authors are fully aware that interviews cannot be strictly divided into three parts (because interviewers move fluidly between stages), the risk of incorrect division was minimized by having the coding process verified. In addition, when there was a considerable move to a previous stage (e.g., from C to E), the text was coded accordingly. For instance, interview 2 concerned two crimes committed on two different occasions; the interviewers therefore dealt first with one crime before proceeding with the other one, which means that the interview pattern was E–A–E–A–C instead of the more common E–A–C.

The second stage of the analysis (quantitative analysis) involved quantifying the interviewers' contributions according to the number of their respective turns in the interview phases. The third stage of the analysis, the final qualitative analysis, aimed to identify patterns of cooperation as well as illustrate turn-taking management between the two interviewers and the function of second interviewers' questioning turns.

Results

The results of the quantitative analysis offer insight into the distribution of interactional space between two interviewers and their degree of participation in different phases. The overall mean ratio between the first interviewers' (Int1) turns and the second interviewers' (Int2) is listed in table 7.1 along with the mean number of turns (the results for individual phases are discussed in the following sections).

The sample of interviews contains varied response lengths: there are, on average, 378 questioning turns per interview, with the median being 248 questioning turns per interview. The results of the ratio of interviewers' turns illustrate that the lead interviewer plays a more active role in the interviewing process, with 75 percent of questioning turns, as opposed to 25 percent for the second interviewer. More important, however, is the distribution of interactional space in the three interview

TABLE 7.1 **Ratio of interviewers' turns**

	Int1	Int2	Number of questioning turns
Mean	75%	25%	378.6
Median	75%	25%	248.5
Standard deviation	0.04	0.04	61.5

phases: (1) engage and explain, (2) account clarification and challenge, and (3) closure. Further quantitative results are presented alongside qualitative analysis according to individual interview stages. Discussion of the key aspects of tandem interviewing is presented in the sections "The Role of the Second Interviewer" and "Passing the Floor" below.

Engage-and-Explain Phase

In the engage-and-explain phase, interviewers generally aim to elicit an open account from an interviewee by asking open questions (those that begin with, e.g., "Tell," "Explain," "Describe") and then following up with probing questions (e.g., "What," "When," "Where," "Who," "Why," "How") (Oxburgh, Myklebust, and Grant 2010: 50). Because the interviewee is encouraged to contribute to the reconstruction of events, the potential for the second interviewer's participation during this phase is limited. Figure 7.1 illustrates the normal frequency distribution of the ratio of the second interviewers' turns in the data (e.g., in eight interviews the ratio of the second interviewers' turns is below 5 percent).

The great majority of interviews display up to 10 percent of second-interviewer turns, with the arithmetic average ratio amounting to approximately 12 percent. The highest ratio of second-interviewer's contributions (50 percent) comes from an interview in which there were no clear distinctions between the two interviewers throughout the whole interview. The most frequent function of the second interviewer's turns in this first interview phase is to clarify and check the previously elicited information (see excerpt 7.1).

Excerpt 7.1: Interview 7 (clarifying questions posed by the second interviewer)

1 Int1: (26.0) Name, just for the time being\ up to (.) the flat\
2 Int2: hmm\

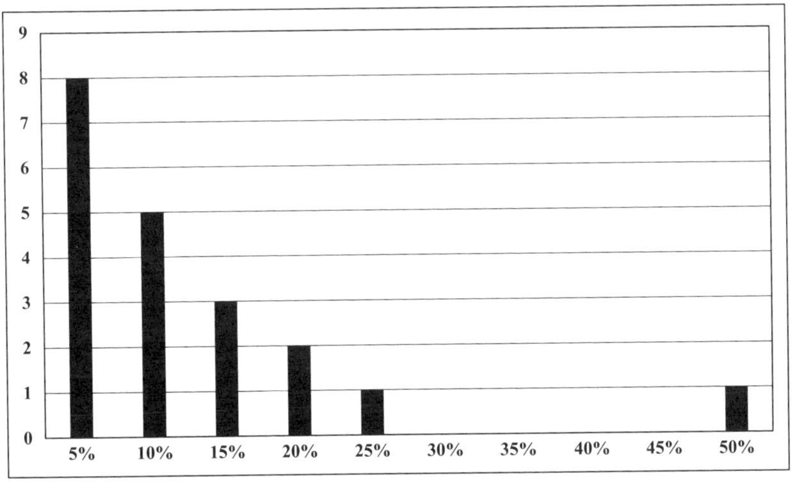

FIGURE 7.1. The normal frequency-distribution histogram for the second-interviewer turn ratio during the interview phase of the first E (engage and explain). The weighting of each interview part is 100 percent.

3 Int1: (. . .) Got anything?\
4 Int2: Uh: who has access (.) to your flat?/
5 S: (5.0) How do you mean?
6 Int2: (.) So, is there anyone else that ca::n go in freely, has a key that can go in to your
7 flat?/
8 S: No\=
9 Int2: =OK/ has there ever been?/
10 S: No\
11 Int1: (16.0) OK?/
12 Int2: Yep\
13 Int1: (6.0) Now/ (. .) we- we've talked about the flat and the flat i::s (.) u:m/ very important\
14 because i::t's been described to us/ and pointed out to us by\ (victim)\ as being where (. .)
15 u:m, these offenses occurred basically\

Excerpt 7.1 illustrates that the second interviewer pursues one specific line of questioning to clarify a detail of the topic previously explored in the interview (lines 4, 6–7, and 9). The turn-taking management between the interviewers is well organized: in lines 1 and 3 the lead interviewer checks with the second interviewer to see if he or she has any questions; in line 11 the lead interviewer checks whether the clarifying questions regarding the topic are completed before moving to a short summary of previously elicited information (lines 13–14) and the subsequent elicitation of another topic (lines 14–15). The second interviewer is thus given a limited amount of time to ask clarifying questions on a specific topic. All of the second interviewer's questions are closed-ended questions: one closed *wh-* question (line 4) and two yes-or-no questions (lines 6 and 9). The questions asked are in line with the role assigned to the second interviewer here, that is, clarifying issues on a specific topic. Thanks to the fact that the second interviewer's role is clearly signaled to the suspect, the interaction between them proceeds without any problems.

The interviews with a higher ratio of participation by second interviewers display one similarity: they require more turns than in excerpt 7.1 for passing the floor as both interviewers discuss the process in front of the suspect (see excerpt 7.5) and ask the questions interchangeably (see excerpt 7.2). Neither of the approaches benefits a clear interview structure.

Excerpt 7.2: Interview 9 (discussions about the questioning strategy)

Int: taxi/- (.) straight back to yours/ or a::ny stops at all on the way?/=
S: =no\, straight back yea\
Int1: (. . .) *coughs* (. .) NAME, I'm not/ (. .), you know I've gone through the night out I wasn't really gunna touch too much further on that, unless you have anything to: a:sk about the (.) drinking etc\
Int2: no/- no I was/, you know I was just gunna ask if anybody fell out then you covered it with your last question/ . . .
Int1: [yea/
Int2: [so u:m/, th- th- there we go
Int1: ok/
Int2: (. . .) ju:st there is some- some background about the friends/, I don't know wh- when/, about how long people have know:n/ . . .
Int: [yea we . . .
Int2: [each other and stuff like that/, I don't know whether you wanna come back later or?/=
Int1: =I think so yea/, we- we'll do that after we just . . .
Int2: [yea . . .

19 Int1: [skipped through the account, shall I make a note of that then?\
20 Int2: Yep/
21 Int1: (. . .) we'll be chatting aside like that u::m\=
22 S: =that's fine yea\

Excerpt 7.2 illustrates lengthy discussions between interviewers related to the topics to be covered (lines 3–20). There is frequent overlapping speech occurring in lines 9–10, 14–15, and 18–19 when the second interviewer briefly confirms the explanation of the strategy presented by the lead interviewer (lines 9, 11, 14, 18, and 20). In line 21 the lead interviewer clarifies to the suspect that they will be having these discussions "aside." Such elaborations of details in front of the suspect are undesirable and should be resolved in the preparatory stage of the interviews (Ord, Shaw, and Green 2011: 54). The suspect may potentially feel conspired against, left out, or not in control of his or her own testimony, which could be detrimental to their emotional and psychological condition. Although the suspect confirms that it is not a problem, the discussions do bring out the police interviewers' institutional power and place it in a negative light, which could potentially be further exposed in court.

Account Clarification and Challenge Phase

In comparison to the previous interview phase, the account clarification and challenge phase allows the second interviewer to be more active—challenging the suspects' accounts, complementing the first interviewers' questions, and checking that all preplanned aspects and newly arising issues are fully covered (see fig. 7.2).

The average ratio of second interviewers' turns is 22 percent, which is almost twice as high as their average ratio in the previous stage (i.e., 12 percent of second interviewers' turns). Similarly to the engage and explain phase, there is one interview that stands out, with 85 percent of turns, owing to a problematic distribution of the interviewers' roles. The predominant majority of the interviews, however, is positioned in the spread between 1 percent and 40 percent. This is mainly because second interviewers have specific topics to deal with, which are either preplanned during the stage of preparation and planning or arise during the critical listening and note-taking processes (Ord, Shaw, and Green 2011: 53).

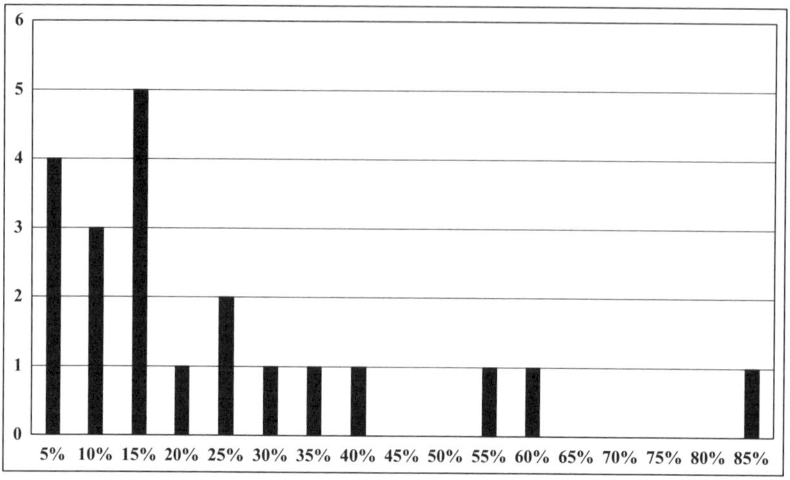

FIGURE 7.2. The normal frequency-distribution histogram for the second interviewer for the interview part of A (account clarification and challenge). The weighting of each interview part is 100 percent.

Similarly to excerpt 7.1, extracted from the engage and explain stage, in this more challenging phase there are many instances of the first interviewer's passing the floor to the second interviewer, who then asks specific clarifying questions on a predetermined topic. Second interviewers often pursue a specific line of questioning by asking short closed or restricted open questions ("You've babysat quite a lot because we've talked about that in the previous interview, haven't we?" or "What does [name redacted] wear to bed?" in interview 2). Clarification of arising issues is thus a very common role for the second interviewer. Another type of collaboration pattern occurring in the phase of "Account Clarification and Challenge" is for the second interviewer to have specific preplanned topics to cover at the interview (see excerpt 7.3).

Excerpt 7.3: Interview 3 (preplanned topic for the second interviewer)

1 Int1: okay/ (.) and so we got an account:/ from all of these people/
2 S: yeah/
3 (. . .)
4 Int1: =we are going to tell you now what other people have said/ and (Int: 2)/ is
5 going to tell you what: (name of victim's mother)\ said/
6 S: yeah\

Alongside presenting a clear plan for the interviewing process (lines 4–5), the lead interviewer also highlights the institutional power of the two police officers acting in collaboration through the use of the collective pronoun "we" in lines 1 and 4. At a later stage of the interview, the pronoun gains an additional meaning of professional experience and accountability when the lead interviewer provides the rationale for children not disclosing abuse to their parents:

> If something happens when u:m, somebody else in the family is involved, we often find that they won't- children will not tell their mum, they won't tell their grandmother, they won't tell any other member of the family\ they will tell their teacher/, or a friend\ (. . .) that's what we find happens/, and we are (. .) specialists in—in what we deal with, which is child abuse\

The word "specialist" resonates with the frequent use of the pronoun "we" and the detailed explanation of their expertise and findings, which strengthens the police officer's institutional voice of authority and power. In addition to having more resources available for critical listening and note-taking when there are two interviewers present, interviewing in pairs enables the team of police officers to appear *as* a team, with institutional power and professional expertise. Both advantages are reflected in the higher frequency of second interviewers' turns in the stage of account clarification and challenge.

Closure Phase

The interview phase of closure is the shortest interview phase; it comes when suspects are given an opportunity to provide additional information and ask questions. Given that this phase lasted for approximately only six minutes on average in the analyzed interviews, it was more likely that only one of the interviewers participated in the process, as evidenced in figure 7.3.

The phase is predominantly conducted by one interviewer, and the ratio of turns is therefore considerably higher for either the lead or the second interviewer. No distinct cooperation strategies were found during closure because interviewers followed previously applied procedures. The following sections summarize two aspects essential to be considered for tandem interviewing: the role of the second interviewer and passing the floor.

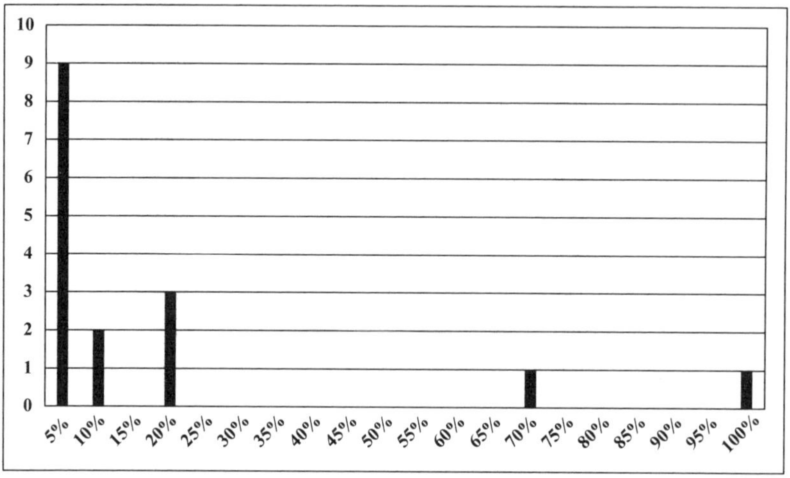

FIGURE 7.3. The normal frequency-distribution histogram for the second interviewer for the interview part of C (closure). The weighting of each interview part is 100 percent.

The Role of the Second Interviewer

As discussed above, there are two main patterns of collaboration found in the dataset: the lead interviewer conducts the interview and the second interviewer (1) covers preplanned topics (see excerpt 7.3) and/or (2) asks clarifying questions at the end of established topics and before the beginning of new topics (see excerpt 7.1). In any of these patterns, critical-listening skills are essential in order for the second interviewer to recognize details that were deliberately left out and only ask clarifying questions related to previously discussed issues (Ord, Shaw, and Green 2011: 54). One of the interviews that was excluded from the analyzed dataset was an interview of a suspect in a case of sexual assault of a minor conducted by one interviewer: it was the only interview of a high-interest suspect with just one officer. An extract from that interview serves as an illustration of how difficult the proceedings are without the input of the second interviewer: "Right at the moment, I just want to go away and think about whether I need to ask you any more questions but ultimately you've admitted kissing and fingering her yesterday" (interview 21).

The presence of the second interviewer was found to affect the following aspects of the interview:

1. as an institutional reinforcement of professional expertise (e.g., as strengthened by the use of "we" in excerpt 7.3);
2. as a way of strengthening the expression of empathy and compassion (e.g., the use of collective pronoun in "[we] do understand\ (.) that it was a big up for you finding out that" in interview 18);
3. as a source of the reiteration of the seriousness of the situation (e.g., "I have to make this clear, [suspect's name], they are there (. . .) [Interviewer 1] has made it absolutely clear that one of the issues with this sort of material is that the person looking at that material if they are doing it on purpose may have a sexual interest towards children and we have a duty to ensure that children are protected, so we are going to give you one more opportunity, it's really quite serious, (. . .)" in interview 17);
4. and, most important, as a mechanism for quality assurance of communication.

Whereas the first three features are related to the psychological advantages of the role of interviewers (i.e., the physical overbalance or prevalence of two officers over one suspect as well as long-standing, institutionally supported and developed expertise and specialism), the latter aspect is of particular importance to the communication process. As an active listener, the second interviewer is in a good position to recognize any potential misunderstandings, as shown in the following.

Excerpt 7.4: Interview 10 (second interviewer's quality assurance of the communication process)

1	Int1:	Yeah ok\ (. .) a::nd u:m what did you tell her exactly?/
2	S:	(. . .) In words?/
3	Int1:	(. .) Yeah\
4	Int2:	(.) You're not going to remember the exact words, are you?/
5	S:	Yea::h/ (. .) I can't remember the exact words/ but\ (. . . .) I said to my wife\,
6		she noticed that I wasn't like\, she said are you ok\ I said well (. .) I kissed a woman\
7		oh but was it just kissing or- like in a conversation/ the conversation was going, oh
8		we had a fumble\ (. .) you know/,(. .) I had sex/, obviously she was upset/ and stuff
9		like that\, I couldn't remember the precise words/ (.) like I can't give you word for

10		word yeah\
11	Int1:	(. .) Ok DC any questions about this account?/ I was going to go onto
12		my agenda now unless you've got any questions?/ (5.0) Ok\, had you met this girl
13		before?/
14	S:	(. .) No\
15	Int1:	That's the first time you've seen her?/
16	S:	Yeah\
17	Int1:	Ok\ (7.0) how do you know that she consented/ (.) to the sex\?
18	Int2:	(. . .) Do you understand the question/, I'm concerned about the words\
19	Int1:	Yeah/
20	Int2:	You understand what the officer is saying?\=
21	S:	=How do I know/ she has agreed/ (.) to have sex with me?/
22	Int1:	Yeah\ (6.0) [others speaking—INAUDIBLE] (4.0) how do you know that she
23		wanted to have sex with you?/
24	S:	(8.0) What/, after we kissed she, I licked her\, and she gave me a blow job
25		and everything\ (. . .)

In line 4 the second interviewer identifies a possible misunderstanding on the part of the suspect (line 2) and ensures the suspect does not feel obliged to provide a verbatim account of his words: the human memory processes the gist of the message and cannot recreate verbatim accounts (Lim 1993). Similarly, in line 21 the second interviewer checks the comprehensibility of the lead interviewer's question referring to the concept of consent. This prompts the suspect to explain the term (line 21) and the lead interviewer to rephrase the question (lines 22–23). Once common ground and correct terminology have been established, the interview proceeds. The role of quality assurance of communication shows the difference the second interviewer can make to ensure the objectivity, fairness, and clarity of the interviewing process. According to Ord, Shaw, and Green (2011: 54–55), the role of the second interviewer should not be seen as less demanding than or inferior role to that of the lead interviewer: both roles contribute to the proceedings in equal shares, albeit from different perspectives.

Passing the Floor

The most frequent strategy for passing the floor between the interviewers is when the lead interviewer asks the second interviewer whether he or she has any additional questions about a specific topic (e.g., "Have you got anything DC [name extracted] about the walk down (.) and just ending at the walk there?" in Interview 14; "Ok\ (. .) DC [name extracted] any questions at this point?/" in interview 10). Once the second interviewer finishes his or her line of questioning, the lead interviewer proceeds to the following topics or stages (similar to examples 7.1 and 7.2 above). Passing the floor follows the scenario.

Excerpt 7.5: Interview 7 (passing the floor)

1	**Int1:**	**(26.0) Ames, just for the time being\ up to (.) the flat**
2	**Int2:**	**hmm**
3	**Int1:**	**(. . . .) Got anything?**
4	**Int2:**	**Uh: who has access (.) to your flat?/**
5	S:	(5.0) How do you mean?
6	Int2:	(.) So, is there anyone else that ca::n go in freely, has a key that can go in to your
7		flat?/
8	S:	No\=
9	Int2:	=OK/ has there ever been?/
10	S:	No\
11	Int1:	**(16.0) OK?/**
12	Int2:	**Yep**
13	Int1:	**(6.0) Now/ (. .) we- we've talked about** the flat and the flat is:: (.) u:m/ very
14		important\ because it's:: been described to us/ and pointed out to us by\ (victim)\ as
15		being where (. .) u:m, these offenses occurred basically\

Thanks to the CA transcription, it is evident that once the first interviewer passes the floor, the second interviewer is ready to take the floor as there are no pauses between lines 3 and 4 (apart from the hesitation marker "uh," signaling the change of the interaction pattern). The smooth process of passing the floor requires an effective strategy for note-taking and critical listening, which are a part of rigorous planning and efficient teamwork. Not all instances of passing the floor were equally smooth: in fact, three interviews in the analyzed dataset included long and frequent discussions between interviewers on questioning strategy (which is why figs. 7.1 and 7.2 show high ratios of second interviewers' turns in some interviews).

Excerpt 7.6: Interview 9 (interviewers' discussing questioning strategy)

1	Int1:	yeah\, I- I- it sort of leads quite nicely into/ (.) discussing about ho:w well friends:
2		that they have been and were/but I don't know whether it leads into discussing about
3		the friendship now/or- or whether just going straight on into the/= . . .
4	Int2:	=I- I think that=
5	Int1:	=the account/
6	Int2:	I'd rather cover the account\ and then we'll/
7	Int1:	[yeah, ok/]
8	Int2:	we'll talk about your relationship with her\
9	S:	ah-hmm\=
10	Int2:	=after that because you'll be:/ you've got something about the other friends et cetera/
11	Int1:	[yeah exactly]
12	Int2:	. . . and so I think so we'll keep that as a separate topic\
13	Int1:	[ok], (. .) so you've had this conversation/and- and you've been talking about
14		several different topics/ . . .
15	S:	ah-hmm/

In the excerpt, the interviewers indicate what evidence they have (lines 10–11) and reveal the topics they want to cover as well as the order of topics to be covered (lines 2–3, 5, 8, 10, and 12); the discussions happen in front of the suspect. The lack of pre-interview planning and lengthy discussions on the questioning strategy can confuse suspects and create an impression of an unprofessional approach to interviewing. It is crucial for police interviewers to be aware of the fact that interviews have multiple uses and are aimed at a variety of audiences (Haworth 2013). Audio recordings and verbatim transcripts of interviews are constantly being reinterpreted and recontextualized during follow-up interviews, interviews with other people involved in the case, and, potentially, court hearings and appeals. Explicit discussions of the interview topics could be reinterpreted, for instance, as an ambiguous coercive strategy. The default position of the interviewer is that of power, because it is the interviewer who both holds institutional power and controls such aspects as question design, choice of topics, sequence of topics, third turns, and turn-taking (Thornborrow 2002). In addition, the well-being of the suspect and therefore the ethos of the PEACE model cannot be supported under the stressful circumstances when the interviewee may feel that he or she has no control over the course of the interview and that interviewers may be intentionally discussing the procedure to show the amount of evidence the police could have.

Conclusion

The results of the pilot study illustrate that there is more incentive for the second interviewer to contribute to the questioning during the account-challenging phase than the other stages. But the importance of the second interviewer's role is paramount throughout the whole proceedings. The roles they conduct range from note-taking and critical listening to following a specific line of questioning. Efficient preparation and teamwork allow the police officers to highlight the seriousness of the charges, express compassion, reinforce their professional expertise, and safeguard quality assurance of communication. Tandem interviewing nonetheless has its pitfalls, mostly caused by poor preparation or ineffective critical listening, which may result in, for instance, inappropriate discussions about the questioning strategy before the suspect. Given the lack of clear guidance on cooperation strategies, the aims of further research should include raising awareness of different options available to interviewers and the effect different tactics could have, as well as establishing clear guidelines on cooperation strategies in tandem interviewing. Further research into the topic is particularly needed because interviewing in pairs is conducted with high-interest suspect groups and can thus have an impact on establishing rapport, managing communication, detecting deception, and employing empathy.

References

Carter, Elisabeth. 2009. "Policing Talk: An Investigation into the Interaction of the Officer and the Suspect in the Police Interview." *International Journal of Speech, Language and the Law* 16(1): 165–168.

Centrex. 2004. Practical Guide to Investigative Interviewing. London: Central Police Training and Development Authority.

Dando, Coral J., and Gavin E. Oxburgh. 2016. "Empathy in the Field: Towards a Taxonomy of Empathic Communication in Information Gathering Interviews with Suspected Sex Offenders." *European Journal of Psychology Applied to Legal Context* 8(1): 27–33.

Dando, Coral. J., and Ray Bull. 2011. "Maximising Opportunities to Detect Verbal Deception: Training Police Officers to Interview Tactically." *Journal of Investigative Psychology and Offender Profiling* 8(2): 189–202.

Gamson, Rachel, Jessica Gottesman, Nicholas Milan, and Sitara Weerasuriya. 2012. *Cues to Catching Deception in Interviews.* College Park, MD: START. Accessed 15 February 2016. https://www.start.umd.edu/sites/default/files/files/publications/CuesToCatchingDeception.pdf.

Gibbons, John. 2003. *Forensic Linguistics: An Introduction to Language in the Justice System.* London: Wiley-Blackwell.

Grant, Tim, Jennifer Taylor, Gavin Oxburgh, and Trond Myklebust. 2015. "Exploring Types and Functions of Questions in Police Interviews." In *Communication in Investigative and Legal Contexts: Integrated Approaches from Forensic Psychology, Linguistics and Law Enforcement*, edited by Gavin Oxburgh, Trond Myklebust, Tim Grant, and Rebecca Milne, 15–38. Chichester: Wiley.

Gudjonsson, Gisli H. 2003. *The Psychology of Interrogations and Confessions: A Handbook.* Chichester: Wiley.

Haworth, Kate. 2006. "The Dynamics of Power and Resistance in Police Interview Discourse." *Discourse & Society* 17(6): 739–759.

Haworth, Kate. 2013. "Audience Design in the Police Interview: The Interactional and Judicial Consequences of Audience Orientation." *Language in Society* 42(1): 45–69.

Heydon, Georgina. 2005. *The Language of Police Interviewing: A Critical Analysis.* Basingstoke: Palgrave Macmillan.

Holmberg, Ulf. 2009. "Investigative Interviewing as a Therapeutic Jurisprudential Approach." In *International Developments in Investigative Interviewing*, edited by Tom Williamson,, Becky Milne, and Stephen P. Savage, 149–175. London: Willan.

Lim, Phyllis Louise. 1993. "Meaning versus Verbatim Memory in Language Processing: Deriving Inferential, Morphological, and Metaphorical Gist."

Accessed 19 May 2016. http://arizona.openrepository.com/arizona/handle/10150/186487.

Milne, Rebecca, and Ray Bull. 1999. *Investigative Interviewing: Psychology and Practice*. Chichester: Wiley.

Newbury, Phillip, and Alison Johnson. 2007. "Suspects' Resistance to Constraining and Coercive Questioning Strategies in the Police Interview." *International Journal of Speech, Language and the Law* 13(2): 213–240.

Ord, Brian, Gary Shaw, and Tracey Green. 2011. *Investigative Interviewing Explained*. Australia: LexisNexis Butterworths.

Oxburgh, Gavin E., Trond Myklebust, and Tim Grant. 2010. "The Question of Question Types in Police Interviews: A Review of the Literature from a Psychological and Linguistic Perspective." *International Journal of Speech, Language and the Law* 17(1): 45–66.

Rock, Frances. 2013. "Every Link in the Chain": The Police Interview as Textual Intersection." In *Legal-Lay Communication: Textual Travels in the Law*, edited by Chris Heffer, Frances Rock, and John Conley, 78–103. Oxford: Oxford University Press.

Shepherd, Eric, and Andy Griffiths. 2013. *Investigative Interviewing: The Conversation Management Approach*. Oxford: Oxford University Press.

Thornborrow, Joanna. 2002. *Power Talk: Language and Interaction in Institutional Discourse*. London: Longman.

Vrij, Aldert, Ronald Fisher, Samantha Mann, and Sharon Leal. 2009. "Increasing Cognitive Load in Interviews to Detect Deceit." In *International Developments in Investigative Interviewing*, edited by Tom Williamson, Becky Milne, and Stephen P. Savage, 176–189. London: Willan.

Williamson, Tom M. 1994. "Reflections on Current Police Practice." In *Suspicion and Silence: The Rights of Silence in Criminal Investigations*, edited by Derek Morgan and Geoffrey M. Stephenson, 107–116. London: Blackstone.

CHAPTER EIGHT

Supporting Competing Narratives

A Membership Categorization Analysis of Identity Work in Police-Detainee Talk

David Yoong and Ayeshah Syed

Introduction

Police engagements with "wrongdoers," whether in the interrogation room or during stop and search,[1] are sites of formalized social control (Leo 1994: 95–98). In these asymmetric engagements, police officers wield considerable authoritative and discursive power, manifested in the way they reconstruct events to fit "categories of crime" (Edwards 2008: 183), where individuals are formally represented as "law abiders" or "offenders." The high stakes of police interviews have prompted considerable research on interaction in this setting. For example, scholars have examined officers' use of various tactics, including deception and psychological coercion to elicit information or confessions (Leo and White 1999; Shuy 2005; Leo 2008), asserting authority and dominance through linguistic choices (Ainsworth 1993; Yoong 2010; Gaines 2011), and controlling the lines of inquiry in the reconstruction of narrative events (Coulthard 2000; Komter 2007).

Interrogation techniques commonly used to elicit confessions include confronting suspects with evidence, which is comparable to the practice of "giving a source" to support epistemic claims in ordinary conversation (Pomerantz 1984: 607–624), and offering moral justifications (Leo 1996: 278; Frantzen 2010). Komter (2003: 437–464) shows how a Dutch police officer succeeds in eliciting a confession from a detainee by minimizing the moral implications of the crime, describing the detainee as a "good" person, and finally inviting the detainee to demonstrate her moral character by confessing. That morality is a feature of police talk is unsurprising given the roles and obligations tied to the police officer's institutional identity, where the aim of police interviews is to discover information, or "the truth," and where the outcomes of these interactions would result in the categorization of people and events with respect to legal stipulations of "right" and "wrong." However, research has shown that identity can also be a resource for detainees in upgrading their own claims and resisting the officer's actions in police interviews. For instance, Haworth (2006) shows how a murder suspect resists the discursive power of the police interviewer by asserting his professional identity as a doctor and by undermining the interviewer's status as an officer and the questioner. Identities are also used by detainees as persuasive devices to convince questioning officers that they are not guilty of crimes (Clifton 2009), to make denials (Stokoe 2010), to mitigate their offenses (LeCouteur and Oxlad, 2010: 13–16; Stokoe 2012: 293–295), or even to admit guilt to an offense.

Although Bronitt (2004) states that there is now a greater emphasis on "covert policing" as a result of law enforcement's shift from coercion to deception, there has been little discussion on interviews resulting from undercover sting operations, owing possibly to a lack of access to such data. In sting operations, an individual is convicted of committing a crime that is covertly created or facilitated by the authorities, which aids in the collection of evidence but also poses ethical questions concerned with the "manufactured" nature of the crime (Hay 2005: 388). Such operations hinge on undercover officers' presenting identities—for example, as buyers or sellers of illegal items, or as decoys to invite illegal activity such as theft or rape attempts (ibid.). In the present study, the sting operation involves an undercover officer posing as an occupant of a cubicle in a public bathroom that had been identified as a location for illegal solicitation of sex. The detainee, who was arrested for soliciting sex through hand and foot signals made to an undercover officer, is later interviewed by the same officer. The officer is accompanied by a colleague, whose participation in the interview is minimal. With no audio or video recording of the incident, two competing versions of events emerge: one presented by the detainee and the official version as reported by the undercover officer.

We draw on membership categorization analysis (MCA) to analyze the interaction between the detainee and police officer in pursuing their conflicting goals in the interrogation room. This incident is unique not only because of its context in an undercover sting operation, but also because the interaction involves a dispute between a police officer and a detainee whose professional identity as a politician carries considerable power. Our analysis demonstrates how identity categories are used by the speakers to accomplish their interactional goals in this site of social control, where the detainee's unwillingness to admit guilt calls into question the officer's version of events. The discussion covers the ways the speakers proffer, resist, reject, accept, and exploit categories related to their identities, and how they contest certain identities projected on them by the other.

Membership Categorization Analysis

MCA originates from the work of Sacks (1995) in the 1970s and has since been advanced by scholars including Jayyusi (1984), Housley and Fitzgerald (2002, 2009, 2015), and Stokoe (2010, 2012) as an ethnomethodology for examining how people create, use, and interpret cultural and societal categories as part of their local reasoning, in order to organize "social orders" and actions and to accomplish interactional objectives. MCA is most useful in examining (1) how people invoke and interpret identities in real time from the speakers' viewpoints, (2) the ways speakers navigate society through the "commonsensical" descriptions of their social and local worlds, (3) the moral and practical "typing" or labeling of people, and (4) how people predict, describe and justify their behavior and the behavior of others (Fitzgerald 2012; Housley and Fitzgerald 2015). Indeed, owing to its usefulness in understanding situated real-time social behaviors and problems, MCA has been used for various investigative purposes. This includes looking at how categories are used to make moral judgments of a man who committed mass murder (Rapley, McCarthy, and McHoul 2003), how gender categories are used to make denials in police-suspect interactions (Stokoe 2010), how categories are used to account for actions and decision making (Housley and Fitzgerald 2009), and how categories are used in dispute talk to make a persuasive case (Stokoe and Wallwork 2003).

The following concepts are parts of the MCA framework that enable one to examine identities in interaction:

- *Identities and categories*: Sacks uses the terms *categories* and *identities* synonymously in his lectures. He regards categories as references to label a person or group of people, and these categories exist in relation to other categories in situated and relevant devices. Categories emerge in social environments where interaction takes place. Along the lines of Turner, Hogg, Oakes, Reicher, and Wetherell's (1987) self-categorization theory and Tajfel and Turner's (1986) social identity theory, these social identities are dynamic categories that people use to classify themselves in situational contexts. Analysts should not be concerned with the epistemic, objective truths of these identities and categories. Rather, they should, among other things, look at how people use them to make sense of role and status relationships with other people and how they manipulate outcomes. Examples of identities and categories are "criminal," "bad guy," "police officer," and "good guy."
- *Members*: Members are "objects" to refer to individual units (mainly people) that fit the prototypical description of a category or sets of categories: for example, a person who is a "sexual deviant" (category) is one who solicits sex with strangers in a public restroom (member). Members' identities are associated with category-bound activities.
- *Category-bound activities*: These are activities associated with specific categories (and members). According to Sacks (1995: 241), "If an activity is category-bound, it is bound to some category that is in a positioned collection"—e.g., sexual deviants (category) solicit sex (activity). Sacks also gives an example of how category-bound activities can be used to denigrate (or praise) somebody: "The way we construct the denigration of somebody is to propose about them that they are doing something that is bound to some category that has a lower position than theirs" (ibid.). Activities are prototypical behavior of the category. Analysts should be sensitive to the ways speakers do "hinting" or provide activities that are associated with particular categories.
- *Membership categorization devices*: When categories and relevant actions or activities are clustered together into a set, that set forms a *device*—e.g., "immoral people" (device) consists of "sex offenders" and "criminals" (categories).
- *Inference-rich membership category device:* People in interactions make inferences based on their existing prototypical and/or stereotypical mental

schemas. Certain members of categories will invoke other categories and meanings. Commonly, speakers would put a name into a category—e.g., "John did X (solicited sex)" in order to mean, "Such-and such did X." Hearers make inferences about John (he is a sexual deviant).

- *Category-tied descriptions*: Descriptions of categories are often expressed as adjectives and often collocate with the category. For example, sexual deviants (category) are "disgusting" and "creepy" (predicates).

It is also important to note that one of the ways to interpret the meaning of these elements is to examine how the speakers react to each other's utterances and propositions in real time. In other words, as analysts, we should mitigate our own symbolic interpretations and rely on the ways the speakers themselves engage in examining and interpreting categories in their interactions. By looking at the perlocutionary effects, for instance, we are able to determine the hearer's understanding of the speaker's intent.

The methods of applying MCA in this study draw inspiration from various sources. Although Stokoe (2012: 280) states that an analysis should collect data across different domestic and institutional settings, MCA analysts have also examined categories in single case designs (e.g., Housley 2002; Clifton 2009; Butler and Fitzgerald 2010)—an approach that is also taken here. We build a collection of explicit mentions of categories and memberships while looking at category-resonant descriptions and the sequential positions of each categorical instance within the interaction. By examining the design and action orientation (including looking at how the speakers orient themselves to the categories and devices and make inferences), we are able to see how categories are used in order to accomplish certain goals. Successful analysis requires an awareness of the context of interaction. In the following section, we briefly discuss the case of Larry Craig.

The Larry Craig Case

In mid-2007 U.S. Senator Larry Craig was arrested by an undercover police officer for allegedly engaging in lewd conduct in an airport bathroom. The officer was conducting an investigation prompted by public complaints about sexual activity in the men's bathroom of Minneapolis airport (McArdle 2007). Following the arrest, Craig was processed at the Minneapolis Airport Police Department, where he was interviewed. During this interview he disputed compromising details in the officer's account of the events leading to his arrest. A month later Craig entered a guilty plea to charges of disorderly conduct. He was fined and given a 10-day jail sentence, which was stayed, and one year's probation. Despite pleading guilty in court, once news of the case became public, the married Republican politician maintained his innocence in press statements, describing the incident as a misunderstanding ("Craig: 'I Did Nothing Inappropriate in Airport Bathroom'" 2007; McArdle 2007). The arrest, along with allegations of homosexuality from the previous year, contradicted Craig's openly conservative politics, which included supporting legislation against same-sex marriage and opposing legislation to protect gay rights. In the face of pressure to resign, Craig nevertheless served out his term as senator until 2008, all the while making attempts to clear his name. However, the incident effectively ended his political career, and he did not run for reelection.

The data used in this chapter are derived from the audiotape recording of Craig's post-arrest interview, which was released by the Minneapolis Airport Police Department in response to questions about the arrest amidst the controversy that followed the news of the arrest ("Craig Resigns over Airport Bathroom Sex Sting" 2007). The transcription method used provides a close-up view of the interaction as it unfolds, by including nonlinguistic features of interaction such as overlaps, pauses, volume, and laughter (Jefferson 2004). The next section provides an overview of the interaction.

Using Identities in a Police-Detainee Interview

This chapter focuses on interaction between the detainee (D) and the arresting police officer (O1). The second police office (O2) who is present does not participate much verbally. The nine-minute interview can be divided into three main sequences: the opening (lines 1–61), the "interview" (lines 62–316), and the closing (lines 317–326). Shortly after the recording begins, the officer performs institutionally required procedures, framing the interaction as a police interview. After recording the details of the interaction and its participants, the officer delivers the Miranda warning and the detainee gives his consent to be interviewed. What follows is the interview proper, during which the officer asks the detainee to provide a narrative of the incident. This research focuses on the second sequence.

Deploying Categories to Support Competing Versions of Events

In the section that follows the opening sequence, the interaction becomes less structured. The activity in this second section revolves around retelling the event that took place. Our analysis covers six moves: (1) deploying categories in accounts and denials, (2) projecting and claiming morally implicative identities to elicit a confession, (3) invoking a physical category as an account, (4) using category-implicative predicates in accusations and denials, and (5) invoking categories to reject accounts and to support an accusation.

DEPLOYING CATEGORIES IN ACCOUNTS AND DENIALS

Having acquired D's consent to continue with the interview, O1 prompts D to provide a narrative of the event using a story-formulation phrase (see Stokoe and Edwards 2006), which indicates the potential for competing versions (your side), as shown in line 63 of excerpt 8.1. What follows is D's strategy in deploying certain categories to create an account that he is innocent and to deny O1's arrest charges.

Excerpt 8.1: Recording time 1:38–2:13

O1: (0.65) Okay (0.31) u:::m (0.76) I just wanna start off with
u:h your side of the story, oka:y? (0.54) So, u:h=
D: =(Well) I go into the bathroom here as I normally dhho:=
=£I'm£ a commuter too here.
O1: Oka:y,
D: I sit down, u::m(1.74) t' go to the ba:throom. (1.08)
and u:h,(0.99) you said our feet bumped I believe
they di:d, (0.76) a::h because I reached down and
scooted over. A:nd u::m, (1.01) the (.) next thing I
kne:w, under the (0.98) bathroom divider comes a
card that says Police, (2.21) No:w, u::m,(1.26) hhh

In beginning his narrative, D foregrounds his membership of the category "commuter" and normalizes his visit to the bathroom, framing the event he is about to describe as a routine bathroom visit. The category claim is preceded by exhalation (line 64) or "laugh particles" (Potter and Hepburn 2010) and a "smiley" voice (line 65), indicating suppressed laughter (Jefferson 2004), where laughter is a resource used to manage delicate or potentially face-threatening situations (Haakana 2001) or problematic sequences. By representing himself with the neutral category of "commuter," he also attempts to distance himself from the "detainee/offender" category imposed on him by the interactional context. With pauses and hesitation, D describes his performance of "normal" bathroom activities ("sit down . . . go to the bathroom," line 67) and includes particular hand and foot actions ("feet bumped," "reached down," lines 68–69). Although vaguely alluding to O1's problematization of his foot movement ("you said our feet bumped I believe they did," lines 68–69), D's narrative represents the event as a commuter's mundane visit to a public bathroom, suddenly contrasted against the legal issues implied by the undercover officer identifying himself as "Police" (line 72). This continues in the following excerpt.

Excerpt 8.2: Recording time 2:13–2:53

D: 'n that's about as far as I can take it, I don't
know of anything else:, uh your foot came
toward mine, mine came toward yours, was that
natural?=I don't kno:w, did we bump?=Yes, I think
we did=You said so:,=
O1: =↑hhh= (cough)
D: =I don't disagree with that.
O1: >Okay.< (2.34) hhh (1.37) I don't want to: (.) get into a
pissing match here.=
D: =We're not going to.
O1: Good. U:[:m],
D: [I] don't (0.38) a- a- a- I- I am not gay I don't
do these kinds of things, and um=
O1: =It doesn't matter, [I] don't care about=
D: [(well)]
O1: >sexual preference or anything like that<>Here's
your stuff [back sir<]
D: [Thank you]
O1: U:m (0.4) I don't care about sexual=
=prefe[rence]=
D: [↑I]know you do:n't, you're out to enforce
the la:w_

O1: Right
D: But you shouldn't be out to entrap people either.

D continues his narrative, elaborating on foot movements in lines 73–77. He uses "foot" as the active subject, instead of attributing the foot movement to a person (agent), and describes his actions as mirroring those of O1 ("your foot came toward mine, mine came toward yours," lines 74–75). This representation supports a claim of innocence, as it contradicts O1's version (on the official report), which describes D's use of foot signals to solicit sexual activity. O1's responses, a cough (78) and the disaffiliate statement ("I don't want to get into a pissing match here," lines 80–81), indicate that D's narrative is unsatisfactory. With a latched response, D assures O1 that they are not about to argue, presenting an affiliative stance. However, D continues to support his claim of innocence by making a category-based denial ("[I] don't a- a- a- I- I am *not* gay I *don't do these* kinds of things," lines 84–85, emphasis added), where denials are performed through character, disposition, or identity claims (Stokoe 2010). D's statement (84) invokes a category (gay) that binds homosexuals and offenders (people who do "these kinds of things") while distancing himself from the offender category through his claim of being "not gay." O1 interrupts D's turn and dismisses his sexual-identity claim as irrelevant ("It doesn't matter, [I] don't care about sexual preference or anything like that," lines 86 and 88), which effectively rejects D's binding of sexual preference and offender categories. This act also asserts O1's power in determining what is relevant to the discussion, as an interaction concerned with legality versus illegality. This is accepted by D, who does not bring up this category again. However, with his category claim treated as irrelevant, he indirectly accuses O1 of entrapping him ("But you shouldn't be out to entrap people either," line 96). This characterizes O1 as being immoral.

PROJECTING AND CLAIMING POSITIVE MORAL CATEGORIES TO ELICIT A CONFESSION

In the face of D's continued unwillingness to admit fault, O1 then shifts the topic to D's hand gestures, using a question that topicalizes a potentially incriminating detail.

Excerpt 8.3: Recording time 2:53–3:25

O1: This isn't entrapment. (all right?) (0.53) U::m, (2.0)
y- you're skipping some parts here, but what-

99 what about your hand.
100 (0.54)
101 D: What about it. I reached down, my foot like this:?
102 (1.67) there was a piece of paper on the floor,
103 I picked it u:p? (0.2)
104 (1.81)
105 O1: ((sniff)) Oka:yh
106 D: What about my hand.
107 O1: Well, you're not being truthful with me I'm kinda
108 disappointed in you Senator. (0.4) 'm rea:l disappointed
109 right now. (1.24) Oka:y, .hh I'm not, (0.61) just so you
110 know, (0.59) just like everybody?
111 D: Yea:h?
112 O1: I, I, I, treat with dignity: I try ta: (.) pull 'em
113 away from the situation=
114 D: =[I appre-]
115 O1: =[And not] embarrass them,
116 D: And I appreciate that.

In responding to O1's question, D maintains a representation of events that supports his innocence. In line 102, after a silence, he offers a possible account for his hand's being visible under the cubicle wall, which O1 responds to with a delayed unmarked acknowledgment token (line 105) accompanied by a sniff. D's confrontational question in line 101 ("What about my hand"), marked by stress on the word "about," shows his orientation to O1's last turn as withholding acceptance of his account. This is confirmed when O1 does not answer D's question, but responds by describing D with a morally implicative predicate, as "not being truthful," thereby rejecting his representation of events. O1 also expresses his disappointment and makes a personal disclosure that appears to contrast with his formality in using D's official title, "Senator" ("I'm kinda disappointed in you Senator;[I]'m real disappointed," lines 107–109). It is also worth noting that such a direct face threat indicates O1's disrespect for D's status as a senator. O1 follows D's negative predication with a contrasting characterization of himself ("Okay, I'm not, just so you know, just like everybody?," lines 109–110), as having positive moral attributes in his treatment of other detainees ("I treat with dignity . . . and not embarrass them," 112–115). D accepts O1's self-characterization. This continues in excerpt 8.4.

Excerpt 8.4: Recording time 3:35–4:13

O1: [I've] never had to bring anybody to jail, because everybody's been truthful to me.=
D: =I don't want you to take me to jail and I think that [(you-)]
O1: [I'm] not gonna take you to jail
D: [(All right)]
O1: [(as long)] as you'll be cooperative but I- .h I'm not gonna lie I w- [we]
D: [Did] my hand come below the divider, ↑yes, it di::d
O1: Okay. Sir. (0.49) We deal with people that lie to us every day.
D: I'm, sure you do.
O1: We deal with- and we [deal with]
O2: [I'm sure] you do too sir=
D: =And gentlemen, so do I.
O1: I'm sure you do. (0.56) We deal with a lot of (0.45) people that are (0.24) very (.) bad people,. hh you're not a bad person.=
D: =No::_ I don't think [I am.]
O1: [Okay] so what I'm telling you, I don't want to be lied to=
D: =O:kay.
O1: Oka:y? (0.61) So we'll start over, you're gonna get out of here. You're gonna have to pay a fine and that will be it. Okay?=
D: =Fine=
O1 =I don't call media, I don't do: any of that type of crap.

O1 continues to speak on the morally implicative topic of being truthful, predicating truth telling as a normative behavior for detainees and the reason he has never had to take anyone to jail (line 119). By introducing the topic of jail, O1 alludes to the power of his official identity, which D acknowledges in making known his desire not to be taken to jail (line 121). The policeman makes an indirect threat by positioning "be[ing] cooperative" (lines 125–126) as a condition for avoiding jail. By contrasting cooperation against lying ("but . . . I'm not gonna lie," lines 125–126), O1 implies that for D to be cooperative, he would need to be truthful, which casts an assessment on the narrative that D has given so far. With a rushed turn in line 127, D brings up hand gestures, indicating his recognition of the response that O1 seeks from him. However, his increased volume and varied pitch ("↑yes, it di::d," line 128) shows disalignment and heightened emotion. In addition, D's response presents his hand movements as involuntary, rather than using an alternative formulation that would place himself as the agent—for example, if he had said, "I put my hand below the divider."

With the confession he is pursuing not forthcoming, O1 changes topic in line 129 and invokes an abstract, morally implicative category of "people that lie" using the collective "we" to refer to himself, and possibly his colleague, as part of a larger group: police officers who are accustomed to dealing with dishonest people ("Okay. Sir. We deal with people that lie to us every day," lines 129–130). These categories present a "moral contrast" (Housley and Fitzgerald 2009: 350–353), with O1 and his colleagues on the "right" side and the people who lie on the "wrong" side. Following D's acceptance of this, the second officer (O2) alludes to D's occupational identity, as a congressman and lawmaker, creating an opportunity for him to align himself with the morally right category ("I'm sure you do too," line 133), which he does (line 134). Before prompting D to retell his narrative (line 142), O1 reinvokes the negative moral category of people encountered by policemen, this time referring to this group as "very bad people" (line 136). He projects a contrasting identity for the congressman ("You're not a bad person," line 136), distancing him from this undesirable category. D accepts this projected category. As O1 follows his positive categorization of D with a prompt to "start over" with his narrative, it creates an impetus for D to demonstrate his membership in the desirable group by retelling the events to match O1's version. There is not much of a choice for D here: if he continues to perform the dispreferred action of contradicting O1's version of events, he will be acting as a "very bad [person]." In lines 143–146, O1 makes further efforts to elicit the confession by describing the benefits of D's cooperation ("You're gonna have to pay a fine and that will be it," lines 143–144), orienting to D's occupational identity as a public figure ("I don't call media," line 146).

INVOKING A PHYSICAL CATEGORY AS AN ACCOUNT

To support his claims that his actions were accidental, D invokes a physical category. He argues that his large build and kinesic mannerisms are why his foot got close to O1's.

Excerpt 8.5: Recording time 5:11–5:49

179 O1: Okay hh 'n when you went in the stall, then
180 what
181 D: (1.06) Sat do:wn?
182 O1: Okay. D'you do anything with your feet?
183 (1.51)
184 D: Positioned them? I don't know, I don't know at the
185 time.
186 (1.64)
187 D: I'm a fairly wide guy, I-
188 O2: Mhmm ((clears throat))
189 O1: >I understand<
190 (You [can't be)]
191 D: [I had] to spread› my le:gs, <=
192 O1: Okay,
193 D: =›When I lower my pants, so they won't slide.‹
194 O1: >Okay,<
195 D: Did I slide them too close to yours? Did I, I
196 looked down once, your foot was close to mine.
197 (1.18)
198 O1: Yes
199 D: Did we bump? A:h, you said so. I don't recall
200 that, but apparently we were close.
201 (0.75)
202 O1: °Ye:ah°
203 (1.19)
204 O1: Well y- your foot did touch mine, on my side
205 of the stall.
206 D: All ri:ght,

D commences retelling his account of the event, prompted by questions from the officers. In line 182, O1 asks a polar question, focusing again on foot movements. Although the question requires a yes-or-no response, D responds with a statement ("Positioned them?," line 184). This displays epistemic uncertainty through his delayed turn and a rising intonation, followed by a claim of not knowing. Drew (1992: 480–486) has shown how such claims of not remembering or not knowing allow witnesses under cross-examination to avoid confirming potentially incriminating details. Similarly, D refuses to confirm or deny making particular foot movements and then offers a self-description using the physical category "a fairly wide guy" (line 187), which is accepted by O1. D continues to build this self-categorization into an alternative account for his foot touching that of O1 ("I had to spread my legs," lines 191–193). He then expands his account to include the perspective of O1 ("Did we bump? Ah, you said so," line 199) but represents his actions as involuntary movements necessitated by his large build, thereby supporting his claim of innocence. Throughout these turns, O1 allows D to complete his account, contributing mainly continuers ("Okay," "Yeah"); however, his delayed turns, compressed talk (line 194), and quiet voice (line 202) indicate disagreement.

ACCUSING AND DENYING USING CATEGORY-IMPLICATIVE PREDICATES

After a prolonged exchange, during which D maintains his innocence, O1 employs a category-implicative predicate to make an indirect accusation.

Excerpt 8.6: Recording time 7:04–7:32

245	D:	Right, okay. h My left hand was (.) in the direct
246		opposite of the stall from you.
247		(0.76)
248	O1:	Okay (0.64) Y- you travel through here=
249		=frequently, sir?=
250	D:	=I do:. (0.7) U::m almost weekly.
251		(1.23)
252	O1:	Have you been successful in these bathrooms here
253		befo:re
254		(1.99)
255	D:	I go to that bathroom regularly, [(in the)]
256	O1:	[(I mean] for
257		any type of other active[ties]
258	D:	[No] Absolutely
259		not. I don't (.) s:eek activity in bathrooms.
260		(4.32)
261	O1:	's embarrassing.
262	D:	↑Well it's embarrassing for both=

With the two parties failing to reach agreement on D's performance of hand and foot gestures, with their implications on his guilt or innocence, O1 initiates the topic of D's routine use of the airport. He follows this neutral question (line 248) with a category-implicative question ("Have you been successful in these bathrooms here before?," lines 252–253). This polar question is designed to solicit a yes-or-no response. Yet, with its categorically implicative predicate, which depicts the recipient as someone who regularly solicits sex in the airport bathroom, even a negative response would imply guilt. After a short silence, D responds, neither providing a yes/-or-no response nor addressing the content of the question (line 255). His statement that he regularly visits the bathroom misunderstands the question, intentionally or otherwise. O1 repairs this in lines 256–257 by explaining that he was referring to bathroom visits made for "other activities." Although O1 does not explicitly refer to sexual activity, D's strong rejection of this ("No. Absolutely not," lines 258–259) shows that he orients toward the categorical implications of O1's question (being gay and an offender), and he follows with a contrasting self-characterization. This is an upgraded category-based denial from the one shown in excerpt 8.2, where D defines the rejected predicate more explicitly ("I don't seek activity in bathrooms," line 259), than he did earlier ("I don't do these kinds of things," lines 84–85) in his attempts to remain consistent with his earlier dispositions. There is a significant silence before O1 says "'s embarrassing" (line 261). O1 categorizes D's argumentative behavior and refusal to admit guilt as a kind of faux pas or "embarrassment," as D's actions contravene his own identity as a morally respected public servant. Though not disagreeing with O1, D's response in 262 attempts to equate the imbalance implied by O1 by attributing "embarrassment" to both himself and O1 ("It's embarrassing for both," line 262). If both parties are within their rights to be embarrassed, then D is not the only one who is morally accountable.

INVOKING AN INSTITUTIONAL IDENTITY TO REJECT AN ACCOUNT AND SUPPORT AN ACCUSATION

Following D's explicit denial of guilt, O1's talk becomes increasingly marked by increases in volume, indicating heightened emotions. Before providing his version of events, O1 invokes his own institutional identity to reject D's account and support his own.

Excerpt 8.7: Recording time 7:32–8:03

264 D: =I'm not gonna fight ↑you=
265 O1: =I know you're not going to fight me. But that's

not the POINT.hh I would resPECT, you and I still
respect you. I don't disrespect you but I'm
disrespected right now and I'm not trynna act like
I have all kinds of POwer or anything, but you're
sitting here LYING to a police officer.
D: I, I, [I, don't]
O1: [But it's] not (a testimony) that I'm
getting from somebody else .hh I'm ((inaudible))
O1: [((Inaudible))]
D: [((Inaudible))]
O1: I was trained in () and I know what I am doing.
D: Did I=
O1: And I saw you put your hand under there and
you're going to sit there [and]
D: [I]admit I put my
hand down.
O1: You put your hand and rubbed it on the bottom of
the stall. (.) With your LEFT HAND
D: Now, ↑wait a moment.

D says that he does not want to fight O1 (line 264), which seems to be an attempt to repair the disaffiliation caused by their competing versions. However, this is dismissed as irrelevant by O1 ("But that's not the point," lines 265–266), who makes a series of statements that position himself as being on the receiving end of dispreferred behavior, presumably referring to D ("I'm [being] disrespected," lines 267–268). He then indirectly asserts his institutional rights with a category-linked predicate ("I'm not try[ing to] act like I have all kinds of power," lines 268–269), and refers to himself in the third person using his institutional identity while directly accusing D of lying ("You're sitting here lying to a police officer," lines 269–270). O1's tone throughout this talk is heightened, marked with multiple word stresses and increased volume. There are several instances of overlapping speech as D attempts to respond, with hesitation and repeated speech. O1 maintains control of the talk, and in line 276 he makes a claim of expertise ("I was trained . . . and I know what I am doing") before narrating his version of events (lines 278–279 and 282–283). D admits to the first action that O1 describes (line 280) but expresses disagreement by interrupting O1 ("Now, wait a moment," line 284) when his narrative depicts D performing a potentially incriminating act (lines 282–283).

Discussion and Final Remarks

One of the challenges in studying how identities are operationalized in interaction is demonstrating how these identities are made relevant and consequential to the participants themselves (Butler and Fitzgerald 2010), particularly in the absence of explicit use of categories or categorical devices. Yet, MCA research in both institutional and ordinary talk has shown how identities tied to larger social structures are made relevant through the analysis of category-bound activities, which illustrates Fitzgerald's point (2012: 307) that "the strength of MCA is found in its analytic flexibility and hence its potential relevance to any discipline interested in aspects of identity and social knowledge."

Our findings demonstrate how both D and O1 utilize identity categorical resources to perform social actions, and how these practices are influenced by the goals of the interactions. Although categorization itself is normative through its prescription of rights and responsibilities of members (Sacks 1992; Housley and Fitzgerald 2002), much of O1's categorical work is morally implicative, either explicitly ("we deal with very bad people," "you're not a bad person") or implied ("I treat people with dignity," "you're not being truthful," "I'm real disappointed in you"). Although earlier studies of morally implicative talk in police interviews have generally involved projections of moral categories or notions onto the interviewee (e.g., Komter 2003; Housley and Fitzgerald 2009), our findings depict the officer's positive self-characterization. This may be an attempt to play the affiliative "good" cop, to encourage the detainee's cooperation, but it could also be attributable to the context of the interview as occurring after an undercover operation. The detainee's withholding of a confession also casts a moral judgment on the officer himself through contradicting the details reported by the officer in the official record. This carries the implication that the officer is wrong or even lying. In other words, these categories, which are used by both D and O1, evoke commonsense ideas of what is righteous and what is morally wrong. It is desirable for individuals to be associated with the former category and not the latter. These practices essentially reveal how identities are used by the speakers to locate and anchor themselves and each other in their social worlds through their inclusion or exclusion of categories that carry moral attributes (Simon 2004).

We wish to make two final points. First, different theoretical and conceptual lenses of identity—for example, the dimensions of background and foreground modes (Schlenker and Pontari 2000), constant and evolving identities (Simon 2004), personal and relational selves (Brewer and Gardner 1996), and/or even "face" (Goffman 1967)—would yield unique analytical interpretations if applied to this data. However, using the MCA approach on this single case of conversational data, we have explored how a police officer and detainee work with identities in real time to accomplish specific interactional objectives.

Secondly, it must be noted that our analysis is limited by the quality of the available audio recording, which was at times unintelligible. In addition, where it was unclear which officer was speaking, we relied on the officially released transcript. Moreover, to identify patterns of category use in context would require expanding beyond the single case to a larger collection, comprising interviews in which the police interviewer and detainee have conflicting versions or claims. Additionally, data from ordinary conversations where speakers are disputing competing claims could enable further identification of interactional practices in claim disputes. Such findings may be useful to police interviewers in engaging with and pursuing confessions from detainees.

Note

1. Based on reasonable suspicion, police officers have the authority and discretion to stop and search any person they believe to be violating the law. This power enables officers to detect criminal activity and end it. Stops and searches are contentious because they involve police officers infringing the liberty and privacy of suspects.

References

Ainsworth, Janet E. 1993. "In a Different Register: The Pragmatics of Powerlessness in Police Interrogation." *Yale Law Journal* 103(2): 259–322.

Brewer, Marilynn B., and Wendi Gardner. 1996. "Who Is This 'We'? Levels of Collective Identity and Self Representations." *Journal of Personality and Social Psychology* 71(1): 83–93.

Bronitt, Simon. 2004. "The Law in Undercover Policing: A Comparative Study of Entrapment and Covert Interviewing in Australia, Canada and Europe." *Common Law World Review* 33(1): 35–80.

Butler, Carly W., and Richard Fitzgerald. 2010. "Membership-in-Action: Operative Identities in a Family Meal." *Journal of Pragmatics* 42(9: 2462–2474.

Clifton, Jonathan. 2009. "A Membership Categorization Analysis of the Waco Siege: Perpetrator-Victim Identity as a Moral Discrepancy Device for 'Doing' Subversion." *Sociological Research Online* 14(5): 8. https://doi.org/10.5153/sro.2002.

Coulthard, Malcolm. 2000. "Whose Text Is It? On the Linguistic Investigation of Authorship." In *Discourse and Social Life*, edited by Srikant Sarangi and Malcolm Coulthard, 270–287. Harlow, Essex: Pearson.

"Craig: I Did Nothing 'Inappropriate' in Airport Bathroom." 2007. CNN, 28 August. Accessed 7 June 2015. http://edition.cnn.com/2007/b/08/28/craig.arrest/.

"Craig Resigns over Airport Bathroom Sex Sting." 2007. MSNBC, 30 August. http://www.nbcnews.com/id/20467347/#.V-yRYJN97zI.

Drew, Paul. 1992. "Contested Evidence in a Courtroom Cross-Examination: The Case of a Trial for Rape." In *Talk at Work: Social Interaction in Institutional Settings,* edited by Paul Drew and John Heritage, 470–520. Cambridge: Cambridge University Press.

Edwards, Derek. 2008. "Intentionality and *mens rea* in Police Interrogations: The Production of Actions as Crimes." *Intercultural pragmatics* 5(2): 177–199.

Fitzgerald, Richard. 2012. "Membership Categorization Analysis: Wild and Promiscuous or Simply the Joy of Sacks?" *Discourse Studies* 14(3): 305–311.

Frantzen, Durant. 2010. "Interrogation Strategies, Evidence, and the Need for Miranda: A Study of Police Ideologies." *Police Practice and Research: An International Journal* 11(3): 227–239.

Gaines, Philip. 2011. "The Multifunctionality of Discourse Operator Okay: Evidence from a Police Interview." *Journal of Pragmatics* 43(14): 3291–3315. https://doi.org/10.1016/j.pragma.2011.06.005.

Goffman, Erving. 1967. *Interaction Ritual: Essays on Face-to-Face Behavior.* New York: Pantheon.

Haakana, Markku. 2001. "Laughter as a Patient's Resource: Dealing with Delicate Aspects of Medical Interaction." *Text—Interdisciplinary Journal for the Study of Discourse* 21(1–2): 187–219. https://doi.org/10.1515/text.1.21.1–2.187.

Hay, Bruce. 2005. "Sting Operations, Undercover Agents, and Entrapment." *Missouri Law Review* 70: 387–431.

Haworth, Kate. 2006. "The Dynamics of Power and Resistance in Police Interview Discourse." *Discourse & Society* 17(6): 739–759. https://doi.org/10.1177/0957926506068430.

Housley, William. 2002. "Moral Discrepancy and 'Fudging the Issue' in a Radio News Interview." *Sociology* 36(1): 5–21. https://doi.org/10.1177/0038038502036001001.

Housley, William, and Richard Fitzgerald. 2002. "The Reconsidered Model of Membership Categorization Analysis." *Qualitative Research* 2(1): 59–83.

Housley, William, and Richard Fitzgerald. 2009. "Membership Categorization, Culture and Norms in Action." *Discourse & Society* 20(3): 345–362. https://doi.org/10.1177/0957926509102405.

Housley, William, and Richard Fitzgerald. 2015. "Introduction to Membership Categorization Analysis." In *Advances in Membership Categorization Analysis*, edited by William Housley and Richard Fitzgerald, 1–22. London: Sage.

Jayyusi, Lena. 1984. *Categorization and the Moral Order*. London: Routledge.

Jefferson, Gail. 2004. "Glossary of Transcript Symbols with an Introduction." In *Conversation Analysis: Studies from the First Generation*, edited by Gene H. Lerner, 13–34. Amsterdam: John Benjamins.

Komter, Martha. 2003. "The Interactional Dynamics of Eliciting a Confession in a Dutch Police Interrogation." *Research on Language and Social Interaction* 36(4): 433–470. https://doi.org/10.1207/S15327973RLSI3604_5.

Komter, Martha L. 2007. "The Suspect's Own Words: The Treatment of Written Statements in Dutch Courtrooms." *International Journal of Speech, Language and the Law* 9(2): 168–192. https://doi.org/10.1558/sll.2002.9.2.168.

LeCouteur, Amanda, and Melissa Oxlad. 2010. "Managing Accountability for domestic Violence: Identities, Membership Categories and Morality in Perpetrators' Talk." *Feminism & Psychology* 21(1): 5–28. https://doi.org/10.1177/0959353510375406.

Leo, Richard A. 1994. "Police Interrogation and Social Control." *Social & Legal Studies* 3: 93–120. https://papers.ssrn.com/sol3/papers.cfm?abstract_id=1141372.

Leo, Richard A. 1996. "Inside the Interrogation Room." *Journal of Criminal Law and Criminology* 86(2): 266–303. https://doi.org/10.2307/1144028.

Leo, Richard A. 2008. *Police Interrogation and American Justice*. Cambridge, MA: Harvard University Press.

Leo, Richard A., and Welsh S. White. 1999. "Adapting to Miranda: Modern Interrogators' Strategies for Dealing with the Obstacles Posed by Miranda." *Minnesota Law Review* 84: 397–457.

McArdle, John. 2007. "Craig Arrested, Pleads Guilty Following Incident in Airport Restroom." *Roll Call*. 27 August. www.rollcall.com/news/-19763–1.html?pg=2.

Pomerantz, Anita M. 1984. "Giving a Source or Basis: The Practice in Conversation of Telling 'How I Know.'" *Journal of Pragmatics* 8(5): 607–625.

Potter, Jonathan, and Alexa Hepburn. 2010. "Putting Aspiration into Words: 'Laugh Particles', Managing Descriptive Trouble and Modulating Action." *Journal of Pragmatics* 42(6): 1543–1555.

Rapley, Mark, David McCarthy, and Alec McHoul. 2003. "Mentality or Morality? Membership Categorization, Multiple Meanings and Mass Murder."

British Journal of Social Psychology 42(3): 427–444. https://doi.org/10.1348/014466603322438242.

Sacks, Harvey. 1995.*Lectures on Conversation*. 2 vols. Edited by Gail Jefferson, with an introduction by Emanuel A. Schegloff. Malden, MA: Blackwell.

Schlenker, Barry R., and Beth A. Pontari. 2000. "The Strategic Control of Information: Impression Management and Self-Presentation in Daily Life." In *Psychological Perspectives on Self and Identity*, edited by Abraham Tesser, Richard B. Felson, and Jerry M. Suls, 199–232. Washington, DC: American Psychological Association.

Shuy, Roger W. 2005. *The Language of Confession, Interrogation, and Deception*. Thousand Oaks, CA: Sage.

Simon, Bernd. 2004. *Identity in Modern Society: A Social Psychological Perspective*. Oxford: Blackwell.

Stokoe, Elizabeth. 2010. "'I'm Not Gonna Hit a Lady': Conversation Analysis, Membership Categorization and Men's Denials of Violence towards Women." *Discourse & Society* 21(1): 59–82. https://doi.org/10.1177/0957926509345072.

Stokoe, Elizabeth. 2012. "Moving Forward with Membership Categorization Analysis: Methods for Systematic Analysis." *Discourse Studies* 14(3): 277–303. https://doi.org/10.1177/1461445612441534.

Stokoe, Elizabeth H., and Derek Edwards. 2006. "Story Formulations in Talk-in-Interaction." *Narrative Inquiry* 16(1): 56–65. https://doi.org/10.1075/ni.16.1.09sto.

Stokoe, Elizabeth H., and Jodi Wallwork. 2003. "Space Invaders: The Moral-Spatial Order in Neighbour Dispute Discourse." *British Journal of Social Psychology* 42(4): 551–569. https://doi.org/10.1348/014466603322595275.

Tajfel, Henri, and John C. Turner. 1986. "The Social Identity Theory of Intergroup Behavior." In *Psychology of Intergroup Relations*, edited by S. Worchel and W. G. Austin, 7–24. Chicago: Nelson Hall.

Turner, John C., Michael A. Hogg, Penelope J. Oakes, Stephen D. Reicher, and Margaret S. Wetherell. 1987. *Rediscovering the Social Group: A Self-Categorization Theory*. Oxford: Blackwell.

Yoong, David. 2010. "Interactional Norms in the Australian Police Interrogation Room." *Discourse & Society* 21(6): 692–713. https://doi.org/10.1177/0957926510381223.

SECTION III

Discursive Transformations in Bilingual Police Interviews

CHAPTER NINE

Narrative Construction in Interpreted Police Interviews

Ikuko Nakane

Introduction

Discourse of police interviews has been analyzed from a number of perspectives, one of which approaches interviews as narrative construction processes (Linell and Jönsson 1991; Heydon 2005; Johnson 2006, 2008). Heydon (2005) discusses how versions of events are told and contested through interactional strategies in various participation frameworks of police interviews. The interview usually has "free narrative" and "elicited narrative" sections (Johnson 2006: 669). Although police and suspect narratives are not always conflicting, it is in the elicited narrative sections that versions of events tend to be co-constructed, contested, and at times manipulated through the interviewer's use of questioning strategies and the suspect's resistance strategies. Examples of such questioning strategies include formulation, contrast, and interruptions (e.g., Johnson 2002; Heydon 2005; Holt and Johnson 2010), although suspects may resist police-preferred narratives or narratives that increase the level of culpability by using discourse strategies of resistance. Newbury and Johnson (2006: 231) identify a number of such resistance strategies in their analysis of a notorious murder case in the United Kingdom, which includes contestation, correction, avoidance, and refusal.

With mobility and multilingualism on the rise in our globalizing world, there is also a greater demand for interpreting services in many legal contexts—including police interviews. In such interviews' role as narrative-construction processes, the question arises of what happens when the interview is mediated by an interpreter. Analysis of questioning strategies in interpreted police interviews by Wadensjö (1997) reveals that strategies of "recycling of information" (40), such as formulation, were affected by the process of interpreting. Some studies have also found that the pragmatic force of questions may be reduced through interpreting. For instance, Berk-Seligson's (1990) study of interpreter-mediated courtroom questioning found that interpreting at times softened the coercive effect of questioning. Komter's (2005) study of misunderstanding in interpreted police interviews showed that interpreters can mitigate highly face-threatening utterances made by the police interviewer. These alterations in questioning strategies and pragmatic force have implications for narrative-construction processes in police interviews.

Another important aspect of the interpreter-mediated interview is turn-taking. Russell (2002) discusses the complexities of turn-taking in police interviews that employ a consecutive mode of interpreting. In this mode of interpreting, primary speakers stop after producing a small segment of talk, and the interpreter's rendition follows. When the rendition has been completed, the next primary speaker takes a turn, and so forth. Russell (2002) analyzes a number of situations in which overlapping talk occurs and discusses interpreter strategies in those situations. Importantly, the author points out that not only is the overlapping talk problematic for the interpreter, but also the record of interview is "degraded" by the time it is transcribed for the trial (119). As Haworth (2010) states, because police interviews have both investigative and evidential functions, interviewing officers are aware of the audience in the ensuing legal processes. Narratives are vulnerable to distortion and misrepresentation through the recontextualization from the interview room to the courtroom, but the layer of interpreter mediation adds further complexities to the recontextualization process.

This chapter attempts to elucidate those complexities and the impact of interpreter mediation on the construction of narratives in police interviews. To this end, several aspects of tripartite interaction relevant for narrative construction are analyzed: turn-taking, questioning strategies, and resistance strategies. The chapter also explores challenges for interpreters in achieving a pragmatic equivalence of force and quality of strategies. It concludes by highlighting the importance of recognizing challenges in training interpreters and police officers in ensuring the quality of evidence obtained through mediated interaction.

The examples used in this chapter have been drawn from two Australian Federal Police interviews conducted in 1992 and 2002 that required Japanese-English interpreting. The durations of the analyzed interview discourse are approximately 4.5 hours for interview 1, and 2 hours for interview 2. Audio recordings of the interviews were transcribed by the author.[1] The suspects in both interviews are native speakers of Japanese alleged to have imported illegal narcotics. Both suspects denied the allegation, claiming that they had no knowledge of the substance they were carrying: one said that her own suitcase was stolen and a replacement given to her contained bags of narcotics in the double bottom; the other said that the bottle of alcohol that contained narcotics was given to him as a souvenir by a work contact. The former was convicted and the latter was acquitted.

Turn-Taking and Narrative Construction

In monolingual interviews, narrative construction processes may be impacted by the turn-taking behavior of the interviewer and the interviewee. In this situation, two interlocutors' turns may overlap. In interpreter-mediated interviews, one of the three interlocutors (interviewer, interpreter, and interviewee) may be interrupted by one or two others. Although the primary speakers in interpreter-mediated interviews usually need to hold off turn-taking until the interpreter delivers a rendition of the other speaker's turn, it is not uncommon to observe one of the primary speakers interrupting either the interpreter during a rendition or even the other primary speaker, who is speaking in the language that he or the first speaker does not understand. Another issue is the deliverable turn length for interpreters. Narratives produced in a long turn or a series of long turns burden the interpreter's memory capacity, which consequently may affect the accuracy of the rendition. However, because it is beyond the focus of the study, this latter issue will not be discussed in this chapter.

Interpreters' renditions of primary speakers' turns may at times be blocked by a primary speaker's interruptions. In the extract below, the suspect is asked to give a description of a bag she claims she had with her before it was replaced with a suitcase, which is in the interview room.

P1a and P1b are the two police interviewers in interview 1; I1 is the interpreter in interview 1; and S1 is the suspect in interview 1.[2]

Excerpt 9.1: Interview 1

1 P1a: How big was it compared to the maroon suitcase we have situated over by the wall?
2 I1: *Mukoo no wainreddo no suutsukeesu to kurabetara ookisa wa dono gurai deshita ka.=* (How big was it compared to the burgundy suitcase over there?)
3 S1: *=Aaiu yatsu janai n desu.* (.) *To chigau no.* (It's not like that. Different from that.)
4 (0.5)
5 I1: It wasn't that one over there.
6 S1: *Suutsu[keesu ja nai.* (It's not a suitcase.)
7 P1a: [No. I'm aware it wasn't that [one but-
8 I1: [Yeah I know that.
9 P1a: What does it look like compared to that in size,
10 I1: *Sono suutsukeesu to kurabeta ra ookisa teki ni, ano donna suutukeesu deshita ka?* (Compared to that suitcase, size-wise, um, what kind of suitcase was it?)
11 S1: *Motto:* (0.2) *haba ga aru n desu yo.* (It was wider.)
12 (0.4)
13 I1: It was wider.

The suspect's response to the first question does not refer to the size of the luggage, which the interviewer was seeking to learn. However the suspect was trying to correct the assumption that her luggage was a suitcase, as we can see in her elaboration in line 6. The rendition (line 5) does not contain "like," which leads the interviewer to think the suspect has misunderstood the question. Thus, although the suspect elaborates her initial response (line 6), the interviewer reacts in line 7 to the interpreted response (line 5). This interviewer turn overlaps the suspect's elaboration and extends to clarification (line 8). The interpreter renders neither the suspect's elaboration nor the interviewer's clarification but speaks of his own accord in the side sequence (Jefferson 1972) in English (line 10). This excludes the suspect from participating in the clarification concerning the reference to luggage.

In this interaction, the participants follow the normative format of turn-taking in consecutive interpreting up to line 5. However the suspect's turn is interrupted by the interviewer's (line 7), which continues on to line 8. This prevents the interpreter from rendering the suspect's expansion turn (line 6) immediately following the normative format. Furthermore, because the interviewer turn concerns a misunderstanding based on mistranslation, the interviewer makes the clarification process a side sequence, excluding the suspect from the interaction. When the questioning resumes (line 9), the pronoun "it" becomes "suitcase" in the rendition (line 10). However, the suspect does not attempt to correct this but responds by addressing the question of luggage size. As a consequence, the questioning proceeds with the assumption that they are talking about a "suitcase." A number of turns later (not included in the excerpt), the misunderstanding still persists on the interviewer's part, while the interviewee is unaware of it. This is an example of the cumulative effect of interruptions (in addition to inaccurate translation) on the trajectory of the information-eliciting process.

The excerpt below shows another example of the interpreter and primary speakers competing for the floor, resulting in overlapping talk and segments of narrative being lost in English-language evidence. With the question at the beginning of the excerpt, the officer asks the suspect about numbers and Japanese words on a piece of paper (the personal names appearing in the excerpts hereafter are pseudonyms).

Excerpt 9.2: Interview 2

1 P2a: Mr. Sato this person here? I can- (0.3) to me that is OMIYAGE oh em ai
2 *[wai a g] e omiyage*, .h is to um: (0.8) that appears to be a telephone number?
3 S2: [*omiyage* (souvenir)
4 I2: *Kore wa denwabangoo desu ka koko ni kaite aru no wa*= (Is this a phone number, what's written here?)
5 S2 =*to omoimasu.* (I think so.)
6 I2: Ye[s I think so=
7 P2a: [Yes?
8 P2a: =Okay, U:m
9 S2: *Ma boku ga kakeru kotow a nai* [(*daroo kedo*) (But I don't think I will be calling.)
10 P2a: [and that number=
11 I2: =but I don't think I will call him.

12 P2a: a(h)ll(h) right. Okay, now that number is zero zero (0.5) uh possibly a one or a slash?
13 oh four oh one zero three seven nine six two. (0.4) the name underneath that telephone
14 number is uh: Mr. KEN spelled kei ii en. Who wrote that on (0.5) that document?
15 I2: *Hai. .hhh de koko no kami ni kakareteiru kore nan desu keredomo darega okaki*
16 *ni nari mashita ka*? (Yes. So, this, written on this paper, who wrote it?)
((15 turns))
31 P2a: Okay. And when were you told to call this person.
32 I2: *De, itsu koko no hito ni renraku o toru yooni tte iwaretemasu ka.* (Okay, when are you told to contact this person?)
33 (0.5)
34 S2: *Ya, renraku ga nakereba* (No, if I don't hear from him.)
35 I2: .hh so, if ff (0.5) if I don't get any (0.3) uh the contact
36 P2a: uh huh,
37 (1.0)
38 S2: *soo desu renraku ga nakereba kakete.* (That's right, if I don't hear from him I am to make a call.)

After the initial exchange about a telephone number, the interviewer closes this question-and-answer adjacency pair with "Okay" in line 8 and seems to initiate the next question. However, before he could ask the question, the suspect self-selects his turn to elaborate on the earlier response, saying "But I don't think I will be calling." In a normative consecutive interpreting mode, this turn should be followed by the interpreter's rendition, but it is overlapped by the interviewer's utterance. The interpreter nevertheless orients to the suspect's utterance and initiates the rendition in line 11, interrupting the interviewer's question turn.

When the interpreter's turn is completed, the interviewer immediately takes a turn to acknowledge the interpreted response with a soft laugh, suggesting his interpretation of the suspect's utterance to be *sarcastic*. The problem here is that the interpreter had to block the new question, and the suspect was not able to continue even had he wanted to do so. The officer's interpretation of the suspect's utterance in line 9 was misguided, which becomes clear after a number of exchanges, because of the interruptions here.

The interviewer tries to collect more information on the paper and asks the next question regarding the name mentioned there. Following this, 15 turns of exchange occur before the interviewer asks the suspect when he was told to call the person whose name is on the note. The response is "if no one contacts [me]," which suggests that the suspect meant to say he was expecting to receive a call but not call the number himself. The suspect's version of events in this case was that his contact had told him to go and collect information on the working conditions of migrant workers and asked him to take a bottle of an alcoholic beverage as a souvenir, and that he did not know anything about the illegal substance in the beverage. The fragmentation of his narrative here because of the nature of consecutive interpreting may have disadvantaged the suspect's case. A complete narrative could have made the point that he was a passive participant without any knowledge of the crime, but the fragmentation of his narrative seems to bring into the questioning an assumption that he was actively involved in the criminal network, at least at one point in the above interaction.

Previous studies of interpreter-mediated interaction such as Wadensjö (1998), Roy (2000), and Russell (2002) have demonstrated challenges that interpreters face in managing renditions without the loss of primary speakers' utterances and consequences of losing some elements of interaction. Similarly, Angermeyer (2015) shows that in consecutive interpreting, the turn-taking system may disadvantage speakers of languages other than the official language of the court. The interpreter's rendition of interviewee turns does not necessarily indicate the end of the interviewee's answer, so the rendition allows the interviewer to press on with the next question even if the suspect's narrative has not been completed.

Questioning Strategies

The second focus of the discussion is police interviewers' questioning strategies. Here formulations and contrast strategies are examined. The following examples show how the distortion of questioning strategies through interpreter-mediated interaction could affect the narrative construction effort by police interviewers and impact the suspects' narratives. When formulation is used in police questioning, it often provides the version of events the interviewer wants to confirm with the interviewee (Heydon 2005; Johnson 2002). On the other hand, projection formats such as "so you are saying . . ." or "you think . . ." might also be used when the interviewer is skeptical of the veracity of the interviewee's narratives, especially if an earlier account contradicts or fails to convince the interviewer. Below, the interviewer probes the suspect about her claim that her suitcase was switched without her knowledge.

Excerpt 9.3: Interview 1

1 P1a: How does she know that va:n. (0.6) How does she know her suitcase went in that van.
2 I1: *Naze ano:* (0.3), *Tanaka san no suutsukeesu wa sono ban: ni tsumeta no ka wakarimasu ka.* (Why, uh do you know that they put your suitcase in the van?)
3 S1: *Wakarimasen.* (I don't know.)
4 I1: I don't.
5 (1.5)
6 P1a: So she's saying when she arrived at Kuala Lumpur and they (.) went through Customs,
7 (0.3) went outside, (0.3) she gave her suitcase to somebody, and she didn't see it again.
8 I1: .hh *soshite, zeekan o tootte, ano*: (0.5) *deta tokini, darekani Tanaka san- Tanaka san*
9 *wa dareka ni suutsukeesu o agete kara, moo nidoto mita kotoga nai desho*: *ka.* (Then, when you came through the customs and came out, to someone you- after you left your suitcase to someone, you never saw it again.)
10 S1: *Ie* (0.4), *a* (0.6) *hai.* (0.5) *soo desu.* (No, ah, yes, that's right.)

The interviewer uses the formulation "so she's saying . . ." to challenge her story. In the interpreted version in line 8, the formulation is lost because of the omission of the discourse marker "so" and the projection frame "she's saying." The omission of projection frames such as this has been discussed by Hale and Gibbons (1999) in their courtroom interpreting study as a loss of "primary reality"—in other words, what happens in the courtroom where two versions of events are contested. Consequently, the rendition does not achieve pragmatic equivalence, because it does not carry the challenge posed to the suspect. Additionally, the affirmative sentence (lines 6–7) is rendered as a yes-or-no interrogative. This forces the suspect to respond with a yes or no to the proposition, rather than to the challenge to her version of events. For the interviewer, this is a positive outcome because the suspect yielded to the challenge, whereas the suspect is likely to have understood her agreement as a confirmation of her claim.

The next excerpt shows another instance of formulation. The suspect initially claims she does not remember whether someone spoke with Takashi, her acquaintance, in a restaurant (line 4). However, after some exchanges in relation to the restaurant and people who ate with her, she says Takashi did speak with someone. After a 1.2-second pause, the interviewer makes a critical comment using the formulation "you think he did talk to someone now." This also adopts the strategy of "format tying" (Goodwin 1990), where the speaker recycles the format of the previous speaker's utterance. One function of this is to counter the previous speaker's position (ibid.).

Excerpt 9.4: Interview 1

1 P1b: Did anyone speak to him, (0.2) whilst you were at that restaurant?
2 I1: *Sono resutoran ni (0.3) ita aida ni dareka ga ka, ano, Takashi to, (.) Takashi san to*
3 hanashimashita ka? (While you were at that restaurant, did anyone, um, talk to Takashi, to Takashi?)
4 S1: Mm: (6.5) Sore wa: oboete nai desu. (Mm I can't remember that.)
5 I1: I can't remember.
((24 turns))
29 I1: No, I don't know anything about Mark, but I- I think he did talk to somebody.
30 (1.2)
31 P1b: You think he did talk to someone now.
32 I1: Ah: dare, ano: Taka san wa dareka to hanashita to omoimasu ka. (Uh who- um do you think Taka spoke with someone?)
33 S1: U:n. (0.2) Sore wa: dareka to hanashita to omo:- omoimasu. (Uh it's- I think he spoke with someone.)
34 (0.2)
34 I1: I did think he talked to somebody.

The rendition (line 32) of the interviewer's formulation utterance (line 31) maintains the projection "you think," but "now" at the end of the turn is omitted. This "now," along with the format-tying strategy, adds a tone critical of the fact that the suspect has changed her claim: she did not remember whether anyone talked to Takashi but *now* she thinks he talked to someone. The loss of "now" through interpreting means that the suspect is not likely to get the metamessage—that she is not a reliable interviewee.

The loss of the pragmatic effect of formulation through interpreting shown above could impact the trajectory of the interview. The interviewer's attitude to the suspect's story is not communicated, which in turn deprives the suspect of his or her opportunity to offer explanations or counternarrative. Any future audience of this evidence will only see the suspect's narrative presented as unreliable through these formulations, unless they understand both languages.

Contrast Strategy

In his analysis of courtroom discourse, Drew (1990) identifies a "contrast" strategy, where counsel uses a series of questions to highlight a contrast between facts A and B in relation to the witness's character, actions, or accounts. Although this strategy is used in Drew's study to discredit the witness in court where the audience is present, it may be used in police interviews for a future court audience, or for putting the suspect on the spot. In the excerpt below, the interviewer attempts to highlight the inconsistency between the suspect's indication on the landing card that he was unemployed and his claim that he was a businessman.

Excerpt 9.5: Interview 2

1 P2a: .hh uh:m on the reverse sa- side of the card there's a box there that says "what is
2 your *usual occupation."*
3 I2: Hai (Yes)
4 P2a just .hh you've completed that and you've written "businessman."
5 I2: Hai de koko niwa ichioo bijinesuman tteyuufuuni shokugyo: no tokoro ga kaite arimasu. (Okay, and actually it is written businessman here in the occupation section.)
6 S2: E: e: [demo ma] (Yees but well)
7 P2a: [you've-] earlier you stated that uh: you've been un[employed for five] years
8 S2: [sore saisho saisho]
9 koko ni noo tte kaita ndesu hehe (For that one I initially, initially wrote No here heh heh)

10 I2: *Ah::, but I I wrote it down "no"*
11 P2a: *Yeah,=*
12 I2: *=first, but scrubbed it.*
13 P2a: *Yeah, but why did you scrub it and write businessman.*
14 I2: *Soide dooshite: noo tte kaita noni[: kaite (Then why, although you wrote No, after writing-)*
15 S2: *[Iya sono hh ha gamen ni mitetara bijinesuman toka (Well the thing is hah watching the screen, it said businessman)*
16 *[atta kara haha bijinesuman [no hoo ga ii no kana to [omotte] (and so on, so hah hah I wondered if businessman might be better)*
17 I2: *[ah: ah: [ah:*
18 P2a: *[is your visa for a business?*
19 *[or is it just to c- for a holiday*
20 I2: *[biza wa bijinesu biza ja nai desu yone, (Your visa is not a business visa, is that right?)*
21 S2: *Nai desu. (No, it isn't.)*
22 I2: *No, not on the business visa,*
23 P2a: *Right.*
24 I2: *but it's because of the videos*
25 P2a: *Yeah,*
26 I2: *it says the businessman so maybe sounds better*
27 P2b: *[Okay]*
28 P2a: *[Okay], all right.*
29 S2: *Suutsu o kiteru noni bijinesuman ja [nai no hen da to omotte. (I thought it would be strange not to be a businessman when one has a suit on, so . . .)*
30 P2b: *[So is th- is this the ticket that you traveled*
31 *here today o*n?
32 I2: *De kyoo wa kono kookuuken de yattekita wake desu yone?* (So today you came here on this ticket, is that right?)

In creating a contrast, two contradictory facts are presented. In the above exchange, from the police interviewer's perspective, and in the communication in English, there are two sets of contrast.

(Contrast sequence 1)

—You wrote "businessman" for your occupation on the landing card. (line 4)

—You said you have been unemployed for five years. (line 7)

(Contrast sequence 2)

—You initially wrote "no" for your occupation and then wrote "businessman." (line 13)

—Your visa is not for a business, but you saw on the plane a video with a businessman and thought that would be better. (lines 18, 21, 24, 26)

After the first part of the contrast sequence 1 has been interpreted (line 5), the suspect agrees but attempts to offer an explanation with "but well." The suspect seems to preempt the forthcoming second element, which contradicts his own earlier interview statement regarding his occupational status. However, in line 7 the interviewer proceeds with the second element of the contrast strategy and interrupts before the suspect's explanation is given. The interpreter is not able to take a turn, because the primary speakers' turns overlap in lines 7–9. The suspect takes a turn at line 8, blocking the second part of the contrast from being interpreted, saying he initially wrote "no" (to indicate he did not have a job). This interruption by the suspect leads to non-rendition of the second part of the interviewer's contrast strategy (line 7) into Japanese. This does not mean that the police officer's utterance is lost from the interview record, since the official language of the court is English. However, from the suspect's point of view, he successfully blocked the contrast sequence from completion in Japanese.

There is another contrast sequence in the above interaction. As the interviewer probes the inconsistency, he presents the fact that the suspect still wrote "businessman" (line 13). The suspect explains that the inflight instruction video showed a businessman, which he thought would be a better option for him. However, the interviewer takes a turn to ask about the nature of the suspect's visa (line 18), preventing the interpreter from rendering the suspect's explanation. This interviewer turn presents and confirms the fact that the suspect is not on a business visa, which serves as the second part of contrast sequence 2 above. The interpreter renders the suspect's uninterpreted utterance after rendering the interviewer's visa question and the response to it. This type of delayed rendition is not uncommon when interpreters are faced with primary speakers' overlapping talk in consecutive interpreting (Russell 2002). When we look at the above interaction in terms of evidence in English, the contrast strategies create a narrative implying the suspect tried to deceive the authorities about his occupation.

However, the suspect's Japanese version looks more like narrative contestation. The suspect agrees that he wrote "businessman" on the card, but by interrupting the interviewer's statement about his unemployed status (lines 8–9) and saying he wrote "no" (= no employment) initially, the second part of contrast sequence 1 is blocked. Then, asked why he changed "no" to "businessman," the suspect refers to the video instruction. While the suspect's response denies that he was on a business visa (line 21), which completes the contrast sequence, he adds an explanation that it would be appropriate to write "businessman" because he was in a suit. This explanation is not entirely unreasonable in the suspect's version of events, as he tells the interviewers later on in the same interview that he was paid to assess Thai migrant workers' work conditions. Thus, in his narrative, he was visiting on business, and wearing a suit as a "businessman." Furthermore, "businessman," as a Japanese loan word from English, does not necessarily mean someone who has their own business but is often used as an equivalent of "white-collar worker." Also, the suspect was promised payment for this job, although it was a one-off assignment, according to his narrative. Thus, as we can see below, the second part of contrast sequence 2 was accompanied by an explanation that was in line with his version of events. However, this explanation is interrupted by the interviewer's new question turn and not rendered into English, which silences the resistance against the contrast strategy.

(Contrast sequence 1)

—I wrote "businessman" for my occupation on the landing card. (part 1: line 6)

—However, I initially wrote "no." (part 2 blocked: lines 9–10)

(Contrast sequence 2)

—I changed "no" [to "businessman"] because I saw a video with a businessman and thought it might be better. (part 1: lines 15–16)

—My visa is not for a business, but I wore a suit so I thought it would be odd not to write "businessman." (part 2 with explanation: lines 20–21, 29)

The suspect's Japanese narrative projects a story line in which his actions can be considered more reasonable than in the English version. When the court examines this record of the interview, however, it is likely only the English version will be considered.

Resistance Strategies

Correction

This section explores suspects' resistance strategies such as correction and contest. The analysis illustrates that the pragmatic force of suspects' resistance may not always be rendered, weakening suspects' version of events. In excerpt 9.6, the suspect corrects what she thinks is implied in the question: that she took an active role in getting a hold of a replacement suitcase.

Excerpt 9.6: Interview 1

1 P1a: I'd like to show you the suitcase again that you saw (0.7) dismantled by members
2 of *our physical evi- evidence unit,*
3 (0.3)
4 I1: Mm =
5 P1a: =just um a while ago,
6 I1: Mm.
7 P1a: U:m (0.4) can she now explain to me how that suitcase came into her possession.
8 I1: Ichioo, sakkino sore wa, a:no: minna ga sore kaitaishita suutsukeesu:: no hanashi (Actually, going back to what we talked about that one previously um that-)
9 ni ano, modori masu keredomo, dooiufuuni,(0.3) a: teni hairi mashita ka?, (the suitcase people dismantled, how uh did it come into your possession?)
10 S1: H(h)a(h), (0.4) atashi wa are o teni ireta nja arimasen. (What, I didn't obtain that.)
11 I1: Un. (0.5) dooyuufuu?= (Yeah. How?)
12 S1: =Nusumareta tokini, = (When they were stolen,)
13 I1: =Hai. (Yes.) (0.3)
14 S1: Tsugino hi ni:, ano keesu ni haitte, yoofuku ga modottekita ndesu. (The next day, my clothes were brought back to me in that case.)
15 I1: U:m what actually happened was the very next day after the case got stolen,
16 that case was- was given back with all of my things in it.

The suspect may have confused the phrase *te ni hairu* (to come into one's possession), in an accurate rendition in line 9, with a similar phrase, *te ni ireru* (to obtain), with the transitive verb *ireru* (instead of the intransitive verb *hairu*). The former does not suggest that the suspect had agency in getting a new suitcase; rather, it implies that she was hoping to receive one. Thus, the suspect may have heard the rendition correctly but not distinguished the meaning of the two phrases. They can be confusing. The latter presupposes her active role in obtaining a replacement suitcase, and the suspect corrects the presupposition with exasperation.

This correction, however, is not rendered in line 11; instead, after a response token *un* (yeah) and a pause, the interpreter repeats "how," a part of the previous rendition. This utterance can be treated as a "self-repair" of the initial rendition, but the problematic phrase that the suspect corrected is omitted. The suspect's latched utterance (line 12) may have blocked a potential expansion of this interpreter turn, but the rising intonation at the end of "how" suggests it was the end of the turn. The omission of correction makes the assumption of the question (which the suspect corrected) irrelevant. An important point here is that the correction was not rendered, even though it may have been based on the suspect's misunderstanding of the phrase in the original question. A more faithful rendition—"I did not obtain the suitcase"—would have provided another opportunity for the suspect to highlight the main line of argument for her innocence: that she was a passive member of the tour group and had no knowledge of the crime.

From the interpreter's perspective, three sources of misunderstanding are possible: the source utterance is unclear, the interpreting is inaccurate, or the primary speaker misunderstands. In this case, the interpreter may have mistaken the primary speaker's misunderstanding for interpreting inaccuracy. Interpreters may attempt to sort out issues without the knowledge of the primary speakers to avoid appearing incompetent, even when the problem is with the speaker of the source utterance (Shlesinger 1991), and this may be the case here. The multiplicity of possible sources of miscommunication in interpreter-mediated interaction may have affected the suspect's resistance strategies.

Contest

In the following examples, the suspect resists by contesting the investigator's evaluation of the story. However, this is weakened through interpreting. In the first example, the interviewer challenges the suspect's story that her tour group was taken to a restaurant an hour and half away from the hotel accommodation. The suspect initiates her response by rebutting the challenge.

Excerpt 9.7: Interview 1

1 P1a: But why would she: or the tour guides take them,
2 I1: Mm,
3 P1a: to a restauran*t an hour and a half from where they were staying,*
4 I1: Mm hm,
5 P1a: when there was a restaurant across the road? (.) Does she think that seems funny?
6 I1: Ano, naze, gaidosan wa, otomari no hoteru kara ichi jikan mo hanarteiru resutoran ni (Um why would the guide take you to a restaurant an hour away from your hotel)
7 tsureteitte, shokuji, .hhh o totta deshoo ka. (.) Toyuuto ano resutoran no mukaigawa ni (and you ate there. I say this because um across the restaurant, ah close by there are)
8 a: sugu chikakuni sooyuu resutoran, arimasu. Dakara. (0.4) Okashii to omoimashita ka? (those kinds of restaurants. So did you think it was strange?)
9 S1: Zenzen omoimasen=wakarimasen mon. (0.4) Atashi wa, moo yohakkiri iimasu kedo: (Didn't think so at all, because I wouldn't know. I no lon- let me make this clear,)
10 .hh tsuite kita dake nandesu (I only followed along with them.)
11 I1: Um=
12 S1: =Nannimo wakannai ndesu. (I don't know anything.)
*13 I1: No I don't know, (.) because um I don't understand because I don't know any*thing
14 because I was just taken on a holiday so (1.2) u:m I followed along with everybody.

The suspect's response was an outright denial—"Don't think so at all"—but without any gap she produces an ambiguous "I don't know." The interactional particle *mon* indicates emotive explanation; therefore, the two sentences here have a causal relationship. For some reason, there is no rendition of this, possibly because the source utterance is in the present tense despite the interviewer's question concerning the past, and it does not indicate what she does not understand. The rendition does not occur until the suspect produces two more sentences (lines 9–10). Although the second sentence of the source turn is rendered accurately, the first sentence, "Don't think so at all," is reduced to "No," followed by "I don't know" in the rendition. It is either a mistranslation of *omoimasen* (don't think so) or a false start of the rendition of *wakarimasen* (I don't know). Furthermore, the strong denial with *zenzen* (not at all) is also weakened in a simple "No." The lack of rising intonation for a boundary after "No" makes "No I don't know" sound like a weak denial with hedging. The interpreter faces a dilemma: if rendition is held until the meaning becomes clear, the pragmatic force of the contestation may be lost or weakened; if clarification is sought at the point of confusion, this risks a premature end to the suspect's narrative, changing the trajectory of the interaction.

The next example also contains the suspect's contesting move, but in this case it is expressed by sarcasm. The interviewer asks if the suspect intends to contact the person who arranged for the suspect's trip.

Excerpt 9.8: Interview 2

1 P2a: Are you intending to be in contact with Kit (.) in the next few days?
2 I2: *De .hh korekara ni san niche no aida ni, Kit san ni renrakusuru yotee wa arimasuka? (So do you have a plan to contact Kit in the next two or three days?)*
3 (0.4)
4 S2: Moo renrakushinai to komarimasu yo ne, kore. (Well, I do need to contact her, don't I, with all this.)
5 I2: =Mmm I- I- I guess I have to tal- talk to he:r,
6 P2a: Mm hm?
7 I2: U:m
8 P2a: Okay. U:m (0.7) I just ask now if Federal Agent (0.5) Morris has any
9 [questions he would like to ask]
10 S2: [Moo demo kore mo kore mo] taberenai kara komatta mon desu yone. (This, and this, they can't be eaten any more, so it's a problem, isn't it?)
11 (0.4)
12 P2b: Ahm I do,
13 (0.8)
14 S2: (Sore wa boku ga) tsukamacchatta tte yuu shikanai deshoo. (Of course there is no way but to tell them (I've) been arrested, you see.)

15 *I2: Uh so I- I- I think I have to tell her that I: I- I'm su- suspended at the airport.*
16 *(1.2)*
17 *P2a: U:m well is that -Did she give you any instructions if you were: (.) detained,*
18 *I2: Mm* hm,
19 P2a: That wh- (was there) anything that you were supposed to do?

The rendition of the suspect's response (line 5) does not communicate the sarcasm of the source utterance, and as a consequence implies he is an accomplice in the crime. The interviewer's ensuring turn with a rising intonation (line 6) suggests that he expected more speech from the suspect (Schegloff 1982), but the interpreter does not have any further rendition. The "Okay" in line 8 signals a shift to a new topic, but in line 10 the suspect interrupts the interviewer and explains why he needs to contact Kit. It is possible that he sensed that the sarcasm was lost in the interpretation, so he may have made a self-incriminating comment, and by showing his concern about food souvenirs with which Kit had entrusted him his innocence may be demonstrated. He makes another comment in line 14, ignoring the second interviewer's turn in line 12, but again the pragmatic force of its sarcasm is lost. The false starts and the interpreter's addition of "I think" reduces the level of assertion and takes away the rhetorical effect. This leads to a pause of 1.2 seconds, where the first interviewer revisits the contact with Kit and asks a question to check the suspects' prior knowledge of the crime. In response (not in the excerpt), the suspect denies the allegation and claims he thought it was a joke that the bottle he carried contained narcotics.

Conclusions

This chapter has explored the impact of interpreter mediation on narrative construction in police interviews. The examples analyzed above illustrated how an extra layer of interaction in the tripartite interaction may at times alter the effect of questioning and resistance strategies, complexifying narrative-construction processes. A tripartite interaction structure may at times lead to the interpreter's interrupting primary speakers, or vice versa, and primary speakers' interrupting each other, which puts the interpreter in a difficult situation. The analysis also shows that the process of interpreting itself could alter the impact of narrative-construction strategies if the rendition does not maintain the level or quality of pragmatic force of the source utterance. Undoubtedly the interpreter's competence, both in terms of turn-taking skills and the ability to maintain equivalence, is a crucial factor in preserving as much as possible the dynamics of narrative-construction processes in the mediated interview. Interpreter training in these areas, and discourse-level awareness of the police interview as a genre, will help in addressing the challenges discussed in this chapter. There is also a case for training police investigators in how to collect evidence in a fair and effective way through interpreter mediation. Nevertheless, the nature of tripartite interaction and dual-language use in interpreter-mediated interviews tends to make their narrative-construction processes more complex and fragile than in monolingual interviews. It is also important to recognize that the future audience of the interpreted interview at trial will rely on utterances in the language of the investigators, as in many jurisdictions it is the only dominant language. This is not to suggest that the interviewee's utterances should always be prioritized in interpreting overlapping utterances. Non-rendition of investigators' utterances may leave the interviewee unaware of the line of inquiry, thus depriving him or her of opportunities to offer his or her version of events. Interviewers can also be trained to recognize and rectify missed opportunities for eliciting possibly important information. Although turn-taking and interaction strategies are often more unconsciously and subtly recognized aspects of interpreter-mediated interaction, they should be given more attention in order to ensure and improve evidence-gathering practices in police interviews.

Notes

1. The author was given access to the records of these interviews through the attorneys, who released them with some participants' names anonymized.

2. All speakers in the transcripts are identified by their role in the interview for confidentiality. Pseudonyms are used for the names mentioned in the interviews.

References

Angermeyer, Philipp Sebastian. 2015. *Speak English or What? Codeswitching and Interpreter Use in New York City Courts*. Oxford: Oxford University Press.

Berk-Seligson, Susan. 1990. "Bilingual Court Proceedings: The Role of the Court Interpreter." In *Language in the Judicial Process*, edited by Judith N. Levi and Anne Graffam Walker, 155–201. New York: Plenum Press.

Drew, Paul. 1990. "Strategies in the Contest between Lawyer and Witness in Cross-Examination." In *Language in the Judicial Process*, edited by Judith N. Levi and Anne Graffam Walker, 39–64. New York: Plenum Press.

Goodwin, Marjorie Harness. 1990. *He-Said-She-Said: Talk as Social Organization among Black Children*. Bloomington: Indiana University Press.

Hale, Sandra, and John Gibbons. 1999. "Varying Realities: Patterned Changes in the Interpreter's Representation of Courtroom and External Realities." *Applied Linguistics* 20(2): 203–220.

Haworth, Kate. 2010. "Police Interviews as Evidence." In *The Routledge Handbook of Forensic Linguistics*, edited by Malcolm Coulthard and Alison Johnson, 169–181. London and New York: Routledge.

Heydon, Georgina. 2005. *The Language of Police Interviewing: A Critical Analysis*. Basingstoke: Palgrave Macmillan.

Holt, Elizabeth, and Alison Johnson. 2010. "Socio-pragmatic Aspects of Legal Talk: Police Interviews and Trial Discourse." In *The Routledge Handbook of Forensic Linguistics*, edited by Malcolm Coulthard and Alison Johnson, 21–36. London and New York: Routledge.

Jefferson, Gail. 1972. Side Sequences. In *Studies in Social Interaction*, edited by David Sudnow, 294–337. New York: Free Press.

Johnson, Alison. 2002. "*So*. . . ?": Pragmatic Implications of *So*-Prefaced Questions in Formal Police Interviews. In *Language in the Legal Process*, edited by Janet Cotterill, 91–110. Basingstoke: Palgrave Macmillan.

Johnson, Alison. 2006. "Police Questioning." In *Encyclopedia of Language and Linguistics*, edited by Keith Brown, 661–671. Oxford: Elsevier.

Johnson, Alison. 2008. "'From Where We're Sat . . .': Negotiating Narrative Transformation through Interaction in Police Interviews with Suspects." In "Narrative Analysis in the Shift from Texts to Practices," edited by Anna De Fina and Alexandra Georgakopoulou. Special issue, *Text & Talk* 28(3): 327–349.

Komter, Martha. 2005. "Understanding Problems in an Interpreter-Mediated Police Interrogation." In *Ethnographies of Law and Social Control*, edited by Stacy Lee Burns, 203–224. Sociology of Crime, Law and Deviance 6. Amsterdam: Elsevier.

Linell, Per, and Linda Jönsson. 1991. "Suspect Stories: On Perspective-Setting in an Asymmetrical Situation." In *Asymmetries in Dialogue*, edited by Ivana Marková and Klaus Foppa, 75–100. Hemel Hampstead: Harvester Wheatsheaf.

Newbury, Phillip, and Alison Johnson. 2006. "Suspects' Resistance to Constraining and Coercive Questioning Strategies in the Police Interview." *International Journal of Speech, Language and the Law* 13(2): 213–240.

Roy, Cynthia B. 2000. *Interpreting as a Discourse Process*. Oxford: Oxford University Press.

Russell, Sonia. 2002. "'Three's a Crowd': Shifting Dynamics in the Interpreted Interview." In *Language in the Legal Process*, edited by Janet Cotterill, 111–126. New York: Palgrave Macmillan.

Schegloff, Emanuel A. 1982. "Discourse as an International Achievement: Some Uses of 'Uh Huh' and Other Things That Come between Sentences." In *Analyzing Discourse: Text and Talk*, edited by Deborah Tannen, 71–93. Washington, DC: Georgetown University Press.

Shlesinger, Miriam. 1991. "Interpreter Latitude vs. Due Process: Simultaneous and Consecutive Interpreting in Multilingual Trials." In *Empirical Research in Translation and Intercultural Studies: Selected Papers of the TRANSIF Seminar, Savonlinna, 1988*, edited by Sonja Tirkkonen-Condit, 147–155. Tübingen: Gunther Narr Verlag.

Wadensjö, Cecilia. 1997. "Recycled Information as a Questioning Strategy: Pitfalls in Interpreter-Mediated Talk." In *The Critical Link: Interpreters in the Community*, edited by Silvana E. Carr, Roda P. Roberts, Aideen Dufour, and Dini Steyn, 35–52. Amsterdam: John Benjamins.

Wadensjö, Cecilia. 1998. *Interpreting as Interaction*. New York: Longman.

CHAPTER TEN

Interactional Management in a Simulated Police Interview

Interpreters' Strategies

Sandra Hale, Jane Goodman-Delahunty, and Natalie Martschuk

Introduction

Police interviews are interactional and complex (Wakefield, Kebbell, Moston, and Westera 2014). When the interviewee does not speak the language of the interviewer, an interpreter is needed to bridge the language gap. However, because the interpreter is another participant in the interaction, his or her presence and actions will inevitably change the dynamics of the interview. Despite the importance of the police interview in the criminal justice legal process (Cotterill 2000), little research has been conducted to ascertain the influence interpreters may have on achieving the goals of the interviewer. Some research showed no differences in the performance of interpreters with experience versus bilinguals in an interview setting in terms of the number of details reported (Ewens, Vrij, Leal, Mann, Jo, and Fisher 2014), although the results may have been due to a low sample (12 interpreters, 5 with experience) and to the fact that the experienced interpreters were not necessarily trained. Conversely, small-scale discourse-analytical studies of police interpreting have shown that interpreters may interfere to varying degrees with the interviewing techniques (Lai and Mulayim 2014; Nakane 2014). The degree of interference may depend on a number of factors, including the interpreter's level of training and experience.

In addition to interpreting the interlocutors' utterances, interpreters in "mediated-institutional contexts" (Pöchhacker 2012: 52) need to adequately manage and coordinate the interaction following accepted protocols. This chapter reports on data collected in the course of a large, multidisciplinary, mixed-methods study of interpreter performance in a simulated police interview in Sydney, Australia. One aim of that study was to analyze interpreters' interactional and management skills and the ways in which these affect the goals of the interview and participants' perceptions of the interpreter. To address this question, the performances of 100 Spanish-English interpreters with varying levels of interpreting qualifications and experience were analyzed using qualitative and quantitative methods.

Participant Roles in the Police Interview

Using Goffman's (1981) participation framework to describe the police interview, Heydon (2005) proposed that a police interview comprises three main sections: opening, information gathering, and closing. During the opening, in particular, police are institutionally bound to inform interviewees of the caution that whatever they do or say may be used in evidence and of their rights. This, Heydon suggested, makes the police officers take on the role of "animator" to comply with and utter a legal requirement that explains the interviewee's rights and obligations under the law. The role of principal and/or author is attributed to the institution. Throughout the information-gathering section of the interview, the police mostly take on the role of author, but not principal, if they are following guidelines on what questions to ask and how to ask them in order to elicit voluntary responses. At times they may interject comments, such as rapport-building utterances, that make them principal authors.

The same participant roles can be attributed to interpreters. As a general rule, when interpreting accurately, professional interpreters do not take on the role of principal, because they are interpreting others' utterances (see Dressler 1994; Clark 1996; and Wadensjö 1998 for different analyses of the interpreter's role). However, they still need to author the target-language versions by deciding how best to interpret an utterance accurately, in order to achieve the same effect and goal as the original. The interpreting process is not mechanical and requires the interpreter's own judgment and decision making. There will be times when interpreters will take on the role of animator, as for example when they cite their code of ethics or explain their role, based on the requirements set by a higher authority (their professional association or code of ethics). At times interpreters also take on the role of principal, for various reasons, when they speak for themselves. As Pöchhacker stated, "The interpreter is a participant at the event level with a specific purpose, which (as any code of professional ethics would prescribe) is not to make his or her own case or express an opinion but to enable the interlocutors to do so. However, performing this role at the utterance level (where codes of professional ethics are less straightforward to apply) may well require self-initiated turns (e.g., clarification questions) and any other discursive action necessary to fulfil the purpose of enabling communication in line with institutional requirements" (2012: 52–53).

This chapter examines these instances when interpreters speak for themselves, rather than when they interpret for someone else. It highlights the differences in the interventions by trained interpreters and untrained bilinguals and their impact on the interaction between the police interviewer and suspect.

Interpreted Interview Structure

When an interpreter attends a police interview, an extra layer of interaction is added to the underlying police structure, as described by Heydon (2005). Before the actual police interview commences, professional interpreters engage in a pre-opening, in which they are introduced, the protocols are established, and the interpreter explains his or her role according to their code of ethics, commonly referred to by interpreting scholars as the "contract" (see Tebble 1998, 2012; Bancroft and Rubio-Fitzpatrick 2011; Rudvin and Tomassini 2011). During the information-gathering section of the interview, apart from the need to stop after every turn to allow the interpretation to take place, there may be situations when the interpreter will stop the interview to seek a clarification or repetition or make a clarification him- or herself. There may also be times when interpreters need to stop the speakers to ask them to slow down or reduce the duration of their utterances or to reemphasize their role and instruct the participants about the best way to use their services (Hale 2007). The closing of the police interview includes an additional statement when the interpreter is thanked. Our study analyzed the different ways interpreters and bilinguals dealt with each of these phases of the police interview.

Interpreters as Coordinators of Turns

In triadic situations, such as interpreted police interviews, interpreters are required to coordinate turns between participants. Wadensjö (1998) identified two types of coordinating activities. One is "implicit coordination," the core of the interpreter's job: taking every second turn at talk at appropriate intervals to interpret the previous utterance into the target language. The other is "explicit coordination," which includes what Wadensjö calls "non-renditions." These include any turns originated by the interpreter to seek clarification or ask for repetition, or to explicitly ask the speaker to stop in order to interpret. Baraldi and Gavioli (2012) observed that the implicit and explicit coordination functions may overlap, because the explicit non-renditions are often related to the interpreter's ability to interpret accurately. In other words, when it comes to professional, competent interpreters, any interruption they initiate will be relevant to the interpreting task. This, however, may not be the case with nonprofessional interpreters, who may interrupt or enter into side conversations with either party that they are not intending to interpret. Such interruptions cannot be classified as interpreter-coordination attempts because they contravene the professional ethical obligations of interpreters (see Australian Institute of Interpreters and Translators 2012). It is this type of intervention that is regarded by Tebble (2012: 27) as acts of unjustified interference.

Few studies have systematically assessed the performance of professional versus ad hoc interpreters working in institutional contexts. One small study compared an ad hoc interpreter with a professionally trained interpreter in a medical consultation in Spain (Valero Garcés 2005). The ad hoc interpreter (husband of the patient), interpreted only two out of nine questions (22 percent) and asked three questions of his own during one consultation; he answered 12 out of 28 questions directly (43 percent) and interpreted only three (11 percent) in another consultation. The professional or trained interpreter, on the other hand, interpreted all questions and had one instance of a non-rendition in the form of a request for a clarification (Valero Garcés 2005: 202). An Austrian case study compared ad hoc interpreting by a Turkish teenage family member at an outpatient clinic with that by a paid experienced interpreter at a legal asylum hearing (Pöchhacker 2012). Results showed that the ad hoc interpreter omitted much of the information in her summaries to the other participants, disempowering the main interlocutors. The paid interpreter, on the other hand, sought clarification and added information, becoming more active in the interaction, although not necessarily following accepted protocols used by Australian trained interpreters, with instances of what Tebble (2012) calls interference rather than interpretation.

Most studies of community interpreting performance have either failed to specify the interpreters' level of training or have analyzed untrained interpreters' practice, even though they are regarded as professional by virtue of being employed and paid (e.g., Davidson 2002; Angelelli 2004; Gavioli and Baraldi 2011). This is generally due to the fact that in most countries, community interpreters are untrained or training is not a prerequisite for practice. In Australia, formal training is available at the tertiary level for community interpreters in a range of languages, although it is not yet compulsory in order to practice. In 2018, however, the National Accreditation Authority for Translators and Interpreters (NAATI) introduced the requirement for compulsory precertification training and postcertification professional development. Our study specifically looked at the difference training made in the way interpreters interacted with the other interview participants.

Interpreter Protocols

Trained interpreters are taught the protocols to apply during their work. These include how to introduce themselves and explain their role, the mode of interpreting to adopt according to the situation, the use of the direct approach, using the first and second grammatical persons, the need to seek leave from the interviewer to ask for a repetition or clarification and to keep everyone informed of what is happening, and the requirement to interpret everything that is said, impartially, even when it may be offensive. In reference to interpreted medical consultations, three opportunities for interactional management by an interpreter were distinguished: according to Tebble, "norms of professional conduct which promote ease of participation and full participation in an interpreted dialogue can be implemented in three ways: during the briefing, which occurs prior to the medical consultation; during the contract, which occurs near the beginning of the consultation; and through the operational guidance on how to cope with the actual interpreting process" (2012: 27). Our study was concerned with the contract and the protocols used throughout the interview.

Trained interpreters are also taught to use discourse markers to indicate clearly the role they are assuming during an interpreted interaction. When they are taking on the role of principal, they make it clear that they are speaking as the interpreter, either by referring to themselves as "the interpreter" (e.g., the interpreter requires repetition) or by stating they are now speaking as the interpreter (e.g., "I'm now speaking as the interpreter. Could I please ask for a repetition?"). At times body language and intonation will be sufficient cues to indicate they are speaking as principal. When they are taking on the role of author or animator of others' utterances, they interpret directly, using the same grammatical pronouns as the original speakers. Bilinguals who are not trained tend to summarize others' utterances using the indirect approach, such as "He said" followed by their own summary (e.g., Gavioli and Baraldi 2011).

The Study

The study assessed interpreting accuracy and competence of trained interpreters and untrained bilinguals and the interactional effects in a simulated police interview in which the roles of the English-speaking interviewing detective and a Spanish-speaking suspect were played by professional actors. The "trained interpreters" were Spanish-speaking bilingual participants who had received formal interpreting training, or were in training at the time of the study, and/or were NAATI-accredited practitioners (hereafter referred to as interpreters). The "untrained bilinguals" were Spanish-speaking bilingual participants who reported no formal interpreting education or accreditation, but who may have had experience interpreting on an ad hoc basis (hereafter referred to as bilinguals).

Participants

A call for participants to interpret in a simulated police interview was put out using a professional recruitment company as well as via AUSIT,

TABLE 10.1 **Interpreters' and bilinguals' formal training and experience**

Participant number	Training	Legal interpreting training	NAATI accreditation	Interpreting experience
42	Master of Interpreting degree	√	Professional	√
29	Master of Interpreting student (final year)	√	–	√
104	Master of Interpreting student (first year)	–	–	–
34	Untrained bilingual	–	–	√
75	Untrained bilingual	–	–	–
133	Untrained bilingual	–	–	–

the national professional association for translators and interpreters, and through NAATI, who sent out the call to all accredited Spanish interpreters in NSW. A total of 56 Spanish-English bilinguals and 44 Spanish-English interpreters participated in the study. Seventy-five percent were female and 25 percent were male. Three-quarters of the interpreters (75.3 percent) and more than half of the bilinguals (61.8 percent) held a university degree. Spanish was the first language for most participants (68.0 percent), followed by English (26.0 percent), Portuguese (4.0 percent), and French (2.0 percent). Participants were de-identified by allocating a number to each in accordance with research ethics confidentiality requirements.

For this study, we present examples from three interpreters and three bilinguals from the study sample to illustrate the expertise among both groups. Table 10.1 summarizes their formal training and experience.

Study Materials

THE EXPERIMENTAL POLICE-SUSPECT INTERVIEW

The stimulus material for the study consisted of a simulated interview by an English-speaking detective of a Spanish-speaking suspect based on an actual case in which the suspect was charged with possession of illegal drugs. The baseline interview contained approximately 60 question-and-answer exchanges (about 1,650 words).

The police-suspect interview was scripted in consultation with police practitioners and experts in interpreting to ensure that the content tested a series of realistic interpreting challenges by incorporating examples drawn from linguistically informed interpreting studies. The interpreting challenges included issues of (1) propositional content; (2) legal discourse and terminology, including questioning style; (3) pragmatic force of discourse; (4) management and coordination of turn-taking between speakers; and (5) ethical interpreting protocols. This chapter reports results of the management and coordination of turn-taking between speakers and compliance with ethical interpreting protocols.

Approximately half of the interpreting challenges appeared in the questions asked by the interviewer and half in the suspect's responses. Further, the police-suspect interview included ethical dilemmas for interpreters, requiring them to make decisions about the best way to perform.

POSTEXPERIMENTAL WRITTEN SURVEY

After the interview concluded, the two actors who interacted with the participants independently rated their perceptions of the interview and the credibility of the participant on a 10-point semantic differential scale called the Witness Credibility Scale (WCS; Cronbach's $\alpha = .95$; Brodsky, Griffin, and Cramer 2010).

Main Dependent Measures

The major dependent measures were the quality of interpretation in terms of (a) interpreting accuracy and (b) indicators of competent and incompetent interpreting. This chapter reports on aspects that fell into category (b), regarding interactional management and ethical protocols.

ASSESSMENT OF INTERPRETING PERFORMANCE

Interpreting performance was assessed using a rigorous method of coding and rating developed by the research team based on protocols to test and accredit professional interpreters at the first author's university. This assessment took into account both verbal and nonverbal communication, in line with an established theoretical model that examines the interaction between the interviewer and interviewee. An overall rating or global assessment score was generated by combining weighted scores for seven criteria. Two of the assessment criteria relevant to this chapter were (a) "use of correct interpreting protocols," given a weighting of 10 percent, and (b) "management and coordination skills," also with a 10 percent weighting. These are the only two criteria reported in this chapter. The criteria were assessed according to the following guidelines:

1. *Use of correct interpreting protocols*: Use of the direct approach (first person); interpreting everything that is said; seeking repetition when needed in the right way; transparency (keeping everyone informed if a repetition or clarification is required).
2. *Management and coordination skills*: Establishing the interpreter's contract; switching to simultaneous mode when needed; turn management.

Research Design

A between-subjects design compared trained interpreters and untrained bilinguals.

Experimental Procedure

One participant was scheduled for one interview session at a time, each lasting between 20 and 30 minutes. The data were collected in realistic interview settings in three different locations in the greater Sydney area.

The actors worked from scripted questions and answers; however, they were instructed to adapt questions and answers according to participants' interpretations or explanations. The actors were blind to the participants' background. Participants were instructed to facilitate the communication between the police officer and the native-Spanish-speaking suspect by interpreting everything that was said. All interviews were video- and audio-recorded and later transcribed by a group of trained transcriptionists who were also trained Spanish interpreters and translators. The transcription style was verbatim (i.e., orthographic) but also included the repetitions, hesitations, fillers, pauses, and intonation of every turn. This was deemed adequate to conduct an in-depth analysis of the conversation between the speakers and the interpreting performance.

Data Analyses

Transcription, translation, coding, and discourse analyses were conducted blind to the experimental condition and participants' training and qualifications. Participants' questionnaire responses and the coded data were subjected to statistical analyses, including descriptive (e.g., means and standard deviations, percentages) and inferential statistics (i.e., analysis of variance for mixed designs, post hoc paired comparison tests, and nonparametric tests where necessary).

Results

Quantitative Results

INTERPRETING PERFORMANCE

Overall, the quantitative analyses demonstrated that participants' interpreting performance was dependent on their training, as is shown in figure 10.1. Interpreters achieved a higher total mark than bilinguals. Relevant to this chapter, the study found that interpreters were more likely to use correct interpreting protocols and demonstrated significantly better management and coordination skills than the bilinguals.

CREDIBILITY OF THE PARTICIPANTS AS PERCEIVED BY THE INTERVIEW PARTICIPANTS

Analyses were performed to test the influence of participant type on their professional credibility as rated by the detective and the suspect. The credibility of the participants was dependent on their training, independent of the rater. The expertise of the interpreters was rated by the actor role-playing the detective as significantly more credible than that of bilinguals, and similarly by the actor role-playing the suspect, on all credibility factors: trustworthiness, confidence, likability, and knowledgeability.

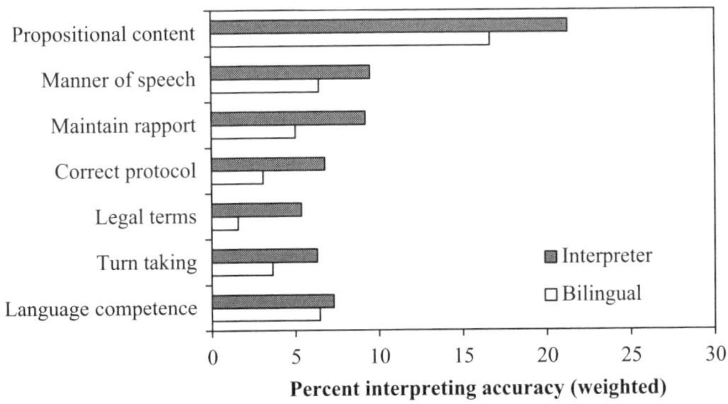

FIGURE 10.1. Interpreting performance by trained interpreters and untrained bilinguals

Discourse Analysis

INTERPRETER INTRODUCTIONS

A comparison of opening approaches showed that the participants in the sample used a variety of strategies. Some were very passive, waiting to be told what to do, whereas others were proactive and established their contract before the interview commenced. Invariably, the interpreters were more proactive and assertive, explained their role and their obligations under their professional code of ethics, and warned the speakers that they would interpret everything without exception. Some interpreters spent more time explaining to the police, while others spent more time with the detainee. The main points they covered in their introduction were: (1) their role entailed interpreting everything faithfully; (2) they advised the speakers not to say anything they did not wish the other side to hear; (3) they asked the speakers to communicate in short segments to allow consecutive interpretation; and (4) they asked the speakers to speak directly to each other (using first- and second-person pronouns).

PROFESSIONAL INTRODUCTIONS

The data were coded for professional introductions that contained most or some of the four aspects listed above. In all cases, the detective spoke to the interpreter first and explained why he or she was called. If the interpreter did not offer to explain his or her role, the detective asked him or her to do it. The bilinguals simply stated they were there to interpret or help.

Among the professional introductions, interpreters used three main approaches, illustrated in excerpts 10.1–10.3 below. Excerpt 10.1 shows one approach by an interpreter who offered a simple explanation of her role to both participants. Although the detective stated that he had worked with interpreters before, the interpreter responded that she still wished to clarify her role (turn 3). This interpreter did not specifically cite the code of ethics but covered the basic protocols.

Excerpt 10.1: Interpreter 29

1 I: Mh, uh first of all I would like to say, like, what is my role as an interpreter, I don't know if you have worked (↑) with interpreters before (↑).

2 P: Yes, yes, I have.

3 I: But, yeah, I just want to . . . clarify.

4 P: Sure, go ahead.

5 I: So uhm, my role as interpreter, I'm gonna interpret everything, faithfully.

6 P: Yes.

7 I: Uhm please keep your . . . sentences short, so I can do my, my, my job [properly.

8 P: [OK, I'll try.

9 I: And speak, uh speak directly to the client uhm so I, and, speak in the first person, and I will, translate it in the same way, now I will uh [tell, tell him.

10 P: [Very good, thank you

11 I: ((to L)) *¿Cómo está?* (How are you?)

12 L: *¿Qué tal? ¿Tú hablas español?* (How are you? Do you speak Spanish?)

13 I: *Sí.* (Yes.)

14 L: *Bien, [gracias.* (Good. Thanks.)

15 I: *[Gracias, soy el intérprete eh le quiero explicar mi rol ah, voy a interpretar todo lo que usted diga, de una forma, lo más fiel que yo pueda, ah por favor, hable con él directamente eh no se refiera a mí sino refiérase a él, en primera persona.* (Thanks, I'm the interpreter and I want to explain my role to you, uh, I'll interpret everything that you say, in the most faithful way I can, uh, so please talk to him directly, uh, don't refer to me, just refer to him, in the first person.)

16 L: *Que no hable contigo, [sino con él, aha.* (So not to speak to you, but to him, OK.)

17 I: *[No, sino hable directamente con él, y mantenga sus frases cortas, de manera que pueda interpretar, de una forma correcta.* (Correct, talk directly to him, and keep your utterances short, so that I can interpret correctly.)

In the second excerpt the interpreter was more assertive, using more forceful language and citing her obligations under the code of ethics (e.g., "Let me just remind you" in turn 3). Whereas the first interpreter, a master of interpreting student in her final year of school, used some features of powerless speech (Conley and O'Barr 1990) such as hesitations, upward intonation, and fillers and hedges such as "like" (e.g., turns 1 and 2), the second interpreter, who was a graduate already accredited by NAATI, spoke in a powerful style, with no such features.

The second interpreter provided her entire explanation in one turn (turn 3), whereas the first interpreter broke it into segments and received more feedback from the participants. Both interpreters managed their turns by interrupting the other speakers at the appropriate time to maintain their turns and stop the others, especially the Spanish-speaker, from introducing irrelevant information (e.g., turns 15 and 17 in excerpt 10.1 and turn 7 in excerpt 10.2). In line with what appeared to be a more confident and experienced professional role, the second interpreter introduced herself by name, shook the interviewee's hand, and addressed him as "Mr. Lopez" (L).

Excerpt 10.2: Interpreter 42

1 I: Before we start, have you worked with interpreters before?

2 P: I have, yes.

3 I: Let me just remind you that I'm bound by a code of ethics and everything that is said I'll interpret and everything that you say I'll interpret . . . and so . . . if there's anything that you don't want the suspect to hear, please don't say it, because I will have to interpret everything faithfully. Please speak directly to him as if I were not here . . . and yes. That's all. Try not to speak in very long chunks . . . so I can relay all the meaning. May I introduce myself to the suspect . . . ?

4 P: Yes . . . Please. Mr. Lopez.

5 I: *Buenos días, Sr. López. Mi nombre es X ((shaking hands with L)). Voy a ser la intérprete hoy.* (Good morning Mr. Lopez. Mi name is X. I will be your interpreter today.)

6 L: *Gracias, buenísimo . . . , no entiendo nada . . . yo que se.*] (Thanks, that's great, I don't understand anything, I know that.)

7 I: [. . . *Antes de empezar, para trabajar conmigo le voy a pedir que no me hable a mí, sino que le hable directamente al detective Christos . . . er . . . cualquier cosa que no quiera que el detective oiga simplemente no la diga . . . porque yo estoy obligada por un código de ética . . . háblele directamente a él y trate no hablar demasiado largo . . . en una sola oración . . . así puedo transmitirle toda la información. ¿Podemos empezar?* (Interviewee nods.) (Before we commence, to work with me I'll ask you not to speak to me, but to speak directly to Detective Christos . . . uh . . . anything you don't want the detective to hear, just don't say it . . . because I'm bound by a code of ethics . . . speak directly to him and try not to speak

for too long . . . one sentence at a time . . . so that I can transmit all the information. Can we start?) ((I to P: we are ready to start now.))

The interpreter in excerpt 10.3, also a student, fell between the performance of the interpreters in excerpts 10.1 and 10.2. Although assertive and confident, she used a more polite style, evident in the use of indirectness in English (e.g., turn 3: "Do you mind if I clarify the role . . . ?"). This interpreter also cited the code of ethics but was less assertive than the interpreter in excerpt 10.2. Interestingly, this may be the reason the detective interrupted her at turn 6. However, the interpreter took control quickly at turn 7 by interrupting the detective. This demonstrated the interpreter's assertion that this was her time to speak as a professional; the detective's time had not yet started. This was also evident in turn 9 ("and if I think that you are speaking longer sentences, I might ask you to pause") and turn 11, where she asked for the name of the interviewee. This interpreter also addressed the interviewee as "Mr. Lopez." The third interpreter was the only one to mention impartiality and confidentiality, and the register she used was slightly more formal than that of the other two.

Excerpt 10.3: Interpreter 104

1 I: Yes, uhm I wanted to ask you before, have you worked with interpreters before?

2 P: I have, yes.

3 I: OK, do you mind if I clarify the role of the interpreter for you?

4 P: Go ahead.

5 I: OK, so uh, I'm here to interpret everything and anything that's being said. If you don't like anything being translated into Spanish, please don't say it, because I'm under the ethical obligation to translate it. Please speak loud and clear. Make short, concise sentences, and allow me for uhm translation after you've rendered your utterances. Uhm, and if you allow me, I will explain the role of [the interpreter].

6 P: [Before you do, will you be uh will you be interpreting as I speak or will you be, will you make, [spaces.

7 I: [If you can allow for a time for me to interpret after each sentence, Uhm.

8 P: [OK.

9 I: [That would be better, and if I think that you are speaking longer sentences, I might ask you to pause.

10 P: That's fine.

11 I: OK. Uhm what is the name of the interviewee?

12 P: Mr. Lopez.

13 I: ((takes note of the name)) *Buenas tardes señor López, soy el intérprete, eh como le acabo de decir al detective, voy a explicarle cuál es mi eh rol como intérprete. Voy a interpretar todo lo que se diga, porque estoy sobre, bajo la obligación ética de decir todo, entonces si usted quiere que no se diga algo, por favor no lo mencione, hable en primera persona, dialogue directamente con el es-, con el detective, voy a tratar, en mi mejor saber y entender, decir todo tan completa y fidedignamente como ehm se esté pronunciando, ehh cuando esté hablando por favor hable en, enunciados concisos y permítame el tiempo de interpretar en inglés para el detective. Eh todo lo que yo escuche lo voy a interpretar de manera fidedigna e imparcial, y confidencial. ¿Tiene alguna duda?* (Good afternoon Mr. Lopez, I'm the interpreter, uh, as I've just told the detective, I will explain what my role is as interpreter. I will interpret everything you say, because I have the ethical obligation to say everything, so if you don't want anything said, please don't say it. Speak in the first person. Speak directly with the. .with the detective. I'll try, according to the best of my skill and ability, to say everything as completely and faithfully as uh it is said. Uh, when you speak, please speak in concise segments, and allow me time to interpret in English for the detective. Uh, everything I hear I will interpret faithfully and impartially and confidentially. Do you have any questions?)

INFORMAL INTRODUCTIONS

In contrast to the foregoing examples, bilinguals' introductions were informal. Some of the bilinguals were prompted by the detective to explain their role to the interviewee; others were not. Invariably, they did not know how to establish a professional contract and either simply said "hello" or stated only that they were there to interpret or to help.

Excerpt 10.4: Bilingual 34

1 P: [First name]. Nice to meet you . . . I am Detective Christos, and we've asked you here this afternoon, to interpret, for Mr. Lopez, who doesn't speak English. ((I to P: OK.))

2 I: ((to L)) *¡Hola!* (Hello!)
3 L: *Gracias por . . . ¡Qué bien!* (Thanks for . . . that's great!)
4 P: OK . . .
5 L: ((to I)) *¿Cómo te llamas?* (What's your name?)
6 I: [Julia or Andrea][1] . . [Andrea] . . .
7 P: Are you ready to commence?
8 I: Yes.

The interpreter in excerpt 10.4 did not introduce herself at all. All she said was "Hello" (turn 2) and responded to the interviewee's request for her name, to which she provided two alternative names, but no surname (turn 6). In excerpt 10.5, the detective prompted the interpreter to introduce herself and explain her role, in response to which she gave her first name (turn 2) and said that she would be "helping" (turn 8). She also used the interviewee's first name, "Carlos." The exchange became a friendly chat between the interviewee and the interpreter. This led the interviewee to ask further personal questions, such as "Where are you from?" (turn 11). Although this exchange may appear harmless and conducive to establishing rapport between the interviewee and the interpreter, no professional distance or ground rules were established, which led to a loss of control by the interpreter later in the interview. In fact, at no point did the interpreter explain that she was an interpreter or a professional, which prompted a question from the interviewee in turn 3: "Do you speak Spanish?"

Excerpt 10.5: Bilingual 75

1 P: So uh, so if you could introduce yourself and let him know why you're here.
2 I: *OK, mi nombre es [first name].* (OK. My name is [first name].)
3 L: *¿Hablas español?* (Do you speak Spanish?)
4 I: *Sí.* (Yes.)
5 L: *Sí, qué bien.* (Yes, that's good.)
6 I: *¿Y tu nombre?* (And what's your [informal] name?)
7 L: *Es Carlos.* (It's Carlos.)
8 I: *Carlos, OK, estoy aquí porque te voy a ayudar hoy ahm interpretar en español y en inglés.* (Carlos, OK, I'm here because I'm going to help you today, uh, interpret in Spanish and in English.)
9 L: *Ah OK.*
10 I: OK?

11 L: *¿Tú eres de dónde?* (And where are you from?)
12 I: *De, yo nací aquí, mis padres de España.* (From, I was born here, my parents from Spain.)
13 L: *Ah, ya.* (OK.)
14 I: *¿Y tú de dónde eres?* (And where are you from?)
15. L: Colombia.

The interpreter in excerpt 10.6 was the most casual and least professional of the group. She was prompted by the detective to introduce herself and explain her role, at which point she introduced herself by her first name and stated that she was there "to help you speak with the officer" (turn 2). She code-switched to English when unable to access the correct word in Spanish, which was supplied by the interviewee (turn 5). The introduction was very colloquial in register, commencing with a "Yep" (turn 1), repetitions, and hesitations, using first names and the informal pronoun in Spanish to address the suspect.

Excerpt 10.6: Bilingual 133

1 D: Do you mind please introducing yourself and telling him why you're here?
2 I: Yep. *Hola me llamo [first name], estoy aquí, estoy aquí para ayudarte a hablar con la, el* officer. (Hello, my name is [first name], I'm here, I'm here to help you speak with the, the officer.)
3 L: *Con el . . . ?* (With the . . . ?)
4 I: *Con ehm . . .* (With uh . . .)
5 L: *Detective.* (Detective).

Interpreter Protocols and Turn Control

The way the interpreters introduced themselves and set the ground rules affected to a large extent the way they were able to manage the rest of the interaction, in particular with regard to challenging situations, where the suspect spoke directly to the interpreter, where both the detective and suspect said things they did not want interpreted, or where the interlocutors did not respect the turn-taking rules that allow interpretation. At these moments, the interpreters had to make professional judgments about how to manage the situation. We found a consistent pattern across the sample of 100 interpreters, illustrated with examples from the same six interpreters as above.

MANAGING UTTERANCES ADDRESSED TO THE INTERPRETER

On a few occasions Mr. Lopez, the suspect, spoke directly to the interpreter rather than to the detective. On these occasions, interpreters needed to decide whether to reply to the suspect, summarize what he said to the detective, or interpret faithfully regardless of whom the speaker intended to address. The trained interpreters, who had set the ground rules at the start of the interview, generally opted for the last option, as shown in excerpts 10.7 and 10.8.

Excerpt 10.7: Interpreter 29

1 L: *Tú le podrías preguntar por qué necesita todo esta información, por qué quieren todos mis datos, yo no entiendo qué está pasando aquí, yo no sé por qué estoy aquí, pregúntale por favor.* (Could you please ask him why he needs all this information? why they want all my details? I don't understand what's happening here, I don't know why I'm here, ask him please.)

2 I: Um (. .) Could- could you ask him why am I here, why he's asking so many questions, uh I don't- I don't know what I'm doing here, could you please ask him that?

Excerpt 10.8: Interpreter 104

1 L: *¿Crees que le puedas preguntar por qué necesita todo esta información? Porque yo no- no entiendo qué es lo que está pasando aquí.* (Do you think you could ask him why he needs all this information? Because I don't- don't understand what's happening here.)

2 I: Do you think you can ask him if uhm why does he need all this information, because I don't understand what's happening here.

In excerpts 10.7 and 10.8, both interpreters maintained Mr. Lopez's form of address, following the mandate to interpret in the same person as the original. Owing to space constraints, we have not presented every example from every interpreter, but we can confirm that the performance of the trained interpreters was consistent across the study sample.

The bilinguals, on the other hand, invariably switched the form of address and summarized the interviewee's request in reported speech, as shown in excerpt 10.9. Whereas the response of the interpreters forced the two interlocutors to speak to each other, the bilinguals encouraged two parallel conversations—one between the suspect and the bilingual, and the other between the bilingual and the detective. The role of the interpreter is to remove the language barrier so that the two main participants speak to each other. The professional interpreters in our sample achieved this. The untrained bilinguals became an extra involved participant and interfered with the two main participants' interaction. By speaking to Mr. Lopez in Spanish, the detective is being excluded, and by speaking to the detective about Mr. Lopez in English, Mr. Lopez is being excluded. In addition, when the bilinguals summarize, they leave a great deal of information out, thus breaching the ethical requirement for a faithful interpretation of everything that was said.

Excerpt 10.9: Bilingual 34

1 L: *¿Tú le puedes preguntar primero . . . por qué necesita todo esto . . . todas estas preguntas y todo esto? . . . Yo no entiendo para qué estoy aquí . . . ni nada . . . de eso . . . de verdad . . .* (Can you ask him first why he needs all this, all these questions and all this? I don't understand why I'm here or any of this, really . . .)

2 I: OK . . . ((to P)) He wants to know why . . . uh . . . you're asking all these questions . . .'cause he doesn't understand . . . why he's here . . . ((rising intonation)).

Built into the interview was an interpreting challenge in which the suspect tried to appeal to the interpreter and create a sense of solidarity by virtue of their sharing a language and culture. The interpreters responded in somewhat different ways. In excerpt 10.10, the interpreter (turn 1) took on the role of animator by reminding Mr. Lopez of the original contract—that he should not speak to her but should direct his comments to the detective (turn 2)—and then relayed to the detective in reported speech what she had just done (turn 3).

Excerpt 10.10: Interpreter 42

1 L: *Perdón . . . perdón. Dígale, por favor, mire yo no quiero ser grosero, pero yo estoy un poco, como, me estoy poniendo como nervioso. Tú sabes, somos de . . . del . . . del mismo idioma . . . pero . . .* (Sorry, sorry. Tell him, please, look, I don't want to be rude, but I'm a bit, like, I'm getting a bit nervous. You know how we are, from, from the same language, but . . .)

2 I: *Sr. Carlos, le voy a pedir, por favor, que no me hable a mí, sino que le hable directamente al detective Christos.* (Sir, Carlos, I'll ask

you please not to speak to me, but to speak directly to Detective Christos).

3 I: I've just asked him, Carlos, "Please don't talk to me," speak directly to you . . . He's just saying he's very nervous.

This approach was not very effective because the first part of Mr. Lopez's utterance was omitted and the detective did not hear it. A slightly different approach was taken in excerpt 10.11, where the interpreter first sought the permission of the detective to remind Mr. Lopez of her role; by so doing, however, she excluded Mr. Lopez from the short exchange between herself and the detective.

Excerpt 10.11: Interpreter 29

1 I: ((to P)) Excuse me, could I, speak as interpreter, for a second.

2 P: Yes.

3 I: Uhm I wanna say it in Spanish and then in English.

4 P: OK.

5 I: *Señor, por favor, podría dirigirse solamente al, al pol-, la pol-, al policía que lo está entrevistando, ya que yo- todo lo que usted me diga a mí, yo lo tengo que traducir.* (Mr. Lopez, please, could you speak directly to the- the police, the policeman who is interviewing you, because I am- everything you say to me, I have to translate).

The interpreter in excerpt 10.12 adopted a more successful approach, starting her intervention by saying "Speaking to the interpreter" first, to make clear to the police who Mr. Lopez was addressing, and then interpreting everything faithfully. It was the detective who then reemphasized the role of the interpreter and asked Carlos not to engage the interpreter in conversation.

Excerpt 10.12: Interpreter 104

1 L: *Mira tú entiendes mi idioma, por favor ayúdame con esto porque de verdad que no entiendo qué es lo que está pasando, no, tú sabes que en Colombia la- la- la policía es un poco corrupta y todo esto y es- es un poco difícil.* (Look, you understand my language, please help me with this because I really don't understand what is happening, no, you know that in Colombia the- the- the police are a bit corrupt and all that, and it's- it's a bit difficult.)

2 I: Uh speaking to the interpreter- you have to help me, you speak my same language, you know, in Colombia all the police are corrupt, can you tell me what's happening?

3 P: OK, firstly, Carlos, please do not engage the interpreter in conversation, he's not there to answer your questions for you, he's here simply to interpret everything faithfully.

By contrast, the bilinguals entered into conversations with the suspect before relaying anything to the detective in summarized form, as in excerpt 10.13.

Excerpt 10.13: Bilingual 75

1 L: *Tú le puedes decir que, tú me entiendes lo que estoy diciendo [y, por qué—*. (Can you tell him that, you understand what I'm saying, and why.]

2 I: [Mm

3 L: *—no le dices que es que en Colombia la policía es un poco ruda y es un poco corrupta, y- y a mí me da un poco de miedo esta entrevista aquí, tan encerrados.* (would you tell him that in Colombia the police are a bit rough and a bit corrupt and- and it makes me a bit scared to be in this interview, so enclosed.)

4 I: OK.

5 L: *Por favor, dile que estoy como nervioso, que por qué no acabamos esto rápido, ¿sí?* (Please, tell him I'm a bit nervous, why don't we finish quickly, will you?)

6 I: OK.

7 L: *Gracias.* (Thank you.)

8 I: He wants you to know that he's a bit nervous, he wants to try and finish this fairly quickly, back in his country, in Colombia, the police there are very uhm like, corrupt, and he just doesn't feel very comfortable at the moment, very nervous.

9 P: OK, uh Carlos, firstly, please uh you cannot engage the interpreter in conversation, ok? She is not here to uh answer your questions for you, she's here simply to interpret everything faithfully.

The experimental interview contained another instance wherein the detective made a sarcastic comment to the other police officer in the room in response to the suggestion by Mr. Lopez that someone else may have put the white powder in his apartment. The detective made it clear to the interpreter that his utterance was not meant to be interpreted (see turn 2 in excerpt 10.14). Such a request conflicts with the interpreter's role, which had been reemphasized earlier by the detective himself and by the interpreter. The experiment deliberately included these two instances of attempts by the interlocutors to align with the interpreter in order to ascertain whether the interpreters would maintain impartiality and interpret all utterances, regardless of the principal author. The trained interpreters in the sample did not seem deterred by this request and interpreted faithfully, at times reminding the interlocutors that they were bound to interpret everything (see turn 8 in excerpt 10.14). The bilinguals, on the other hand, simply did as the detective instructed and omitted the utterance altogether.

Excerpt 10.14: Interpreter 29

1 I: Uh I don't know what to think about that, I don't know anything ((sigh)) uh this is, this may be a joke, this has to be a joke, I never had anything to do with drugs, my fa-, in my family nobody does drugs, uh probably somebody got into my house and put the bag in there, I don't know, I don't know what is going on, and this can't be true!
2 P: ((sigh)) ((to P2)) How many times have we heard that one?
3 N: Yeah.
4 I: [*Cuántas veces hemos*] (How many times have we])
5 P: [Please don't translate that, though, uhm [Mr. Lopez.
6 L: [*¿Qué pasó?* (What happened?)
7 I: [*Cuántas veces hemos sentido esto* (How many times have we heard this)
8 I: ((to P1)) e- excuse me, I- I need to interpret everything.

Interpreter 42 (the most experienced and the only graduate), in excerpt 10.15, approached this in a different way. Without reminding anyone of her role, she interpreted everything (see turn 4 in excerpt 10.15) and let the interlocutors deal with the consequences (see turns 5 and 6 in excerpt 10.15). This interpreter also used the simultaneous mode to manage this difficult situation. Instead of waiting for Mr. Lopez to finish his angry outburst in turn 5, she simultaneously interpreted to allow the detective to respond straight away (turn 5).

Excerpt 10.15: Interpreter 42

1 P: ((to P2)) How many times did we hear that?
2 I: *¿Cuántas veces hemos escuchado esto?* (How many times have we heard this?)
3 P: Please, don't translate that.
4 I: *Por favor, no interprete esto.* (Please don't interpret that.)
5 L: *¿Cómo así . . . ? No, no, no espere un momento ¿Por qué está allí diciendo que no traduzca las cosas, señor?* ((I: Why are you saying the interpreter shouldn't interpret?)), *¿Por qué le está diciendo a la señora que no traduzca esto? Yo no estoy diciendo mentiras.* ((I: Why are you telling the interpreter not to translate this? I'm not telling lies.))
6 P: Mr. Lopez, please, sit down.

Finally, excerpt 10.16 demonstrated that Mr. Lopez wanted to know what the detective had said but was ignored and therefore not given the opportunity to respond. In contrast, when the trained interpreters relayed everything, Mr. Lopez was able to respond and demand an explanation.

Excerpt 10.16: Bilingual 75

1 L: *Alguien tuvo que haber puesto eso ahí, alguien* (Someone must have put that there, someone)
2 I: Someone must've put that there.
3 P: ((to P2)) How many times have we heard that?
4 L: *¿Qué dijo?* (What did he say?)
5 P: Uhh please, don't translate that
6 I: ((nods)) OK
7 L: *¿Qué?* (What?) ((keeps looking at I))

When interpreters are hired, challenging situations will arise if one of the interlocutors acts unethically or inappropriately, as in our experiment. If the contract is established at the outset, interpreters can interpret faithfully without hesitation, because they are not the principal authors of the utterances and cannot be held accountable for them. The results of the post-interview questionnaire show that although the trained interpreters interpreted the inappropriate remarks from the police and from Mr. Lopez, the two interlocutors consistently gave the trained interpreters a higher score when asked how comfortable they felt with their performance.

Conclusions

Most prior linguistic research has analyzed the performance of interpreters in terms of interpreting accuracy, at both the propositional and the pragmatic levels (Hale 2004; Berk-Seligson 2009; Lai and Mulayim 2014). This study advanced that perspective by evaluating the performance of trained interpreters and untrained bilinguals on two other key aspects of the interpreter's task: the management of turns and ethical propriety. By focusing on the skill required by interpreters to manage the flow of information between speakers across numerous exchanges, requiring spontaneous adaptations of the script by the actors in response to the interpretations provided by the participating interpreters, a realistic picture was obtained of the difference training can make in the context of a police interview. The results showed a considerable gap in the expertise on ethical protocol use, with bilinguals achieving about 40 percent of skills demonstrated by trained interpreters. The disparity in managing turn-taking was smaller, but there was nonetheless a significant gap, with bilinguals achieving 60 percent of the expertise demonstrated by trained professionals. The results showed the way that the interpreters' interventions affected the dynamics of the interaction. The better trained and more experienced interpreters allowed the interlocutors to speak to each other, build up rapport between themselves, but also resolve their own conflicts. The trained interpreters allowed interviewer and interviewee to communicate directly with each other with no interference in the process. The untrained bilinguals, on the other hand, interfered with the interlocutors' ability to communicate effectively by omitting or adding information or holding separate side conversations with each of the interlocutors, to the exclusion of the other.

These results show the risk that police departments face with untrained bilinguals or ad hoc interpreters. Although in Australia the police should give preference to NAATI-credentialled interpreters, training in legal interpreting is not yet compulsory. The situation is even more tenuous in other countries where very little specialist training is available. To safeguard against these risks, training for police interviewers should include familiarization with interpreting standards, as well as the importance of ground rules, ethical obligations for interpreters, and management of turns for consecutive interpreting.

Police practitioners are advised to secure the services of trained and/or credentialed interpreters, preferably those who specialize in legal interpreting, in order to minimize interpreter interference and ensure the most equitable outcomes.

Note

1. Names have been changed.

References

Angelelli, Claudia. 2004. *Medical Interpreting and Cross-Cultural Communication.* London: Cambridge University Press.

Australian Institute of Interpreters and Translators. 2012. "AUSIT Code of Ethics and Code of Conduct." AUSIT. Accessed 11 April 2018. http://ausit.org/AUSIT/Documents/Code_Of_Ethics_Full.pdf.

Bancroft, Marjory A., and Lourdes Rubio-Fitzpatrick. 2011. *The Community Interpreter: Professional Interpreter Training for Bilingual Staff and Community Interpreters.* 5th ed. Columbia, MD: Culture and Language Press, Cross-Cultural Communications.

Baraldi, Claudio, and Laura Gavioli. 2012. "Understanding Coordination in Interpreter-Mediated Interaction." In *Coordinating Participation in Dialogue Interpreting*, edited by Claudio Baraldi and Laura Gavioli, 1–21. Amsterdam and Philadelphia: John Benjamins.

Berk-Seligson, Susan. 2009. *Coerced Confessions: The Discourse of Bilingual Police Interrogations.* Language, Power, and Social Process 25. Berlin: Walter de Gruyter.

Brodsky, Stanley L., Michael P. Griffin, and Robert J. Cramer. 2010. "The Witness Credibility Scale: An Outcome Measure for Expert Witness Research." *Behavioral Sciences & the Law* 28(6): 892–907.

Clark, Herbert H. 1996. *Using Language.* Cambridge: Cambridge University Press.

Conley, John M., and William M. O'Barr. 1990. *Rules versus Relationships: The Ethnography of Legal Discourse.* Chicago: University of Chicago Press.

Cotterill, Janet. 2000. "Reading the Rights: A Cautionary Tale of Comprehension and Comprehensibility." *Forensic Linguistics* 7(1): 4–25.

Davidson, Brad. 2002. "The Interpreter as Institutional Gatekeeper: The Social-

Linguistic Role of Interpreters in Spanish-English Medical Discourse." *Journal of Sociolinguistics* 4(3): 379–405.

Dressler, Wolfgang U. 1994. "The Text Pragmatics of Participant Roles in Oral Interpretation and Written Translation." In *Atti della Fiera Internazionale della Traduzione II, Forum di Forlì, 3–6 dicembre 1992*, edited by M. A. Lorgnet, 97–110. Bologna: CLUEB.

Ewens, Sarah, Aldert Vrij, Sharon Leal, Samantha Mann, Eunkyung Jo, and Ronald P. Fisher. 2014. "The Effect of Interpreters on Eliciting Information, Cues to Deceit and Rapport." *Legal and Criminological Psychology*: 1–19. https://doi.org/10.1111/lcrp.12067.

Gavioli, Laura, and Claudio Baraldi. 2011. "Interpreter-Mediated Interaction in Healthcare and Legal Settings: Talk Organization, Context and the Achievement of Intercultural Communication." *Interpreting* 13(2): 205–233.

Goffman, Erving. 1981. *Forms of Talk*. Oxford: Basil Blackwell.

Goodman-Delahunty, J., Sandra B. Hale, Mandeep K. Dhami, and Natalie Martschuk. 2015. *Effects of Situational and Relational Variables on Interpreting in High Stakes Police Interviews*. Washington, DC: United States Federal Bureau of Investigation.

Hale, Sandra Beatriz. 2004. *The Discourse of Court Interpreting: Discourse Practices of the Law, the Witness and the Interpreter*. Amsterdam and Philadelphia: John Benjamins.

Hale, Sandra Beatriz. 2007. *Community Interpreting*. Basingstoke: Palgrave Macmillan.

Heydon, Georgina. 2005. *The Language of Police Interviewing: A Critical Analysis*. Basingstoke: Palgrave Macmillan.

Lai, Miranda, and Sedat Mulayim. 2014. "Interpreter Linguistic Intervention in the Strategies Employed by Police in Investigative Interviews." *Police Practice and Research* 15(4): 307–321.

Nakane, Ikuko. 2014. *Interpreter-Mediated Police Interviews: A Discourse-Pragmatic Approach*. New York: Palgrave Macmillan.

Pöchhacker, Franz. 2012. "Interpreting Participation: Conceptual Analysis and Illustration of the Interpreter's Role in Interaction." In *Coordinating Participation in Dialogue Interpreting*, edited by Claudio Baraldi and Laura Gavioli, 45–69. Amsterdam and Philadelphia: John Benjamins.

Rudvin, Mette, and Elena Tomassini. 2011. *Interpreting in the Community and Workplace: A Practical Teaching Guide*. London: Palgrave Macmillan.

Tebble, Helen. 1998. *Medical Interpreting: Improving Communication with Your Patients*. Canberra: Language Australia.

Tebble, Helen. 2012. "Interpreting or Interfering?" In *Coordinating Participation in Dialogue Interpreting*, edited by Claudio Baraldi and Laura Gavioli. Amsterdam/ and Philadelphia: John Benjamins.

Valero Garcés, Carmen. 2005. "Doctor-Patient Consultations in Dyadic and Triadic Exchanges." *Interpreting* 7(2): 193–210.

Wadensjö, Cecilia. 1998. *Interpreting as Interaction*. London and New York: Longman.

Wakefield, Shellee J., Mark R. Kebbell, Stephen Moston, and Nina Westera. 2014. "Perceptions and Profiles of Interviews with Interpreters: A Police Survey." *Australian & New Zealand Journal of Criminology*: 1–20.

CHAPTER ELEVEN

Non-Native Speakers, Miranda Rights, and Custodial Interrogation

Bethany K. Dumas

Introduction

Much linguistic research about custodial interrogation of criminal suspects focuses on the interrogation strategies used by police (e.g., Haworth 2010). Linguists have identified significant problems with both interrogation strategies and the use of interrogation statements as evidence at trial. Special problems are often identified in cases involving the interrogation of suspects who are not native speakers of the language of interrogation (Berk-Seligson 2002). Research by sociolinguists makes it clear that interrogation techniques designed to elicit statements showing guilt have the effect of restricting a respondent's ability to provide information (Shuy 1997, 1998; Berk-Seligson 2009, 2011). In the three cases discussed here, linguists were retained by both prosecution and defense, and all submitted reports.[1] Furthermore, they were all asked to examine documents and/or analyze audio recordings of interrogations of the accused persons in order to ascertain whether their English proficiency at the time of interrogation was sufficient for them to understand all their Miranda rights, including the right to have an attorney present. The cases are discussed separately because of the different levels of English-language proficiency of the three defendants.

The data discussed in this chapter comes from work in several cases.[2] This chapter explores how discourse analysis can assist linguists in better understanding the issue of language proficiency in police interviews. In the first case discussed, proficiency in English is deemed high; in the two additional cases, it is deemed very low.

The chapter concludes by making recommendations for the giving of warnings to non-native English-speakers and for assessing delivery adequacy. It briefly addresses issues of conversational structure, interpreting, and bilingualism, but it focuses primarily on defendants' discourse proficiency during custodial interrogation, a scenario in which power differences are built in. It is not the defendants' academic proficiency that is at issue, but their ability to understand and respond appropriately.[3] Custodial interrogation normally occurs only in criminal cases and can lead to charges, conviction, and sometimes death (in capital cases).

Miranda Rights and Non-Native Speakers of English

The primary issue addressed in the chapter is the constitutional right of the arrested person to refuse to answer questions and to have the assistance of a lawyer during further questioning (at state expense, if necessary). Non-native speakers of English often face insurmountable obstacles with respect to the language of interrogation. They may not know even the ordinary meanings of English words used in the Miranda warning as given, let alone the specialized sense in which the words are used in the context of custodial interrogation. Berk-Seligson's 2009 book analyzing the discourse of police interrogations involving U.S. Hispanic suspects offers a detailed examination of the tactics employed by police officers with some knowledge of Spanish as they interrogate suspects and suggests that such police officers should not serve as interpreters at custodial interrogations. Such techniques as closed-ended questions, restrictions on subject matter, and references to a need to hurry often restrict suspects' ability to provide information and thus to some extent thwart the Miranda requirement.

The requirement for the giving of the Miranda warnings stems from the 1966 Supreme Court opinion in *Miranda v. Arizona* (1966; 384 U.S. 436). The opinion by Chief Justice Earl Warren opens with these words: "The cases before us raise questions which go to the roots of our concepts of American criminal jurisprudence: the restraints society must observe consistent with the Federal Constitution in prosecuting individuals for crime." That Supreme Court opinion does not specify the exact text that must be delivered, but a legally adequate version of the Miranda warning must include these elements:

—You have the right to remain silent.

—Anything you say can and will be used against you in a court of law.

—You have the right to have an attorney present before any questioning.

—If you cannot afford an attorney, one will be appointed to represent you before any questioning.

And the accused must also be asked this question:

—Do you understand these rights?

Much research over the years suggests a discrepancy between native English-speakers' understanding of Miranda rights and the understanding of non-native speakers of English. Specifically, research suggests that most English-speaking adults probably understand the warnings. But this is not good enough. The warnings must actually be understood by all interrogated suspects, including minors, people with mental problems, and those who do not speak English or do not speak it well (Solan and Tiersma 2005: 75).

Thus comprehension of Miranda rights is often a major issue in criminal cases. The position of the National Association of Judiciary Interpreters and Translators (NAJIT), for example, is that an understanding of "basic English" is not sufficient when an individual is confronted with the criminal justice system.[4] This chapter presents verifiable audio or transcript data from the three cases discussed to illustrate problems, such as misunderstanding and confusion, that can arise during custodial interrogations of non-native speakers. It also examines discourse techniques used in the cases, focusing on the effectiveness of police discourse with defendants possessing different levels of English proficiency. As will be shown, problems can arise from a lack of comprehensibility of the syntactic complexity of English and unfamiliarity with certain kinds of interrogation questions, particularly yes-or-no questions. In one of the cases discussed, analysis supported adequate comprehension of Miranda; in the other two, data supported limited understanding of the interrogation questions.

Tennessee Murder Case

A 2000 murder case in Tennessee involved assessment of the English proficiency of a native speaker of Spanish (from Honduras) at the time of his arrest with respect to whether it was sufficient for him to understand his Miranda rights as presented. Assessment was also made with respect to whether his English proficiency was sufficient for him to understand information in the summary statement and the admonition and waiver document that he signed. The warnings were presented in English and Spanish; the signed documents were in English. Officers conducted two custodial interrogations, a brief one with two officers present and, two days later, a much longer one with three officers present.

Two linguists were retained by the prosecution; both were originally from Texas. One was bilingual and the other could use conversational Spanish, though she was not fully bilingual. One had a great deal of experience as an expert witness in court cases; the other had little experience. They were retained in opposition to a defense claim that the defendant, charged with the murder of his girlfriend, could not have understood his Miranda rights as delivered. All evidence supported the conclusion that he understood his Miranda rights as delivered in English and Spanish. He eventually confessed, then later filed an appeal. He dropped his request for an appeal during a hearing at which the prosecution linguists were to testify. Interestingly, as the linguists waited to testify with other potential witnesses, they learned that for many years the defendant had taught an adult Sunday-school class in English in Robertson County, Tennessee.

The prosecution linguists analyzed the following documents and recordings:

1. tapes and police transcriptions of two interviews conducted with the defendant, one at the time of his arrest and one two days later (both are accompanied by certificates of translation);
2. a summary statement and an admonition-and-waiver document signed by the defendant;
3. taped copies of 24 fairly brief—each less than five minutes—telephone conversations between the defendant and family members, friends, and professional personnel related to his case while he was incarcerated at the Riverbend Maximum Security Institution;

4. the expert report submitted by the defense linguist;
5. a transcript of the evidence from a previous court case involving the defendant; and
6. copies of letters (in English and Spanish) written by the defendant.

Analysis of the language of the documents and recordings revealed to the linguists that the defendant was sufficiently fluent in English to understand his Miranda rights; this conclusion was stated in their expert report. All conclusions were reached by means of an independent assessment of the defendant's ability to understand, speak, and possibly read English at the time of his arrest based on his turn-taking strategies and his choices about which questions to answer.

The linguists for the prosecution analyzed the report from the defense linguist with respect to the appropriateness of the analytic methods employed and the accuracy of its conclusions. They stated that conclusions about the level of the defendant's English proficiency at the time of his arrest were inaccurate. Those conclusions were based on the use of inappropriate instruments, unsound practices of analysis, inaccurate conclusions about the discourse practices exhibited in the two interviews, and conclusory statements that amounted to no more than unsubstantiated claims. Clearly, the defense linguist was not an expert in sound testing mechanisms.

In both custodial interviews, responses supplied by the defendant, comprehension checks by interrogators, translations provided by one of the officers present, repeated repetitions of Miranda rights, and the general English competency of the defendant indicated that he comprehended English and Spanish well enough to understand his Miranda rights and spoke English well enough to confirm or supply information related to the night of the murder.

During the custodial interviews the defendant consistently and strategically answered all questions so long as the answers did not implicate him. He responded three times with a "Yeah, sí and sí" to the questions asked by officers regarding whether he understood his rights. He stated at three different times that he understood what was being said to him—once when he was asked, "Do you pretty much understand what I'm saying, right?" His immediate response was "Yes" (in English). The second time was after an interrogator explained why he was thought to have committed the crime. The officer said, "Because the evidence at the scene and witnesses at the scene clearly show that he did this without a doubt." At this point an officer asked the accused "¿Lo entiendes?" (Do you understand him?); he replied "Sí entiendo." ("Yes, I understand"). This second admission of understanding what was being said is not in the transcription of the audio, but it is on the audiotape and can be heard clearly. The third time the defendant admitted to understanding what the officers were saying was when he said, "Yo sé lo que me están hablando pero yo no sé lo que está pasando" (I know what they are saying, but I don't know what's going on). This response could have referred to his suspicion that he was being asked to supply implicating information, for the interrogator had focused not on *whether* he had committed the crime but on *why* he had committed it.

In response to the interrogators' questions the accused consistently provided linguistically appropriate responses to questions. His answers gave no indication of being random, compliant agreement statements; they were contextually appropriate. Furthermore, recorded telephone conversation between the defendant and a cousin provided additional evidence that he was able to use English strategically and to manipulate discourse to his advantage.

The interrogator often inserted comprehension checks after statements, occasionally through the use of "okay?"—typically pausing after the "okay." If there was a response, indicating that the defendant either understood or did not understand, the officer moved on to the next agenda item. If there was no response, only silence or a mumbled phrase, the interrogator usually rephrased his statement, as in the following example:

1. TBI Agent: Let me ask you this, was it after they . . .
2. Defendant: [unintelligible response]
3. TBI Agent: Let me ask you this, when she took them home, the rest of the night were you two the only ones there?
4. Defendant: Yeah, me and my girlfriend.

After reading his Miranda rights to the defendant at the beginning of the second interview, the officer checked that they had been understood by saying "okay," a word sometimes used as filler—something that fills space but has no semantic meaning. The intonation at this point suggests that the officer is using the word "okay" to mean "Okay, you understand" or "Okay, can I go on" rather than using it as a mere filler. The pause after the "okay" allows for a response, as in the following example, where "okay" seems to function as a topic marker.

1. Detective: Do you remember running through a big field?
2. Defendant: I don't remember which way I run.
3. Detective: Do you remember running through a field and then having to jump over a fence like maybe where you hurt your ankle?
4. Defendant: I remember there was a fence.
5. Detective: Okay. Is that where you hurt your ankle?
6. Defendant: Yeah.
7. Detective: Okay. Do you remember there's a house right over you jumped over the fence, there's a house over there on [name of street deleted] Street and you ran up there and knocked on a guy's door and asked him for the keys to his car. Do you remember that?
8. Defendant: [No response.]
9. Detective: Okay. You really don't remember that you told the guy- said I need the keys to your car.

The officer serving as the interpreter was available to facilitate the accused's comprehension of his Miranda rights, often by rendering questions and answers, usually in the occasionally nonstandard English of ordinary conversation in Tennessee (see Labov, Ash, and Boberg 2006; Wolfram and Schilling-Estes 2006). At one point, for instance, the interrogator said, "Me and him have talked just like you and me are talking before." The statement successfully communicates information, even though the grammar is not standard. Later he asked, "Do you know what your rights is?" This is prescriptively ungrammatical, but it is comprehensible. The key word is "rights," particularly because the officer explained that the accused had the right to silence and the right to a lawyer, that a lawyer would be appointed for him if he did not have one, and that he would not be forced to speak to the interviewing officers. When the defendant was arrested in Nashville, his Miranda rights had been read to him in English, so this was not the first time he had heard them. Later, he was again advised of his rights in both English and Spanish. He was told (in Spanish), "You know that you have the right to have a lawyer. If you don't have a lawyer, one will be given to you. If you do not want to talk to us, you do not have to. Do you know this? You know that we cannot force you to speak with us." Again, there is a discrepancy between the transcription and the actual taped conversation. The reference to an attorney's being appointed for the defendant if he does not have one is not on the official transcription, but it is on the audiotape. And the first 18 of the 50 exchanges that took place during that first interview were clearly an attempt to be certain that the accused understood his legal rights. When an interrogating officer told him to respond "yes" or "no" to the question "You know that you have rights? Remember that I was talking to you about that," the translator was not satisfied with that option; he interrupted to ask, "Does he understand them?" He asked in Spanish, "Do you know that you have rights in the United States?" The response was "Sí," indicating that the defendant did know that. The interpreter probed further, repeating his questions. Again the response was "Sí." The interpreter then informed him that he did not have to talk and that no one could force him to talk. The accused then informed the interpreter that he would not be talking.

The officer proceeded to establish how long he and the accused had known each other and asked whether they had ever had any problems. The subtext may be that they have known each other long enough for the officer to know that the defendant understands what is being said to him and that he speaks well enough to be able to answer ordinary questions. The subtext may also be that the officer has known him long enough to know that murder is not characteristic behavior for the man. The defendant answered by saying first, "Casi tres años," and then, "about three years." The official transcription indicates that it was an officer who interpreted what the defendant had said, but this is not factual; it was the defendant. Perhaps because this question appeared to have nothing to do with the charge of murder, the defendant answered the question.

The question "How long have I known you?" is linguistically complex, but the defendant had no problem answering it. The officer's response was "About three years, that's right. And in that time have you and I ever had a problem?" The immediate response (in English) was, "I never had no problem with you." The defendant was clearly capable of understanding and of replying in something other than memorized utterances.

One officer attempted to get the defendant to talk about the events preceding the murder by mentioning the sale of weed and cocaine, but he stated also that the evidence showed that he had committed the crime. The officer stated that all he wanted to know was "what caused what happened." The response was, "I'm not going to say nothing about that right now. Till I get somebody." This was the first time he suggested that he wanted to speak to "somebody." The officer asked what he meant by "get somebody."

The defendant responded, "Talk to somebody first." The officer asked, "Who do you want to talk to?" The defendant replied (in Spanish), "Tell him that I am not going to talk to them. I am not going to say nothing about anything right now. So you see that I don't know what is going on or nothing." (The translation in the official transcription does not provide a complete and correct translation of what the defendant actually said.)

Next an officer attempted to assess what the defendant did not understand. The defendant said that he did know what was being said ("What you are talking about") but did not know why they thought he committed the crime. When evidence was cited, he acknowledged that he had understood by beginning his response with "But," as in, "Even so, I still want to speak to someone." At this point the officer stopped the recorder.

Discourse from the first interview shows that the officers attempted to confirm that the defendant understood his Miranda rights, that they had no reason to believe that he did not understand those rights, and that he did indeed understand the questions that he was being asked, since he answered them or refused to answer them, probably based on the kind of information he was willing to give them. An interpreter further explored the defendant's understanding of his Miranda rights by using both Spanish words for lawyer: *abogado* and *licenciado*.[5] His pronunciation of both words was appropriate for a native speaker of Spanish.

The officer proceeded to focus on the defendant's behavior prior to the murder, framing his questions in the guise of trying to figure out what led to the defendant's behavior. He ended with this statement: "I mean, do you want people to think you're just some kind of cold-blooded murderer or do you want to get your side of this in? Something had to happen inside that room to cause this." The defendant's response, in English, was, "I'm not going to say nothing about that right now. Till I get somebody."

Again, the defendant's response is a linguistically and contextually appropriate response to the officer's comments, and it is strategic in that he refuses to engage in an exchange of information that might implicate him. He seems to understand that the officer is trying to elicit a confession. In this exchange the defendant's English is typical of oral language fluency in that he forms contractions: "I am" becomes "I'm," "until" become "till."

The officers also attempted to obtain clarification of what the defendant meant when he said that he would not speak until he "gets somebody." Asked who that somebody would be, he stated in English that he simply is not going to talk—"I don't want to right now." The defendant then called upon the interpreter, saying (in Spanish) "Tell him . . . Tell him that I am not going to talk to them. I am not going to say anything. So you see that I don't know what's going on." This information was conveyed to the attending officers in English and then the defendant interjected the following statement in Spanish: "I know what you are talking about but I don't know what's going on. I need to talk to somebody." He said that what he didn't understand was why they thought he had committed the crime. When they explained, by referring to evidence at the scene and the fact that he was seen running away with a gun in his hand, the defendant again stated (in Spanish), "But, right now I am not going to talk." His response here was strategic. The "but" suggests an understanding of their discourse, such as "Okay I understand but I'm still not going to talk." At this point the officer stopped the recorder.

Analysis of the second custodial interview further illustrates the defendant's level of competence in English at the time of his arrest, his ability to give strategic responses to questions, and his active participation in recreating the events on the night of the murder. He willingly offered information about the victim's behavior the evening she was murdered but responded "I don't know" and "I don't remember" to questions that implicated him. He may not have remembered all the events that relate to the shooting because of a lack of sleep, his use of crack, and heightened levels of adrenaline or endorphins, but his responses strongly suggested that he understood the questions posed to him. The defendant thus assisted the interrogating officers in constructing events about the murder with respect to all details except those that would explicitly implicate him.

One of the few times that the defendant used Spanish in that session was when he narrated the events leading up to the arrest. He began the narrative in Spanish and ended it in English, using a form of code switching characteristic of bilinguals who have some level of fluency in two languages. He began the narrative with "No se olviden que I was driving pero yo no tenía licencia" and ended it saying "So I stop at a gas station and they pulled behind me. . . ." Other instances of code switching occurred in his telephone conversations, as when he used the word "jail" in English, instead of *la carcel*. Code switching can be an indication of comfort and ease of manipulations between two languages, though it may also, of course, reflect the defendant's desire to please the interrogator.

The first interview contains examples of the defendant's linguistic competence in English. At one point he was asked, "Who do I give that car back to?" He replied, "What car?" The officer responded, "The Geo that was sitting there." The defendant replied, "Uh, do y'all got the car?" The officer explained that the owner needed to pick it up, and the defendant said, "I was just talking to him just now. Let me call back." The defendant's comprehension and speaking abilities were clearly strong enough to construct complex sentences and successfully exchange information with native speakers of English.

The prosecution linguists were given a report stating that Miranda rights were read to the accused in Spanish before the tape recorder was turned on. Later, before the defendant made the phone call referred to above, the interrogating officer suggested that they take care of the business at hand, stating, "I'll let you call back, let's knock this out right here first." He then reiterated the Miranda rights. After that, he stopped to confirm that these were the same rights that had been read to him earlier. Missing from the audiotaped interview, of course, are the communication exchanges that can occur through physical gestures, such as a shaking of the head for "no" or a nodding of the head for "yes."

The officer then said, "The only thing I want to do now is reduce down to writing what you told me, okay? And just help me out, I'm going to tell you what I think that you've said, okay. That you were in the room, you'd been smoking some crack and you'd been drinking some. . . ." The defendant did not interrupt the narrative until the officer stated, "She had lifted a drawer, pulled the front off a drawer so she was pretty mad, too, and then something just kind of. . . ." At this point, the defendant stated, "Screamed and then she just like opened that thing for everybody, you know, for everybody to see."

The officer clarified what "that thing" was by responding, "Oh, she was trying to open the curtains, okay?" The defendant confirmed that. The officer continued, "She did open them. Okay. And then when you shot the first time, how was she turned in the room, do you remember where . . ." Embedded in this response is the implication that the defendant shot the gun. The defendant immediately said, "I don't know. I don't remember nothing." Anytime the defendant was asked a question that would implicate him, he responded by saying "I don't remember" or "I don't know." He thus maneuvered through the interview questions strategically. Below are some statements initially stated or confirmed by the defendant during interrogation:

1. You were in the room, you'd been smoking some crack and you'd been drinking some. More crack than drink. And you and your girlfriend got into an argument. You were trying to leave but she wouldn't let you leave.
2. [She] had been drinking, but no crack.
3. You were arguing every day, all day. [Stated in English by the defendant.]
4. You really wanted to leave. [Stated in English by the defendant.]
5. [She] was blocking the door and opened the curtains. [Stated in English by the defendant.]
6. [She] was always threatening to call the police on you to get you arrested. [Confirmed by the defendant, who said, "She always did that."]
7. You had a Beretta black pistol [Stated by defendant, but missing from transcript.]
8. You don't remember which way you ran. [Stated in English by defendant.]
9. You remember a fence. [Stated in English by defendant.]
10. You remember throwing the gun out of the car. [Confirmed by defendant.]

In response to the following statements, the defendant claimed no recollection:

1. You shot the gun the first time.
2. You pulled the pistol from your waistband.
3. Where [she] was standing when you first fired the gun for the first time.
4. Bumping into a guy and telling him to get back into the room.
5. Running through a field. [The defendant's response was "I don't remember which way I run."]
6. Whether your mind was going in a lot of different directions.
7. Where you threw the gun out. [The defendant's response was "I'll think about it."]

The defendant's summary statement includes, with one exception, only information that the defendant himself had stated or confirmed. The exception had to do with a statement about riding in a car to Nashville. The officers may have seen physical confirmation of this statement, even though the transcriber did not include it. The interchanges that occurred in this interview clearly provide a reconstruction of events with the defendant in the driver's seat, for all the details were provided or confirmed by him. No evidence supports the defense linguist's claim that the summary statement was "pieced together by the officer using his own theories, conclusions, and ideas, with rare confirmation." Further claims that his English skills were so remedial that he was not "linguistically present" are not supported by evidence.

The defense linguist's report based its conclusions on the use of a four-hour interview during which she administered a language background questionnaire, the mini-questionnaires, and an oral proficiency interview (OPI). She claimed to have assessed and evaluated his reading ability as well but provided no information about the procedure used for this. She also used instruments to assess English comprehension that are not targeted indicators of comprehension skills (reading or listening), choosing instead to use the OPI, a speaking test.

The defense linguist also administered two self-report questionnaires. Such questionnaires may sometimes provide useful information, but they should not be used to assess an individual's level of proficiency, especially when the results of the questionnaire can implicate a suspect. A self-report questionnaire lends itself to manipulation by the person filling it out. The defense linguist claimed that the defendant's "lack of English impeded him from being linguistically present during the interrogations [*sic*] and to authentically express his knowledge about this case." There is clear evidence that the defendant was linguistically present during the interrogations. The defense linguist appears to have conflated proficiency with grammatically standard speech. She claimed that nongrammatical statements lead to a breakdown in communication; the discourse in the case does not sustain this assessment.

Attempted First-Degree Murder Case in Tennessee

In a 2012 case of attempted first-degree murder, a linguist was retained by the defense and asked to listen to a recording and study the transcription of a partial record of custodial interrogation by a police officer of a man accused of attempted first-degree murder of his wife. The goal was to ascertain whether the man, a non-native speaker of English, understood the language used by the interrogator, particularly with respect to whether he understood his Miranda rights. The linguist studied relevant documents and custodial recordings and interviewed the defendant. A plea agreement was reached before trial in 2014.

The audio recording and transcript provided to the linguist did not contain any explicit transmission of a statement of Miranda rights to the defendant or any explicit waiver of those rights:

1. . . . we have read you your rights. Is this the Rights sheet that I read to you prior to__
2. Yes.
3. —us speaking and you agreed to go ahead and speak to me—
4. Yes.
5. —without an attorney present, is that correct?
6. (no audible response)

This exchange presents several problems. The transcript contains an inaccuracy in suggesting that there is "no audible response" to the last question, for there is no *spoken* response. Further, no information was provided about the contents of what the officer called "the Rights sheet" during this interview or whether the accused was permitted to examine it before answering the question. Also, there is only a brief allusion to a prior statement of rights; the records show no information about exactly what was said to him earlier and what he had agreed to. There is no information about whether the entire text of the admonition-and-waiver document was read to him. There is no information about whether the meanings of terms such as "admonition," "waiver," and "coercion" were explained. Thus there is no evidence that efforts were made to ensure that the accused fully understood his Miranda rights and also understood the exact nature of what he was doing by waiving those rights.

During the interview with the linguist, the defendant supplied examples of ordinary words that he had been puzzled by; they included the expression "two bits," meaning "25 cents" and also the word "ill," meaning "sick." He said that he had attempted to enter U.S. military service but was disqualified because he failed an aptitude test on relationships among English words. He said that he knew so few of the words that he had to guess at many answers. He also said that he found slang hard to understand.

He claimed to have functioned fully in two languages other than English prior to moving to the United States, German and Spanish (while living in Germany and Peru); he also knew some Polish and Ukrainian. Equally important is the nature of the questioning and other interview techniques used by the interrogating officer. As noted above, research makes it clear that questioning techniques used during custodial interrogation often have the effect of restricting a respondent's ability to provide information; that was clearly the case here. Below are some of the many closed-ended questions asked on August 20 as recorded in the transcript:

1. Is this the Rights sheet that I read to you prior to- without an attorney present, is that correct?
2. Is that correct?
3. is that correct?
4. Did something happen in the past week or two that upset you that- that you want to—
5. Did she file for a divorce from you?
6. Is that correct?
7. But you didn't want to get divorced. Is that right?
8. But that was a source of concern for you?

In addition to using primarily closed-ended questions during interrogation, the officer further restricted the respondent by instructing him not to say some things; at one point he said, "I don't want to know what people said. I want to know what you did and what happened concerning the explosion." Finally, the officer rushed the interrogation by saying, "we need to hurry because that- the jail staff is waiting on us, okay?"

In summary, three techniques that were used during the interrogation of the defendant restricted his ability to provide information: closed-ended questions, restrictions on subject matter, and references to a need to hurry. During the linguist's one-hour interview with the defendant, he was fully cooperative, answering all questions and agreeing to read a one-page text that he was told he did not have to read. He complained about the earlier custodial interview, stating that he did not have an opportunity that day to provide information he wanted to provide and that he had never been asked whether he wanted a lawyer. He said that he did not know what a Miranda warning was. He said that the officer had lied to him when he told him that he would not go to jail.

Based on analysis of the materials provided to the linguist, it was clear that the accused did not fully understand the implications of all statements made to him during custodial interrogation, and that he was not able to knowingly, voluntarily, and intelligently waive his Miranda rights.

Possession of a Controlled Substance (Heroin) with Intent to Sell or Deliver

In a 2015 drug case, a linguist was asked to interview the defendant, a young female Spanish-speaker from Mexico, to determine whether she could have understood the English language used by interrogators at the time of her arrest, particularly with respect to whether she could have clearly understood all her Miranda rights and knowingly and intelligently waived them. The linguist spent two hours with the defendant, and the conversation was recorded. There was no indication during the interview that the defendant was attempting to conceal evidence of the level of her comprehensibility of English, which seemed very low. An interpreter was scheduled to be present during the interview; she showed up for only the final minutes of the interview.

The linguist was told that the detectives and/or officers who arrested her claimed to have delivered the Miranda warning, though only in English, during the interrogation, but that they did not record their delivery. In a recording of court testimony of one of the arresting officers, he testified that the defendant claimed that she understood the Miranda warning. He also testified twice that when questioned about whether officers could search her car she had replied "Check, check." There is no recording to verify this. There is also no evidence that the English words "check, check" constitute an affirmative response when uttered by a Spanish-speaker who knows little English. During court testimony of the officer, he said that the two of them "were able to communicate" but offered no evidence. Given the defendant's low level of comprehension of English, it is quite possible that she assumed the officers only wanted to check to make certain that her car was safe to drive; she in fact suggested that at one point during the interview with the linguist.

During the linguist's interview with the defendant, she appeared to understand very few English words. And there is no evidence in the interview with her or with any of the materials provided to the linguist showing that efforts were made to explain her rights so that she understood them fully. Given her education (through the eighth grade, in Mexico) and her recent social history of living in U.S. neighborhoods where the population is mostly Hispanic and Spanish-speaking, it is unlikely that her level of English competence allowed her to understand the statements at issue. At one point she said that all she knew about Miranda was that it is "a word."

She had never been arrested before and thus had no experience with patterns of police discourse. There is evidence that an interpreter was used at all of her court hearings and at all meetings with counsel. Furthermore, her social class and educational level suggest that she considered herself subservient to authority, particularly that of police identified as such, as the arresting officer was, since he was wearing a vest that had the word "Police" on it.

There is also evidence that the typical Miranda statement may require at least a 10.5-grade reading level for the overall statement and as high as a 17.3-grade reading level for the waiver of rights—and that is for native speakers (e.g., van Naerssen 2012). The only evidence of her comprehension of English is an opinion statement by an officer who did not speak Spanish and who had no qualifications for gauging the English competence of a native Spanish-speaker.

In her interview with the defendant, the linguist asked mostly open-ended questions and asked whether the defendant could read a one-page text in English. She could not. The only part of the English text that she claimed to recognize was the word "chicken." When asked if she could read more, she simply shrugged her shoulders and remained silent. Here are some of the questions asked by the linguist:

1. Will you tell us a little bit about yourself? Un poco?
2. What's your favorite food?
3. Had you heard about the Miranda warning before that day?

During the initial part of the interview, the defendant's attorney and the linguist spoke to her primarily in English. Both her body language and periods of silence during that time suggested that she did not understand what was going on. Their questions were innocuous—such as "What's your favorite food?"—so there was little reason for her to refuse to answer them. Even after they began using some Spanish, she responded to questions and statements with a few yes-or-no responses in English, a few other English words, many statements in Spanish, a great deal of body language, laughter, and occasional silence. Such uniformly nonlinguistic cues are strong evidence of noncomprehension. During the final part of the interview, when the interpreter was rendering both the questions and responses, the defendant displayed less negative body language and no silence at all.

All evidence indicates that the defendant did not have sufficient proficiency in English to understand most statements made and questions posed during the linguist's interview with her. Thus it is very unlikely that she understood the vocabulary and legal implications of the Miranda warning that arresting officers claim were given to her in English the night she was arrested.

The defendant filed a motion to suppress evidence seized, and the linguist testified at the hearing. Based partly on the fact that the interpreter assigned to the interview showed up for only the final minutes of the two-hour interview, the judge ruled that the linguist's testimony did not substantially assist the trier of fact, saying at one point that "the Court cannot put much if any weight on her testimony due to the circumstances surrounding the interview." The motion was denied.

Conclusions

Many factors are at play when a non-native speaker of English undergoes custodial interrogation in a criminal case in the United States. Based on the three cases discussed above, it seems clear that the assessment must be done in such a way that legal professionals, including judges, understand both the assessment techniques used and the conclusions reached.

A recent document by an international group of 21 linguists, psychologists, lawyers, and interpreters entitled "Guidelines for Communicating Rights to Non-Native Speakers of English in Australia, England, and Wales, and the USA" includes seven recommendations for such communications:

—Use standardized version in plain English (clear English)

—Develop standardized statements in other languages

—Inform suspects about access to an interpreter at the beginning of the interview

—Present each right individually

—Do not determine understanding by using yes or no questions

—Adopt an in-your-own-words requirement

—Video-record the interview

To these excellent guidelines should be added:

—Be aware that delays or absences of scheduled interpreters may play a role in how evidence is received.

Notes

1. All linguists were university professors with previous experience completing such analysis.

2. For reasons of confidentiality, names of parties discussed in this chapter will not be disclosed.

3. Archibald (1998).

4. Language Assistance for Law Enforcement, 31 March 2006. https://najit.org/wp-conten/uploads t /2016/09/LanguageforLawEnforcement2006.pdf.

5. The word *licenciado* may be used for "attorney."

References

Archibald, Alasdair Neil. 1994. *The Acquisition of Discourse Proficiency: A Study of the Ability of German School Students to Produce Written Texts in English as a Foreign Language.* Frankfurt am Main: Peter Lang.

Berk-Seligson, Susan. 2002. *The Bilingual Courtroom: Interpreters in the Judicial Process.* Chicago: University of Chicago Press.

Berk-Seligson, Susan. 2009. *Coerced Confessions: The Discourse of Bilingual Police Interrogations.* Berlin: Walter de Gruyter.

Berk-Seligson, Susan. 2011. "Negotiation and Communicative Accommodation in Bilingual Police Interrogations: A Critical Interactional Sociolinguistic Perspective." *International Journal of the Sociology of Language.* 207: 29–58.

Communication of Rights Group. 2016. *Guidelines for Communicating Rights to Non-Native Speakers of English in Australia, England and Wales, and the USA.* http://www.aaal.org/?page=CommunicationRights.

Haworth, Kate. 2010. "Police Interviews as Evidence." In *The Routledge Handbook of Forensic Linguistics*, edited by Malcolm Coulthard and Alison Johnson, 169–181. London and New York: Routledge.

Labov, William, Sharon , Ash, and Charles Boberg. 2006. *The Atlas of North American English*. Berlin: Mouton de Gruyter.

Miranda v. Arizona. 1966. 384 U.S. 436.

National Association of Judiciary Interpreters and Translators. 2006. *Language Assistance for Law Enforcement*. https://najit.org/wp-content/uploads/2016/09/LanguageforLawEnforcement2006.pdf.

Rogers, Richard, Kimberly S. Harrison, Daniel W. Shuman, Kenneth W. Sewell, and Lisa L. Hazelwood. 2007. "An Analysis of Miranda Warnings and Waivers: Comprehension and Coverage." *Law and Human Behavior* 31(2): 177–192. http://www.english.illinois.edu/-people-/faculty/debaron/584/584reading/rogers miranda.pdf.

Rogers, Richard J., Jill E. Rogstad, Jennifer A. Steadham, and Eric Y. Drogin. 2011. "In Plain English: Avoiding Recognized Problems with Miranda Miscomprehension." *Psychology, Public Policy, and Law* 17(2): 264–285.

Shuy, Roger W. 1997. "Ten Unanswered Language Questions about Miranda." *Forensic Linguistics* 4(2): 175–195.

Shuy, Roger W. 1998. *The Language of Confession, Interrogation, and Deception*. Thousand Oaks, CA: Sage.

Solan, Lawrence M., and Peter M. Tiersma. 2005. *Speaking of Crime: The Language of Criminal Justice*. Cambridge: Cambridge University Press.

van Naerssen, Margaret. 2012. "The Linguistic Functions of 'Knowingly' and 'Intelligently' in Police Cautions." *IAFL Porto 2012 Proceedings*, 157–169. http://ler.letras.up.pt/uploads/ficheiros/13605.pdf.

Wolfram, Walt, and Natalie Schilling-Estes. 2006. *American English: Dialects and Variation*. 2nd ed. Malden, MA: Blackwell.

SECTION IV

The Discursive Journey and Institutional Applications of Police Interviews

CHAPTER TWELVE

"Tell Me in Your Own Words . . ."

Reconciling Institutional Salience and Witness-Compatible Language in Police Interviews with Women Reporting Rape

Nicci MacLeod

Introduction

It is a well-established tenet of discourse analysis that the primary recipient for many types of institutional talk is not the participants who are physically present, but an absent "overhearing audience" (Heritage 1985). In the case of investigative interviews, the talk is relevant to a wider context—it is "performed for a higher authority, a judge and jury" (Johnson 2008: 330). In England and Wales, interviews with "significant witnesses," that is, those who were immediate to the event in question or have a particular relationship with the victim, including victims themselves, are identified as requiring particularly thorough and proceduralized interviews (Rock 2010) and routinely have their police interviews video-recorded (Ministry of Justice 2011; ACPO 2013). They are then entitled to have the video recording stand in for their direct examination at a subsequent trial, meaning the interview is an evidential object as well as an investigative aid (see Haworth 2010). The influence of this future audience over the unfolding talk and the communicative challenges posed by this unusual audience design (Bell 1984, 2001), often unrecognized by the naive interviewee (IE), have been explored thoroughly (Stokoe and Edwards 2008; Haworth 2013). But negotiating the needs of multiple audiences is not the only challenge faced by interviewers (IRs) seeking institutionally useful accounts of events from lay witnesses. A further potential constraint associated with contemporary, cognitive, interview-based training models such as PEACE is the recommendation for the IE to be allowed to tell their story "in their own words" (see Milne and Bull 1999; Milne 2004, 2016), uninterrupted and with minimal input from the IR. As highlighted by Heydon (2005), in Goffmanian (1981) terms this equates to a preference for IEs to be aligned as principal and author, as well as animator, of their own accounts—in other words, they hold sole responsibility for the content and form of their story. Evidence of IRs' preference for such a framework often appears in the form of explicit promotion of it, such as "Would you care to tell me in your own words . . . ," but they also work to maintain the footing in more subtle ways, such as by feigning ignorance of certain facts in order to elicit an on-the-record answer to a question, as though the IE were the sole owner of the "new" information. IRs are also heard reactivating elements of IEs' accounts in order to carry out probing around specific topics, attempting to do so within a framework wherein the IE's status as principal and author is not jeopardized.

The salience of the overhearing audience and the preference for an account in which the IE, uninitiated in the routines of police interviewing, has her principalship and authorship preserved thus presents a double-pronged challenge for IRs. Their aims are conflicting; while the central goal of an investigative interview is to draw out and fix an institutionally appropriate account of events, IRs experience a simultaneous pressure to ensure that this account is rendered in the words of the IE—words that are unlikely to be deemed institutionally appropriate. IRs are tasked with negotiating a telling that will be compatible with its roles within the criminal justice system while avoiding potential criticism that they themselves have unduly influenced the telling. How these seemingly contradictory objectives are reconciled is the key focus of this chapter.

The problems are further complicated in the context of interviews with complainants in rape cases. The achievement of justice in rape cases has long been recognized as a substantial challenge within the criminal justice system (see Westera, Kebbell, and Milne 2016), and one that is inextricably tied up with prevalent and deep-seated attitudes toward sexual violence, its perpetrators, and its victims (Gregory and Lees 1999; Anderson and Doherty 2008). Western society has been described as a rape-supportive culture, and such support is realized through all levels of the social structure, including the legal system (Matoesian 1993) and the police (Page 2008). Questions therefore arise about how such ideology might be realized and oriented toward investigative interviews—if rape-supportive ideas are a feature of institutional attitudes toward sexual violence, what are the concrete implications of this for the negotiation of an institutionally appropriate account of a rape?

In this chapter I focus on formulation (Garfinkel and Sacks 1970) and reported speech as sites where IRs can variously be heard to orient to the absent audience and to maintain the IE's authority, and as interactional resources IRs draw on in order to fix meaning and establish institutional salience. I examine the processes by which IEs' reportings of events come to be restated by interviewers and in the process are negotiated such that they provide a good fit for addressing their primary aim. I identify tensions between the seemingly conflicting goals of institutional propriety and maintenance of IE principalship and conclude with some observations on the impact of these patterns for rape victims' experiences of the criminal justice system.

Participation Frameworks and Reflexive Language

This chapter is concerned with the extent to which IEs' status as authors of their own accounts is truly maintained when IRs use reflexive language, or metadiscourse, in significant witness interviews. The data drawn on here were collected from an English police force in 2008 for research purposes; video-recorded interviews are archived by the police as a matter of routine and are eligible for release to researchers under section 33 of the Data Protection Act (1998). All names and identifying information were changed at the time of transcription, which was carried out by the author.

Both formulations and reported speech are devices used to reactivate or maintain topics while ensuring that IEs retain principalship, or authority, for the content of the message, but both are sites for potential rewordings that pose a threat to the IE's status as author. The process has been noted as "a powerful instrument in mystifying . . . principalship" (Bublitz and Bednarek 2006: 552). Thus, final versions of accounts are likely to contain descriptions of events in the words of IRs, attributed to

IEs. Given the risks associated with rape victims' accounts in court not matching exactly their accounts during their interviews, this is an issue that should be viewed with some concern.

Switching between the available production and reception roles, or shifts in "footing" between various "participation frameworks" (Goffman 1981), are managed with the use of cues that indicate the producer's and receiver's relationship to the utterance(s). In the police interview we might expect several footings to be activated, and these are managed in several ways. A recurrent feature of the opening phases of the interviews, for example, is the identification of the IR by name, rank, and badge number, along with a statement summarizing the time, date, and location. Rather than being the words and sentiments of the individual officer spoken for the benefit of the ostensible addressee, the IE, these utterances are in fact produced on behalf of the police institution for the benefit of the ultimate audience of the tape. During questioning, however, the situation is likely to be quite different. IRs are not provided with scripts for use during this stage—rather, they are expected to be flexible and adapt their questioning according to the interviewee's responses.

Garfinkel and Sacks define formulations as points within conversation where a participant takes the opportunity to "describe that conversation, to explain it, or characterize it, or explicate, or translate, or summarize, or furnish the gist of it." (1970: 350). Thus, formulations provide a resource for participants to reach an agreement on the meaning of what has gone before: "the introduction of a formulation enables co-participants to settle on one of many possible interpretations of what they have been saying" (Heritage and Watson 1974: 123). Although rare in "ordinary" conversation, formulations are typical of many types of institutional, audience-directed interaction (Heritage 1985) and demonstrate the authority a powerful participant has to gloss the meaning of preceding talk. Third-turn positions in the talk of trials, news interviews, and police interviews are typically occupied by these utterances, which allow questioners to "decline the role of report recipient while maintaining the role of report elicitor" (Heritage 1985: 100) and reporting the speech of others as a means by which an IR "detaches her/himself from the proposition in the reporting clause, since s/he attributes to somebody else the responsibility of averring what comes after the reporting verb" (Caldas-Coulthard 1987: 152).

Formulations are directed at the overhearing audience, ostensibly to summarize the gist of preceding talk but selectively re-presenting the content in the process and inviting the IE to minimally confirm or deny the modified version. One important function of formulations is the translation of the interaction into something "preservable and reportable" (Heritage and Watson 1974: 149). They have three central properties: preservation, deletion, and transformation (125). Identifying the elements that are preserved, deleted, and transformed has the potential to reveal underlying assumptions of the IRs and the police institution as a whole. With reported speech, too, it is inevitable that some elements of the original account will be absent from the re-presented version, and the elements that remain are likely to have undergone some degree of transformation. The actual words chosen by the IR to represent propositions previously expressed by the IE have the potential to construct meanings that differ from those the IE may have originally intended.

Johnson (2008) shows how police IRs, in translating lay accounts into institutionally appropriate ones through formulation, necessarily do not "take up" all the elements that are provided. Instead, they focus on those elements that emphasize suspects' involvement and responsibility, from which they negotiate a new version, which the suspect is then encouraged to support. Haworth points out that an IR often "alters the [interviewee's] words subtly but significantly, re-casting the scene described in a different light" (2009: 200).

As well as potentially feeling that the negotiation process has produced a skewed portrayal of events, there is the possibility that IEs whose own words have been inaccurately attributed to them feel some pressure to acquiesce to the inaccurate statement nonetheless.

As well as making explicit one participant's understanding of what is being or has been said, formulations require this understanding to be ratified by the other participant(s). More specifically, formulations fill the first pair part slot in adjacency pairs, where a confirmation or disconfirmation is expected to fill the second pair part slot. As with many other actions, a positive response—that is, a confirmation—is the preferred reception. A direct and unmitigated disconfirmation has the potential to disrupt the ongoing talk and "initiate a search for a fresh basis on which concerted comprehension can be established" (Heritage and Watson 1974: 144). As a result, disconfirmations are often combined with confirmatory elements, much as rejections of invitations incorporate justifications for the rejection in order to soften the negative effects of such dispreferred utterances. Given the asymmetrical nature of the interaction and the fact that formulations by their very nature ostensibly preserve the IE's principalship, it is worth questioning how frequently formulations and reported speech are challenged by IEs. I will go on to show how many instances of reflexive language, though inaccurate (sometimes potentially damagingly so), are nevertheless accepted wholesale by IEs as an accurate representation of their own words.

Cooperative Reorientation and Defining the Crime

An IR's repetition or paraphrasing of part of an IE's account functions to direct the IE to a particular part of that account in order to ask specific questions about it. Recapitulating prior talk as a point of departure for subsequent probing in this way might be viewed as cooperative activity, assisting the IE in navigating her account and mitigating the impact of what might otherwise appear to be a highly disjunctive interaction. Since it is an effective means of breaking down the account for further questioning while avoiding interruption, the sequence of reported speech plus open information-seeking question is a commonly used strategy and one that succeeds in smoothly eliciting descriptive accounts, as shown in the following excerpt. Note that in all extracts, line numbers reflect where the segment appears in the original interview transcript.

Excerpt 12.1

655 IR: no. (1.0) •hhh so can you describe to me **y- you've**
656 **mentioned about a can of Carling** (.) can you describe
657 what happened there.
658 (1.0)
659 IE: um (.) I think I was still watching (2.0) er the League of
660 Gentlemen (.) and he came in (1.5) and gave me the can of
661 Carling that was already open and then sat down (0.5) and
662 I: (.) started to drink it (2.5) u:h don't know if he
663 started coming on to me (.) while I was drinking it (.)
664 o:r if I (.) put it down (.) and then he started.

Excerpt 12.1 provides evidence of the IR's awareness that reporting the IE's earlier talk back to her is likely to assist her by reestablishing the context in which further questions are about to be asked. Beginning with an open-ended, information-seeking question on line 655, she initiates a self-repair and instead elects to direct the IE to the relevant section of her free report before producing the originally intended question. Although it would be feasible to ask her to "describe what happened with the can of Carling," the reporting of the earlier part of the account allows the IE to become aware of the IR's intentions much earlier.

The cooperative recycle is one function of formulations explored by Heritage (1985) in the context of new interviews, and this can also be identified in police interviews. Consider the following excerpt, for example, where a formulation from the interviewer is treated as "accurately and agreeably re-present[ing] the interviewee's stated position" (Heritage 1985: 106). The IE has just explained that she had been advised not to drink alcohol while taking her prescribed antidepressant medication.

Excerpt 12.2

IR: okay •hh is that purely because it stops the medication
working or does it have any adverse effects with the
alcohol.=
IE: =um (.) well alcohol is a depressant=
IR: =mm [hmm]
IE: [so]it
(.) it just makes (.) um medication useless really.
IR: okay (1.0)**so it's th- it's- it's- sort of u:m (.)**
counteracting the antidepressant with a depressant.
IE: yeah.

The IR's formulation on lines 810–811 represents a more formally worded, institutionally appropriate, yet unproblematic gloss of the IE's contribution at lines 806 and 808–809, which the IE subsequently confirms on line 812. The IE has not used the words "counteracting" or "antidepressant" in her attempt to describe the effects of alcohol on her medication, but the IR introduces these terms in her own gloss of the description. This extract also demonstrates the preference structure associated with formulations, with a confirmation preferred, as is evident from the IE's instantaneous and unqualified response. Thus, reflexive language can be a means of assisting an IE in conveying her message, by offering a paraphrase of prior talk that agreeably represents the stated position. There are obvious potentially negative implications of this, to which I shall return later.

Some occasions of reflexive language function to project a topic over a further turn, standing alone to invite the IE to elaborate on an aspect of her account. By restating IEs' statements, IRs are able to draw out particular elements and preserve them as a topic of further talk, presumably on the basis that these elements are of particular salience within the institutional context of a rape investigation and potential prosecution. In the following excerpt, the IR produces a stretch of reported speech and then a formulation, both of which prompt elaboration from the IE on the topic of the suspect's hair.

Excerpt 12.3

IR: °okay° •hhh you've described him as having (0.5) short
dark hair (.) sort of shaven.
IE: mmm (.) u::m (1.5) like a n- a number four or five.
IR: okay (4.0) so that's sli- slightly longer than having it
like shaven (.) to the head.
IE: no it wasn't (.) like that but it wasn't sort of floppy
(.) hair.

The IR begins on line 348 with a stretch of reported speech, directing the IE back to the part of her earlier account where she had described the suspect's hair. The IE responds to this first with the minimal response "mmm," indicating a confirmation of the re-presented information, followed by a pause before she elaborates on this description. Thus, IRs' intentions when reporting IEs' speech are often immediately obvious to the interviewee, to the extent that the questions being set up are sometimes not required at all; the IE provides further detail in response to the restatement alone. Since these kinds of utterances from IRs have previously been categorized as confirmation-seeking questions (Newbury and Johnson 2006), it is of interest that they can also provoke such elaborate and informative responses. The IR's formulation on lines 351–352 can be heard as prompting the IE to elaborate, in that it indicates her description on 350 as having altered, albeit slightly, the initial description of the hair as "shaven," thus requiring further explanation. In producing the formulation, the IR signals that the description has been modified from what might have been understood from the IE's original. The formulation is accepted by the IE on lines 353–354, and she goes on to place her description somewhere between "shaved" and "floppy." Thus, although the formulation in this extract has been designed and responded to as a prompt, it also functions to assist the IE in the construction of an accurate, and thereby institutionally useful, account of events.

IEs understandably often exhibit difficulty in describing the rape itself, but the police obviously are strongly motivated to establish the facts of this central action in order to investigate further and refer it to the CPS. Formulation is one way to achieve the fixing on the record that an action legally defined as rape took place. An example appears in excerpt 12.4, where three extracts relating to the telling of the central event are reproduced: A is from the IE's initial free report, B from the subsequent questioning phase, and C from the next phase of questioning, labeled in the guidance as the "investigatively important questioning" phase.

Excerpt 12.4

A	113	IE:	an then after <u>that</u>~ (1.0) •HHH HH •HH um •HHHHHHH~I
	114		don't know where it was but (.) mm (.) a male •hhh
	115		mm **obviously (0.8) did what he did** HH (.) and then
	116		(0.8) I just closed my eyes through **it all.**
	((around 17 pages omitted))		
B	1043	IR:	you did. (.) right okay (0.3) so: (1.0) what did he do
	1044		next?
	1045	IE:	•hhh (0.5) hhhh (0.4) I don't know (1.3) um
	1046		((•shih)) (0.4) **I think it was <u>sex</u> I'm not sure**
	1047	IR:	okay=
	1048	IE:	=whether it was his hand or not.
	((57 lines omitted))		
C	1105	IE:	°I got° he was too <u>strong</u> (1.4) so I just (.) gave
	1106		up (1.3) and let him do it?
	1107		(5.3)
	1108	IR:	°okay° (4.8) so (0.6) **he actually penetrated your**
	1109		**vagina yeah?**
	1110		(0.7)
	1111	IE:	yeah.

During her free report (A), the IE relies on an assumed shared frame of reference—she is, after all, in a police station reporting a rape—in order to explain what happened to her. The use of "obviously" alongside the vague "did what he did" supports this interpretation. During the first questioning segment (B), the IR uses a relatively open information-seeking question (lines 1043–44) to successfully move the IE to the less ambiguous, but still decidedly vague, "I think it was sex I'm not sure . . . whether it was his hand or not." During the investigatively important questioning phase (C), when leading questions are permitted in order to address specific gaps in the account, the IR formulates the IE's contributions to the unambiguous "he actually penetrated your vagina" and offers this for her confirmation. In doing so he has established that there can be no doubt that what she is reporting is penetration against her consent, which is clearly prosecutable as rape under UK law.

The extracts discussed here highlight the differences in the ways interviewers and interviewees view the purposes of the interaction. Because interviewees are naive as to the position of the interview in the investigative and evidentiary chain, they attach equal importance to all the details they recall. Interviewers, on the other hand, because they are familiar with the institutional role and goals of the interview, attach more importance to some details over others. One way in which this manifests itself is in the use of formulations to foreground particular elements of interviewees' reports, often drawing them out as topics for further discussion into subsequent turns. Inevitably this occurs at the expense of other details, which are backgrounded by virtue of exclusion from interviewers' formulations. Thus, although the implications of interviewees' talk for the investigation and collection of evidence are often highlighted, other matters deemed less relevant for the pursuit of institutional goals are obscured.

I have so far demonstrated the relatively straightforward and unproblematic use of formulating and speech-reporting practices, with interviewers making use of them in order to summarize and direct the discussion in particular directions—a manifestation of their power at the local level, but not in any obvious way a threat to the credibility of the IE. I will continue by examining ways in which IRs use reflexive language to transform IEs' accounts into objects of value to the criminal justice system, thus demonstrating institutional power in a wider context. These practices also reveal particular ideological assumptions inherent in this wider context, in terms of what is deemed to be of institutional value.

Reflexive Language and Threats to Authorship

That reflexive language is a routine means by which IRs signal the IE's status as the principal behind a message has been touched upon, as has the fact that, in formulating or constructing a stretch of reported speech,

IRs give the impression that the interviewee also stands as author in relation to the message—in other words, that it is a verbatim account of what she has already said. When alterations are made to IEs' wording, there is potential for negative effects on their credibility or on the evidential quality of the interview. Let us look at some examples.

Excerpt 12.5

A 88 IE: •shih (3.0) he bought me two drinks sat at the table
89 (1.0) two big bottles of cider it was (3.0) u::m (2.0)
90 •shih **they were passing (.) u:m cocaine between**
91 **(.) him and Gary (0.5) quite frequently going to the**
92 **toilets with this small bag**, (.) •shih (10) •shih
((around 87 lines omitted))
B 179 IR: all right **you'd said that they'd u:m had this: (.)**
180 **bag of coke that they'd passed between them had**
181 **<u>you</u>: taken anything?**
182 IE: no (.) I'm on medication so I wouldn't •shih take
183 any drugs (1.5) a few of my friends take them but
184 •shih I don't.

Excerpt 12.5 shows the IR producing a stretch of reported speech (lines 179–180) and following it up immediately with a closed question on the topic of whether the IE had taken drugs on the night in question. Let us compare the reported speech to the IE's initial account. Earlier, the IE stated that the men she was with "were passing [. . .] cocaine" (line 90). When the IR attempts to direct her back to this segment for probing, she asserts that "you'd said that they'd [. . .] had this bag of coke," using a colloquial term for the drug that one might assume to be institutionally dispreferred. This alteration gives cause for concern. First, the words of the IR are attributed to the IE with the use of "you'd said" (line 179). Secondly, the IE has no opportunity to challenge this attribution: the stretch of reported speech is not a question to be answered, or even a formulation to be confirmed or disconfirmed; it is a precursor to a question, and as such is followed up, immediately and without pause, by the part of the turn to which the IE *is* expected to respond. The asymmetrical nature of the interview and the sequential organization of reported speech make it difficult for IEs to launch challenges. Of crucial importance is the possibility that the IR's words, masquerading as those of the IE, are the ones to appear in the negotiated, final version, thereby creating the potential for challenge from cross-examiners. Since, arguably, referring to cocaine as "coke" suggests some higher degree of familiarity with the substance than using its full name, the possible implications for this in terms of the IE's perceived credibility are obvious. It should surely remain a matter of concern that IRs are able to misrepresent IEs' accounts in this way and remain unchallenged.

A further example of institutional assumptions being made latent in the restating contributions of the IR appears in excerpt 12.6. The relevant earlier segment from the IE's free report is included, as well as the later exchange in which the IR directs her back to the report. "Nathan" is the pseudonym given to the IE's partner, who was asleep next to her at the time of the attack. "Paul" is the pseudonym given to the suspect.

Excerpt 12.6

1093 IE: he sat and told me to shush. (4.8) and when Nathan woke
1094 up he obviously didn't (0.6) he was just like (0.4) what's
1095 going on and **I'm screaming to tell him to get away from**
1096 **me and •hh not to let him hurt me.** (2.5) started crying
1097 and then (0.8) hitting Paul.
((sixteen lines omitted))
1113 (1.4)
1114 IR: °mmm° (34.2) **you said you were saying (1.0) don't hurt me**
1115 **or don't let him hurt me** (0.4) what made you think (0.6)
1116 that he was gonna hurt you [or that]
1117 IE: ['cause he] was having sex with
1118 me and I didn't want to. (11) and that <u>is</u> hurting me.

After a long gap on line 1113, the IR restates the IE's claim that she had, on waking to discover the suspect engaging in intercourse with her, attempted to wake her partner by "saying don't hurt me or don't let him hurt me." It is interesting to note that although IE's account uses the words "*screaming* to tell him," the IR has altered this to the more neutral verb "saying." It would be problematic for the IE to challenge this rephrasing—first, the words are being presented as her own, and secondly she is given no opportunity to confirm the accuracy of the IR's version before he moves into the particularizing question on 1115, "What made you think. . . ." To ask "What made you think . . ." is itself worthy of further discussion, suggesting as it does that the IE's reasons for reaching that conclusion are not immediately obvious. The premise of the question on lines 1115–1116 appears even more anomalous when we consider that the IE has already provided the information that during this time, the suspect was engaging in intercourse with her without her consent. The IR has displayed a reliance on an interpretive repertoire of forced penetration being distinct from "hurting" someone—of rape as distinct from violence. This IE launches a challenge to this interpretation on lines 1117–1118, but it is easy to see how much simpler it would be to acquiesce, and indeed this IE ultimately does.

Another theme that has frequently been identified in discourse-analytical studies of rape is that of "appropriate" resistance (see Fairclough 1995; Ehrlich 2001). At one time in the United States there existed a legislated "utmost resistance" standard for convicting of rape—that is, a woman had to demonstrate that she resisted to the utmost of her capabilities if she wanted to claim that she did not consent. Despite no longer being official, it has been demonstrated that the standard still fully functions below the surface, and that resistance is a factor that should be established on the record if a case is to proceed successfully.

Excerpt 12.7

904 IR: °°right°° (1.8) and (0.8) whilst all this (0.5) was
905 happening (1.3) **you said you had your hands on his chest**
906 (0.8) was there anything else that you did (1.0) that you
907 felt (0.8) woul- °dunno what I'm trying to say here° (3.8)
908 y- you're saying that- **you obviously reported this to the**
909 **police that you didn't want this to happen.**
910 IE: ((shaking head)) ((°°unclear°°))
911 IR: okay (1.0) how do you think that h- th- that you portrayed
912 that to him?
913 (2.8)
914 IE: u:m (3.9) °don't know° (1.6) [a l-]
915 IR: [when um]
916 IE: a lot of people (1.0) take advantage that I wear a short
917 skirt when I go out that I'm- (0.5) I'm (.) easy? (1.7)
918 but I've never (1.7) I've never given anybody the come
919 on.

As the interviewer's use of "this" on line 904 indicates, it is not a topic much earlier in the interview that is being revisited, but rather the current topic that is being continued. However, "you said you had your hands on his chest" (line 905) is referring the IE to a specific aspect of the current topic: her resistance. The question that this statement sets up proves problematic for the IR to construct, as flagged by the noticeably quieter aside on line 907. The content of the aside suggests that the IR is attempting to avoid betraying an expectation of more resistance—an expectation he nevertheless does eventually betray. He changes tack and uses another reflexive statement on line 908–909, "You obviously reported this to the police that you didn't want this to happen," rather than producing a question right away. This reflexive statement is quite obviously produced as a basis for the question that follows on lines 911–912, "How do you think that . . . you portrayed that to him?" This question implies, first, that it would be expected for a woman in this position to give more indication that she did not want intercourse; and secondly, that there are set ways of portraying a lack of desire to have intercourse (including having one's hands on his chest, as is evident from the first attempt at formulating the question on line 906, "Was there anything *else*" [my emphasis]). Of further interest is the emphatic stress on "him," suggesting that, while *the IR* understands the meaning of the IE's actions, the attacker is not necessarily expected to have interpreted the pushing in the same way. The substantial gap on line 913 and the filler and pause on 914 before the IE's noncommittal reply indicates that these assumptions do not correspond with her own, or at least that she is having trouble understanding exactly what kind of answer the IR is expecting. As the IR begins to try to assist her, she finally attempts an answer, finding it necessary to justify her behavior on lines 918–919: "I've never given anyone the come-on." In effect, she is forced into denying the opposite behavior from where the sequence started. For the IE, not having "given the come-on" is evidence enough for her lack of consent. The IR seemingly abandons the line of questioning and moves on to another part of the IE's account.

IRs' assumptions about which details hold greater evidential value than others can be shown to be closely related to institutional attitudes toward sexual violence as a whole. A close examination of the details from IEs' narratives that are preserved, deleted, and transformed has the potential to demonstrate this. An example of a potentially problematic gloss appears in excerpt 12.8.

Excerpt 12.8

296 IR: and then what happened?
297 (.)

298 IE: they said "ah s- can we come back to your house" (.) and
299 **I said "ok fine it's not very often I get company" (.)**
300 **didn't have a problem with it.**
301 (5.0)
302 IR: so how had you felt about the night so far with=
303 IE: =okay (.)
304 no problems at all.
305 (3.0)
306 IR: **and you'd said yes because you were w- w- enjoying the**
307 **c[ompany,]**
308 IE: [yeah][I felt safe.]
309 IR: [so then] **you felt safe** •hh what u:m what
310 happened after that then how did you get (.) [home?]

Fairly dramatic changes are made to the IE's account of how the suspect ended up at her home. She directly quotes herself as saying on the night that "it's not very often I get company" and the negative statement "[I] didn't have a problem with it" on lines 299–300, implying that having "a problem with it" might be expected given that one of the men went on to rape her. This is transformed by the IR to "*enjoying* the company" (my emphasis). The contrast between the two is stark, yet the IE issues an instantaneous ratification of the IR's version of events. The fact that the IR restates the reason the IE has given for allowing the men into her home suggests some importance is attached to this element of the story, and that this is behavior requiring explanation. Rather than focusing on the men's reported behavior, for example with a formulation such as "and they'd asked to come back to your house," which might seem more logical given the circumstances (potential evidence of premeditation), the IR instead foregrounds the IE's actions of *allowing* them to come back. This is revealing of a pervasive ideology that places great import on the actions of a woman who makes a claim of rape, particularly when those actions involve inviting the suspect into one's home; the suspect's actions appear to be secondary to this.

Concluding Remarks

I have shown that reflexive language has the potential to be revealing not only of institutional priorities, but also of the ideological assumptions on which those priorities are based. Of course, it could be argued that IRs are attempting to test IEs' accounts with counterclaims that could potentially be made by the suspect or his lawyer (see Antaki, Richardson, Stokoe, and Willott 2015). Nevertheless, the discussion here highlights the fact that police-interview discourse conforms to well-established norms of discourse around sexual violence, particularly in respect of its foregrounding of victims' behavior and obscuring of perpetrator culpability. Formulation and stretches of reported speech function to construct an institutionally beneficial object out of the lay tellings of naive interviewees—a translation process that in itself can prove highly revealing of institutional assumptions about the nature of the crime. As well as displaying IRs' orientation to the absent audience, reflexive practices are highly revealing of what they perceive to be of most value, in that they systematically select elements from IEs' accounts that support or refute particular versions of events. When an IR chooses to reiterate that a victim "said yes because [she] was enjoying the company," or to question what the IE had done to demonstrate that sex was unwanted or what had given the IE the impression that a man in the process of raping her might hurt her, for example, it is useful to explore their motivation for doing so—what potential "versions of events" do these reiterations support?

Reflexive language may be problematic for interviewees to refute in that the words, or at least the force of the message, have been attributed to the interviewees themselves. Although the changes often seem minor and of little consequence, some of the excerpts in this chapter show that simply substituting one word for an apparent synonym can have a significant impact on the way events or people are portrayed. At the micro-level, the very fact that elements of interviewees' reports are presented as the words of the interviewee, through the use of "you said . . ." or 'you mentioned . . . ," makes them particularly difficult to challenge. This difficulty is further compounded by the often swift following-up of reported speech with a question, meaning that any response from the interviewee is expected to relate to the question and not the reported speech, the proposition in which therefore remains unchallenged (and unchallengeable). Although in the case of formulations the rewording is almost invariably offered back to the interviewee for confirmation, the nature of the discourse situation is such that rejection is likely to present difficulties. In terms of those formulations that are produced to display understanding, it is useful to consider the situations in which this has been considered necessary. To produce an utterance whose main purpose is to check mutual understanding is to suggest that intended meaning or intention is not immediately obvious. Thus, when an interviewer produces a third-turn receipt to the effect of "you invited him back because . . . ," it is clear he or she considers the behavior to require an explanation—to the overhearing audience, if not to the interviewer. Therefore, as well as considering the elements that have been preserved, deleted, and transformed in each case, that the formulation was produced at all is in itself revealing of "commonsense" assumptions. That interviewers often perceive victims' behavior to be of more interest than perpetrators' is consistent with the culture of victim blaming that has long been identified by feminist scholars. As Anderson and Doherty point out, "Agency and responsibility are removed from the alleged rapist by casting the victim as the rightful guardian and regulator of his behaviour" (2008: 3). Asking a victim why she allowed two men to come back to her house, rather than attempting to establish why the men wanted to come back to her house, fits neatly into this perception. The significance of these processes cannot be overlooked. Rape victims often face criticism during cross-examination on the basis of inconsistencies between their statement and their testimony. This chapter demonstrates just two of the means by which these supposed inconsistencies might arise.

References

ACPO. 2013. *Advice on the Structure of Visually Recorded Witness Interviews*. 2nd ed. http://library.college.police.uk/docs/APPREF/ACPO-Witness-Interview-Structure-2013.pdf.

Anderson, Irina, and Kathy Doherty. 2008. *Accounting for Rape: Psychology, Feminism and Discourse Analysis in the Study of Sexual Violence*. London: Routledge.

Antaki, Charles, Emma Richardson, Elizabeth Stokoe, and Sara Willott. 2015. "Police Interviews with Vulnerable People Alleging Sexual Assault: Probing Inconsistency and Questioning Conduct." *Journal of Sociolinguistics* 19: 328–35.

Bell, Allan. 1984. "Language Style as Audience Design." *Language in Society* 13: 145–204.

Bell, Allan. 2001. "Back in Style: Reworking Audience Design." In *Style and Sociolinguistic Variation*, edited by Penelope Eckert and John R. Rickford, 139–169. Cambridge: Cambridge University Press.

Bublitz, Wolfram, and Monika Bednarek. 2006. "Reported Speech: Pragmatic

Aspects." In *Encyclopedia of Language & Linguistics*, edited by Keith Brown, 550–553. Oxford: Elsevier.

Garfinkel, Harold, and Harvey Sacks. 1970. "On Formal Structures of Practical Actions." In *Theoretical Sociology: Perspectives and Developments*, edited by John C. McKinney and Edward A. Tiryakian, 337–366. New York: Appleton-Century-Crofts.

Caldas-Coulthard, Carmen Rosa. 1987. "Reporting Speech in Narrative Written Texts." In *Discussing Discourse*, edited by R. M. Coulthard, 149–167. Discourse Analysis Monographs 14. English Language Research, University of Birmingham.

Ehrlich, Susan. 2001. *Representing Rape: Language and Sexual Consent*. London: Routledge.

Fairclough, Norman. 1995. *Critical Discourse Analysis: The Critical Study of Language*. London: Longman.

Goffman, Erving. 1981. *Forms of Talk*. Philadelphia: University of Pennsylvania Press.

Gregory, Jeanette, and Sue Lees. 1999. *Policing Sexual Assault*. London: Routledge.

Haworth, Kate J. 2009. "An Analysis of Police Interview Discourse and Its Role(s) in the Judicial Process." Ph.D. diss., University of Nottingham.

Haworth, Kate, 2010. "Police Interviews in the Judicial Process: Police Interviews as Evidence." In *Routledge Handbook of Forensic Linguistics*, edited by Malcolm Coulthard and Alison Johnson, 169–194. Abingdon: Routledge.

Haworth, Kate. 2013. "Audience Design in the Police Interview: The Interactional and Judicial Consequences of Audience Orientation." *Language in Society* 42(1): 45–69.

Heritage, John. 1985. "Analyzing News Interviews: Aspects of the Production of Talk for an Overhearing Audience." In *Handbook of Discourse Analysis*, Vol. 3, *Discourse and Dialogue*, edited by Teun van Dijk, 95–117. London: Academic Press.

Heritage, John, and D. Rod Watson. 1974. "Formulations as Conversational Objects." In *Everyday Language: Studies in Ethnomethodology*, edited by George Psathas, 123–162. New York: Irvington.

Heydon, Georgina. 2005. *The Language of Police Interviewing: A Critical Analysis*. Basingstoke: Palgrave Macmillan.

Johnson, Alison. 2008. "'From Where We're Sat . . .': Negotiating Narrative Transformation through Interaction in Police Interviews with Suspects." In "Narrative Analysis in the Shift from Texts to Practices," edited by Anna De Fina and Alexandra Georgakopoulou. Special issue, *Text & Talk* 28(3): 327–349.

Matoesian, Gregory M. 1993. *Reproducing Rape: Domination through Talk in the Courtroom*. Chicago: University of Chicago Press.

Ministry of Justice. 2011. "Achieving Best Evidence in Criminal Proceedings: Guidance on Interviewing Victims and Witnesses, and Guidance on Using Special Measures." http://www.cps.gov.uk/publications/docs/best_evidence_in_criminal_proceedings.pdf.

Milne, R. 2004. "The Enhanced Cognitive Interview: A Step-by-Step Guide." [Unpublished police manual.] https://researchportal.port.ac.uk/portal/en/impacts/surrey-police-use-interview-guide-made-by-uop-staff(29bac711-2070-4442-b008-23bfb6b26f4f).html.

Milne, Rebecca. 2016. *CREST Guide: The Cognitive Interview*. https://crestresearch.ac.uk/wp-content/uploads/2016/05/16-006-01.pdf.

Milne, Rebecca, and Ray Bull. 1999. *Investigative Interviewing: Psychology and Practice*. Chichester: Wiley.

Newbury, Phillip, and Alison Johnson. 2006. "Suspects' Resistance to Constraining and Coercive Questioning Strategies in the Police Interview." *International Journal of Speech, Language and the Law* 13(2): 213–240.

Page, Amy D. 2008. "Judging Women and Defining Crime: Police Officers' Attitudes toward Women and Rape." *Sociological Spectrum* 28(4): 389–411.

Rock, Frances. 2010. "Witnesses and Suspects in Interviews. Collecting Oral Evidence; The Police, the Public and the Written Word." In *Routledge Handbook of Forensic Linguistics*, edited by Malcolm Coulthard and Alison Johnson, 126–138. Abingdon: Routledge.

Stokoe, Elizabeth, and Derek Edwards. 2008. "'Did You Have Permission to Smash Your Neighbour's Door?' Silly Questions and Their Answers in Police Suspect Interrogations." *Discourse Studies* 10(1): 89–111.

Westera, Nina J., Mark R. Kebbell, and Becky Milne. 2016. "Want a Better Criminal Justice Response to Rape? Improve Police Interviews with Complainants and Suspects." *Violence against Women* 22(14): 1748–1769.

CHAPTER THIRTEEN

"Are You Saying You Were Stabbed . . . ?"

Multimodality, Embodied Action, and Dramatized Formulations in "Fixing" the Facts in Police Interviews with Suspects

Alison Johnson

Introduction

Police work involves multiple activities in which talk and questioning play key roles: roadside stops (Linfoot-Ham 2007), witness statement-taking (Rock 2001), custody suite interactions (Rock 2007), and interviews with suspects under arrest, which are the focus of this chapter. Questions seek primarily to elicit evidence in relation to an alleged crime, but they also construct an evidential record. Despite forty years of research on questioning in the judicial process, both in police interviews and in courtroom discourse (e.g., Atkinson and Drew 1979; Watson 1983; Matoesian 2001; Heydon 2005; Komter 2006; Stokoe and Edwards 2008; Holt and Johnson 2010; Haworth 2010), only recently has there been an examination of the embodied actions of gesture that accompany speech in the legal process (e.g., Komter 2003; Matoesian 2005, 2010; González-Martínez 2006; Kidwell 2006; Stokoe 2009; Licoppe and Dumoulin 2010; Matoesian and Gilbert 2016). This recent work marks what Nevile describes as "the embodied turn" in interactional research in a wide range of conversational and institutional settings, a turn that reflects "increasing scholarly sensitivity and recognition for how we are always in our bodies" (2015: 141).

I start this chapter by outlining two major problems with police-interview recording practice, which in its current state fails to take into account the bodily nature of interaction. First, because much linguistic research on legal discourse is done by making a written transcript of an audio recording, assigning contextual information such as gestures to minimal comments placed in double brackets, it largely neglects many of the multimodal aspects of meaning-making. For instance, the suspect's second turn below may be transcribed as a three-second silence that is noted as "no reply."

P: So you're saying that Joey's made up this story
S: For all I know yeah
P: which happens to coincide exactly with two statements off two very frightened gi::rls
S: (3.0) ((no reply))

However, when transcribing the combined audiovisual recordings used here, we can see that many of these silences are, in fact, filled with gesture. In the example above, taken from excerpt 13.1 below, the suspect's silence is filled with an emphatic rejection of the implication that he is lying, as he shakes his head from side to side. Other turns may be transcribed with multiple pauses, as we will see in excerpt 13.6, where the police interviewer interrupts the suspect's narrative:

P: [Can I- can I just stop you there (0.5) Danny

(1.0) You say you made a grab for the knife (1.0)

Are you saying you were (2.0)

ss- stabbed with the knife (1.0)

or are you saying you (0.5) grabbed the ↓knife?

This turn has no fewer than six so-called pauses that might suggest the interviewer is planning his speech very carefully (see the Goldman-Eisler hypothesis, 1968, 1972, of pauses as a reflection of cognitive activity). However, a look at the visual record shows us that each of these silences is filled with spectacular gesture (where the interviewer produces stabbing and grabbing actions), in what I am calling a *dramatized formulation*, as the turn is filled with gesture and is one that is prefaced with "You say," repeating the gist of the suspect's words. A multimodal analysis acknowledges the combined spoken and gestural turn as a continuous stretch of communication, rather than speech fragmented by silence. The second problem is that the legal system privileges written interview records (often a summary made by non-linguists) over audio or audiovisual recordings, a "reliance" (Chalmers 2014: 122) that overlooks the embodied talk. In this chapter, therefore, I argue that records that focus only on speech—logocentric records—ignore many important aspects of meaning, and that these records are always limited, imperfect representations of reality. I examine audiovisually recorded interviews to see what is multimodally accomplished in order to establish what is absent from logocentric analyses and records. I focus on sequences containing SAY questions and their accompanying gestures, such as "Are you saying that you were stabbed . . . ?," delivered with a stabbing action or where "you" is accompanied by hand beats that "emphasise salient words" (McNeill 2005: 38). Although SAY indicates a report of speech, we will see that it also combines with gestural actions that turn saying into doing. I therefore argue that the current focus on logocentric records compromises our understanding of meaning and action and undermines justice.

The pragmatic complexity of SAY interrogatives is first created through the metadiscursive phrase "you say/are you saying" (occasionally "tell/telling"), within a yes-or no or declarative question that summarizes a narrative segment from the suspect's prior talk, usually in a recent or previous turn, but occasionally over a large stretch of talk. A SAY question that focuses on a recent or previous suspect's turn constitutes a shift in "footing" (Goffman 1981) from lay telling to institutional asking, challenging suspects on details of their own narrative. Matoesian tells us that the effect of this kind of footing shift "legitimate[s] discursive authority and shape[s] affective meaning in the performance of legal knowledge" (2001: 134). Where the formulation is of a much earlier narrative element, it refocuses the talk, subjecting the suspect's narrative to more challenging scrutiny. Either way, the institutional speaker strategically shifts the direction of the talk, as if rewinding the tape, rather than letting the talk flow forward. The "you say/are you saying" "metadiscursive expression" (Craig and Sanusi 2000: 425) is notably in the simple present tense or the present progressive (the past tense "you said" is very infrequent in the data), marking it as repeating a suspect's talk, the repeat signaling trouble from the interviewer's point of view, a phenomenon illustrated by way of introduction in excerpt 13.1 (SAY questions are indicated by → in the extracts, as in line 1 below). This extract involves an alleged kidnapping of two prostitutes by three suspects, two of whom have been arrested in a house from which the two women escaped while the men were asleep. One suspect is being interviewed and has been read a section from one complainant's statement, giving an account that is materially the same as that of the other arrested suspect, but that differs from his own. Gesture lines are in italics and interleaved between the speech. The speech and gesture should be read as occurring simultaneously. Immediately prior to his first turn, the police interviewer moves forward in his chair, from his listening position holding a complainant statement on his knee in both hands, to a more challenging one, bringing his gaze and the statement closer to the suspect. (The police interview data are introduced fully later.)

Excerpt 13.1: Kidnapping (recording time 20:30:34–20:31:22)

→ P: So you're saying that Joey's made up this story
On "you're" holds out right hand toward S and holds gesture to end of turn. On "this story" looks down at statement and up again.
S: For all I know yeah
S sitting back in chair, arms folded, right leg crossed over left.
P: Which happens to coincide exactly
On exactly points with right hand to statement in left in bouncing movement and looks down at statement and then up again to return gaze to S.
with two statements off two very frightened gi::rls
Holds gaze with S to elicit response.
S: (3.0) ((no verbal reply))
Shakes head from side to side to indicate rejection of allegation.
P: Mmm?
Continues to hold gaze with right hand up to mouth and holds statement in left hand, displayed vertically in front of him under mouth.
S: (2.0) ((no verbal reply))
Shakes head from side to side to indicate continued rejection and silence.

P: It's a bit too much to expect really. Don't you agree?
Statement lowered in left hand and right hand up to mouth.
S: N- not really.
Shakes head from side to side.
P: You don't really agree with that?
Keeps right hand up to mouth; then strokes left cheek with
right index finger.
S: No
S is immobile but gazing at police with arms folded.
P: W- would it help you to-to um (2.0)
Adjusts posture: crosses left leg over right in (2.0).
if I showed you the video (1.0)
Moves back in chair and moves gaze away from S and
toward recording equipment.
or part of the video of Joey's interview
Statement held down on knees again.
would it help you to accept what I'm saying↑
Holds statement vertically in front of him and then up to hide
mouth. Looks back at S while waiting for response; holds gaze.
S: (5.0)
Shakes head side to side throughout (5.0) and returns gaze.
→ P: So what you're saying is
On "you" extends left hand in point.
that what Joey has said is lies↑
On "Joey" makes a double waving beat.
S: Yeah
Nods down once in a beat on "yeah."
P: I put it to you that you're↑ not telling me the truth↓
Extends left hand on "you" and beats on "you're."
S: (0.5) You're entitled to your own opinion.
Shrugs in (0.5).
P: Mm↓ (4.0)
Drops gaze with suspect and returns to papers to start next
point.

The repeated SAY question (line 1, continued on lines 7–12 and 43–46) challenges the suspect to consider the impossibility of his claim, recruiting both the complainant's statement by pointing to it in order to display and objectify it (lines 8, 17, and 39), and the co-suspect's video interview (lines 33–36), and using gesture (pointing) and gaze to amplify the persuasive confrontation. Gestural enrichment of the formulations and their immediate environment includes: beating hand gestures and deictic pointing, emphasizing *you* (excerpt 13.1, lines 8, 44, and 46); changing posture to coincide with a tactical change of approach (immediately before line 1 and lines 32 and 34); and, at the end of the formulations, to confront the suspect with the trouble and seek a response (lines 10, 12, 16, and 40). In contrast to the "you're saying" formulation, the suspect refers to "Joey," "the girls," and what "I'm saying," making the conflicting accounts persistently salient.

Taking Matoesian's notion of "production media" (2001: 133), which draws attention to the means of producing intertextual authority through reported speech, we can see that the police formulations in excerpt 13.1 draw attention to the suspect's contradictory position by presenting the co-suspect's story as "lies," a word not used by the suspect. The proposition is produced by the police as being doubtful, through combinations of words (the two complainants give "ex<u>act</u>ly" the same version of events), prosody (emphasis on the dominant syllable of ex<u>act</u>ly), gestures (pointing deictically to the statement in his other hand), and mobilizing the material object of the statement as an artifact, which becomes the "center of attention" (Matoesian 2013: 635), thereby morally evaluating the suspect's position as untenable. The formulations are dramatized to problematize the suspect's position and cue his reconsideration. Long silences (such as the five seconds in line 41) may be interpreted as the suspect's exercising his right to silence, when in fact he is actively signaling a rejection of the proposition by shaking his head throughout. This brings new relevance to the right to silence: gestures indicate that the suspect has something to say here, and the interviewer should have made a verbal note that he was shaking his head.

Formulations

In reported speech, what is repeated is a quotation or paraphrase; however, Tannen (1989: 17) uses the term *constructed dialogue* to indicate that there is no report at all, but a recontextualization of some verbiage that *replays* the prior interaction (Clift and Holt 2007: 7). A formulation should also be treated as constructed dialogue rather than quoted speech. Komter found that formulations are an important resource for stating "the record-thus-far" in police records (2006: 201). For Garfinkel and Sacks, a formulation is the treatment by a conversational participant of some part of it "as an occasion to describe that conversation, to explain it, or characterize it, or explicate, or translate, or summarize, or furnish the gist of it" (1970: 350). For Heritage and Watson, studying news interviews, formulations "characterize states of affairs already described or negotiated . . . in the preceding talk" (1979: 126). And in an earlier work they describe formulations as manifesting three central properties, which indicate the powerful ideologically motivated work they do: *preservation* (of *selected* aspects), *transformation*, and *deletion* of some aspects (Heritage and Watson 1977: 2–3). That these occur in police interviews, then, is unsurprising, as they have the power to take a suspect's preceding talk and transform it into a more powerful institutional version, selecting only those elements that are ideologically important, persuasively controlling meaning and repositioning the suspect. Heydon found that they are powerful because, although they appear to summarize to achieve understanding, the selections, transformations, and deletions "systematically introduce terms of violence and intentionality that were not present in the original utterances" (2005: 141). We will see that they also introduce gestural violence. The present tense or progressive aspect—"you say/are you saying"—also marks a real-time contest, combining physical and verbal struggle. For Drew, in a formulation, a speaker "offer[s] his or her interpretation of what the other meant" (2003: 296), generally taking the form "(So) what you mean/are saying is . . . ," as we see in the data here. In this chapter I show how gestures that accompany formulations dramatize the evidence production, hence *dramatized formulation*, to challenge, contest, and undermine suspects' self-proclaimed nonculpable identity and attempt to transform suspects' actions from routine, defensive, or true to deviant, offensive, and lies.

Gesture and Bodily Interaction

For both McNeill (2005: 22) and Goodwin (2000: 1498), gesture is not a mere accompaniment to talk, nor is it redundant. For Streeck (2009, 2010), too, gesture is central to the human way of being in the world and for "manufacturing meaning" in what he calls "ecologies of gesture." Gesture is something that speakers work into their talk, making speech and gesture "semiotic fields that participants demonstrably orient to" (Goodwin 2000: 1490). In this way "the human body is made publicly visible as the site for a range of structurally different kinds of displays implicated in the constitution of actions of the moment" (Goodwin 2000: 1492; see also Kendon 2004). Gesture and talk are not discrete properties of interaction, but are "integrated components of a common process for the social production of meaning and action" (Goodwin 2000: 1490). Gesture is social because it "requires that not only the party producing an action, but also that others present, such as its addressee, be able to systematically recognize . . . what is occurring." McNeill talks of speech and gesture's "unbreakable bond" (2005: 24–26) and shows empirically that they are transferred to memory interchangeably; gestures can be remembered as speech and vice versa (see also McNeill 1992).

For McNeill (2005: 38–39), there is a quartet of gesture categories: iconic ("images of concrete entities," which are "picturable"), metaphoric ("images of the abstract"), beat (hand beats to highlight salient words), and deictic (pointing to objects or people in the context). Gestures can be loaded with one or more of these categories at once. Each gesture has an *anatomy* that defines its start, progress, and end. This can be shown with {optional} parts and one obligatory *stroke*, which we can show as: {preparation} ^ {pre-stroke hold} ^ stroke ^ {stroke hold} ^ {poststroke hold} ^ {retraction} (31–33). *Preparation* involves the limb moving away from a rest position and *retraction* returns it to a rest position. The interviewer's preparation in excerpt 13.1 is to change posture before pointing on "you" with his right hand and then holding that hand out in appeal. It is only retracted fully after the second formulation, when he returns to looking at his papers (line 54). Held gestures stop the movement to wait and synchronize it with "a specific linguistic segment" (32), such as "you." In both of the interviews that we examine suspects usually sit with arms crossed, as if tensing their bodies against leaked gestures. McNeill also describes two *gestural viewpoints*: a first-person or character viewpoint and a third-person or observer viewpoint (34); these work particularly in iconic gestures (see also Kopp, Tepper, and Cassell 2004), such as stabbing, as we shall see.

Since the police interview record performs "a number of very important functions in the criminal process—to enable Crown Prosecutors to make their decisions, to be disclosed to the defence and to be used in court" (Baldwin and Bedward 1991: 673), the layered meanings that are created and then, as we will see, lost are a matter of concern.

The Police Interview Record in the Judicial Context

The Police and Criminal Evidence Act (1984; PACE) required police in England and Wales to audio-record interviews with suspects in criminal cases, outlawing the previous use of contemporaneous written notes. When a suspect is charged with an offense and committed for trial, a written Record of Taped Interview (ROTI), a summary of the interview, is usually prepared by the police from the audio recording; this is the preferred form for use in court, since it can easily be copied and handled. Recordings are rarely played, except in the case of special measures for vulnerable and intimidated witnesses to give their evidence on video, made possible by the Youth Justice and Criminal Evidence Act (1999). The more general audiovisual recording of most witness interviews or suspect interviews is not the usual practice in England and Wales, or in many parts of the world, although since 2010 (PACE Code F 2010) audiovisual recordings of interviews with suspects have been allowed where suitable equipment is available.[1]

We know that gaps and errors occur during the creation of the ROTI from the audio recording (see Baldwin and Bedward 1991; Haworth 2010), but the audio recording itself discards the visual semiotic channel, making this practice doubly problematic. This has real-world implications, since these monomodal "facts" are "fixed in the legal discourse"; furthermore, once the oral record is converted to text, it "creates a singularity of meaning" that "not only makes discourse appear factual, but also objectifies it" (Kozin 2008: 220). Since police interviews have resonance and reverberations that gain in strength as they "travel" (see Heffer, Rock, and Conley 2013) throughout the judicial process, treated as a courtroom object (Johnson 2014), we should consider the value of the whole event: speech with embodied action, not just speech written down.

Transcription of audio- and videotape is problematized by Goodwin (1994: 607) and Bucholtz (2000: 1439), who draw our attention to the "politics of representation/transcription." Bucholtz mentions forensic linguistic studies that have "pointed out the real-world consequences of choices made during the transcription process" (1439) outlining a case in which she was involved as an expert. She shows how "interpretive decisions" in transcribing the videotape mean that a police officer "comes across as an honorable fellow," "compassionate," and "a man of his word," while, on the other hand, a "criminal eagerly confess[es] to his crime" (1444). Transcription, she says, is partial and powerful. Goodwin's (1994: 606–620) multimodal analysis of an amateur video of Rodney King's police beating in 1991 and the subsequent trials of four police officers in 1992 and 1993 draws our attention to the "practical problem" of transcription practices that produce a "professional vision," one that is "selective" and "contested," and arrived at through "socially organized ways of seeing and understanding events that are answerable to the distinctive interests of a particular social group." As Goodwin also notes, his and my analysis both make "extensive use of the very same practices it is studying," and "the rich record of complicated vocal and visual events . . . provided by a videotape must be transformed into something that can silently inhabit the printed page" (1994: 607). It is therefore necessary to say something below about transcription.

Police interview structure, as seen in these interviews, has five stages: (1) dealing with the tapes, participant introductions, stating the reason for arrest, cautioning; (2) collecting background information on the suspect's life; (3) free narrative, where the suspect is invited to tell the story in his or her own words with minimal interruption or questioning; (4) questioning, which in both interviews includes reading excerpts from witness interviews; and (5) closing and dealing with the tapes. It is stages 3 and 4 that produce the dramatized formulations that are the focus of this chapter.

Data and Methodology

The two video-recorded interviews are from a collection made in England between 1989 and 1990 (reported in Baldwin and Bedward 1991; Baldwin 1992, 1993); some of these were made available for this research with permission from one police force. The interviews represent two investigations that were carried out in the same police station by different interviewing officers in November 1989. Although the interviews are now old, their use is justified here, as there are consistencies in interviewing practice between then and now—that is, interviews are all post-PACE, video-recorded police interviews are rarely available to researchers, and the data have not previously been analyzed in terms of the multimodal elements. Multimodal analysis is particularly relevant to this context, as there has been scant application, as detailed above. A qualitative discourse analysis of the videos is conducted, revealing multiple examples of dramatized formulations and allowing microanalysis of the phenomenon and its pragmatic effects.

Interview 1 (*Kidnapping*) concerns an allegation of kidnapping two prostitutes by three men and holding the women against their will; there are two suspects in custody. It is in two parts, with a break in between stages 3 and 4 (in which the other suspect is interviewed), and lasts nearly two hours in total. All of the dramatized formulations are in stage 4. Interview 2 (*AttMurder*) concerns an allegation of attempted murder. It lasts an hour and thirty minutes and covers stage 1 to partway through stage 4, where the officer breaks, intending to further interview later in the day. I do not have a second videotape, but the incompleteness of the interview does not affect the analysis, as I trace two formulations that are linked between stages 3 and 4. Both interviews are conducted by two male detectives; in *AttMurder* the suspect is accompanied by a solicitor (called an attorney in the U.S. system). In one of the extracts a second police officer, a note taker, appears in a gestural turn; at all other times they are silent.

The video image shows the interview room from two angles: (1) a close-up of the suspect in the upper left and (2) a fish-eye view of the whole room showing all participants, allowing for observation of gaze (between interviewer and suspect), gesture, and note-taking, as shown in figure 13.1. There are a number of objects pointed out: ashtray, trash can, recording stand, pens, and papers. These come into play in the interviews and form part of the gestural and ecological field.

Speech transcription is carried out according to Jefferson's conventions (2004).[2] There are a number of multimodal transcription systems; McNeill (2005) uses square brackets around the word(s) that coincide with gestures, and Goodwin (1994) uses transcripts accompanied by drawings. I have decided to use interlinear notes in italics for gesture lines. This choice shows the oral and gestural channels separately, allowing the reader to see what would be missed if the transcript were simply of the speech. However, they can also be read simultaneously, emphasizing the synchronized layering of talk, prosody, and gesture.

FIGURE 13.1. Video image from the interview room from two angles

Doing Things with Words, Gestures, and Objects

In both interviews, there are many examples of SAY questions, occurring in stage 4 (the questioning stage), making this a phenomenon primarily of interrogation. We first examine the use of dramatized formulations (excerpts 13.2–13.5), all from *Kidnapping*, to show how they contribute to the intensification of contested meaning over time. Excerpt 13.1, introduced above, fits chronologically into the sequence of extracts below: 2, 3, (1) 4, 5. We then look at a second phenomenon in *AttMurder*. Here, a formulation that is produced in stage 3 (excerpt 13.6) is returned to for more rigorous treatment in stage 4 (excerpt 13.7). In all occurrences the interviewer uses the question to mark a problem with a detail in the suspect's narrative and to subject it to scrutiny.

The pragmatically highlighted trouble in each extract points to the suspect's account as unbelievable or implausible (excerpt 13.2), disputed, and therefore a lie (excerpts 13.1 and 13.3), incredible (excerpt 13.4), and untruthful and impossible (excerpt 13.5). At the same time, the other witnesses' accounts are presented as the truthful ones, including the co-suspect's. "Say" questions therefore signal institutional disbelief. The suspect's version is contrasted unfavorably with the other accounts and also overtly assessed as "incredible" (excerpt 13.4), "impossible" (excerpt 13.5, line 20), and "not true" (emphasized in three mentions in excerpt 13.5, lines 30, 32, and 35). Although "you say" is a paradigmatic choice that implicitly invokes a contradictory "I/we/he/she/they say," we see that these other voices are also explicitly and multimodally drawn in, increasing the pressure on the suspect to reconsider his story: "they" (the two female complainants in excerpt 13.2), "Joey" and "the two girls" (excerpts 13.1 and 13.3), "these three people" (excerpt 13.4), and "everyone" (excerpt 13.5). Prosodic and gestural emphasis draws the suspect's attention to the "presence" of these people in the room, and the interviewer confirms, "I can verify the version of events" (excerpt 13.5, line 6).

Excerpt 13.2: Kidnapping, 20:25:01 (offering the complainants' version)

1 P: Do you agree that this description
2 *Left-hand beat on "agree" while looking at statement in right*
3 *hand on knee.*
4 is very similar to you? Coffee-colored skin, mustache,
5 *Reads from one complainant's statement from "coffee."*
6 gold chains, wearing a pleam- (1.0) cream and black jumper [sweater]
7 that was oblong and checked and chunky.
8 S: (2.0)
9 *Shakes head back and forth slowly in (2.0), indicating no*
10 *comment.*
11 P: That's very similar to you, isn't it.
12 *Looks directly at suspect.*
13 In fact you've just said just now that it was so similar to you
14 *Deictic pointing at suspect on "you" held. Beat on "said" and*
15 *"now."*
16 that you thought they've ((complainants)) looked at you in the
17 *Deictic pointing at suspect on "you."*
18 bedroom and given that description to try and implicate you

(2.5)
S: ((grunts))
Nods agreement.
→ P: That's what you're saying↑?
Gazes at suspect; left- hand beat on "say"; statement in right.
S: Mhm
Nods agreement.

Excerpt 13.3: Kidnapping, 20:26:54 (offering the co-accused's version)

P: Would you like me to show you the video of Joey
Left hand to side of mouth; on "show" offers it out open toward S.
(0.5) describing the versions of events (1.0) saying that he met
Beats toward suspect on "describing" and "met."
you on Friday night that you went out together on Saturday↑
Beats toward suspect on "went."
S: What you're telling me I believe you but it's not-
On "tell" extends left hand palm up toward interviewer and holds.
it's no use me saying- watching the video 'cause I know it would-
No.
Continues hold and beats on "No"; retracts to refold arms.
→ P: So are you saying that Joey's lying and he's invented
all this?
Moves forward in seat, uncrosses legs and holds statement with both hands during lines 6 and 7.
S: I don't know. I don't know. That's [why-
Shakes head.
P: [What are you saying?
Moves papers to left hand and puts right hand up to mouth.
S: What I'm saying is that I was not in ((place))
On "not" and ((place)) nods head down.
and I was not driving no car.
On "no" shakes head.
P: So why would Joey say that? (0.5)
Sitting forward, holds statement with left hand: on "Joey" waves left hand at S.
S: I don't know↑.
Shrugs right shoulder and shakes head.

P: Why would the two gir::ls say that? (1.0) Mm?
Still sitting forward with statement in left hand; points to it on "girls."
S: I don't know. I don't know.
Shakes head slowly back and forth.
P: OK. I'll carry on.
On "OK" snaps right hand fingers; holds statement with both hands; sits back.

Excerpt 13.4: Kidnapping, 20.43.26 (incredulity)

Interviewer and suspect are both sitting forward in their chairs. Suspect is holding a plastic cup in his left hand (tea was brought at 20:13:00) and cigarette in right hand clasped together in front of him.

→ P: Are you saying that these three people have (0.6)
On "these three" flaps the statement with left hand.
conspired to set you up↑?
S: Yeah for all I know it could be yeah
On "could" extends both arms wide in front of him and holds until interviewer finishes next turn.
(0.3) I don't know.
P: Don't you think that's a bit (0.1) incredible?
Gazes at S who on "incredible" reclaps hands, cup and cigarette; looks down.
S: No.
Shakes head.

Excerpt 13.5: Kidnapping, 21:12:11 (reconsider the truth because your version's impossible [gestures are included only from line 16 on])

P: I'll put it to you once again (0.3)
we:re you in that car when these two girls were picked up?
S: No::(4.0) I was never in no car.
P: A- I'll a::sk you once more to- to reconsider what
→ you're telling us for the reasons I explained earlier and I'll
explain them to you again. I can verify the version of events
[that I've given t' you
S: [No (0.3) I'm not changing. No. (6.0)
P: Would you like to think very carefully about why::
I'm asking you to do that (0.2) simply because the version of

11 events you're giving me (0.2) the fact that everybody describes
12 you being there when it happens and you yourself admit that
13 you were at the house.
14 S: Yeah
15→ P: But (1.0) you then sa::y (1.0)
16 *Holding statement with both hands. On "but" points up with*
17 *right index finger to beat and down to left hand.*
18 you weren't driving the car when you picked up the girls (0.2)
19 *On "you" points right hand at S and holds.*
20 you weren't in the car on the way down to London
21 *Continues hold; beats on "you" and holds again with hand*
22 *vertical.*
23 (0.2) and you slept ↑pea::cefully all night in that house
24 *Continues hold; on "slept peacefully" sweeps hand from right*
25 *to left and holds.*
26 and never knew anything was happening.
27 *Continues hold.*
28 S: Yes.
29 *Suspect gazing at interviewer.*
30 P: That (0.1) version of events is not true (0.5)
31 *Beats right hand on "that" and "events" with palm down.*
32 what you're telling me is not true (0.4)
33 *S hangs head down looking at floor. Interviewer rests*
34 *right hand.*
35 Not only is it not ↑true (0.3) but it is very likely ↓impossible.
36 *On "true" S looks up to left and right toward video camera and*
37 *down again.*
38 S: It's impossible↑
39 *Looks half up at interviewer and shrugs and shakes head.*

In excerpts 13.1 and 13.3 a video recording of the co-suspect's interview is multimodally indexed as an evidential object, showing that interviewers orient to the record-making (see also Mondada 2003) but also make suspects aware of it. The suspect's resistance to changing his story is thereby implied as absurd. In excerpt 13.5, line 8, the suspect orients to this implication, saying "I'm not changing," accepting only that he was in the house, prompting the interviewer to launch a final SAY question, this time prefaced with "but" (line 15), intensifying the adversarial tone and institutional power.

In each of the extracts we can see the importance of interviewer gaze, prosodic emphasis that coincides with gestural beats around "you," deictic pointing to contradictory evidence in the complainant statement, held gestures to keep the important words in play, and change of posture to mark the challenge of the SAY question; furthermore, (in excerpt 13.1, lines 8–11, excerpt 13.2, lines 1-7, and excerpt 13.4, lines 1–2) the complainant statement in the interviewer's hands iconically and metonymically stands in for the three voices that contradict his own. The SAY questions are generally lengthy, and the held and rhythmic gestures, such as in excerpt 13.5 (lines 16–27), help list the problems with the "you say" position. There are three problematic, negative "you" statements, emphasized with three gestures: a right-hand point (line 19), a beat (line 21), and a sweeping gesture from left to right that is held to the end of the turn (lines 24–27). All of these interviewer actions confront the suspect, resulting in responding gestures, such as head shaking, shrugs, and, eventually, gaze avoidance and head hanging, which signal that the import of the questions is recognized by the suspect, though he resists transforming his story. All of this is lost in a logocentric record. Many of these gestures co-occur with prosodic features in the speech or fill apparent pauses or silence, making them crucial parts of the communication.

The SAY question represents a site of challenging institutional struggle, because what the suspect says is contrasted with what other witnesses say. In "Kidnapping" the suspect resists the transformations offered by consistently rejecting the police formulations. Nevertheless, the interviewer has institutionally undermined the suspect's understated role in the alleged crime. A multimodal transcription record shows that, far from being disengaged, silent, and offering no reply to questions, the suspect holds the interviewer's gaze to signal engagement and emphatically rejects and denies the formulations through shaking his head and using downward nods with "no."

Moving to the "AttMurder" interview, unlike in "Kidnapping," where the SAY questions are confined to the questioning stage, there are twelve SAY questions in the free-narrative stage. In excerpt 13.6 I examine one of these instances where the formulation only briefly interrupts the suspect's narration to offer an alternative version, while in excerpt 13.7 we see the formulation restated in stage 4 questioning. The SAY question (in excerpt 13.6, lines 9–24) does not invoke "we/he/she/they say," as in the examples in "Kidnapping," because other voices have yet to enter the interview, but it does mark disbelief. The shift in both participants' footings from storyteller to listener and from listener to interrogator and back represents a brief moment of institutional struggle. In lines 1–10 the suspect is narrating the point at which his girlfriend was stabbed during a fight with him (she is in hospital with 17 stab wounds and two collapsed lungs) following a party at their home, after the guests had left and a female friend and her child had rctired upstairs to sleep. The suspect sits straight and motionless throughout lines 1–10, both feet apart on the floor, his bandaged right hand clasping his left, which is in a cast. The interviewer is also in a resting posture. Then he strategically shifts his posture and produces a SAY question accompanied by a fully formed gestural sequence, consisting of preparation^ pre-stroke hold^stroke^double-stroke hold^retraction, extending over 14 lines (11–24).

Excerpt 13.6: AttMurder, 15:26:32–15:27:38 (from narration to interrogation and back)

S: Uh I remember one of the drawers was pulled out
because I tripped over it (4.0) er (0.5) and we started arguing
(1.0) and she was screaming at me a:nd (4.0) she hit me (1.0)
u::h I think I made a gra::b at her to stop with my left hand (1.0)
a:::nd the next thing I kne::w was that she'd (0.5) stuck a knife
in my hand (2.0) a::nd (1.0) there was bloo:::d. I remember
seeing the bloo:d. I don't know where.
NT: *On "where" stops taking notes and raises right*
hand to mouth.
S: I presume she got the knife off the [draining bo-
P: [Can I- can I just stop you there (0.5) Danny
***Preparation:** on "stop" extends fingers of left hand while still*
*clasped and **holds.***
→ (1.0) You say you made a grab for the knife (1.0)
*Continues with **hold.***
→ Are you saying you were (2.0)
On "were" raises right hand up in a fist; in (2.0) lowers it half
*down; **stroke.***
ss- stabbed with the knife (1.0)
On "ss-" raises right hand; on "stabbed" slaps hand down to
flat left palm.
→ or are you saying you (0.5) grabbed the ↓knife?
On "(0.5) grabbed" fully extends left arm & fist in grab

toward S; ***stroke ends.***
S: No no I think what actually ha::ppened was that
Nods head downward on "no" and looks down at hand.
(1.0) that I made to grab (0.5) he::r with my left ha::nd [(1.0)
On "(0.5) he::r" looks at interviewer and unclasps left, injured
hand and extends it, opening fingers to form a wide grasp in the
space between the suspect and interviewer.
and the next thing I knew was [the] knife
P: [yep]
In resting posture, arms recrossed.
S: had gone into (0.5) my hand.
On "into (0.5)" points with first and second right fingers to his
injury under his left hand's cast.
P: Can you describe the knife?

Let us examine excerpt 13.6 in three parts: suspect narration (lines 1–10); police interruption with a dramatized formulation (lines 11–24); and suspect rebuttal (lines 25–36), before the police move on to return him to narration (line 26). In the narration section, note that there are multiple unfilled silences, during which there is no bodily action by the suspect. His speech is controlled and labored and his body is similarly controlled and closed to action. The interruption section is marked by the police note taker stopping writing, as if signaling a point for interrogation. The synchrony of "stop" with the iconic gesture of the stop sign (line 12) interrupts the suspect, while at the same time the interviewer bodily advances into the suspect's personal space, coordinating the move with verbal encroachment on his narrative. The interviewer's gestures are incrementally built so that he does not immediately become gesturally violent but builds up to it, from an initial left-hand movement while the right hand is still passive (lines 12–13), to engagement with his right hand (line 17) and then both hands (lines 20–21), before returning to listening mode (end of line 24). Most notably, however, the multiple silences are definitely not accounted for by speech planning. Instead, a major, iconic, gestural sequence co-occurs with these silences, producing coordinated, laminated speech and gesture across a turn. A transcription that records only speech and silence ("You say you made a grab for the knife (1.0). Are you saying you were (2.0) ss- stabbed with the knife (1.0) or are you saying you (0.5) grabbed the knife↓?") therefore fails to acknowledge the important communicative weight carried by the gestural layer. The silences are used to enact grabbing and stabbing actions with a knife and to confront the suspect with his own action, the police officer inhabiting the narrative and enacting it from a first-person perspective in which the officer becomes the alleged murderer. Two sequential events from the suspect's narration are taken up by the interviewer: "I made a gra::b at her to stop" (line 4) and "she'd stuck a knife in my hand" (lines 5–6) in his "you say/are you saying" formulations (lines 14, 16, and 22). Here he "animates" the suspect's words and, in the reported speech that follows this "production format" (Goffman 1981), transforms them into "made a grab for the knife" (line 14). Subtle changes to the prepositions—"at (her)" becomes "for (the knife)"—render a defensive action an offensive one, with the noun complements of the prepositions also changing from "her" (unstressed) to "the knife" (stressed), making the knife a more salient "discursive object" (Kozin 2008). "Stop" is omitted altogether. As well as animating the suspect's voice, it also assesses him and his actions for the prosecution's case to come, taking "a moral stance" that reflects the "strategic interests [of the police] in shaping the production and reception of utterances" (Matoesian 2001: 109). Whereas the suspect's narrative featured the grabbing first and the stabbing second (he does not use the word "stab"), the officer reverses the actions, strategically disrupting the narrative and reframing it into one about the suspect's actions and not his girlfriend's. Blame shifts from victim to suspect; the police view is that he grabs the knife for offensive purposes, during which he sustains a self-inflicted injury.

It is not surprising, then, that in the rebuttal section the suspect rejects (line 25) both the change and the implication that his injury was self-inflicted and emphatically denies with a double "no," the second one stressed with an accompanying downward nod (line 26), restating, but emphasizing, his version; "he::r" is stressed and elongated and marked with an iconic grab and a returned gaze at the interviewer, as the suspect begins to dramatize his own speech. He then shifts his gaze from the interviewer to index his injured hand, using an iconic two-finger knife action showing how it entered "into my hand" (lines 35–36). Adding "what actually ha::ppened" (line 25) to his more-than-"no" answer marks his sustained disalignment with the interviewer. A wide and open-fingered hand grasp (line 29) is consistent with grabbing a bulky person, not a knife; the iconic two-fingered knife gesture (line 35) exhibits the blade entering his hand with a small local movement, rather than the high raised hand and violent downward whole-handed stab demonstrated by the interviewer. This extended, multimodal rejection successfully avoids the police's fixing of the facts. In his rebuttal the suspect downplays both the stabbing and the victim's agency—"she'd stuck a <u>knife</u> in my <u>hand</u>" (line 5) becomes "the knife had gone <u>in</u>to my hand" (line 34)—delexicalizing the verb "stuck" and revising to "gone into," and focusing in both speech and gesture on his invasive injury.

The dialogic, institutional contest in the formulation and rebuttal is vigorous and highly charged: each tries to inscribe his own meanings on the narrated events as meanings are multimodally offered, attached, and detached. As Bakhtin (1981: 337) says, "The more extensive, differentiated and highly developed the social life of a speaking collective, the greater is the importance attaching . . . to another's word," since it "will be the subject of passionate communication, an object of interpretation, discussion, evaluation, rebuttal, support." Interpretation, evaluation, and rebuttal are all passionately expressed here through the stressed lexical choices and iconic actions demonstrating each participant's contrasting and competing position. While the interviewer exploits a first-person viewpoint that forces the suspect to view himself performing the action, the suspect responds iconically to unfix the facts, reinforcing his version of events (a self-defense response to the victim's attack on him, rather than his aggressive control of the knife) with speech and action that emphasize his alleged victimhood. The simultaneous prosodic and embodied emphasis by the two speakers "laminates" (Goodwin 2013: 11–12) the interaction with a raised level of passionate communication that constitutes this dramatic change in footing from measured monologic narration and listening to dynamic verbal and gestural action. The interviewer chooses not to pursue the suspect's rejection of the formulation here (because doing so would interfere detrimentally with the free-narrative account), moving back to listener posture. This signals a return to narration, which continues for a further 82 turns.

The SAY questions in stage 3 incrementally lead to an interviewer stance of disbelief that in the questioning stage moves to suggesting that the suspect's account is not wholly true, as he deals first with the female guest's statement and then with that of a male guest who was one of the last to leave. The victim's hospital-bed account is also presented, and then the officer turns to the doctor's statement as the dramatized formulation and the suspect's account of his injury is returned to nearly an hour after its first mention (at 15:27, excerpt 13.7). A "you tell me" formulation is used here (line 5). Interlinear gestures are provided only from line 14. Of note, however, is that the interviewer makes no iconic gestures at the mention of the grabbing or stabbing (lines 6–7), presenting these as already settled facts, sitting in resting mode.

Excerpt 13.7: AttMurder, 16:19:13–16:20:30 (returning to the stabbing and grabbing)

P: Um (1.0) Quite clearly Danny obviously something
has happened between you a- a- and Rosie. I mean that's an
understatement isn't it [(1.0) quite a violent argument.
S: [right]
P: Now you tell me that she attacked you and you had
this incident with your hand that (1.0) you either grabbed the
knife or she stabbed you [(1.0)
S: [right]
P: Uh (1.0) now I've also spoken to the doctor that's
treated you at Hill hospital [(1.0)
S: [right]
P: In an effort to try and clarify how you may have come
by [(1.0) your injuries.
S: [right]
P: Now here again, Mr Johnson ((solicitor)) I haven't
got his statement so I'm going from [memory.
SOL: [right]
P: I was particularly interested to find out as to whether
On "whether" raises left hand up in the air to start stab action,
but abandons.
it was in fact a stab wound (1.0) or whether it was a defensive
wound. By that I mean whether y- she was attacking you-
Lowers hand and rests on folded right arm.
S: (2.0)
Nods.
P: You perhaps may have grabbed the blade of the knife
On "perhaps" raises left hand; on "blade" makes a grab
forward & down.
in a panic. Now in fairness he said that could have happened.
What a::lso could have happened and I put it to you is this (3.0)
that on one of the instances that- (1.0) we accept that you
stabbed Rosie (1.0) that your hand may have slipped
On "slipped" gives vigorous nod beat & on "blade-" raises left

hand to head.
from the blade- (1.0) from the handle down the blade.
Lowers hand down to side of left leg in open clasped
stabbing/slipping action.
S: No.

The extended "you tell me" formulation that invokes the long-distant turn from excerpt 13.6 continues over the entirety of excerpt 13.7, with only minimal responses from the suspect and solicitor. By adding "I put it to you" (line 30), the interviewer introduces a modified hypothesis on the origin of suspect's injury, which is tentatively offered (note "whether," lines 18, 21, and 22; "perhaps" and "may," line 26; "could," line 29; and "may," line 32) and displayed in new words and gestures (lines 32–37). Here, rather than grabbing the knife from the victim, the suspect is presented as being injured as his hand slips from the handle to the blade while stabbing her. The SAY question is also prefaced by the deictic discourse marker "now," signaling the importance of the immediate present as a space in which the interrogation strategy emphasizes what is "important for the establishment of a particular point" (Schiffrin 1987: 8). The suspect responds by preparing for a revelation, taking a drag from his cigarette, leaning down to stub it out in the ashtray on the floor, and exhaling smoke toward the interviewer (during lines 11–14) as he begins to deliver his new hypothesis with "what also could have happened" (line 30). The new hypothesis is consistent with the interviewer's view, supported by invoking the doctor, that the suspect's injury is self-inflicted. Enacted again from a first-person viewpoint, but with a new grabbing and slipping action, it is designed to confront. Although the suspect again rejects the formulation (line 38), there ensues a lengthy two-minute interrogation over these details (compared with the brief 30-second treatment in stage 3) in which the suspect recognizes the significance of the proposition but offers the same animated "what actually happened" explanation with a repeated iconic enactment of the blade entering his hand and then adding "like that," enhancing it by forcefully punching his fist down on his injury, thereby producing an important dramatized denial for his defense. Nevertheless, the hypothesis has entered into the police record with the possibility of corroboration from the doctor.

What the suspect says now, in defense, is a matter for argument in court. "Say" and "tell" are, after all, crucial words in police interviews, given that suspects are asked to "tell in your own words what happened" and cautioned that they "do not have to say anything, but it may harm your defense if you do not mention when questioned something which you later rely on in court."[3] As we have seen, however, nods, shaking of the head, and iconic actions, though important communicative devices, will not count as mentions, since they are often not recorded.

Conclusions

Dramatized SAY (and TELL) questions are powerful adversarial devices that do important pragmatic work: (re)focusing suspects on problematic details of their stories; confrontationally and persuasively bringing other people and objects into the interaction; "doing things with things" (Streeck 1996); marking trouble and disbelief; and shaping, transforming, and contesting suspect narratives. Material objects, such as statements or video recordings, can be shared with or offered to suspects and used as nonshared objects of police authority. Dramatized formulations can occur sequentially in stage 4's questioning, building a context of disbelief (as in "Kidnapping"), or they can appear and reappear across stages 3 and 4 (as in "AttMurder"), first momentarily treating a detail with disbelief but then returning to carry out a more invasive examination. Interviewer first-person enactments of actions with iconic objects (the knife in "AttMurder") produce provocative, multimodal narrative alternatives that force suspects to hear and watch interviewer performances and respond. The combative nature of dramatized formulations is oriented to by suspects, stimulating matched, dueling physical and verbal responses from otherwise rather passive suspects. Though there is little shift in mental position as suspects reject the police formulating moves, at the same time they contest facts, and their disputation is recognized and marked in the record. As Heffer notes of cross-examination questions in court, "the metalinguistic markers of assertion" ("suggest," "put to," "saying") are used to "assert a version of events which conflicts with that of the witness," placing this version "clearly on stage" (2005: 137–138). Using gesture with these markers (SAY, TELL, and PUT TO) enhances visual staging in a rehearsal for the courtroom, providing both prosecuting and defense advocates with material.

There are a number of methodological implications. As Goodwin (1994) tells us, transcription favors a particular view and presents considerable dangers for "professional vision," but there are also benefits. The interlinear transcription of gesture, posture, gaze, and object manipulation exposes the synchronized layers of speech and gesture and highlights what McNeill calls the "double essence" of interaction, where there is a "dialectic" between gesture and speech (2005: 23). Pauses and silences, far from being empty, are integral elements in gestural sequences, part of an unfragmented stream of talk where gestures are prepared for, executed, and retracted in combination with prosodically emphasized words. This is possible only because of the audiovisual mode. Although it is not practical to suggest detailed multimodal transcription for police records or by lawyers, the analysis demonstrates that there is much to be gained from both hearing and seeing what is done in, for example, the contested moments that form dramatized formulations, rather than simply relying on the ROTI.

There are important legal implications. The analysis allows us to reconsider the value of monomodal police records (the ROTI) as currently produced routinely for use in court. Much is lost by transferring multimodal activity into monomodal form. A great deal is accomplished in pointing, beating, head nodding and shaking, and iconic gestures, with implications for all involved. For the prosecution, the deictic "you" with gestural pointing challenges suspects to respond; beating works with prosody to doubly emphasize the salient words in the formulation, referencing contradictory voices and bringing them into the interview room to confront the suspect, boosting the interviewer's resources. Shifting gaze, alternating between the suspect and a statement held by the interviewer, forces the suspect to make a link between the documentary evidence and his own contradictory position and cues engagement and reciprocal action. First-person performance of hypothetical actions gives the interviewer the power to be the suspect and confronts the suspect with himself, making these turns provocatively "double-voiced" (Bakhtin 1981: 324) and demanding a responding and reciprocal performance. And although the formulation begins with SAY, it is not simply saying but also doing that makes these questions crucial. For the suspect, head shaking and gaze avoidance in silences signal rejection, but suspects also engage multimodally, producing responding actions and a held gaze, and there is also recognition of contradictory accounts. For the defense case, formulations form a window into the prosecution's investigative hypotheses and the ways that these are rejected.

There are also implications beyond England and Wales, since other countries that do not yet routinely record interrogations in either audio or audiovisual form might look to England and Wales as a model. Although audiovisual recording was piloted in the 1980s and was made possible by a PACE amendment in 2010, it is still not widely chosen, though it is evident in "Kidnapping" that the interviewer positively orients to it, recruiting it as an ephemeral object to confront the suspect. Using audiovisual material in police interview training could also be productive (a point made in Baldwin 1992),[4] showing how the micro detail of interaction is employed in shaping suspects' stories so that both what is said and what is done may be given in evidence and relied on in court. Even though police officers are trained to note for the audiotape any nonverbal or visual aspects of the interview, such as "the suspect is shaking his head," this is not consistently done, though it is difficult to see where it would stop once started. This underlines the importance of the words "say" and "mention" in the caution, since the caution only refers to speech. As we have seen, doing is integral to saying, but what is said through gesture is currently either lost or ignored in the record, to the detriment of all. The caution is a warning, but it should also be a promise or a commitment to fully record what is said. Saying is not just speech; it is layered with gesture. Recording only one layer neglects the full communicative load of interview interaction. Suspects will believe they have said what they needed to, but if this is through gesture that accompanies silence, it is the silence that will be recorded. Since silence is not always remaining silent, as we have seen, logocentric records therefore compromise our understanding of what is said and potentially undermine justice.

Notes

1. The Terrorism Act (2000) requires interviews with suspects in terrorism cases to be audiovisually recorded, but audiovisual recording interviews for other alleged crimes is a matter of police choice (PACE Code F 2010). I cannot find up-to-date statistics on the number of visually recorded police interviews that take place, though a BBC report (Hudson 2012) states that "90% of the two million interviews carried out in 2011 were recorded on to [cassette] tape," which is audio only. Zander (2010) reports that starting on 1 May 2010, police forces began "the process of changing from tape to digital recording of interviews with suspects." Dixon and Travis (2007), however, report on "the routine use of audio-visual recording in New South Wales, Australia, where such recording has been required" since the turn of the millennium.

2. Following Jefferson (2004), pauses in seconds are shown in parentheses, stressed syllables are shown with underlining, extended syllables with colons, notably rising and falling intonation with up and down arrows, cut-off segments with a dash, and overlap and interruption with square brackets. Where interviewers and suspects refer to other people involved in the alleged offense as suspects or witnesses, these names are anonymized with a pseudonym. Contextual information (other than gestures) is contained in double brackets.

3. At the time of the interviews analyzed here, the police caution was: "You do not have to say anything unless you wish to do so, but what you say may be given in evidence." This was replaced in 1995 with the caution shown here, which makes omissions in the interview more salient than what was simply implied in the earlier caution. Nevertheless, I include the current caution here, to highlight the importance of SAY questions and dramatized formulations in the current context.

4. Stokoe's (2014) conversation analytic role-playing method (CARM) uses audio recordings to train police interviewers; audiovisual recordings could supplement these.

References

Atkinson, J. Maxwell, and Paul Drew. 1979. *Order in Court*. New York: Macmillan.

Bakhtin, Mikhail. 1981. "Discourse in the Novel." In *The Dialogic Imagination*, edited by Michael Holquist, 259–422. Austin: University of Texas Press.

Baldwin, John. 1992. "Video-Taping Police Interviews with Suspects—An Evaluation." Home Office: London Police Research Series Paper 1. Accessed 27 August 2017. www.tna.eurparchive.org/20090120202547/homeoffice.gov.uk/rds/prgpdfs/prg1bf.pdf.

Baldwin, John. 1993. "Police Interview Techniques. Establishing Truth or Proof?" *British Journal of Criminology* 33(3): 325–352.

Baldwin, John, and Julie Bedward. 1991. "Summarising Tape Recordings of Police Interviews." *Criminal Law Review* (September): 671–679.

Bucholtz, Mary. 2000. "The Politics of Transcription." *Journal of Pragmatics* 32: 1439–1465.

Chalmers, James. 2014. "Recording of Police Interviews." In *Post-Corroboration Safeguards Review Report of the Academic Expert Group*, edited by James Chalmers, Fiona Leverick, and Alasdair Shaw, 118–123. Edinburgh: The Scottish Government.

Clift, Rebecca, and Elizabeth J. Holt. 2007. "Introduction." In *Reporting Talk: Reported Speech in Interaction*, edited by Elizabeth Holt and Rebecca Clift, 1–15. Studies in Interactional Sociolinguistics 24. Cambridge: Cambridge University Press.

Craig, Robert T., and Alena L. Sanusi. 2000. "'I'm Just Saying . . .': Discourse Markers of Standpoint Continuity." *Argumentation* 14: 425–445.

Dixon, David, and Gail Travis. 2007. *Interrogating the Images: Audio-Visually Recorded Police Questioning of Suspects.* Sydney: Sydney Institute of Criminology.

Drew, Paul. 2003. "Comparative Analysis of Talk-in-Interaction in Different Institutional Settings: A Sketch." In *Studies on Language in Social Interaction*, edited by P. J. Glenn, C. D. leBaron, J. Mandelbaum, and R. Hopper, 293–308. Mahwah, NJ: Lawrence Erlbaum.

Garfinkel, Harold, and Harvey Sacks. 1970. "On Formal Structures of Practical Actions." In *Theoretical Sociology: Perspectives and Developments*, edited by John C. McKinney and Edward A. Tiryakian, 338–366. New York: Appleton-Century-Crofts.

Goffman, Erving. 1981. "Footing." In *Forms of Talk*, 124–159. Philadelphia: University of Pennsylvania Press.

González-Martínez, Esther. 2006. "The Interweaving of Talk and Text in a French Criminal Pretrial Hearing." *Research on Language and Social Interaction* 39(3): 229–261.

Goodwin, Charles. 1994. "Professional Vision." *American Anthropologist* 96(3): 606–633.

Goodwin, Charles. 2000. "Action and Embodiment within Situated Human Interaction." *Journal of Pragmatics* 32: 1489–1522.

Goodwin, Charles. 2013. "The Co-operative, Transformative Organization of Human Action and Knowledge." *Journal of Pragmatics* 46: 8–23.

Haworth, Kate. 2010. "Police Interviews in the Judicial Process: Police Interviews as Evidence." In *The Routledge Handbook of Forensic Linguistics*, edited by Malcolm Coulthard and Alison Johnson, 169–181. London: Routledge.

Heffer, Chris. 2005. *The Language of Jury Trial: A Corpus-Aided Analysis of Legal-Lay Discourse.* Basingstoke: Palgrave Macmillan.

Heffer, Chris, Frances Rock, and John Conley. 2013. *Legal-Lay Communication: Textual Travels in the Law.* Oxford: Oxford University Press.

Heritage, John C., and D. Rod Watson. 1977. "Recent Developments in the Sociology of Language in Britain." *Sociolinguistics Newsletter* 8: 2–6.

Heritage, John C., and D. Rod Watson. 1979. "Formulations as Conversational Objects." In *Everyday Language: Studies in Ethnomethodology*, edited by George Psathas, 123–162. New York: Boston University Irvington Press.

Heydon, Georgina. 2005. *The Language of Police Interviewing: A Critical Analysis.* Basingstoke: Palgrave Macmillan.

Holt, Elizabeth J., and Alison Johnson. 2010. "Legal Talk: Socio-pragmatic Aspects of Legal Talk; Police Interviews and Trial Discourse." In *The Routledge Handbook of Forensic Linguistics*, edited by Malcolm Coulthard and Alison Johnson, 21–36. London: Routledge.

Hudson, Alex. 2012. "Who, What, Why: Why Do Police Still Use Cassette Tapes?" *BBC News Magazine*, 3 December. http:// www.bbc.co.uk/news/ magazine-20556330.

Jefferson, Gail. 2004. "Glossary of Transcript Symbols with an Introduction." In *Conversation Analysis: Studies from the First Generation,* edited by Gene H. Lerner, 13–31. Amsterdam: John Benjamins.

Johnson, Alison. 2014. "'Dr Shipman Told You That . . .': The Organising and Synthesising Power of Quotation in Judicial Summing-up." *Language & Communication* 36: 53–67.

Kendon, Adam. 2004. *Gesture: Visible Action as Utterance.* Cambridge: Cambridge University Press.

Kidwell, Mardi. 2006. "'Calm Down!' The Role of Gaze in the Interactional Management of Hysteria by the Police." *Discourse Studies* 8(6): 745–770.

Komter, Martha. L. 2003. "The Interactional Dynamics of Eliciting a Confession in a Dutch Police Interrogation." *Research on Language and Social Interaction* 36(4): 433–470.

Komter, Martha L. 2006. "From Talk to Text: The Interactional Construction of a Police Record." *Research on Language and Social Interaction* 39(3): 201–228.

Kopp, Stefan, Paul Tepper, and Justine Cassell. 2004. "Towards Integrated Microplanning of Language and Iconic Gesture for Multimodal Output." In *Proceedings of the 6th International Conference on Multimodal Interfaces*, 97–104. New York: ACM.

Kozin, Alexander V. 2008. "Unsettled Facts: On the Transformational Dynamism of Evidence in Legal Discourse." *Text and Talk* 28(2): 219–238.

Licoppe, Christian, and Laurence Dumoulin. 2010. "The 'Curious Case' of an Unspoken Opening Speech Act: A Video-Ethnography of the Use of Video Communication in Courtroom Activities." *Research on Language and Social Interaction* 43(3): 211–231.

Linfoot-Ham, Kerry. 2007. "Conversational Maxims in Encounters with Law Enforcement Officers." *International Journal of Speech, Language and the Law* 13(1): 23–54.

Matoesian, Gregory M. 2001. *Law and the Language of Identity: Discourse in the William Kennedy Smith Rape Trial.* Oxford: Oxford University Press.

Matoesian, Gregory M. 2005. "Struck by Speech Revisited: Embodied Stance in Jurisdictional Discourse." *Journal of Sociolinguistics* 9(2): 167–193.

Matoesian, Gregory M. 2010. "Multimodality and Forensic Linguistics. Multimodal Aspects of Victim's Narrative in Direct Examination." In *The Routledge Handbook of Forensic Linguistics*, edited by Malcolm Coulthard and Alison Johnson, 541–557. London: Routledge.

Matoesian, Gregory M. 2012. "Gesture's Community: Social Organization in Multimodal Conduct." *Language in Society* 41: 365–391.

Matoesian, Gregory M. 2013. "Language and Material Conduct in Legal Discourse." *Journal of Sociolinguistics* 17(5): 634–660.

Matoesian, Gregory M., and Kristin E. Gilbert. 2016. "Multifunctionality of Hand Gestures and Material Conduct during Closing Argument." *Gesture* 15(1): 79–114.

McNeill, David. 1992. *Hand and Mind: What Gestures Reveal about Thought*. Chicago: University of Chicago Press.

McNeill, David. 2005. *Gesture and Thought*. Chicago: University of Chicago Press.

Mondada, Lorenza. 2003. "Working with Video: How Surgeons Produce Video Records of Their Actions." *Visual Studies* 18: 53–73.

Nevile, Maurice. 2015. "The Embodied Turn in Research on Language and Social Interaction." *Research on Language and Social Interaction* 48(2): 121–151.

Police and Criminal Evidence Act. 1984. Accessed 28 August 2016. http://www.legislation.gov.uk/ukpga/1984/60/contents.

Rock, Frances. 2001. "The Genesis of a Witness Statement." *Forensic Linguistics* 8(2): 44–72.

Rock, Frances. 2007. *Communicating Rights: The Language of Arrest and Detention*. Basingstoke: Palgrave Macmillan.

Schiffrin, Deborah. 1987. *Discourse Markers*. Cambridge: Cambridge University Press.

Stokoe, Elizabeth. 2009. "'For the Benefit of the Tape': Formulating Embodied Conduct in Designedly Uni-modal Recorded Police-Suspect Interrogations." *Journal of Pragmatics* 41: 1887–1904.

Stokoe, Elizabeth. 2014. "The Conversation Analytic Role-play Method (CARM): A Method for Training Communication Skills as an Alternative to Simulated Role-Play." *Research on Language and Social Interaction* 47(3): 255–265.

Stokoe, Elizabeth, and Derek Edwards. 2008. "'Did You Have Permission to Smash Your Neighbour's Door?' Silly Questions and Their Answers in Police Suspect Interrogations." *Discourse Studies* 10(1): 89–111.

Streeck, Jurgen. 1996. "How to Do Things with Things: Objets Trouvés and Symbolization." *Human Studies* 19: 365–384.

Streeck, Jurgen. 2009. *Gesturecraft: The Manu-facture of Meaning*. Amsterdam: John Benjamins.

Streeck, Jurgen. 2010. "Ecologies of Gesture." In *New Adventures in Language and Interaction*, edited by Jurgen Streeck, 223–242. Amsterdam: John Benjamins.

Terrorism Act. 2000. Accessed 27 August 2017. https://www.legislation.gov.uk/ukpga/2000/11.

Watson, D. Rod. 1983. "The Presentation of Victim and Motive in Discourse:

The Case of Police Interrogations and Interviews." *Victimology* 8(1–2): 31–52.

Youth Justice and Criminal Evidence Act. 1999. Accessed 27 August 2017. https://www.legislation.gov.uk/ukpga/1999/23.

Zander, Michael. 2010. "From Tape to Digital Recording of Interviews with Suspects." *Criminal Law & Justice Weekly*, 16 April. Accessed 27 August 2017. https://www.criminallawandjustice.co.uk/features/Tape-Digital-Recording-Interviews-Suspects.

CHAPTER FOURTEEN

Functions of Transmodal Metalanguage for Collaborative Writing in Police-Witness Interviews

Frances Rock

Introduction

Appadurai notes that "it has now become something of a truism that we are functioning in a world fundamentally characterised by objects in motion. The objects include ideas and ideologies, people and goods, images and messages, technologies and techniques. This is a world of flows" (2000: 5). Nowhere is this perhaps more clearly illustrated and more pressing to understand than in relation to law. A primary function of legal contexts is to gather laypersons' stories in order that those stories can inform legal decisions. The process of collecting and recording stories is predicated on transformation in that it is designed to convert laypersons' talk into legally significant evidence (Kozin 2008: 220). This conversion process enables texts to "move through and around" law's institutional processes (Rock, Heffer, and Conley 2013: 4). Yet as well as conferring legal status onto laypersons' words, processes of textual travel and transformation in legal contexts can alter the source texts dramatically. This aspect of transformation has been criticized because it is opaque to lay participants and denies them control of voicing in their narrating, as I will illustrate in the next section. This chapter, however, shows that textual travel and transformation in legal contexts do not inevitably exclude laypersons. It shows, conversely, that the transformation process can be made explicit to lay participants within the legal process. The chapter focuses on witness statements that are usually created through a literacy event in which an extended conversation between a police officer and a witness is used as the basis for a written text that comes to represent the witness later in the legal process. Typically, in these witness interviews, the police officer will write down the statement for the witness rather than, for example, helping the witness to write his or her own statement. This chapter examines how, in police interviews with witnesses, the textual transformation process involved can be made explicit by metalanguage. This metalanguage allows police officers to very clearly display their decisions about what to write when they scribe for witnesses. The chapter reviews the use of metalanguage using a case study that was part of a small linguistic ethnographic project focusing on a group of police interviewers. The case study is of one officer whose literacy practices in interviews were somewhat distinctive in consistently making text-production processes explicit to witnesses. Metalanguage was a key component of establishing this explicitness.

After positioning the transformation of talk in legal contexts through a short review of some key texts on this topic, I introduce the notion of metalanguage and characterize the metalanguage to be examined in this chapter as transmodal. I then position transmodal metalanguage as part of collaborative writing before presenting and analyzing some examples of the literacy practices that constitute transmodal metalanguage in naturally occurring police interviews. The chapter closes with a critical evaluation of the notion of transmodal metalanguage and its place in police interviews with witnesses.

Transforming Texts in Legal Contexts

The transformation of text has become a hot topic across a range of legal contexts owing to its perceived influence on the legal process and the negative consequences that it seems to have for lay participants. For example, *disputes between neighbors* are marshaled through complaint procedures, which create and transform categorizations of social characteristics (Stokoe 2009) and ethnicity (Stokoe and Edwards 2007); these illustrate the potential for key matters to be transformed. Moving to legal interviews specifically, interviews with *asylum seekers* see laypersons' talk transformed by public officials, who "rely on commonsensical, but at times inappropriate, knowledge of social, cultural, and linguistic values to construct, process, and eventually determine the validity of each claim" (Jacquemet 2009: 525). Legal actors' work is difficult yet influential. Laypersons can share the challenge of textual travel. In *lawyer-client interviews*, attorneys and their clients topicalize items extracted from the legal record and reformulate them repeatedly in talk before compressing them into written notes, where the different versions compete (Kozin 2008: 229). Ultimately a legal case constitutes a grid of representations that combine to satisfy a "specific context-imposed purpose" such as creating a case to answer or, in due course, a defense (Kozin 2008: 235). In *protective order application interviews*, through which abusive partners might be legally constrained, the paralegal and victim jointly construct a "story of abuse to make it fit the criteria required by a protective order affidavit" (Trinch and Berk-Seligson 2002: 395). Even though this process is "undoubtedly" collaborative, Trinch and Berk-Seligson's work illustrates that the interviewer drives the elicitation and recording process. Moving to policing, institutional actors have been seen to be highly influential. In *interviews with suspects*, police officer–initiated negotiation becomes an "institutional resource to reshape, evaluate, and transform narrative" in ways which might alter allocation of responsibility and the strength of evidential claims as the narrative travels through interviews (Johnson 2008: 346). Likewise, in *interviews with witnesses*, officers can apparently become the source of even such details as what times and durations are recorded on paper on the witness's behalf (Rock 2001). These studies, representative of the many that consider transformation and travel in legal contexts, indicate the potency of change, the significance of the institutional actor on this change, and its potential to have predominantly negative outcomes for laypersons.

A key problem with these processes of change is that when institutional actors are called upon to scribe with, for, or about members of the public, they frequently do so in ways that deny the layperson opportunities to engage with the text under production. This is frequently facilitated, if not caused, by the ways in which writing processes interpose with talk in literacy events (Heath 1982). Both Komter (2002, 2006) and van Charldorp (2011, 2013, 2014) have investigated the influence of recording through writing, in their case through typing, in Dutch police interviews with suspects. They find that the default means for gathering information in these interviews is the Question-Answer-Typing (QAT) structure, in which officers ask a question, suspects deliver an answer, and then typing ensues. I have shown how a similar structure features in police interviews with witnesses in England and Wales. Adapting their terminology, I have called it a Question-Answer-Writing (QAW) structure (Rock 2017). This writing phase is illustrated in the example below, from data I have collected. In the transcript, W (writing) phases, when the officer writes silently, and their duration in seconds are given in italics (all data have been anonymized). I suggest that this silent writing excludes the witness from the writing process:

Excerpt 14.1: Interview 23

P: so on Tuesday the third of July you'd spent
most of the day at a hospital in Town X
with your husband and (.) sister-in-law =
W: = yep
P: *{. . . writes 25.0 . . .}* what's your husband's
name
W: Tim
P: *{. . . writes 11.2 . . .}* and your sister-in-law's
name
W: Jill
P: Jill Green
W: no Gill Hemmingway
P: Hemmingway *{. . . writes 7.7 . . .}* you'd been
visiting your (.) mother-in-law
W: yeh
P: who ((was detained at //the hospital?))//
W: // yep //
P: *{. . . writes 16.7 . . .}* so y- you were left there
at (.) early evening to return to City X
W: we did yes yep
P: *{. . . writes 10.3 . . .}* and you traveled in
your husband's Focus is it
W: yep it's a Focus yeah
P: *{. . . writes 13.2 . . .}*

In excerpt 14.1, the witness endures considerable periods of silence whilst the officer writes in lines 5, 8, 13, 18, 21, and 24, following a QAW structure in the preceding talk. The officer's silence during the writing phase disconnects the witness from the activity of writing and prevents her from knowing what is being written. My field notes show that as the officer wrote silently, the witness multimodally displayed this disconnect by gazing around the room (a room in her own home), frequently scrutinizing her hands and skirt, and watching the officer "with curiosity or disdain" (field note 23). Toward the end of the interview, her cat began meowing loudly at the door, and this door became a focus of her visual attention during the officer's periods of silent writing. Like van Charldorp's suspects, she was "waiting for the typing [writing] to end" (2013: 225). Like van Charldorp's officers, the officer here maintains control of the writing process and creates asymmetry by using "the typing activity to select what information he hears and writes" (2011: 75). Only the officer knows "the substance of the typing" (Komter 2006: 220). Due to the mismatch between the duration of witnesses' turns and the duration of officers' subsequent typing, witnesses cannot even guess what is being written. Thus, the witness was involved in telling her story but not in that story's representation on the page.

Both Komter and van Charldorp note that it is possible for officers to do this work differently. In an earlier work (2017) I illustrated various processes through which witnesses can be actively engaged in the literacy practices of statement taking through the officer's suggesting words for inclusion, reading words aloud as they are written and recapping the words just written. In this chapter I consider an additional strategy through which officers who interview witnesses go further still. This is the use of explicit metalanguage about the writing activity, which allows witnesses to know, during the construction of the text, not only *what* is written, but also *why* it is written.

Metalanguage

Metalanguage is an umbrella term for a set of devices that enable communicators to comment on the very system of communication in which they are engaged. It is often referred to as "talk about talk" (Hodson 2014: 147) but can also—of particular relevance here—be taken to denote "talk about text" (Kitade 2008: 66), because "an oral metalanguage may be used to refer to aspects of writing" (Olson 1991: 261). To better acknowledge the functionality of metalanguage, we might more specifically stress its reflexive potential (Lucy 1993) and more informatively see it as "language in the context of linguistic representations and evaluations" (Jaworski and Galasiński 2004: 4). The devices under metalanguage's umbrella have been variously catalogued and divided. Gombert (1992), for example recognizes metaphonological (relating to sounds), metalexical/semantic (word structures/meanings), metasyntactic (syntax), metapragmatic (relating to appropriate language use), and metatextual (relating to text structure). To this list we can add, for example, metapropositional (labeling and categorizing propositional content; Caldas-Coulthard 1994: 305–306) and metadiscoursal, perhaps the most divisive of these subterms in being used by some for the direction, purpose, and structure of texts and by others as the projection of self into communication (Hyland 2015: 1). For some, *metalinguistic* denotes only that talk about language which uses the terminology of linguistics. Whilst such talk does happen in police interviews, particularly talk about spelling and handwriting, here I use a broader definition, after Johnson and Johnson, who say that not only are "grammars, dictionaries, linguistics and applied linguistics are all metalinguistic; so are mundane remarks like 'what does this word mean?' This reflexiveness allows language to be both the means and the object of study" (1998: 212).

In this chapter the term *metalanguage* is used to denote all metaphenomena under discussion, because metalanguage's functions and its negotiation, rather than its forms, are the focus of the analysis. This focus is possible because, as well as using metalanguage to refer to language's sounds, structures, and meanings, speakers can also use it to refer to "strategic purposes in talk" (Jaworski and Galasiński 2004: 3). It can even be employed as "a resource for strategic communication" as speakers "make active and local use of the metalinguistic function of language in goal-directed ways in communicative acts and events" (4). Such metalanguage "can work at an ideological level, and influence people's actions and priorities in a wide range of ways, some clearly visible and others much less so" (3). In this chapter, then, the *meta* is recognized as part of "the ubiquitous social processes through which norms and meanings for communication are continually negotiated" (Craig 2008: 3707).

Lucy stresses that metalanguage is a form of reflexivity that can be used in many ways, such as pointing out regularities in language use, reporting or referring to speech, and explaining how speech should be interpreted (1993: 9–10). He stresses that speech is "permeated by reflexive activities" (11). This ubiquity has led some scholars to question the value of studying metalanguage (e.g., Verschueren 2004: 54) as even "the claim in a language that a proposition in that language is 'true' is a reflexive statement" (Lucy 1993: 11). Indeed, there is a risk that discussing metalanguage in police interviews with witnesses can become meaningless owing to the ubiquity of metalanguage. The statement-taking sessions can appear to be entirely metalinguistic, because every word said is implicitly about the construction of written text, with each question or suggestion from the officer and each assertion from the witness being seen as metalinguistically suggesting a wording for the written text. Even before the writing itself begins, initial small talk is concerned with establishing a communicative space in which writing can occur. Once the crime itself is under discussion, every word the witness says is implicitly a suggestion for incorporation in writing. This becomes even more obvious once the officer begins writing. Some of the metalanguage is more explicit, however, because talk "ranges along a continuum from the relatively blatant verbal framing moves . . . to relatively unconscious cues (such as a slightly noticeable word choice, vocal emphasis, or facial expression) in which [metalanguage] may be hardly distinguishable from first-level discourse" (Craig 2008: 3707). The focus in this chapter, then, is explicit metalanguage through which one or both participants orient directly to text construction. This makes it possible to examine how metalanguage becomes "simultaneously a means of communication and a tool for thinking" (Swain and Lapkin 1998: 320), being vital to collaboration between witness and police officer. The data here feature a reflexivity that is highly functional and can be seen as co-reflexivity—reflexivity about language that involves two people.

When people collaborate in talking about text, institutional and interpersonal benefits can accrue. These benefits have been explored most thoroughly in relation to language teaching and learning—for example, where metalanguage has been shown to help speakers to learn to reflect (Wells 1999), improve their writing (Villamil and de Guerrero 1998), and develop their writing process (Corden 2007: 280). More generally, however, as Bateson explains: "Sometimes if both people are willing to listen carefully, it is possible to do more than exchange greetings and good wishes. Even to do more than exchange information. The two people may even find out something which neither of them knew before" (1999: 12). My contention is that in the witness interview, talk about text affords the witness a greater understanding of what is being written on their behalf and, in the case of explicit metalanguage, permits insight also into why.

Metalanguage and the reflexivity it entails are central to textual travel and transformation in legal contexts. Trinch and Berk-Seligson note that "perhaps the most obvious technique employed by interviewers to establish the appropriate narrative form for . . . abuse accounts is . . . use of metalanguage" by the interviewers (2002: 396). Although the authors do not directly display this metalanguage, they suggest that metalanguage they observe from institutional actors is not only directive in telling the laypersons who testify how to talk, but also indexical in suggesting that the lay talk will not otherwise be legally recognizable. They assert that through metalanguage and other devices "paralegals in effect convert narratives that are insufficient or inadequate, from the court's perspective, into ones that will be convincing to a judicial authority" (411). They note that whilst this helps clients to communicate their case to the court, it leads the paralegal to predetermine the case through selectivity, which frees judges from "the burden of obtaining the relevant facts" (412). They note that there is a didactic element to this process as victims "learn that the courts require specificity in regard to such facts as the dates and times of abusive incidents" (412). Auburn's work on reflexivity in crime narratives told by prisoners on a rehabilitation program examines explicit metalinguistic utterances such as "I mentioned that because it . . .'as got some relevance" (2005: 704) and "it's important to say that cuz the jacket comes into it in a moment" (708). This metalanguage enabled the narrating prisoners to break off from providing a sequence of events in order to draw hearers' attention to or divert it away from inferences. This was useful to the speakers because it allowed them to manage threats to face and ultimately fulfill an institutional aim of graduating from the rehabilitation program by positioning appropriately in relation to its aims. In this way, offenders contrasted their state at the time of the offense with their current state of awareness. This allowed them to shift footing as they explained, calling on Schiffrin's examination of metatalk (1980).

The evaluations directed to one's own utterances, however, also display a change in footing—a change in the speakers' alignment in relation to themselves. When individuals substantiate their claims and justify their assertions, they establish principals—those whose positions are given by the words spoken and who have committed themselves to what those words say. When individuals comment on their talk through metatalk, however, a different part of self is projected; here the individual is projecting an animator, the part of the self active in the role of utterance production. Meta-talk allows a speaker to exercise control over the principal at specific junctures during its production by projecting an animator who will bracket the expressive implications of what is being said (Schiffrin 1980: 231).

The metalanguage in this chapter plays with the boundaries between the production format roles that Schiffrin describes as the officer invites the witness, through metalanguage, to becomc involved in all stages of production short of holding the pen him- or herself.

Transmodality

"Reflexive use of language may involve two distinct, named language codes (e.g., a comment in English about Chinese) or the reflexivity may operate more narrowly within a single such code (e.g., a comment in English about English)" (Lucy 1993: 9). The data examined here feature a single code, English, but multiple modalities. Shifting between these modalities is accomplished through and around this reflexivity, and the term *transmodal* captures this dimension. Transmodality is central to the work of the interviewer and witness and is ripe for scrutiny. As Park and Bucholtz note, "While the special status of the written record has been well recognized in previous research on institutional power, the specific role that the speech-to-writing transmodality of entextualization plays in modern institutions is less explicitly acknowledged" (2009: 486).

Pennycook (2007) uses the term *transmodal* to refer to the rich performances that draw on a complex of modalities to make meaning, such as those of hip-hop artists. For Newfield, too, transmodal representational practices are those which call on a "range of semiotics modes" in meaning-making (2015: 267). Transmodality in this sense captures police officers' work during witness interviews, wherein speech, writing, gesture, and facial expression, for example, combine in the performance and accomplishment of entextualization. However, I use the term in a richer sense too, because the notion of *trans-* very accurately captures the fact that the police officer's metalinguistic work provides a passage between modes rather than just a co-occurrence of modalities. My use of the term foregrounds this with particular reference to speech and writing. This sense is captured by Newfield, who refers to transmodal sequences as "the routes along which representations migrate and mutate." Observing these makes it possible to understand how meaning makers' "ideas are formed, developed and change" (267). The notion of transmodal sequences recognizes that meaning-making occurs through "complex, interconnected situated practices" (268). Thus the term becomes both a relatively static description of the multiplicity of communicative practice across an event (Pennycook's sense) and a dynamic term that captures the transformational potential of metalanguage in achieving movement between modalities (Newfield's sense)—in this case, between modalities clustering around speech and the written mode. The notion of "transmodal remaking" also echoes this usage of *trans-*, for it denotes "refashioning an entity that has already been given with the resources of a different means of expression" (Mavers 2015: 284). *Trans-*, as it is used in this chapter, is also reminiscent of Jacquemet's term *transidiomatic*, which denotes the use of "an array of both face-to-face and long-distance media . . . [which] produce and reproduce . . . social hierarchies and power asymmetries" (2009: 527). I have not used the term *transidiomatic* itself because it entails the use of multiple languages in transnational environments, which is not the focus of this chapter. This use of *trans-* also meshes with Kress's term *transduction*, which names the process of moving meaning-making from one mode to another, including speech to writing (2010: 125). I do not use the term *transduction* itself, first because I take a more interactionist approach than is typical in the social semiotic framework with which Kress's usage associates, and secondly because this chapter explores how transformations are accomplished rather than what is transformed.

Data, Methods, and Analytic Approach

As I noted above, this chapter uses a case study rooted in an examination of 25 interviews between police officers and witnesses to crimes in England and Wales. The chapter uses four of these interviews in addition to the one drawn on in the introduction. Most prominent is an interview with a witness with whom the officer had a professional affinity: a male hospital security guard. He had witnessed a criminal incident of disorder in which a drunken man was being violent and aggressive in a hospital's emergency department. He reported his direct involvement in removing the man from the hospital (interview 13). Of the other three interviews, two are with women who both witnessed a single incident also involving an abusive, violent man who was customer in a pub where the witnesses both worked; the remaining one is with a male hospital nurse who also encountered a violent person, this time a hospital visitor. I audio-recorded and attended the interviews, taking field notes, and was able to discuss the interviews with participants and to undertake wider ethnographic work with some of the interviewers, observing and shadowing in police stations and their other workplaces and participating in work-related social environments. I transcribed the interview talk and those aspects of its relationship to writing activities that are relevant to the analysis (a key is appended). Field notes taken during the interviews recorded some gestures and facial expressions, details of writing activities, and contextual information according to Hymes's SPEAKING mnemonic (1974: 55 ff.), as well as my impressions of interpersonal and interactional aspects of the interviews. Informed consent, achieved through spoken and written procedures at the beginning and end of each interview, was obtained from all participants. Additionally, the research was approved by the police forces involved and the relevant university ethics panels and legal advisors.

The data have been analyzed from a broadly discourse-analytic and social-interactionist stance that incorporates focus on literacy practices informed by a social-practices approach to reading and writing and attention to processes of textual transformation. This has afforded an examination of talk, writing, and other sense-making activities in combination. In this chapter I present naturally occurring data from police interviews in combination with short excerpts from research interviews with officers and witnesses.

The data were analyzed by identifying and analyzing all examples of explicit metalanguage. This was then categorized and analyzed according to the function of each instance of metalanguage and the mechanism through which that function was achieved. All of the metalanguage here combined with other practices that also drew the witness into the officer's text construction, such as reading aloud whilst writing. These other practices are mentioned here only when they are relevant to the functions and mechanisms of metalanguage (they are discussed in Rock 2017).

Analysis

Openings: Transmodal Metalanguage as Framing

Following small talk and the recording of contact information, the real business of interviewing begins when officers shift to eliciting the witness's narrative and drafting the statement. In the interviews examined here, this shift was framed (Goffman 1974) with talk that was metalinguistic in referring to talk and writing and transmodal in referring across modes and initiating a transition from talk in itself to talk that authored text. This metalanguage, exemplified in excerpts 14.2 and 14.3 below, occurred at the very outset of elicitation (excerpt 14.2) and drafting (excerpt 14.3). It therefore sets the ground for extended writing.

Excerpt 14.2: Interview 16

1 P: right uh before we start writing (.) will you just tell me (.) what you saw

Excerpt 14.3: Interview 21

1 P: okay (.) now are you single?
2 W: yes
3 P: yeh (.) we'll start by saying (.) I'm a single person (.) and I live at the address supplied to the police

Besides the metalinguistic request in excerpt 14.1 "will you just tell me . . . ," which is not transmodal so not our focus here, both excerpts feature transmodal metalanguage when the officer says "before we start writing" (excerpt 14.2) and "we'll start by saying" (excerpt 14.3). These turns foreground the writing process and, through the pronoun *we*, cast writing as collaborative. Through the metalanguage, the officer involves the witness in the writing task either implicitly (excerpt 14.2) or explicitly by stating the words he intends to write (excerpt 14.3). In excerpt 14.4, below, from the same point in a different interview, the officer uses metalanguage too. Here, he combines it with a strategy mentioned earlier and discussed elsewhere (Rock 2017), reading aloud what he writes, as he writes:

Excerpt 14.4: Interview 13

1 P: now are you a single or a married man
2 W: I am a married man
3 P: right *I am a married man I live* [inaud.]
4 ((*family*)) *I am employed-* (.) uh (.) **you**
5 **see I don't want ((to dictate it but))**
6 **this is (.) your life story in (.) three lines** //[inaud.]//
7 W: //[laughs]//

Metalanguage appears in lines 5–6 ("I don't want to dictate it but this is your life story in three lines"). It is much more extensive than in the previous two excerpts and, unlike them, mitigates the officer's textual intervention rather than baldly presenting it. Excerpt 14.4 is from the interview with the hospital security guard, who frequently gives police statements about workplace confrontations. Throughout the interview the officer orients to his professional commonalities with the security guard and the guard's extensive experience as an interviewee. Nonetheless the officer evidently decides to begin the statement in a standardized way. This standardization risks threatening the witness's positive face by appearing not to value any wording he might prefer and his negative face by apparently impeding his autonomy in presenting his own perspective (after Brown and Levinson 1987: 66). The metalanguage in lines 5–6 provides a way to manage this face threat by orienting to the task at hand and by distancing from the standardized aspect of the writing task by presenting it as not what the officer himself wants. Humor in the presentation of such a brief life story supports this mitigation.

In educational contexts, there may be benefits in "demonstrating metatalk to students before asking them to complete tasks jointly" (Storch 2008: 111). These excerpts have illustrated how, from the very start of text construction, metalanguage functions to involve the witness, foreground writing, cast writing as collaborative, establish common ground, and manage and mitigate face threat. Thus here the officer's use of metalanguage in the course of involving the witness sets up what is to come. I now move on to show how witnesses responded to metalinguistic invitations to contribute and how the officer justified textual decisions through metalanguage.

Lexical Checking: Transmodal Metalanguage as Elicitation

In the next set of examples, the officer's transmodal metalanguage is oriented toward arriving at lexical items for the statement. This orientation is founded on soliciting information in a way that draws the witness into collaborative text construction and attends to the witness's lexical selections. These examples are, then, metalinguistic in that they ask about language choices and transmodal in that they provide a bridge for the witnesses' spoken suggestions to travel into the written statements. Excerpt 14.5 illustrates lexical checking about a job title.

Excerpt 14.5: Interview 13

W: ((it was Saturday yeah))
P: uh "I was posted to work" (.) *and at 1 am* (.)
Saturday 1 am (.) *together with* (1.9) **do**
you call yourselves Security Officers
or S.O.s o::r //do you//
W: // S.O.s //
P: S.O.- *S.O. Lloyd* "S.O. Lloyd" (.) "Lloyd" *I*
was called

In excerpt 14.5, the officer's metalanguage queries the job title of the witness and his colleague. He is not seeking to find out the correct job title by asking, for example, "are you called Security Officers or S.O.s," but rather asks about the witness's way of using the job title with the words "do you call yourselves . . ." (lines 3–5). The officer's metalanguage is partly about him incorporating what he called, during informal conversations with me, "the right words" into the witness statement, words that the witness would use. At the same time, this talk allows the officer to perform valuing of the witness's perspective by attending closely to detail. Implicitly, this communicates to the witness that the statement should represent him precisely. The witness's suggestion is made recognizably in line 6 and incorporated straightforwardly in line 7.

The next two examples feature the officer checking how witnesses would refer to the activity of beginning a work shift. Here witnesses orient to his metalanguage quite differently. As in excerpt 14.5, his question is not simply soliciting crime narrative but the witnesses' ways of referring. In conversation with me after these interviews, the officer was clear that his decision to insert a metalinguistic check early on was not chance. He said, "I like to make sure I've got their words in at the beginning (.) it shows them that I'm listening and makes it harder for someone to trip them up in court on the basics." His comment suggests that he recognized not only the interpersonal potential of his metalanguage in displaying an orientation to his interlocutor, but also its rich meaning-making potential in considering downstream legal participants and processes:

Excerpt 14.6: Interview 21

P: "Sunday sixteen July" (.) *I was* um:::: (.)
what thing would you use would you
use the word posted or rostered to work between twelve and =

4 W: = yeah
5 P: rostered (.) is that a word you would use
6 W: Yeah
7 P: yeah hhh (.)
8 W: I don't do that shift //anymore now//
9 P: *// rostered // to work twelve midday until* six pm

The officer checks, in his first turn, the witness's lexical preference using the rather opaque *wh-* question "What thing would you use" (line 2) but follows it with the more transparent either-or question "Would you use the word posted or rostered" (lines 2–3). However, the witness seems to answer his first question, offering just "yeah," in overlap (line 4), apparently not focusing on the distinction between the two words exhibiting ambivalence, if not gratuitous concurrence (Eades 2010: 91). The officer does not abandon his attempt to incorporate the witness's choice and accordingly attempts again to elicit it, in line 5, focusing on "rostered." His persistence potentially communicates his determination to attend to the witness. The witness confirms the suggestion, "rostered," from turn 5 although she adds, "I don't do that shift anymore." Perhaps, left to her own devices, she might have produced a formulation that included "shift." However, the officer appears unable to take up this wording. being perhaps already fixed on rapidly incorporating both a start and an end time ("rostered to work . . . until . . ."), which could be accomplished only through circumlocution if "shift" was used. Indeed, the officer later noted in an informal interview that "sometimes they'll say things in a way that doesn't quite fit in." Thus, whilst his metalanguage offered the potential to solicit and incorporate witnesses' words, it sometimes failed to live up to this promise in the rapid, multimodal flow. Nonetheless, the officer has considered the witness's preference closely. Indeed, at the end of this interview the witness, whilst not specifically discussing this turn, commented that the officer "seemed to pay a lot of attention to what I was saying."

Thus, although the officer was enthusiastic about incorporating witnesses' words and saw the utility of presenting that enthusiasm to witnesses, they, in contrast, could be ambivalent about his efforts, showing weak preferences and acquiescence. Similarly, the witness below, offered the choice between "report for work" or "walk on" in lines 2 and 3, selects one of these options, but not without diverting the exchange to purposes other than lexical selection:

Excerpt 14.7: Interview 9

P: Tuesday the 13th of [month] (4.7 seconds)
uh what do you do **do you report for (.)**
for work or (.) walk on or
W: I just walk on duty I mean jus- hhhhh don't
have to worry about that stage =
P: = yes =
W: = he-
he- just turn up about half past eight (.)
and groan and moan about the state of
the place [laughs heartily]

For this witness, a hospital nurse, the interactional takes precedence over the transactional in Brown and Yule's terms (1983: 1). He ignores the opportunity to engage with lexical choice and instead presents himself humorously, as a seasoned medical professional with a particular orientation to work (lines 5 and 9). In this way the witness defers to the police officer, apparently trusting this fellow public servant, to draft appropriately, leaving him free to orient to their common ground.

Not all witnesses shared the ambivalence exhibited in excerpts 14.6 and 14.7, however. The hospital security guard made lexical choices with great care in excerpt 14.8, in which the officer queries the suspect's location. Here it is the witness himself who introduces an explicitly metalinguistic dimension.

Excerpt 14.8: Interview 13

P: where w- where was he? //was he in-//
W: // when he //
// he was //
P: // in the cubi //cles o::r waiting area or
W: this n- uh // **what ((do)) you call it** //
P: // in the surgical area //
W: **I'll tell you what to call it in a sec** (.) says up
on there what it was called [reaches up for
paper pinned to a notice board beside them
(3.9)] that's right (.) it's the treatment room
P: OK it's *in*?
W: the treatment room
P: *the (.) treat-* (.) is that one that's (.) divided up

like cubicles
W: //yeah//
P: //the whole lot's called the treatment room?
W: it's a uh- what it is the whole // area //
P: //is [inaud]//
the treatment room

After a *wh-* question about location (line 1), the officer suggests two options (line 4). These are different locations within the emergency department, not simply alternative lexical variables for the same variant; these are only potentially metalinguistic. However, the witness, in line 5, orients to the exchange as not simply information gathering but rather as a request for lexical specification when he asks himself, "what do you call it," and responds, "I'll tell you what to call it" (line 7). Ultimately he determines the correct location name using hospital documentation (lines 8–10). He thus responds to the officer's turn as metalinguistic and goes to some lengths to provide the institutionally sanctioned term. The witness's orientation to lexical choice and his apparent desire to comply with his own institution's terminological prescriptions introduces a highly metalinguistic element, which the officer pursues in lines 13–19. Whereas the earlier examples saw the officer seeking to incorporate a word that the witness would himself or herself use, here he ends up with an institutional rather than a personal choice, but one that the witness evidently favors owing to his institutional affiliation.

Like the security guard, the witness below apparently took metalanguage to offer a genuine opportunity to contribute wordings to the statement. Excerpt 14.9 concerns a device installed in the pub where the witness worked that calls the police at the touch of a button.

Excerpt 14.9: Interview 16

W: Steven informed Kelly to press the security buttons (.)the
um:: (.) and the bloke was just saying "press
the 4 //button press the button"//
P: //*Steven informed Kelly to// press the* s- s- um hh
we'll call it //personal//
W: // panic //
P: attack alarm **would you call it personal attack**
alarm?
W: yeah panic button

P: **would you call it panic button**
W: yeah
P: to press the (.) panic button (.) that is personal attack
alarm? (.) yeah because yeah

The witness first refers to the device as "the security buttons" (line 1). However, the officer suggests instead "personal attack alarm." He makes this suggestion in two ways. First, he asserts, "we'll call it personal attack alarm" (lines 5 and 7), which, despite the inclusive personal pronoun "we," grammatically allows the witness little choice. Secondly, however, he reverts to consulting the witness: "would you call it personal attack alarm?" (lines 7–8). Rather unusually, this features rising intonation, which could, in the context of his other interrogatives, be heard as a reinforcement of the redress to the bald statement about lexical choice in lines 5 and 7. The witness, who has already said "panic" in overlap with the officer (line 6), agrees to this wording ("yeah," line 9) but offers a further suggestion, "panic button," which the officer queries in line 10. He ultimately incorporates the witness's choice, "panic button" but adds his own gloss through the words "that is personal attack alarm" (line 11). Through metalinguistic talk, the officer incorporates both a term familiar to the witness and one that he understood to be more universal.

These examples show the officer orienting not only to eliciting information but also to eliciting the witness's take on that information; the witnesses respond variously with ambivalence, compliance, and enthusiasm.

Justifying Lexical Choices: Transmodal Metalanguage as Legitimation

Metalanguage did not only serve to introduce and establish the officer's orientation to the interview and to provide lexical specification. It was also used to legitimize the wordings that were incorporated. As Berger and Luckmann explain: "Legitimation provides the 'explanations' and justifications of the salient elements of the institutional tradition. [It] 'explains' the institutional order by ascribing cognitive validity to its objectivated meanings and . . . justifies the institutional order by giving a normative dignity to its practical imperatives" (1966: 111).

The excerpts below evidence the officer's metalanguage invoking the institutional tradition and order and situating formulations in relation to them. The metalanguage here is dynamic in being "about the operating procedure of claiming legitimacy" and in potentially persuading witnesses that the officer's "grasp and manner of speech are appropriate for the position of authority" that he holds (Charaudeau 2002: 314). I suggest in this section that his metalanguage, in legitimating lexical choices, has a wider role in not only persuading but also reassuring, bolstering, empowering, and making decisions.

Excerpt 14.9, at the end of the previous section, closed with the officer saying, "yeah because yeah," which tantalizingly suggested that he may have been considering legitimizing his formulation. The next section explores this phenomenon in more detail. The examples below are metalinguistic because they concern writing motivations, and they are transmodal because they illustrate the officer's representations of those motivations at the moment of converting talk to text. The first example is from near the opening of the interview with the security guard.

Excerpt 14.10: Interview 13

P: how long you been in this job?
W: eight years
P: *a post I have held for* (.) *eight years* **that will**
then tell the (.) people who read it
you've got a depth of experience in this
particular line ((the uh anyway)) if they
can try and trip you up they will but ((I
don't know if they'll bother in there
really)) with the experience you've got

The metalanguage throughout the officer's extended turn ("that will then tell the people . . . with the experience you've got," lines 3–9) reviews his motivations. It presents his aims in terms of the needs of future audiences, "the people who read it" (line 4) and "they" (lines 6 and 7). He does not simply cast the information about the witness's length of service as useful or interesting to these future audiences but rather as a rhetorical device which will evidence the witness's workplace experience and, by implication, his reliability as a witness. He develops this idea in lines 16–18 by adding that not only will this rhetorical device be persuasive but it might forestall attempts to discredit the witness. Thus, the metalanguage enables him to prepare the witness for the downstream legal process by indicating a courtroom scenario in which the witness's version of events is challenged. Corden illustrates that collaborative interchange around writing in classrooms can help children to "develop a sense of audience" (2007: 271), which is an outcome here too. The collaborative interchange in metalanguage here also presents the officer, the witness's scribe, as having the witness's best interests at heart as he is observably designing the statement in order to head-off possible future trouble for the witness. It also allows him to imply admiration for the witness's length of service.

Developing a sense of audience and an orientation to audience was key to much of the transmodal metalinguistic legitimation, particularly in interview 13 with the security guard who the officer noted seeing as *part of the same team* as his own profession. The following examples are predominantly from that interview and show how the legitimizing metalanguage develops in the context of this professional closeness. The next example features legitimizing metalanguage about the term *A & E*. This is an abbreviation for Accident and Emergency Department, long used in England and Wales to denote hospitals' emergency or casualty departments.

Excerpt 14.11

P: I was called (.) to the A & E?
W: yeh ((that's when we found out))
P: to A & E ((desk)) I ((he)) (.) **I'll use the abbreviations**
here because they're legal abbreviations and
people know them (.) and (.) *and to the A & E*
((desk)) because (1.5) uh A MAN WAS CAUSING
TROUBLE **because you don't know what it is at the time?**

The officer's first segment of legitimizing metalanguage occurs at lines 4–5. Here he provides two justifications for using the abbreviation A & E, both of which concern future readers' needs. The first justification relates to the legal status of the abbreviation ("they're legal abbreviations," lines 4–5) and the second to its general familiarity ("people know them," line 5). He also justifies the suggested wording "a man was causing trouble" (line 7). This time, rather than the metalanguage reaching forward to address the needs of future audiences, it reaches back into the witness's experience of the incident. The officer says that he will not specify what kind of "trouble" the suspect was causing at this point in the statement because this was not clear to the witness at this stage in the incident. In this way he heads off future audiences' concerns that the witness is concealing prior knowledge (the risks of this for those giving statements are explored in, e.g., Coulthard, Johnson, and Wright 2017: 168). Throughout, it is as if the officer is inviting the witness as a kind of coworker to share in the legally oriented decisions he is making in his writing.

In excerpt 14.2, the officer and security guard are producing text that describes how the guard removed the suspect from the site of a fracas in the hospital. The officer asks about the removal.

Excerpt 14.12: Interview 13

P: you ejected him did you
W: yeh
P: together with- together with
W: [nods]
P: yeh
W: [inaud. 5 syllables]
P: how would you- you- when you eject somebody
. . . [short discussion of wrist lock techniques] . . .
P: OK yeah [reads] "because of his behavior
the police had been informed" and (.) together
(.) S.O. Lloyd and I took hold of- of his arms (.)
and escorted him off //the premises//
W: //off the premi//ses
P: **always (.) sounds better than "ejected" at the end**
of the day which sounds just uh like a
bouncer *and escorted him out of A & E*

Here the officer refers to the process of removing someone from a building with the word "eject(ed)" (lines 1 and 7) during the talk directed at the witness. However, as he writes the statement aloud, he instead incorporates the word "escorted" (line 12). He legitimizes this selection in lines 14–15, claiming that "escorted sounds better than 'ejected'" and specifying that "ejected" is undesirable because of its connotations, specifically that it "sounds just like a bouncer." This justification is clearly somewhat concerned with the downstream legal audiences of investigators or courtroom participants. However, those audiences may not agree with the officer's view of this word's connotations. Therefore we can see that this metalanguage is also about the professional affinity between the two men. Whilst a security guard may seem like a bouncer to the uninitiated, the officer, before the interview, explained his view that "in the trade" security staff are seen more favorably than bouncers. This formulation reflects that sensitivity and his resulting alignment with the guard.

Sometimes the officer's metalanguage would show what appeared to be unfettered enthusiasm for lexical choices. On one occasion, for example, he congratulated a witness when she, unable to remember whether a suspect's T-shirt was white or gray, said "it was a light-colored T-shirt." He complimented her on circumventing her uncertainty, exclaiming, "Light always good light," in this way noting her achievement in arriving at a wording that is vague yet sufficiently accurate and that he had evidently already found useful in this genre. As in excerpt 14.11, which attended to the court's need to understand the abbreviation "A & E," this attends to their need to be accurately informed. The officer also represented the need to persuade the courtroom in his metalinguistic comments. In excerpt 14.3, he and the witness are constructing text about what ensued when the security guard finally began to expel the suspect from the hospital.

Excerpt 14.13: Interview 13

P: then what happened
W: when he come back on ((our site)) we uh (.) we
then turned him around and put him back on the street
P: *he was* good word this is "again" **carries a lot of**
weight that does in court *again returned* (.) *onto* (.)
the public (.) *highway* yeah?
W: and again we returned back to the hospital site
P: and again (.) we returned back to the hospital yeah?
W: and this I would say had happened a num- a few
times he's coming
backwa//rds and forwards//
P: // okay okay // *this pattern* (.) repeated itself
several times?
W: yep
P: *this pattern* (.) *repeated itself* (.) *several* see in the
police (3.1) once is an accident (.) twice is
persistent you know so [laughs]

A key feature of the events being described is repetition. The witness details that the suspect "come back" onto the hospital grounds (line 2) only to be put "back on the street" (line 3) and that this to-ing and froing happened "a few times" (lines 9–10). The officer reported after the interview that he was keen to record repetition in the man's conduct, because it illustrated that his activities were deliberate; in legal terms, it evidenced intent. His metalanguage in the excerpt foregrounds his interest in highlighting repetition and occurs twice in the excerpt above. First, in lines 4 and 5, he evaluates the lexical choice "again," saying, "good word this 'again' carries a lot of weight that does in court" (lines 4–5) before writing the word "again" in the statement (line 5). In this way he contextualizes his decision to use the word "again" as being motivated by the word's persuasive potential downstream in the legal process. His second metalinguistic comment in this excerpt comes in lines 15–17, where he again evaluates the evidential potential in legal terms, this time noting its significance in the investigation when he says, "see in the police once is an accident twice is persistent." By invoking the legal process and legal reasoning, he explains his authorial decisions to the witness and conspiratorially shares their bases.

The officer's legitimizing metalanguage was sometimes a little tongue-in-cheek. In excerpt 14.14, for example, he humorously invokes the courtroom to justify writing which might have seemed overly detailed. He explains that he is going to introduce the delicate matter of the suspect's exposing himself in public. He includes the witness's word for this, "mooning," but has judged that this word alone would not be sufficient, so he needs to arrive at a way of explaining this word in the statement and to present this addition to the witness in the interview:

Excerpt 14.14: Interview 16

P: with his back towards me and (("he)) bent over"?
W: yeah
P: and he bent over showing his backside to
everyone (.) this is called mooning (.) **I think**
uh everybody knows that but uh
W: yeah // [laughs] //
P: //((there we go))// (.) [wryly] **for the**
benefit of the magistrates who might not know
W: yeah [giggles uncontrollably]

The officer justifies his decision to include a gloss of "mooning" in lines 4–5 and 7–8. He presents the gloss as self-evident but includes it "for the benefit of the magistrate" (lines 7–8). This also serves to other the magistrate by casting him or her as a remote part of the legal system. Through this depiction the officer distances himself from the legal apparatus and casts himself as close to the witness, who, through hearty laughter, receives this enthusiastically.

More disciplinary dimensions of court, and legal processes leading to court, also surfaced in the officer's metalanguage as he explained and negotiated the legitimate content of statements. The officer explicitly called on the downstream legal process in the excerpt below, from the hospital security guard interview. In this instance he is not celebrating an excellent drafting decision, as he did above, but rather is considering and evaluating a potentially controversial one. He is trying to capture the previous talk of the security guard. The witness has said that he arrived at the scene of the incident and made rapid decisions about what was unfolding based on both his observations and his previous contact with the suspect. This notion that the witness drew on his previous experience is problematic for the officer, who has to exercise caution about including evidence in the statement that was not directly perceived at the crime scene. The officer writes and suggests a certain wording:

Excerpt 14.15: Interview 13

P: yeah (.) right (.) OK (2.5) *without being further informed*
by staff I- I could see I- that Hoey (2.3) huh (.) and you-
uh **I think you can say this** (.) "was being his usual
self" having had previous dealings with him I mean we-
hh we- **we can put this in because the CPS they can**
edit out what they do- what- what- "what- is hearsay
what- what's that my Lord"
W: yeah
P: but I think (.) it give- it gives them the flavor (.)
they can (.) take it out leave it in
W: yeah

Here the officer grapples with how, and indeed whether, to include the witness's background knowledge about the suspect. He legitimizes his decision through two phases of metalanguage. First, he calls on an abstract notion of what one "can say" (line 3). At this stage it is not clear whether the modal "can" is deontic, referring to what is permitted within a legal framework, or epistemic, referring to what it is possible to say within the confines of what will be clear and comprehensible in a statement (see Coates 1983 and Perkins 1983 for discussions of epistemic and deontic modality). By line 5, when he again mentions what one "can put in," a deontic reading emerges relating to whether there is an adequate evidential basis for including the witness's claim that he could second-guess the suspect based on familiarity with him. This first phase of metalanguage thus rests on justifying what can be said in terms of the strength of the witness's claims. The second phase of metalanguage turns to justifying on the basis of how the statement might be used downstream in the legal process, focusing particularly on the autonomy of the prosecuting body in England and Wales, the Crown Prosecution Service or CPS, and the judge in any subsequent legal case. The officer presents what the CPS might do with the problematic claim ("they can edit out," line 5, and "they can take it out or leave it in," lines 9–10). He also acts out the part of a lawyer responding to a query from a judge about the status of the evidence ("what's that my Lord"). Thus, in justifying the inclusion of information he represents his decision making in detail. It appears that the officer grapples with what to include, through metalanguage, online whilst taking a statement. Indeed, when I discussed this excerpt with the officer later, he noted: "I sometimes need to think things through and it's better to tell [the witness] about that so that they know what's going on—what my reasons are."

This section has shown how the officer's legitimizing metalanguage allowed him to explain his decisions to witnesses, particularly when affiliating with them. This metalanguage was not only used to legitimize decisions taken but also to think through decisions under way.

Conclusions

This chapter opened with Appadurai's words about "objects in motion" in the "world of flows" (2000: 5). In the police interviews discussed here, this motion and flow were less passive than these words might suggest. The officer actively and creatively made motion and flow explicit in his talk as he created legal text and in the process created opportunities for his interlocutor to become aware of the way that he was processing his or her talk when creating text and his reasons for the decisions he made.

Early in the chapter I noted that much textual travel in legal contexts through scribing for another is criticized for its lack of attention to the lay participant or even attempts to conceal that participant. This process can be particularly malign and powerful because "the permanent and systematized representation of discourse through writing projects itself as objective and disinterested" (Park and Bucholtz 2009: 487). Here, however, I have shown that writing practices that involve transmodal metalanguage can be seen to give laypersons at least some insight into the texts written for them and their motivations.

We could argue that witnesses should not be distracted by officers' metalanguage. However, this concern rests on the unsafe assumptions that silences of the kind illustrated in excerpt 14.1 are not distracting and that being relatively informed is distracting. It also denies the complexity of the officer's task and the potential contribution that witnesses can make to it. Finally, it overlooks the risks in not getting witnesses "on board," as the officer put it, when they see their statements after the writing is essentially complete.

Transmodality is difficult to accomplish in a collaborative writing context. If officers are to do so without such devices as transmodal metalanguage, witnesses must trust their interviewers' textual decisions until they get to see the completed statement at the end of interview, at which stage witnesses may feel that major alterations are not really possible or practicable. They may, alternatively, request that aspects of the text be altered with which they would have been comfortable had the motivations been explained or alternative formulations explored during interview.

The data discussion here was organized around metalanguage, which frames interviews as collaborative and begins to model how they will develop: that which elicits formulations from witnesses where witness responses to transmodal metalanguage were shown to vary considerably, and that which allows officers to display writing motivations and in so doing position themselves in relation to witnesses and to position witnesses in relation to downstream legal processes. Specifically, the transmodal metalanguage in these statements serves the functions listed in table 14.1.

The theoretical contribution of this chapter has centered on consideration of the visible accomplishment of transmodal textual travel in this context, where the writing process is verbalized and thus laid bare. It suggests that for interactants, transmodality is not a black box but rather can facilitate its own progress.

TABLE 14.1 **Functions of the transmodal metalanguage**

Organizing and positioning the interactional activity:
Framing: demarcating the interview proper
Foregrounding writing
Casting the activity as collaborative/joint (in concert with pronoun usage)
Casting the statement as the witness's and himself as scribe\
Foregrounding the importance/functionality of information
Attending to the witness's interpersonal needs:
Attending to face
Mitigation
Showing affiliation/alignment
Reducing social distance
Valuing the witness
Complementing the witness on his or her lexical choice
Doing identity work
Allows the witness to supply his or her own words
Justifying textual work and intervention:
Foregrounding drafting motivations
Representing drafting motivations
Fulfilling legal objectives:
Arriving at formulations that will be familiar to the witness or will communicate the witness's perspective
Producing statements that minimize opportunities for challenge
Attending to downstream audience's:
Questions or concerns
Likely understanding
Possible inferences or responses to connotations
Need not to be misled through overspecificity
Need to be persuaded
Orienting the witness to the downstream legal process they might encounter:
Attending to and representing the wider legal process
Guiding the witness on representing him- or herself before the law
Facilitating the writing process:
Providing the officer with opportunities to think aloud
Providing the officer with opportunities to monitor the witness's view on the writing under way

References

Appadurai, Arjun. 2000. "Grassroots Globalisation and the Research Imagination: Globalisation from Below." *Public Culture* 12(1): 1–19.

Auburn, Timothy. 2005. "Narrative Reflexivity as a Repair Device for Discounting 'Cognitive Distortions' in Sex Offender Treatment." *Discourse & Society* 16(5): 697–718.

Bateson, Gregory. 1999. *Steps to an Ecology of Mind: Collected Essays in Anthropology, Psychiatry, Evolution, and Epistemology.* Chicago: University of Chicago Press.

Berger, Peter, and Thomas Luckmann. 1966. *The Social Construction of Reality*. Harmondsworth: Penguin.

Brown, Gillian, and George Yule. 1983. *Discourse Analysis: Cambridge Textbooks in Linguistics*. Cambridge: Cambridge University Press.

Brown, Penelope, and Stephen Levinson. 1987. *Politeness: Some Universals in Language Usage*. Cambridge: Cambridge University Press.

Caldas-Coulthard, Carmen Rosa. 1994. "On Reporting Reporting: The Representation of Speech in Factual and Fictional Narratives." In *Advances in Written Text Analysis*, edited by Malcolm Coulthard, 295–308. London: Routledge.

Charaudeau, Patrick. 2002. "A Communicative Conception of Discourse." *Discourse Studies* 4(3): 301–318.

Coates, Jennifer. 1983. "Epistemic Modality and Spoken Discourse." *Transactions of the Philological Society* 85: 110–131.

Corden, Roy. 2007. "Developing Reading-Writing Connections: The Impact of Explicit Instruction of Literary Devices on the Quality of Children's Narrative Writing." *Journal of Research in Childhood Education* 21(3): 269–289.

Coulthard, Malcolm, Alison Johnson, and David Wright. 2017. *An Introduction to Forensic Linguistics: Language in Evidence*. 2nd ed. Oxford: Routledge.

Craig, Robert T. 2008. "Meta-Discourse." In *International Encyclopedia of Communication*, edited by Wolfgang Donsbach, 3707–3709. Oxford and Malden, MA: Blackwell.

Eades, Diana. 2010. *Sociolinguistics and the Legal Process*. Bristol: Multilingual Matters.

Goffman, Erving. 1974. *Frame Analysis: An Essay on the Organization of Experience*. New York: Harper & Row.

Gombert, Jean-Émile. 1992. *Metalinguistic Development*. Hemel Hempstead: Harvester Wheatsheaf.

Heath, Shirley Brice. 1982. "What No Bedtime Story Means: Narrative Skills at Home and School." *Language in Society* 11: 49–76.

Hodson, Jane. 2014. *Dialect in Film and Literature*. Basingstoke: Palgrave Macmillan.

Hyland, Ken. 2015. "Metadiscourse." In *The International Encyclopaedia of Language and Social Interaction*, edited by Karen Tracy, 1–11. London: Wiley.

Hymes, Dell. 1974. *Foundations of Sociolinguistics: An Ethnographic Approach*. Philadelphia: University of Pennsylvania Press.

Jacquemet, Marco. 2009. "Transcribing Refugees: The Entextualization of Asylum Seekers' Hearings in a Transidiomatic Environment." *Text & Talk: An Interdisciplinary Journal of Language, Discourse & Communication Studies* 29(5): 525–546.

Jaworski, Adam, and Dariusz Galasiński. 2002. "The Verbal Construction of

Non-verbal Behaviour: British Press Reports of President Clinton's Grand Jury Testimony Video." *Discourse & Society* 13(5): 629–648.

Johnson, Alison. 2008. "'From Where We're Sat . . .': Negotiating Narrative Transformation through Interaction in Police Interviews with Suspects." *Text & Talk: An Interdisciplinary Journal of Language, Discourse & Communication Studies* 28(3): 327–349.

Johnson, Keith, and Helen Johnson, eds. 1998. *Encyclopaedic Dictionary of Applied Linguistics*. Oxford: Basil Blackwell.

Kitade, Keiko. 2008. "The Role of Offline Metalanguage Talk in Asynchronous Computer-Mediated Communication." *Language Learning & Technology* 12(1): 64–84.

Komter, Martha. 2002. The Suspect's Own Words: The Treatment of Written Statements in Dutch Courtrooms." *Forensic Linguistics* 9(2): 168–192.

Komter, Martha. 2006. "From Talk to Text: The Interactional Construction of a Police Record." *Research on Language and Social Interaction* 39(3): 201–228.

Kozin, Alexander V. 2008. "On Positionality and Its Comparability in the Legal Context." *International Studies in Sociology and Social Anthropology* 114: 195–220.

Kress, Gunther. 2010. *Multimodality: A Social Semiotic Approach to Contemporary Communication*. Abingdon: Routledge.

Lucy, John A. 1993. "Reflexive Language and the Human Disciplines." In *Reflexive Language: Reported Speech and Metapragmatics*, edited by John A. Lucy, 9–32. Cambridge: Cambridge University Press.

Mavers, Diane. 2015. "Remaking Meaning across Modes in Literacy Studies." In *The Routledge Handbook of Literacy Studies*, edited by Jennifer Rosswell and Kate Pahl, 282–294. London: Routledge.

Newfield, Denise. 2015. "The Semiotic Mobility of Literacy: Four Approaches." In *The Routledge Handbook of Literacy Studies*, edited by Jennifer Rosswell and Kate Pahl, 267–281. London: Routledge.

Olson, David. 1991. "Literacy as Metalinguistics." In *Literacy and Orality*, edited by David Olson and Nancy Torrance, 251–270. Cambridge: Cambridge University Press.

Park, Joseph Sung Yul, and Mary Bucholtz. 2009. "Introduction, Public Transcripts: Entextualization and Linguistic Representation in Institutional Contexts." *Text & Talk: An Interdisciplinary Journal of Language, Discourse & Communication Studies* 29(5): 485–502.

Pennycook, Alastair. 2007. *Global Englishes and Transcultural Flows*. London: Routledge.

Perkins, Michael. 1983. *Modal Expressions in English*. London: Pinter.

Rock, Frances. 2001. "The Genesis of a Witness Statement." *Forensic Linguistics: The International Journal of Speech, Language and the Law* 8(2): 44–72.

Rock, Frances. 2017. "Recruiting Frontstage Entextualisation: Drafting, Written-ness and the Artefactuality of Writing as Resources in Police-Witness Interviews." *Text & Talk: An Interdisciplinary Journal of Language, Discourse & Communication Studies* 37(4): 437–460.

Rock, Frances, Chris Heffer, and John Conley. 2013. "Textual Travel in Legal-Lay Communication." In *Legal-Lay Communication: Textual Travels in the Law*, edited by Chris Heffer, Frances Rock, and John Conley, 78–103. Oxford: Oxford University Press.

Schiffrin, Deborah. 1980. "Meta-Talk: Organizational and Evaluative Brackets in Discourse." *Sociological Inquiry* 50: 199–236.

Stokoe, Elizabeth. 2009. "Doing Actions with Identity Categories: Complaints and Denials in Neighbor Disputes." *Text & Talk: An Interdisciplinary Journal of Language, Discourse & Communication Studies* 29(1): 75–97.

Stokoe, Elizabeth, and Derek Edwards. 2007. "'Black This, Black That': Racial Insults and Reported Speech in Neighbour Complaints and Police Interrogations." *Discourse & Society* 18(3): 337–372.

Storch, Neomy. 2008. "Metatalk in a Pair Work Activity: Level of Engagement and Implications for Language Development." *Language Awareness* 17(2): 95.

Swain, Merrill, and Sharon Lapkin. 1998. "Interaction and Second Language Learning: Two Adolescent French Immersion Students Working Together." *Modern Language Journal* 82(3): 320–337.

Trinch, Shonna, and Susan Berk-Seligson. 2002. "Narrating in Protective Order Interviews: A Source of Interactional Trouble." *Language in Society* 31: 383–418.

van Charldorp, Tessa. 2011. "The Coordination of Talk and Typing in Police Interrogations." *Crossroads for Language, Interaction and Culture* 8(1): 61–92.

van Charldorp, Tessa. 2013. "The Intertwining of Talk and Technology: How Talk and Typing Are Combined in the Various Phases of the Police Interrogation." *Discourse and Communication* 7(2): 221–240.

van Charldorp, Tessa. 2014. "'What Happened?' From Talk to Text in Police Interrogations." *Language and Communication* 36(1): 7–24.

Verschueren, Jef. 2004. "Notes on the Role of Metapragmatic Awareness in Language Use." In *Metalanguage: Social and Ideological Perspectives*, edited by Adam Jaworski, Nikolas Coupland, and Dariusz Galasiński, 53–73. Berlin: Mouton de Gruyter.

Villamil, Olga S., and María C. M. de Guerrero. 1998. "Assessing the Impact of Peer Revision on L2 Writing." *Applied Linguistics* 19(4): 491–514.

Wells, Gordon. 1999. *Dialogic Inquiry: Toward a Sociocultural Practice and Theory of Education*. Cambridge: Cambridge University Press.

CHAPTER FIFTEEN

Reconstructing Suspects' Stories in Various Police Record Styles

Tessa (T. C.) van Charldorp

Introduction

Written police records play an important role in the future of a suspect. In the Netherlands a police record—the written statement written up by a police officer based on the interrogation with the suspect—can be one of two pieces of evidence needed to convict a suspect of a crime. By law, a police record must be written "as much as possible in the suspect's own words" (Code of Criminal Procedure 1926). However, it is the police officer who solicits the suspect's version of what happened, and it is the police officer who types up the suspect's words. We know from previous research, both from the Netherlands and elsewhere, how police interrogations (or interviews) are structured in various countries (see van Charldorp 2011 for examples from the Netherlands; Heydon 2005 for examples from Australia; and Johnson 2008 and Rock 2001 for examples from the United Kingdom). Suspects' stories are solicited, preferably through open-ended questions such as "What happened?," but more often steered by police officers toward a story that is relevant for the future judicial process (see van Charldorp 2014). Conversation and discourse-analytic research has shown that when spoken police interrogations are rendered as text, several transformations take place (see Jönsson and Linell 1991; van Charldorp 2011).

In the Netherlands and Belgium, police officers are relatively free in how they write up a police record. Van Charldorp (2011) and van Charldorp and Schellingen (2014) have shown that in the Netherlands and Belgium, we nowadays see three different styles in which police records are written up: monologue, recontextualized, and question-and-answer. The computer format and the law place certain restrictions on the manner in which an officer can write up the suspect's story, but he or she is otherwise free to do so in any of these styles. Often police records show a combination of two or three styles. In contrast to police practice in other countries (such as the United Kingdom), full transcriptions (which would be a fourth style) are rare and are made only when there is a recording (this is not standard procedure). In the Netherlands this generally only happens when the case is "big" enough to write up fully.[1]

This chapter focuses on the transformations that take place when an interrogation is written up as a police record. It deals particularly, with how the three different police record styles play a role in the transformation of the suspect's story from spoken interaction to a written record. I will provide an overview of the three different police record styles that are usually found in the Netherlands and Belgium and demonstrate that none of the styles accurately reflects how the suspect's written stories have come about in his or her interaction with police, and that the question-and-answer style in particular may even create a false sense of accuracy.

From Police Interrogation to Police Record

Various phases can be distinguished within the police interrogation. These phases may vary in different countries, but generally a distinction can be made between a preliminary phase (which may include when the suspect and officer meet each other, social talk, filling in a form, and giving the caution), the social and/or case-related phase of the interrogation (during which at least the case for which the suspect has been arrested will be discussed), and the exit phase (which may include reading the document that was drafted, signing it, and ending the interrogation). I will focus on the social and case-related phase during which the suspect is asked not only about his or her background, living conditions, and financial situation (during the social interrogation), but also about the case for which he or she has been arrested (during the case-related phase of the interrogation). During this social and case-related phase police officers write up what was talked about. As was noted in the introduction, this should be done "as much as possible in the suspect's own words" (Code of Criminal Procedure, 1926).

Although there are various rules and regulations regarding the recording of police interrogations worldwide, most interrogations in the Netherlands are not video- or audio-recorded. The judge and other participants in the subsequent judicial process have to rely on the written police record constructed by the police officer who conducted the interrogation. If a second interrogator is present during the interrogation, usually one police officer does most of the interrogating and the other is mainly concerned with typing up the police record. One can imagine that when there is only one police officer, he or she is responsible for conducting a proper and efficient interrogation whilst at the same time producing a readable and truthful police record. Since the document is generally signed at the end of the interrogation (although suspects are not obliged to sign the police record if they do not want to), no changes are made to the record after the interrogation ends.

Summarized Version

An interrogation can easily take an hour or longer, but it might yield only two to four pages of written text. Clearly a lot of interaction is left out, resulting in a summarized version of what was talked about. Jokes, pauses, hesitations, sighs, tears, and coffee breaks are generally not recorded in the written statement. Depending on what style is used in the police record, the words of the police officer in particular may be missing from the police record. Komter (2006: 222) shows that the "interrogator's activities are 'noticeably absent' in [the] text." When reading just the police record, it is therefore difficult to put the suspect's words within the context of how these words came about (also see Rock 2001). What is left is often a structured, logical, chronological story of what happened (van Charldorp 2011). At the same time, the suspect's story has been transformed from a vague story to a more precise version, as if the suspect's actions were a "series of rational and planned actions" (Jönsson and Linell 1991: 434), and from an emotional to a neutral tone (Jönsson and Linell 1991). These authors further show that there is a clear narrative structure present in the written versions of the spoken stories.

At a more local level in police-interrogation interactions, we also see summaries taking place. In conversation-analytic literature, such summaries are also referred to as formulations. According to Heritage and

Watson (1979: 129), "As conversations proceed, members may 'formulate' what it is they have been saying." Not only do these summaries "preserve relevant features of a prior utterance or utterances," but they also "recast" them (129). Summaries of the suspect's words are therefore highly dependent on the individual police officer summarizing the suspect's story on paper. In a Dutch paper, Sliedrecht and van Charldorp (2011) show that formulations act as a midpoint between spoken and written language. Right before or after the police officer begins typing, formulations are common in police interrogations. The officer either summarizes what has been said in his or her own words before typing it up, or the officer first types up the suspect's answer and then summarizes what he or she has just written up.

Police interrogations are not the only place we see such summaries: we see similar changes occur when talk is transformed to text in other (institutional) settings in which "reporting" is a common activity. For example, written news stories based on interviews often leave out the interviewer's questions (see Clayman 1990), or a doctor's report based on a patient's describing his or her symptoms only reports the patient's answers and not the doctor's questions. Furthermore, the institutional demands of the written record play a role in how texts are constructed. Maynard and Schaeffer (2006) demonstrate that survey-interview respondents' answers must "fit" the standardized survey-interview forms. Similarly, the suspect's answers must fit a structure that is created by the police officer conducting the interrogation. Whilst the police record does not have to precisely fit specific answer fields, it does have to fit the institutional demands of the text, because the text will be used in the upcoming judicial process. It will be read by the public prosecutor, lawyers, examining judge, and possibly other judges. In other types of legal systems, a jury may read or hear the police record. These participants will examine the police records as part of the case file, and in the Netherlands specifically, it can even count as one of two pieces of evidence that are required to convict a suspect.

The Five Phases of Police Interrogation

In Dutch police interrogations, officers generally make six global phases relevant during the interaction (van Charldorp 2011): (1) preliminary actions and social talk, (2) filling out of forms, (3) the police caution, (4) the social interrogation, (5) the case-related interrogation, and (6) exit activities.[2]

During the first phase, officers conduct social talk with the suspect while setting up the computer. In the second, the officer will then prepare to write up the record by filling in prerecorded fields such as the suspect's full name, date of birth, mailing address, and so on. Minors are asked additional questions such as the name of their school, their grade level in school, and the like. Generally, after the form has been (partially) filled in, officers give the legally required police caution. Officers tell the suspects that they are not obliged to answer. On the police record the following statement automatically appears: "After I told the suspect that he was not obliged to answer and about what I wished to interrogate him, he declared. . . ." Then officers generally move on to the social phase of the interrogation, where officers ask about the social background of the suspect such as the suspect's family, previous or current education, housing situation, financial situation, and past experiences with the police. This is followed by the case-related phase of the interrogation, in which the facts of the case are discussed and typed in the record. During this phase officers are truly interrogating. The interrogation ends with a number of exit activities, wherein the officer prepares the record for printing by editing and cleaning up the layout. The officer prints the document, the suspect reads through the entire record (when the suspect is a non-Dutch-speaker the document is read out loud by a translator, and when the suspect is [functionally] illiterate it is read out loud by the officer) and the suspect can ask for changes to be made. Both the suspect and the officer sign the document, and the suspect initials every page. The suspect can also choose not to sign the document.

The order of the phases may slightly change, and the social interrogation phase does not, for example, occur during every interrogation. The phases may not be universal across all police interrogations worldwide and may also be labeled differently. For example, Heydon (2005) has defined three phases in Australian police interrogations: opening, information gathering, and closing. Although these phases also apply to Dutch police interrogations, I have chosen to use the six phases defined above because the participants themselves make these phases relevant during the police interrogation in my data (see also van Charldorp 2011).

Transforming Stories

It is clear that changes take place when a suspect's spoken story, generated through interaction, is written up in the computer in police record format. Whereas the social talk and filling out of forms phases may be less relevant in how stories change, the social and case-related phases are of importance for both the suspect and the police officer. Because the written records are typed up during the interrogation, and because there are often no recordings, it is essential that the summarized version be an accurate one. We see different police record styles because police officers have considerable freedom regarding how they document the interaction that went on during the interrogation. In this chapter I will demonstrate how these styles differ from one another and how the suspects' stories are transformed for each of the three most common police-record styles found in Dutch and Belgian police records.

Data

The observations in this chapter are based on the recordings of 15 police interrogations at a police station in Amsterdam and their police records. The interrogations were recorded and observed in 2007–2008 during a six-month period of ethnographic field work that I conducted for my doctoral dissertation. The recordings were transcribed according to conversation-analytic standards and anonymized. Permission to record and study the interrogations and police records was granted by the Attorney-General of the Dutch Ministry of Justice, as well as the local police unit, the individual police officers, and the suspects.

The analyses below are based on three case studies, representing the three different police record styles. The examples that are used are illustrative of both the typical interaction that occurs during the interrogation and the way the interaction is written up in the police record.

Police Record Styles

Before turning to how suspects' written stories are constructed based on what police record style is used, I will first illustrate the three different police record styles that I found in my data: monologue, recontextualized, and question-and-answer (van Charldorp 2011). A fourth possible style, a literal transcription of the interrogation, did not occur in my data. One can imagine that a literal (verbatim) transcription of the spoken interaction would provide the most transparent version of what was said. However, such literal transcriptions take time to produce and read. It is for these (economic) reasons that they are not a standard procedure in the Netherlands and are only used in major cases.

In my data there were one police record fully written in monologue style, two records fully written in recontextualized style, and two records fully written in question-and-answer style. The remaining ten police records were written in two different styles. In these the social interrogation was always written in monologue style and the remainder in a different style. Below follow the characteristics of the three different styles that are present in my data, each illustrated with an example from the data.

Monologue Style

The monologue style can be distinguished from other styles because a police record written in this style is written from the perspective of the suspect (in first person). The questions asked or remarks made by the interrogator(s) do not appear in the record. This style is used quite commonly, especially amongst the older generation of police officers. In all interrogations that include a social-interrogation phase, this phase is written up in the monologue style. Excerpt 15.1 illustrates the monologue style and is taken from the social-interrogation phase with a minor that has been written up by the officer while interrogating.

Excerpt 15.1: Interview 3 (police record)[3]

I have heard and understood that I am not obliged to answer. I am 14 years old. I live with my father. My father's name is Steven Pinas. My mother passed away.

I go to Maas Lyceum Amsterdam. It's not going so well at school. I don't feel like going to school anymore. I want to work and earn my own money. I get five euros a week from my father.

I don't smoke or drink.

I don't have a hobby.

Recontextualized Style

This style also makes use of the suspect's perspective and the first person but at the same time shows in part what questions the interrogator asked.

This style uses a complicated form in which the officer's question is asked from the perspective of the suspect—for example, "You ask me what I want to state about this. I state to you, that yesterday afternoon I was. . . ." It demonstrates in a complicated way that the officer asked, "What do you want to state about this?" Not only are these recontextualized phrases (Komter 2013) lengthy, formal, and complicated, but they may also create the impression that the suspect used this type of complicated language him- or herself. Komter (2013) explains the term "recontextualisation phrase" as the "interrogator [who] reworks his own questions, remarks, or suggestions into the narrative" while still using the first-person perspective and by doing so "ensure[s the officer's] visibility" in the police records. Excerpt 15.2 illustrates three short recontextualized paragraphs that occurred as part of the case-related section of a police record.

Excerpt 15.2: Interview 3 (police record)

You ask me which act I performed.

I state to you that I kept the garage door closed and I also helped pull Mervellino into the garage.

You ask me if a knife was used.

I state to you that no knife was used. At least, not as far as I know.

You ask me if I saw a knife.

I state to you that I only saw a knife when we went to fix the lock of Manilo's garage door. I'm not exactly sure who was in possession of that knife. I think Manilo.

Question-and-Answer Style

The question-and-answer style consists of the police officers' questions and the suspects' answers. In other words, the written text follows a question-and-answer structure. This is generally written as "Q" and "A" or "Question: . . ." and "Answer: . . . ," as can be seen in excerpt 15.3.

Excerpt 15.3: Interview 7 (police record)

QUESTION: In the living room we also encountered some stuff that looks like drugs, whose is that?

ANSWER: I don't know, that is not mine.

QUESTION: Have you ever seen your uncle with a firearm?
ANSWER: No.

QUESTION: Who else comes to your uncle's residence?
ANSWER: My friends and my brother.

Verbatim Transcript

If an interrogation is video- or audio-recorded (which is not standard procedure in the Netherlands), a verbatim transcript can be made based on the recording. Although this may be the most accurate written version of what was said, there can be a wide variety of level of detail within a transcript (see also Bucholtz 2007). For example, whether or not the transcriber includes (measured) pauses, hesitations, laughter, crying, or side conversations can vary. Since there are no verbatim transcripts in my data, I will not include this style in the further analyses.

The three styles found in the data do not reflect the informal conversations that occur in the interrogation room. Nor do they accurately reflect how the suspects' written stories have come about in interactions; this will be demonstrated in the next section.

Constructing Stories in Three Different Styles: The Monologue Style

The police record written in monologue style looks like a volunteered statement by the suspect. Turning back to excerpt 15.1, we see that the first sentence is a first-person account of the caution written as "I have heard and understood that I am not obliged to answer." An abrupt transition follows in which the suspect's age and living situation, as well as information about his parents, are given.

> I have heard and understood that I am not obliged to answer. I am 14 years old. I live with my father. My father's name is Steven Pinas. My mother passed away.

In the next paragraph, information about where the suspect goes to school, what he thinks about this, and how much pocket money he receives is written up from the same first-person perspective.

> I go to Maas Lyceum Amsterdam. It's not going so well at school. I don't feel like going to school anymore. I want to work and earn my own money. I get five euros a week from my father.

What follows are two sentences separated by hard returns.

> I don't smoke or drink.
>
> I don't have a hobby.

Excerpt 15.4 shows the interaction that has led to part of the second paragraph and the last single sentence as shown above. Earlier in the interrogation, the officer asked the suspect where he goes to school. The officer has remembered the suspect's answer and is now typing it up in the record. The text in bold is the text as it occurs in the written police record.

Excerpt 15.4: Interview 3 (minute 9:28)

P: phhhroehmnn.
xxxxxx x x x X
[maas?
[xxxx x x x
S: lyceum amsterdam.
P: x x x x x x x
xx x x x x (2.0)
x x x x x x x
xxxxxxx x X X
x [xxxxxx x x x x x **I go to Maas Lyceum Amsterdam**
[is it going well at school?
(3.0)
not.
S: no.
P: why is that,
(2.0)
S: I don't feel like going to school.
P: you don't feel like going to school,
(4.0)
and what do you feel like?
(2.0)
S: freedom. ((laughing))
P: fourteen years old.
can you handle it,
S: but I don't ↑get it.

26 P: no. (1.0)
27 yes well, (3.0)
28 It's better that way, (4.0)
29 no you you you you g freedom no, (2.0)
30 ↑no look but that's whay I don't get eh,
31 look you're still ↑young.
32 I don't know th- th,
33 t would eh probably be, (1.0)
34 something that is bothering you a bit?
35 hh but take it from me sometimes, (3.0)
36 I wish to be (3.0)your age. (1.0)
37 >> P continues his monologue for 35 seconds (left out of transcription) <<

When the police officer has typed up where the suspect goes to school (lines 2–10), he asks the suspect whether it is going well at school (line 11). After receiving a nonverbal negative response in line 12 and a verbal negative response in line 14, the officer asks the reason for this. The suspect, who is not very talkative throughout the entire interrogation, responds with short answers. The officer often repeats the suspect's answers (for example, line 18) and leaves long pauses (lines 19 and 21). During these repeats, pauses, and further questioning, the officer does not type. Thus there is a change from "doing interrogating" (lines 1–11) to having a more informal conversation (from line 12 onward). We also see this when the suspect laughingly responds to the officer's further questioning (line 22), which is more oriented toward how the suspect feels rather than facts about his social life, such as his age, the name of his school, and so on. From line 26 onward, the officer provides a long (almost one-minute) monologue about the benefits of being young and not having responsibilities. This "moral story," which is filled with fatherly advice, is followed by a couple of question-and-answer sequences and continues for almost three minutes. During this interaction the officer and the suspect talk more about life, working, and earning money.

After these three minutes, during which the officer was "doing being fatherly," the officer types up a summary of what they discussed: "It's not going so well at school. I don't feel like going to school anymore. I want to work and earn my own money. I get five euros a week from my father." This written summary does not show what questions and further conversation elicited this information. Nor does it show the officer's fatherliness toward the suspect, or the suspect's short answers and nontalkativeness. If the officer had not continued questioning the suspect about why he did not want to go to school, the suspect might not have volunteered this information. In fact, the suspect's first reason for not wanting to go to school is that he wants "freedom" (line 22). This is not taken up in the written record. Rather, when only reading the text, a reader might assume that the suspect would rather work hard than go to school. Furthermore, an answer such as "no" in line 14 is written up in a grammatically correct full sentence in the record.

It appears as if the suspect has volunteered all the information in the written text. It also appears as if all the sentences within this paragraph are related—as if his wanting to work and earn his own money is related to "only" receiving 5 euros of pocket money from his father. The interaction that has led to this written record, however, shows that the suspect only responds to questions that are asked, and that the sentences in the record may not be related at all. They are merely answers given in response to questions asked by the officer. In other words, the officer's manner of questioning and advice giving, and therefore the officer's reasoning, play an important role in what is written in the record, as well as how it is written up and in what order.

In sum, the written record is a drastically summarized version of the interaction that preceded it. There are no traces of the officer's questions, suggestions, advice, evaluations, or further questioning. It looks as if the suspect has volunteered all the written text. There are no traces of the suspect's nontalkativeness or any informal conversation. Lacking the context of the talk that went on in the interrogation, a reader of the written record cannot know how the record was constructed. Whereas it reads as if this is the suspect's story, written from his perspective, it is in fact a story initiated by the officer through questioning, advice giving, and evaluating. It is the officer who adapts the talk to written sentences that follow a structure that is created by the police officer himself, but written from the perspective of the suspect.

Constructing Stories in Three Different Styles: The Recontextualized Style

The police record written in the recontextualized style also looks like a volunteered statement by the suspect. However, we do see some traces of the officer's questions in the police record. Turning back to excerpt

15.2, we see that the questions are not written up as questions, but are recontextualized, as if the suspect were responding to the questions asked by the officer. What follows is an answer, also written from the suspect's perspective in first-person monologue style, as the first paragraph from excerpt 15.2 illustrates.

> You ask me which act I performed.
>
> I state to you that I kept the garage door closed and I also helped pull Mervellino into the garage.

The style creates a formal story, owing partly to the complicated recontextualized questions, but also because of the "I state to you" which precedes every answer. Furthermore, it appears as if the suspect volunteered rather elaborate answers consisting of multiple sentences in response to closed questions, as the second and third paragraph demonstrate.

> You ask me if a knife was used.
>
> I state to you that no knife was used. At least, not as far as I know.
>
> You ask me if I saw a knife.
>
> I state to you that I only saw a knife when we went to fix the lock of Manilo's garage door. I'm not exactly sure who was in possession of that knife. I think Manilo.

When we turn to the interaction that led to the written words in the first and second paragraph, we see the following.

Excerpt 15.5: Interview 3 (minute 39:04)

P: and what did you do yourself,
S: I watched a bit? (1.0)
(of [them) helped a bit,
P: [a bit,
huh?
S: I also helped?
P: how [did you help?
S: [( ) kept the door closed,
sometimes i pulled him inside a bit.

10 (2.0)
11 P: x x x x x x xxxxxxxxxxxxxx
12 x x x x x X xxxx x x
13 xxxxxxxxxxxxxxxxxxx
14 (2.0) x X xxxxxxxxxxxxxxxxx x x x x X
15 xx x x x xX xxxxxxxxxxx x x
16 X (1.0) xxxxx (0.5) x x x x x X (0.2)
17 x x x x x x x x x x x x X
18 xxxxxxxxxxxxxxxxx X X X
19 xxxxxxxxxxxxxxxxxxxxxxxxx x x xx
20 xxxxxxx (1.0) **You ask me which act I performed. I state to you that I kept the garage door closed and I also helped pull Mervellino into the garage. You ask me if a knife was used.**
21 X xxx x x x xxxxxx [xxx
22 [was there also a knife used?
23 xxxxx [xx
24 S: [no,
25 [not as far as i know.
26 P: [xxxxxxxxxxxxxxxxxxxx (0.5)
27 xxxxxxxxX xxxxx x x xxxxxxxxxX
28 xxxxxxxxxxxxxx x X X
29 x xxxxxxxxxxxxxxxxxxxxx X [X [X
30 [did [you see a knife?
31 **I state to you that no knife was used. At least, not as far as I know. You ask me if I saw a knife.**

At the beginning of excerpt 15.5 we can see how the first paragraph in the written record has come about. Whereas we see a careful answer from the suspect using "a bit" (lines 2, 3, and 9) and "sometimes" (line 9), we see a straight answer in the text, "I also helped pull Mervellino in the garage," lacking the suspect's nuances . The subtle repeat "a bit huh" from the officer in lines 4 and 5 evokes a more straightforward answer by the suspect in line 6: "I also helped." This is the formulation the officer chooses to use in the written text, rather than the "helped a bit" that was initially given by the suspect.

While typing, the officer continues the case-related phase of the interrogation by asking about whether or not a knife was used (lines 21–22). Whereas the suspect answers only: "No, not as far as I know," this is written up in recontextualized format in full sentences in the second paragraph: "I state to you that no knife was used. At least, not as far as I know." By reformulating the talk to the first-person perspective while showing part of the question as well as the "I state to you" formulation, the written text becomes more formal than the original talk. Furthermore, text is added that was never spoken, in this case the "at least" is added by the officer.

Typical for the case-related phase of the interrogation is that questions and answers follow each other up more rapidly. Whereas we saw a lot of "other" talk in the social-interrogation phase (such as evaluations or advice giving, as demonstrated in excerpt 15.4), the officer is truly interrogating in excerpt 15.5, where questions, answers, and typing follow each other continuously. At the same time, the spoken interaction is often "paused" because of the typing activity (for example, lines 10–21). As the officer asks a new question, it is already being typed up in the record (see lines 21–22 and 29–30). This then shows that the officer expects to write up an answer to the question he has just asked or is about to ask. Again, the officer creates the chronology of the story and the structure on paper by asking questions he deems necessary for the police record story. Even though we do see traces of the questions in this police record style, it also gives a false sense of knowing exactly what questions were asked. As the interaction shows, a question such as the one posed in line 1 ("And what did you do yourself) is transformed into a more formal version: "You ask me which act I performed." Further questions such as "How did you help" (line 7) are not taken up in the record at all.

In sum, although the recontextualized style may include some trace of the questions asked by the officer, this style does not transparently show the interaction that went on during the interrogation. Police officers may have phrased the questions differently and may have asked more questions, as the example above shows. Therefore, not only are the answers reformulated, as we saw in the monologue style, but the questions themselves are also reformulated. Furthermore, the answers given by the suspect appear, as in the monologue style, to have been volunteered, and to have been given in complete, grammatically correct sentences. This creates a false sense of accuracy and does not portray the type of interaction that went on during the interrogation.

Constructing Stories in Three Different Styles: The Question-and-Answer Style

The police record written in question-and-answer style displays an interaction between the officer(s) and the suspect. Questions and answers are marked as such. This style is more commonly used when there are two police officers. In the interrogation below, the two officers had already prepared some questions beforehand by typing full questions and keywords in a document. This document is available on the screen while they are interrogating and typing up the record. As will be shown below, this plays a role in how the interrogation is conducted.

This question-answer style makes the questions the officers ask visible. At the same time, the written record becomes fragmented as questions and answers follow each other up rapidly. As can be seen below, the topic of every paragraph is indicated in the question.

QUESTION: In the living room we also encountered some stuff that looks like drugs, whose is that?
ANSWER: I don't know, that is not mine.

QUESTION: Have you ever seen your uncle with a firearm?
ANSWER: No.

QUESTION: Who else comes to your uncle's residence?
ANSWER: My friends and my brother.

Excerpt 15.6 illustrates how the first two question-and-answer sets in the written record above were constructed in the interaction.

Excerpt 15.6: Interview 7 (minute 20:02)

P2: oh okay.
and also in the: living room?
S: yes?
P2: In the cabinet?
we found the same.
whose is that?
S: that is not mine.
P2: that is not yours.
S: I know that.

10 P2: you know that.
11 (1.0) have you ever seen it there, have you seen it lying there.
12 S: no.
13 P2: no.
14 S: I only know everything going in my room. (1.0)
15 I had everything in my room.
16 P1: ((typing 10 seconds))[4]
17 S: maybe I put it there by accident I dunno.
18 P1: ((typing 19 seconds))
19 (°what do you think of this°)
20 P2: °you say oh° hmn n?
21 P1: ((typing 8 seconds))
22 P2: okay.
23 have you ever seen your uncle with a firearm?
24 that's just a question in ↓between.
25 S: no.
26 P2: NEE?
27 S: no.
28 P1: ((typing 3 seconds))
29 P2: and other persons. (1.5)
30 S: not either.

In this written record we do not see a typical "story" told in narrative format like we saw with the monologue and recontextualized styles, but we see detailed questions with short answers. Questions such as the one posed in lines 2–6 are written up in grammatically correct full sentences, such as "In the living room we also encountered some stuff that looks like drugs, whose is that?" Answers such as the one given by the suspect in 7 and 9 are also reformulated. In the example, the officer adds "I don't know" to the suspect's answer "that is not mine." This suggests that this type of answer (knowing or not knowing) was expected or preferred. The follow-up question in line 11, which receives a negative response, is not taken up in the police record. This occurs again in line 29, which is a follow-up question to the question posed in line 23. This demonstrates that, again, the officers choose which questions to include in the record and which ones to leave out.

In this particular interrogation, some questions were prepared beforehand. In lines 19–20 we clearly hear the two interrogators discussing what question to ask next. There is little of the side talk, laughter, or advice giving that we saw in excerpt 15.4. When an answer is given and "recordable" (Komter 2006), as is shown by the typing, the next question is asked.

In sum, this question-and-answer style in the police record most accurately reflects the questions that were asked during the interaction. This is due in part to the particular question-and-answer style, and in part to the fact that two officers were conducting the interrogation. While one officer (P2) is focusing on "doing interrogating," the other officer (P1) is typing. At the same time, however, not all questions are written up. Again, questions and answers are slightly adapted to make them grammatically correct. We even see an addition to an answer that the suspect never uttered. Although the reader can begin to see how the suspect's story was constructed, the written record still gives a somewhat false sense of the accuracy of what actually went on during the interrogation. After all, it is still the officer who creates the written record and who can choose what to include, how, and in what order.

Conclusions

In this chapter, three styles were discussed that can be found in Dutch and Belgian police records: the monologue, recontextualized, and question-and-answer style. The analyses show that the styles in which the police records are written up contribute to how accurate, formal, and institutionalized the suspect's story becomes. In my data, the social interrogation phase, which generally consists of a lot of informal talk, is always in the monologue style. The case-related phase of the interrogation is written in each of the three styles.

In all styles we see transformations taking place when the interrogation is written up. Generally, we see a summarized version of the talk in the record while the utterances are written up using grammatically correct language. The text becomes more formal and readable for its audience—that is, the participants in the judicial system. At the same time, spoken side talk, advice, and evaluations are left out. Furthermore, the context of the interaction cannot be reconstructed based on the written text alone. Often the police officer's questions are left out. In the monologue style there is no trace of the officer's questions, while in the recontextualized style we see some traces using complex language. Although the question-and-answer style most accurately reflects the questions the officer asked and in what order, not all questions are taken up, and the questions and answers are somewhat reformulated.

Although the question-and-answer style is the most transparent display of how the written record was interactionally constructed, it remains a written version of the interaction as directed by the police officer. We must remember that it is not the officer's job to construct a story: rather, his or her task is to note down, as much as possible in the suspect's own words, what was said in the interrogation room. But because officers seek stories, it may seem logical to construct a narrative on paper. The first-person narrative used in both the monologue and recontextualized styles seems to fit this storytelling idea. But the case studies in this chapter show that the transformations that take place in rendering talk into text are numerous. Such changes can also contribute to how readers of the document place the text within the context in which it was produced. What the exact effects are on the readers within the judicial system cannot be determined based on these qualitative analyses. Research where readers are asked, for example, to rate the believability or trustworthiness of a suspect based on various written versions of their story may provide interesting further insights into the various written styles used in police records.

Notes

1. Generally, this is determined by the type of crime and the maximum punishment one can get for the crime if convicted.

2. This section is based on a more elaborate passage in my doctoral dissertation (see van Charldorp 2011).

3. The translations are mine. The analyses were done on the original Dutch recordings, transcripts, and police records.

4. For reasons of both readability and space, typing is not transcribed with x's.

References

Bucholtz, Mary. 2007. "Variation in Transcription." *Discourse Studies* 9: 784–808.

Clayman, Steven. 1990. "From Talk to Text: Newspaper Accounts of Reporter-Source Interactions." *Media, Culture and Society* 12: 79–103.

Heritage, John, and D. Rod Watson. 1979. "Formulations as Conversational Objects." In *Everyday Language*, edited by George Psathas, 123–162. New York: Irvington Press.

Heydon, Georgina. 2005. *The Language of Police Interviewing: A Critical Analysis*. Basingstoke: Palgrave Macmillan.

Johnson, Alison. 2008. " 'From Where We're Sat . . .': Negotiating Narrative Transformation through Interaction in Police Interviews with Suspects." In "Narrative Analysis in the Shift from Texts to Practices," edited by Anna De Fina and Alexandra Georgakopoulou. Special issue, *Text and Talk* 28(3): 327–349.

Jönsson, Linda, and Per Linell. 1991. "Story Generations: From Dialogical Interviews to Written Reports in Police Interrogations." *Text* 11(3): 419–440.

Komter, Martha. 2006. "From Talk to Text: The Interactional Construction of a Police Record." *Research on Language and Social Interaction* 39(3): 201–228.

Komter, Martha. 2013. "Travels of a Suspect's Statement." In *Legal-Lay Communication: Textual Travels in the Law*, edited by Chris Heffer, Frances Rock, and John Conley, 126–146. Oxford: Oxford University Press.

Maynard, Doug, and Nora C. Schaeffer. 2006. "Standardization-in-Interaction: The Survey Interview." In *Talk in Interaction in Social Research Methods*, edited by Paul Drew, Geoffrey Raymond, and Dan Weinberg, 9–27. London: Sage.

Rock, Frances. 2001. "The Genesis of a Witness Statement." *Forensic Linguistics* 8(2): 44–72.

Sliedrecht, Keun Young, and Tessa van Charldorp. 2011. "Tussen spraak en schrift: De rol van samenvattingen in het politieverhoor." *Tijdschrift voor Taalbeheersing* 33(1): 34–55.

van Charldorp, Tessa. 2011. *From Police Interrogation to Police Record*. Oisterwijk: Boxpress.

van Charldorp, Tessa. 2014. "'What Happened?' From Talk to Text in Police Interrogations." *Language & Communication* 36(1): 7–31.

van Charldorp, Tessa [T. C.], and Rudi Schellingen. 2014. "Het opstellen van een proces-verbaal." In *Verdachtenverhoor: Meer dan het stellen van Vragen*, edited by Rudi Schellingen and Nienke Scholten, 255–269. Mechelen: Kluwer Belgium.

CHAPTER SIXTEEN

Police Records in Court

The Narrative Fore- and Backgrounding of Information by Judges in Inquisitorial Criminal Court

Fleur van der Houwen

Introduction

In Dutch criminal trials the case file plays an important role (Malsch and Nijboer 2005). The case file consists of various documents such as statements by the suspect, witnesses, or experts. Judges as well as the other parties use the case file to prepare for the case. In court the judges have as their task to "find the truth" and investigate whether what the prosecutor has claimed can also be proven. The case file serves as a reference. According to the immediacy principle, judges must base their decisions on the material that they have dealt with in court (Article 301:4 of the Code of Criminal Procedure). In the Netherlands witnesses are normally not heard again in court—their written statements are used instead. The statements of the people involved are therefore not immediate but rather mediated (Nijboer 2008).

Judges need not read all documents out loud, which might in any case be undesirable considering the size of some files; they generally confine themselves to summarizing and verifying what is in the case file (Malsch and Nijboer 2005: 32). Not everything in the case file is equally relevant with regard to the charges against the suspect. Furthermore, there may be repetition, as suspects and witnesses might, for instance, agree on where and when something happened but not on how it happened. The case file therefore contains more information than judges need to put to the court; it also contains some information that is repeated in various documents but that needs to be put to the court only once.

How information is reported or summarized from the case file has implications for what type of information is fore- or backgrounded—that is, what information may be designated as more or less "important." A study on reported speech in American courts (Phillips 1986) shows that direct and indirect speech in the discourse of prosecutors and defense attorneys have a fore- and backgrounding function respectively. Another study on fore- and backgrounding in British courts (Felton Rosulek 2009) shows how prosecutors foreground different types of information from defense lawyers. The prosecution foregrounds the narrative of the criminal charges more than the defense does and also more strongly emphasizes the role of the accused. Unlike prosecutors and defense attorneys, judges have a neutral position in a criminal trial. Whereas prosecutors and defense attorneys can draw on different reporting strategies to strengthen the rhetoric of their statements (see, for example, van der Houwen and Sneijder 2014), judges report from the case file while examining the suspect and are expected to do so objectively.

The analyses are based on a corpus of 34 criminal trials recorded in the Netherlands.[1] The data were transcribed and analyzed using conversation analysis (e.g., Heritage and Clayman 2010). Conversation analysis is a particularly useful method for analyzing the sequential context of the various types of reporting by the judges—that is, analyzing the reports by examining what utterances precede and follow it. Three broad linguistic strategies were found that invoke the content of the case file: summaries or paraphrases, indirect reports, and direct reports. This chapter analyzes how judges report from the case file and what information they summarize, report indirectly, or report directly, and thus how they emphasize for the court some information over other information in constructing a version of what happened and on which the judgment will be based.

Reported Speech

In research on reported speech, a distinction is generally made between direct and indirect perspectives—a distinction based on whether the deictic center is in the current speech or writing situation (e.g., John said that he . . .) or the original context in which the words were or would have been uttered (e.g., John said: "I . . ."). Reported speech has been the object of many studies and has been examined from different perspectives such as those of syntax, semantics, and pragmatics (e.g., Wierzbicka 1974; Coulmas 1986); sociolinguistics and language variation (e.g., Vincent and Perrin 1999; van der Houwen 2012); interactional linguistics (Tannen 1989); and conversation analysis (e.g., Holt and Clift 2007; van der Houwen 2013).

Although many different functions of direct speech have been identified, there appear to be two main ones: the theatrical function of direct speech and involving the audience (e.g., Labov 1972; Banfield 1973; Wierzbicka 1974; Chafe 1982; Tannen 1989); and its "evidential" function, because direct speech, in pretending to report the exact words, would be more accurate, believable, and trustworthy than other forms of reported speech (e.g., Li 1986; Philips 1986; Holt 1996; Wooffitt 2001; Galatolo 2007). For indirect reported speech, fewer functions have been identified, possibly because the focus tends to be on direct speech and its relative functions as compared to indirect speech (more theatrical and more trustworthy than indirect speech). Studies that have compared the two strategies in their own right (Philips 1986; van der Houwen 1998, 2000; Lowe and Hurlimann 2002) have distinguished the two in terms of fore- and backgrounding. This will be elaborated on below.

Interactional studies have generally examined reported speech in narrative context, both in everyday conversations (e.g., Tannen 1989; Holt 1996) and in institutional settings (Baynham 1996), including judicial settings (Philips 1986; Matoesian 2000; Galatolo 2007; D'hondt and van der Houwen 2014). Distinguishing narrative from nonnarrative discourse is not straightforward. In a criminal trial, for instance, judges' task is to find the truth, that is, to put the facts (and not the "story") on the table. But the facts and the narrative are not mutually exclusive; the facts are part of what happened in the narrative. We might expect the evidential function as well as the theatrical and involving character of direct reports to be intertwined in the context of courtroom proceedings. The examination of the facts by the judge follows the indictment; this means that only the guilt of the accused is examined and not his or her innocence. The truth that is sought in the criminal procedure hence is not balanced ("the truth is unbalanced" [de waarheid hangt scheef], Enschedé 2008). How believable the facts and charges are often depends on the narrative context in which it took place, a narrative constructed by the prosecution.

A judicially relevant narrative is not the same as an everyday narrative, but we do find a similar structure. In this study I therefore use Labov's narrative structure (1972) in an explorative way. In an everyday narrative about a bank robbery, it may not be very interesting to know exactly how the suspect got a knife or which one of two bank robbers was holding a gun at a specific moment. In a courtroom narrative however, these tend to be the facts that need to become clear and can have climax status because of their juridical implications. In a narrative, different elements may be fore- and backgrounded. The abstract and orientation of a narrative, for instance, tend to have backgrounding information, whereas the climax is foregrounded. Foregrounded information is "high deictic"—that is, it instructs the audience to pay attention—while backgrounded information is "low deictic," with lesser urging of the audience to do inferential work (García 1975).

In reporting strategies we find a parallel with high deicticism in direct speech and low deicticism in indirect reporting strategies. A study on reported speech in American courts (Philips 1986) shows that direct speech and indirect speech in the discourse of prosecutors and defense attorneys have a fore- and backgrounding function respectively. Lowe and Hurlimann (2002) observe a similar pattern in narrative texts in Cerma, a West African language. In Cerma mental processes are always cited indirectly and function as backgrounding information, because these mental processes do not advance the story line. In interactions in the courtroom, narrative and nonnarrative are strongly intertwined. A mental process—for instance, intention—can function as foregrounding information in a criminal trial. Another study on fore- and backgrounding in British courts (Felton Rosulek 2009) shows how prosecutors foreground different information from defense lawyers, in line with their respective roles. Prosecutors foreground the narrative of the criminal charges more than the defense and also emphasize the role of the accused more than do defense attorneys.

Judges in a criminal trial must, however, maintain a neutral position (but see for instance van der Houwen and Jol 2016) . Whereas prosecutors and defense attorneys can draw on different reporting strategies to strengthen the rhetoric of their statements (see, e.g., Sneijder 2011; van der Houwen and Sneijder 2014), judges read the case file and use it as a reference during the proceedings. For judges, the case file thus serves as both a source from which they can select information that they need to put before the court on which they will base their decision and a basis for further questioning to clarify those documents in the case file that contain diverging accounts of what happened.

Considering the different functions that direct and indirect reporting strategies have in terms of fore- and backgrounding the information reported, this chapter further examines the discourse of judges and how they put information from the case file to the court. The aim is to get more insight into how judges manage information they report from the case file in light of the fore- and backgrounding strategies inherent to reported speech. At the basis of the analysis is deixis—either high or low. It is in the linguistic nature of these reporting strategies to be either high or low deictic, but this difference is not always made clear and can lead to circular reasoning. A judge may choose either high-deictic (cueing the listener to pay attention) or low-deictic (also important but not more important than the surrounding discourse) reporting. The choice (which may or may not be conscious) for one or the other strategy fore- or backgrounds the reported information.

Data

The analyses in this chapter are based on the examination of a corpus of 34 Dutch criminal trials. Five of the trials were videotaped in 2008, and 29 were audiotaped in 1990. Various fragments from the larger corpus will be used to illustrate patterns in the reporting strategies found. Although reported speech is ubiquitous in Dutch criminal trials, for clarity of the analysis most fragments will come from one case. The data were transcribed and organized with the software program Transana (Woods and Fassnacht 2009) following a simplified version of conversation-analytic transcription conventions (Jefferson 2004). In this chapter the original Dutch fragments have been translated into English, staying as close as possible to the original Dutch. Some of the translations may seem awkward or ungrammatical, but the original in those cases was also awkward and ungrammatical. I tried to maintain some of the conventions (such as pauses and hesitations) in order to give the reader something of a feel for the interaction, but most conventions do not allow for smooth translation. Considering the focus on reported speech, this should not get in the way of the analysis.

Criminal trials in the Netherlands are organized as follows (Tak 2008):

1. identification of the accused by the judge;
2. reading of the charge by the public prosecutor;
3. examination of the accused, witnesses and experts by the judge, followed by additional questions of the accused and witnesses by the public prosecutor and defense counsel;
4. the closing statements of the prosecutor and defence counsel;
5. the accused's final statement;
6. deliberation by the judge in chambers; and
7. delivery of the verdict and sentence in open court within two weeks.

For this study the third part, the examination of the accused by the judge, was examined. Instances of various forms of reported speech were collected in the form of clips and then further categorized. The use of reported speech in other parts of the proceedings has been left out of this study (but see van der Houwen 2013 or van der Houwen and Sneijder 2014 for a study that also examines reported speech in other parts of the trial).

Findings

Most examples in the analysis below come from one case in which the suspect is accused of having tried to strangle his fiancée. Using one case makes it possible to show how the narrative structure builds and how it relates to reporting strategies used.

Indirect Perspective

Judges can invoke a document from the case file in various ways using an indirect perspective: summarizing the information in the documents, paraphrasing, or reporting indirectly. The deictic center of this indirect way of reporting lies with the judge (whereas with a direct perspective the deictic center would be with the reported speaker). In this paragraph I give two examples in which the judge reports from an indirect perspective. Excerpt 16.1 gives an example of summarizing, and excerpt 16.2 shows an example of an indirect report. Both fragments come from the beginning of the case after the suspect has been identified and the prosecuting officer has read the indictment.

Summarizing

Excerpt 16.1: Attempted strangulation of fiancée

50:→ J: I will tell a few things that we do not have a discussion about.
51 e:h you have (3.0) lived together with Dorien for a few years,(.)
52 from the summer 1987, (.)
53 first at the Prinsenhof,
54 (.) and later I believe in your student flat,
[. . .]
67 J: there an argument arose,
68 on that day,
69 eh an argument about e:h (.)
70 if maybe you e::h (.) were seeing an eh other girl,
[. . .]
89 J: so in that argument things happened,
90 that should not have happened,
91 and I should now (.) talk to you about this.

In excerpt 16.1 the judge reports information that, as she frames it, is not under discussion (line 50). When information is not disputed it is likely to be the same in different documents (for instance, both the suspect's and the witness's statements give the same information regarding where they lived and that they had an argument). Referring to specific documents (e.g., "at the police station the witness stated. . . . or on page 27 of your statement you say . . .") is then not necessary (compare how in an academic article one generally does not give references for information that has been accepted by the community as common knowledge [Buttny 1998: 45]).

The judge summarizes what she understood from the case file (beginning in line 51). After line 54 ("and later I believe in your student flat") there is a correction with regard to where the suspect lived first (namely, first in the student flat and later at the Prinsenhof). The formulation "I believe" reflects insecurity about the information or the order of events and projects a possible alternative version, which indeed is given by the suspect (following line 54, not included in excerpt). And although where the argument took place is relevant information, it is not disputed. After the correction the judge continues her summary without invoking documents and concludes with a forward reference to what the case is really about (line 89–91). Excerpt 16.1 is therefore an introduction to the case: the judge puts to the court some background facts that the parties involved agree upon in the form of a summary.

Excerpt 16.2 follows a bit after the previous extract. The judge questions the suspect about how things went during the fight. The parties involved still agree about what happened—namely, that at a certain point the suspect sat on top of the victim—but it takes a little more negotiation for the judge to get this part of the narrative on record.

Indirect report

Excerpt 16.2: Attempted strangulation of fiancée

116 J: in that e:h pushing and pulling between you and your girlfriend,
117 she ended up on the bed.
118 (2.0)
119 S: we both ended up on the bed.
120 J: you too.
121 S: yes.
122 J: e::h you on top of her?
123 (7.0)
124 S: that (.) I can (.) not e::h answer exactly if you mean by that
125 [if from the first moment I on top of her—
126→ J: [well (.) you (.) sai:d at the police station
127→ and she says that too,
128 that she at a given moment in that e:h pushing and throwing,
129 e:h ended up on the bed on her back,
130 And that you then on top of her
131 yeah sat down,
132 each side of her body one knee,
133 and (.) so yes
134→ that is her story.
135 is that true?
136 S: Well yes at a given moment that was [of course true
137 J: [(that you at a given moment—)
138 of course,
139 at a given moment,
140 because if you wrestle a bit with one another,

141 then every moment a new situation arises
142 but that did happen then
143 like eh (.) it was said then. (2.0)

The sequential position of the indirect report differs from the summary in excerpt 16.1. The judge in excerpt 16.2 asks the suspect for clarification about the fight, to which the suspect, after a seven-second pause, gives an evasive answer. This prompts the judge to refer to the case file (see also van der Houwen 2013 for a more elaborate analysis of this pattern) and what was said by both the suspect and the witness (lines 126–127), suggesting that the suspect and witness agree. It is not entirely clear whose words are actually being reported: line 126 suggests they are the suspect's words ("you said at the police station"), but line 134 indicates it is his fiancée, the victim, whose words are reported ("that is her story"). The judge appears to establish as much common ground as possible between the parties involved, first by framing the indirect quote as belonging to both parties and then by mirroring the suspect's reasoning about "being on top" ("at a given moment, of course"), thereby establishing that the suspect was on top of the victim at some point ("but that did happen," line 142). So as we are getting closer to the heart of the case, namely whether the suspect tried to strangle his fiancée, the reporting comes closer to the original words in the case file (but not necessarily the suspect's or witness's original words!), though the reporting perspective is still indirect.

Direct Perspective

Just as reporting from an indirect perspective can take different forms (summarizing, paraphrasing, indirect reported speech), reporting from a direct perspective also takes different forms. The direct perspective can be introduced by a *verbum dicendi* (in this corpus, for instance, a form of "say," "tell," or "state") or some other form of framing reference to the written source (for instance, in this corpus, "it says here," "I read here," "on page 13"). The direct report may also occur without a *verbum dicendi* or other framing and may instead stand alone. In that case, the quality of the reporter's voice or gesture cues the audience that perspectives have changed. In the following fragment, from the same case, we see an example of direct reporting (in a "reading out loud" tone).

Excerpt 16.3: Case 9, attempted strangulation of fiancée

176 J: e:h well that is the point
177 that is one of the (.) things that you are accused of by the prosecuting officer
178 that you with a belt put that belt around her neck,
179 And that you pulled it.
180 Do you remember anything from this? (.)
181 S: No I don't remember anything from this. (.)
182 J: ( )
183 (3.0)
184 → myeah you have said,
185 That you at a given moment >at the police station you said that<
[. . .]
192 ((leafing through pages 5 seconds))
193 Page thirty. (7.0)
194 You make—
195 You say (. .) at (.) the police station,
196 I will read it out e:h (.) e:h literally,
197 S: (you do that)

Excerpt 16.3 shows a typical sequential embedding for direct reports in the corpus studied, and it differs from the sequential context of summaries and indirect reports. The judge in excerpt 16.3 introduces the information reported from the case file as the central point of the case (line 176). She puts the version of events in the indictment to the suspect and verifies it with him (line 180). The answer by the suspect, who does not recall (line 181), is dispreferred, at which point the judge resorts to the case file, reading out the suspect's statement regarding the strangulation as written down by the police on an earlier occasion. Thus, we see how the direct report is embedded in a three-part structure, in which (1) the judge verifies a charge as stated in the indictment (lines 176–180), (2) the suspect does not give a confirmation, and (3) the judge reads a relevant fragment out loud from the case file to provide a preferred answer—one that is in line with the version as stated by the prosecuting officer in the indictment (see also van der Houwen 2013).

In sum, what we have seen is a judicial narrative that develops from an orientation (excerpt 16.1) to the complicating action (excerpt 16.2) and the "judicial climax" (excerpt 16.3), with linguistic reporting strategies that fit the narrative development: the summary of documents in the case file (excerpt 16.1) comes at the beginning of the case; the indirect report gives information from the case file that leads up to the "climax" or possibly disputed information (excerpt 16.2). The direct report is used at the "judicial climax" (excerpt 16.3). The larger corpus shows similar patterns in the different cases.

Indirect and Direct Perspectives That Alternate

Indirect and direct perspectives generally do not follow each other as neatly as in the case shown above; rather, direct and indirect perspectives may alternate, especially within the narrative part of the complicating action (if we can freely apply Labov's narrative structure to the courtroom discourse of examining the evidence). Although there are different interactional patterns in which reports occur, I discuss the following pattern in more detail:

1. J: states how something happened and asks question
2. S: does not know/denies/ gives a version that is different from what the judge has stated
3. J: cites from the case file.

We saw this pattern in excerpt 16.2: (1) the judge puts forth a version of what happened before the court and (2) the suspect qualifies this somewhat (they were both on the bed). Steps 1 and 2 are recycled when the judge asks a question for clarification, the suspect does not remember, and then (3) the judge reports indirectly from the case file. We also saw this pattern in excerpt 16.3: (1) the judge announces what the prosecutor has accused the suspect of, followed by a question; (2) the suspect denies it; and (3) the judge reports directly from the case file.

Below I show two more examples, both from a case that involves minors. The suspect, Manilo, allegedly deprived the victim of his liberty twice by holding him in a garage. In excerpt 16.4 the judge reports from the victim's statement how he was held the first time. The suspect disputes this and says it was the second time.

Excerpt 16.4: Case 2b, minors: holding boy in garage

1271 J: Yes because he said the first time
[. . .] [Judge reports directly from the victim's statement]
1279 S: That was the second time

1280	J:	Yes well yes okay
1281		He stated (that differently) that it was the first time

In except 16.4 the judge puts a version to the court in the words of the victim. The suspect does not disagree with the version, but he does disagree that this was the first time he held the victim in the garage. The judge reports what the victim has stated indirectly (line 1281). Both the framing ("yes well yes okay") and the low-deictic, indirect report suggest that the judge does not consider this detail essential and does not put it on record more explicitly using a direct report. After the negotiation about whether this was the first or second time the victim was held (excerpt 16.4), the judge continues his report from the victim's statement in excerpt 16.5, which is a little more complex regarding perspective-taking. To assist the reader in reading the transcript, I have labeled the utterances either DP (direct perspective) or IP (indirect perspective).

Excerpt 16.5: Case 2b, minors, holding boy in garage

1282	J:	DP	And- and he says in the end we came back on the uh street
1283		IP	And then you ask, right, he says
1284		IP	again
1285		IP	eh to go into the box [i.e., the garage]
1286		IP	and uh he then doubts a little
1287		DP	but he says well yes because it only was Mani- Manilo
1288		DP	I did go back
1289	S:		Well that is not true
1290	J:		[hm
1291	S:		[he just
1292			came back himself
1293			he had not said anything at all
1294	J:		hm
1295	S:		He came back just like that
1296	J:		yes
1297	S:		He thought that it was a joke
1298	J:		yes
1299			(1.0)
1300→			Well he said
1301		DP	And then Manilo tried to lock me up in the box [garage] again

1302	DP	I wanted to leave
1303	DP	And then they held me back
1304	DP	By standing in front of the uh uh uh entrance

The judge continues his report from the victim's statement, switching between direct perspectives (DP) and indirect perspectives (IP) (lines 1282–1288). The suspect denies this version and offers an alternative one, which the judge acknowledges. After a short pause the judge reports again from the victim's statement, giving a version of events (lines 1289–1297) that differs from what the suspect has just claimed. The charge that the judge examines is whether this was a case of deprivation of liberty, as stated by the prosecuting officer. The judge follows the indictment and also reports from the document in which this version is given (the victim's statement rather than the suspect's). The information reported is directly relevant for the judgment and is reported with the best-fitting strategy: the high-deictic, direct perspective.

The question is, when do judges choose a direct perspective, and when do they choose an indirect one? The analyses of the larger corpus, as illustrated here with fragments, suggest three things: (1) if judges introduce a (new) fact, they tend to use an indirect perspective to report the relevant introductory information from the case file; (2) if the suspect does not know or disagrees (even in part) with the version the judge puts to the court, an indirect report tends to follow, which "argues" with the suspect, and if the suspect is more adamant, a direct report tends to follow; and (3) if the information is not directly relevant to the judgment, an indirect report is used, while if it is directly relevant, a direct report is used.

Discussion and Conclusions

This study has shown the important role police records play in Dutch criminal courts. Although police records are to be written down in "the suspect's own words," various studies (e.g., Komter 2002; van Charldorp 2011) have shown that transformations take place in the process from spoken to written statements. Further transformation takes place at trial, when information from these statements is reported not only selectively but also in different ways linguistically, which further fore- or backgrounds different aspects of the case. The criminal-trial narrative is fed by the different narratives as they were written down by the police in the various statements on earlier occasions. From these different narratives, judges need to construct a version of events on which to base the judgment, and one way they do this is to draw texts selectively from the case file. As we saw, the judge has different ways of putting information from the case file to the court, by paraphrasing, reporting indirectly, or reporting directly. Depending on the strategy chosen, the information is more or less prominently on record. These various linguistic strategies help judges direct the interaction and create a new and coherent version of what happened.

This case study has exemplified patterns found in the larger corpus: a summary can function to give background information that is (at that moment) assumed to be undisputed, to give a general picture, or to create a version that is supported by more than one statement. Indirect reported speech differs from summaries in that it is closer, or at least pretends to be closer, to the original words. With indirect reports, judges tend to name the person whose statement is cited. Direct speech, on the other hand, appears to be used when it concerns information directly relevant to the charges, to support a specific version—for example, when the suspect's statement in court differs from a statement given earlier, by either the suspect or others. Direct reports also tend to follow denials by the suspect. Examination of how judges put information from the case file to the court is relevant, because this is not a neutral activity, and the reporting strategy chosen will fore- or background the information reported and hence make some elements in a story more or less salient, thereby constructing a version of what allegedly happened that may implicate the suspect to a greater or lesser degree.

Note

1. This study was funded by NWO Programmatic Research in the Humanities, grant number 360–70–240.

References

Banfield, Ann. 1973. "Narrative Style and the Grammar of Direct and Indirect Speech." *Foundations of Language* 10: 1–39.

Baynham, Michael. 1996. "Direct Speech: What's It Doing in Non-narrative Discourse?" *Journal of Pragmatics* 25: 61–81.

Buttny, Richard.1998. "Putting Prior Talk into Context: Reported Speech and the Reporting Context." *Research on Language and Social Interaction* 31(1): 45–58.

Chafe, Wallace. 1982. "Integration and Involvement in Speaking, Writing and Oral Literature." In *Spoken and Written Language: Exploring Orality and Literacy*, edited by Deborah Tannen, 35–53. Norwood, NJ: Ablex.

Coulmas, Florian. 1986. "Reported Speech: Some General Issues." In *Direct and Indirect Speech*, edited by Florian Coulmas, 1–28. Berlin: Mouton de Gruyter.

D'hondt, Sigurd, and Fleur van der Houwen, eds. 2014. Editorial. In "Quoting From the Case File: Intertextuality in Judicial Settings." Special issue, *Language & Communication* 36: 1–6.

Enschedé, Ch. J. 2008. *Beginselen van strafrecht*. Deventer: Kluwer.

Felton Rosulek, Laura. 2009. "The Sociolinguistic Creation of Opposing Representations of Defendants and Victims." *International Journal of Speech, Language and the Law* 16(1): 1–30.

Galatolo, Renata. 2007. "Active Voicing in Court." In *Reporting Talk: Reported Speech in Interaction*, edited by Elizabeth Holt and Rebecca Clift, 95–220. Studies in Interactional Sociolinguistics 24. Cambridge: Cambridge University Press.

García, Erica C. 1975. *The Role of Theory in Linguistic Analysis: The Spanish Pronoun System*. Amsterdam: North-Holland.

Heritage, John, and Steven Clayman. 2010. *Talk in Action: Interactions, Identities and Institutions*. Oxford: Blackwell.

Holt, Elizabeth. 1996. "Reporting Talk: The Use of Direct Reported Speech in Conversation." *Research on Language and Social Interaction* 29: 219–245.

Holt, Elizabeth, and Rebecca Clift, eds. 2007. *Reporting Talk: Reported Speech in Interaction*. Studies in Interactional Sociolinguistics 24. Cambridge: Cambridge University Press.

Jefferson, Gail. 2004. "Glossary of Transcript Symbols with an Introduction," In *Conversation Analysis: Studies from the First Generation*, edited by Gene H. Lerner, 13–23. Philadelphia: John Benjamins.

Komter, Marta. 2002. "The Suspect's Own Words: The Treatment of Written Statements in Dutch Courtrooms." *Forensic Linguistics* 9(2): 168–192.

Labov, William. 1972. "The Transformation of Experience in Narrative Syntax." In *Language in the Inner City*, 354–396. Philadelphia: University of Pennsylvania Press.

Li, Charles. 1986. "Direct and Indirect Speech: A Functional Study." In *Direct and Indirect Speech*, edited by Florian Coulmas, 9–45. Berlin: Mouton de Gruyter.

Lowe, Ivan-Margaret, and Ruth Hurlimann. 2002. "Direct and Indirect Speech in Cerma Narrative." In *Reported Discourse: A Meeting Ground for Differ-*

ent Linguistic Domains, edited by Tom Güldemann and Manfred von Roncador, 71–90. Amsterdam: John Benjamins.

Malsch, Marijke, and Hans Nijboer. 2005. *De zichtbaarheid van het rech: Openbaarheid van destrafrechtspleging*. Deventer: Kluwer.

Matoesian, Gregory. 2000. "Intertextual Authority in Reported Speech: Production Media in the Kennedy Smith Rape Trial." *Journal of Pragmatics* 32(7): 879–914.

Nijboer, Hans. 2008. "Doornroosje wordt wakker." *Expertise en Recht* 6: 203–208.

Philips, Susan. 1986. "Reported Speech as Evidence in an American Trial." In *Languages and Linguistics: The Interdependence of Theory, Data and Application*, edited by Deborah Tannen and James E. Alatis, 154–170. Washington, DC: Georgetown University Press.

Sneijder, Petra 2011. "Citaten in requisitoir en pleidooi: Een retorische structuur." *Tijdschrift voor Taalbeheersing* 33(1): 55–68.

Tak, Peter. 2008. *The Dutch Criminal Justice System*. Wolf Legal Publishers.

Tannen, Deborah. 1989. *Talking Voices: Repetition, Dialogue, and Imagery in Conversational Discourse*. Cambridge: Cambridge University Press.

van Charldorp, Tessa. 2011. *From Police Interrogation to Police Record*. Oisterwijk: Boxpress.

van der Houwen, Fleur. 1998. "Organizing Discourse: Direct and Indirect Speech in Mexican Spanish." *Linguistics in the Netherlands* (January): 123–134.

van der Houwen, Fleur. 2000. "El habla directa vs. indirecta y la organización del discurso." In "Estudio analítico del signo lingüístico: Teoría y descripción," edited by Bob de Jonge. Special issue, *Foro hispánico: Revista hispánica de Flandes y Holanda* 17: 27–40.

van der Houwen, Fleur. 2012. "The Effect of Genre on Reporting Speech: Conversations and Newspaper Articles." *Borealis: International Journal of Hispanic Linguistics* 1(1): 101–130.

van der Houwen, Fleur. 2013. "Reported Writing in Court: Putting Evidence 'On Record.'" *Text & Talk* 33(6): 747–769.

van der Houwen, Fleur, and Petra Sneijder. 2014. "From Text to Talk in Criminal Court: Prosecuting, Defending, and Examining the Evidence." In "Quoting from the Case File: Intertextuality in Judicial Settings," edited by Sigurd D'hondt and Fleur van der Houwen. Special issue, *Language & Communication* 36: 37–52.

van der Houwen, Fleur and Guusje, Jol. 2016. "Negotiating the Right to Remain Silent in Inquisitorial Trials." In *The Discursive Constructions of Consent in the Legal Process,* edited by Susan Ehrlich, Diana Eades, and Janet Ainsworth, 264–286. Oxford University Press.

Vincent, Diane, and Laurent Perrin. 1999. "On the Narrative vs. Non-Narrative Functions of Reported Speech: A Socio-Pragmatic Study." *Journal of Sociolinguistics* 3(3): 291–313.

Vincent, Diane, and Laurent Perrin. 1999. "On the Narrative vs. Non-Narrative Functions of Reported Speech: A Socio-Pragmatic Study." *Journal of Sociolinguistics* 3(3): 291–313.

Wierzbicka, Anna. 1974. "The Semantics of Direct and Indirect Discourse." *Papers in Linguistics* 7: 267–307.

Woods, David, and Chris Fassnacht. 2009. *Transana* 2(41). https://www.transana.org. Madison, WI: Board of Regents of the University of Wisconsin System.

Wooffitt, Robin. 2001. "Raising the Dead: Reported Speech in Medium-Sitter Interaction." *Discourse Studies* 3: 351–374.

Index

Page numbers followed by "f" and "t" refer to figures and tables, respectively.

Abbe, Allison, 54–55
accumulative construction, 90
  of provocation, 90 (*see also under* Truong interrogation)
  of responsibility, 101–6
  of spontaneity, 97–101
Achieving Best Evidence in Criminal Proceedings (*ABE*), 23, 24, 27, 28, 31, 32, 34, 37
affect sharing, 56–57
Alison, Laurence, 43–44
Appadurai, Arjun, 299
appeals-to-self-interest strategy, 66, 67, 71
  minimization, sympathy, and, 78–82
  with and without a time-limited offer, 71, 74–77
"Are you saying X?," 268, 270, 274, 281, 282, 285–87
argumentation stage, 66
asylum seekers, 300–301
attorneys. *See* counsel
audio recording. *See* recording(s) of interrogations
Authorised Professional Practice (*APP*). *See under* College of Policing

backgrounding of information by judges, 350–53, 361–62
Baldwin, John, 45
beating hand gestures, 273, 275, 280, 281, 283, 284
Berk-Seligson, Susan, 4, 306
bilingual police, 10
bilinguals, trained interpreters vs. untrained, 200, 205, 206
  credibility of participants as perceived by interview participants, 209
  discourse analysis
    informal introductions, 214–16
    interpreter introductions, 210
    professional introductions, 210–14
  formal training and experience, 206, 206t
  interpreter protocols and turn control, 216
    managing utterances addressed to interpreter, 217–23
  interpreting performance by, 209, 209f
blame mitigation, 87
  the discourse structure of, 89–106
    the accumulative construction of provocation, 90
  See also minimization
Boeri, David, 108n2
Brandon, Susan, 54–55
Brooks, Peter, 115–16
Bucholtz, Mary, 276–77
Buckley, Joseph P., 90

case-related phase of interrogation, 330, 332–34, 336, 342–43, 346
categories (membership categorization analysis), 159
category-bound activities (membership categorization analysis), 159
category-tied descriptions (membership categorization analysis), 160

challenging. *See under* PEACE model: phases
Cherryman, Julie, 48–49
clarification, 182, 183. *See also under* PEACE model: phases
clarifying questions, 142–44, 148
closed questions/closed-ended questions, 48, 49, 228, 241
closing phases of interview, 76, 161, 201, 202, 277, 333. *See also* closure phase
closure phase (PEACE model), 141, 147
codes of practice, legal and institutional, 23–24
code switching, 216, 217, 236–37
coercive interrogations, 70, 107
  and confessions, 42–44, 85–86, 107–8
  disadvantages, 43, 44
  empathy and, 58, 82
  forms of "mild" coercion, 51
  linguistics, discourse analysis, and, 87, 107–8
  maximization, minimization, and, 86, 87
  moving away from coercion, 45
  overview, 42–44
  PEACE model and, 59–60
College of Policing (England and Wales), 53–54
  principles and standards, 24
    Authorised Professional Practice: Investigative Interviewing (*APP*), 22–24, 27, 28, 38
compassion, 48, 49, 149. *See also* empathy
confession narratives, 113–20, 131–32
  sequences enacted to procure, 120
    tell us what happened, 120–22
    now let me tell you what happened, 122–28
    tell me again what happened, 128–31
  suspect owning the narrative, 128–29
confessions, 132
  coercive interrogations and, 42–44, 85–86, 107–8
  contamination of, 131, 132
  convictions quashed based on "unreliable," 45
  false, 65–66, 85–87, 107, 130, 132 (*see also* Truong interrogation)
  interviewer characteristics and, 52–53
  interview tactics and, 52, 66, 71, 78 (*see also* maximization; minimization)
  nature of, 113–18
  not provided voluntarily, 42–43
  ownership of (*see* ownership, story)
  PEACE model and, 49, 50, 59, 65–66
  storytelling and, 113–17, 126, 128, 131, 132
  suspects' intentions and decisions to (not) make, 44
  techniques used to elicit, 156–57, 164–67
confession-seeking objective of police interviewing, 60, 76–77, 136. *See also* confession narratives
confirmation-seeking questions, 256
confrontational model, 66. *See also* Reid technique
confrontation stage of interrogation, 77
confronting the suspect, 67, 70–77, 79–81. *See also* gestures
connectedness
  defined, 72
  See also separateness: vs. connectedness
constructed dialogue, 273–74
construction
  of events (*see* narrative construction)
  of proof, 2
  See also under Truong interrogation
contradictions and contradictory evidence, 51, 88, 189–90, 284, 292. *See also* inconsistencies
contrast strategy, 188–91
conversation analysis (CA), 26, 108n3, 139, 140, 151, 350
conversation analytic role-playing method (CARM), 294n4
cooperative recycle, 255
cooperative reorientation and defining the crime, 254–58
counsel
  indirect requests/invocations for, 69, 70, 81
  prewaiver invocation for, 68–69
"covert policing," 157
Craig, Larry, 160–61
Craig, Robert T., 304, 305
Criminal Interrogation and Confessions (Inbau et al.), 86
Crown Prosecution Service (CPS), 323

Deese, James, 55
deictic center, 354
deicticism, 352, 353

deictic pointing, 273, 280, 284, 292
deletion, formulation and, 274
denials, PEACE-fully overcoming, 50–51
detectives
  beliefs of experienced, 48–49
  sympathetic, 77–82
direct perspectives (DP), 357–59
  alternating indirect perspectives (IP) and, 359–61
discursive psychology, 4–5
double essence of interaction, 292
dramatized formulations, 270, 274, 278, 286, 288, 291, 292. *See also* "Kidnapping" case
Drew, Paul, 2
drug possession. *See* heroin possession with intent to sell or deliver, 2015 case of
Dutch criminal courts. *See under* Netherlands

ecologies of gesture, 275
"elicited narrative," 179
embodied actions, 268, 276. *See also* gestures; "Kidnapping" case
embodied talk, 270
empathic contagion, 56
empathic understanding, level of, 52
empathic vs. forensic questioning, 31–38
empathy
  ABE and, 27, 28, 31
  communicating, 27–30, 38–39
    and confessions, 52–53, 59
  continuum of types, aspects, and levels of, 56f, 56–57
  definitions, 53, 55, 58
  feigning, 57
  nature of, 55–58
  skill of, 48, 49, 52
  vs. sympathy, 30–31, 58
empathy-altruism hypothesis, 57
empathy continuum, 56, 56f
engage-and-explain phase (PEACE model), 50, 142–45, 143f
England and Wales, 45, 249
  Crown Prosecution Service (CPS), 323
  Police and Criminal Evidence Act 1984 (PACE), 21, 45, 276
  See also College of Policing
environment of the interview, 25–27
epistemic modality, 322–23
epistemic stance, 123–24
epistemic status, defined, 122
ethnolinguistics, 4
exit activities/exit phase of interrogation, 330, 332, 333

false confessions. *See* confessions: false
false-evidence ploys, 71, 86
false sense of accuracy, 330, 343, 346
false vs. true statements, differentiating, 44
first-person viewpoint/first-person perspective, 287–92, 335–37, 341, 343, 347
Fitzgerald, Richard, 172
"fixing" the facts. *See* "Are you saying X?"; "Kidnapping" case
flexibility and adaptability, 44, 48, 52, 252
footing, 115
fore- and backgrounding of information by judges, 350–53, 361–62
foreign language speakers
  "Guidelines for Communicating Rights to Non-Native Speakers of English in Australia, England, and Wales, and the USA," 244–45
  Miranda warning, 228–44
  See also bilinguals, trained interpreters vs. untrained; interpreters
forensic linguistics (FL), 1
formulations, 273–74, 331
  defined, 252
free narrative, 47, 179, 277

Garrett, Brandon, 119
gestural beats, 284. *See also* beating hand gestures
gestural viewpoints, 275
gesture categories, 273, 275, 292. *See also* deictic pointing; iconic gestures
gestures, 268–71, 273, 278, 284–93
  anatomy of, 275
  and bodily interaction, 274–76
  dialectic between speech and, 292
  doing things with words, objects, and, 279–91
  nature of, 274–75
  See also iconic gestures
gesture sequences, 285, 286, 292

"good" cop, playing, 172
Goodwin, Charles, 276–77
guilt-presumptive interrogation phase, 88. *See also* interrogation phase
guilt-presumptive strategies, 81. *See also* interrogation, police: examining the blueprint of a; Reid technique

Haworth, Kate, 3
held gestures, 275, 284
Heritage, John, 2
heroin possession with intent to sell or deliver, 2015 case of, 242–44
Heydon, Georgina, 250
homosexuality, 161, 164. *See also* sex, illegal solicitation of
hostility, 55
"how come format," 35–36, 39
human information gathering (HIG), 59
Hurren, Emily, 44

iconic actions, 287, 288, 290, 291
iconic gestures ("images of concrete entities"), 275, 284, 286–90, 292
identities (membership categorization analysis), 159. *See also* police-detainee interview
immediacy principle, 349
implausibility, implying, 32, 33, 280
imprudence, implied, 32–33, 39
Inbau, Fred E., 90
inconsistencies
  Achieving Best Evidence in Criminal Proceedings (*ABE*) and, 31–34
  challenging and probing, 31–34, 37, 188–90
  presenting and exploring, 31
  in the testimony of sex crime victims, 33–34, 37, 265
  See also contradictions and contradictory evidence
indirect (reported) speech, 350–52, 362
indirect perspectives (IP), 350–51, 354–57
  alternating direct perspectives (DP) and, 359–61
  See also indirect reporting strategies
indirect reporting strategies, 350–57, 362. *See also* indirect perspectives
indirect reports, 360–62
inequivalences of knowledge between interactants, 2–3
inference-rich membership categorization devices, 159–60
information gathering section of interview, 201, 333
"innocence off the table," taking, 66, 81
Innocence Project, 85, 118–19
institutional discourse, defining, 3
intellectual disabilities (ID), 22–23, 36, 38
  defined, 22
  See also learning disabilities
interlinear gestures, 288–89
interpreted interview structure, 202–3
interpreter protocols, 204–5
  turn control and, 216
interpreters, 200–201, 205–6
  code of ethics/contract, 202, 206t, 210–13
  as coordinators of turns, 203–4
  implicit coordination vs. explicit coordination/non-renditions, 203
  ethical obligation to interpret everything, 213, 214, 218
  managing utterances addressed to, 217–23
  roles, 201
  See also bilinguals, trained interpreters vs. untrained
interrogation, police
  examining the blueprint of a, 68–81
  phases/sections in, 179, 201, 277, 330–33 (*see also* PEACE model: phases; *and specific phases*)
  See also interview(s); police-detainee interview; *and specific topics*
interrogation phase, 88, 103, 132
  purpose, 103
  See also social-interrogation phase
interviewer behavior, a major change in, 46
interviewing, investigative
  purpose of, 46
  skills and tactics associated with good/effective, 43–44, 49–53
  See also specific topics
interview records. *See* police record(s)
interview(s), police
  discourse of, 1–2
  framing the, 2–7
  participant roles in, 201–2
  See also interrogation, police; police-detainee interview; *and specific topics*

Jayne, Brian C., 90
Johnson, Alison, 253
judges
 in Netherlands, 349
 neutral position, 350, 352–53
 tasks of, 115, 306, 349–50
  reporting suspect's story to the court, 349–50
  summarizing, 349, 350, 354–59, 362
 See also indirect perspectives; indirect reporting strategies

Kassin, Saul, 86, 89, 117
Kebbell, Mark, 44
"Kidnapping" case, 271–73, 278–84, 291, 293
King, Rodney, 277
knowledge, inequivalences of, 2–3
Komter, Martha, 301–3

language
 of institutions, 2–3
 and the law, 1
 See also foreign language speakers; linguists; metalanguage
language alternation. *See* code switching
lawyer-client interviews, 301. *See also* counsel
learning disabilities, 23–25, 38. *See also* intellectual disabilities
legislation, 21, 24. *See also* Police and Criminal Evidence Act 1984
legitimation, 316
 transmodal metalanguage as, 316–23
Leo, Richard, 43, 86
lexical checking, 311–16
lexical choices, 313–16
 justifying, 316–23
Linell, Per, 2–3
linguists, 227, 242–44
 defense, 231, 239–41
 prosecution, 230–31, 237
Luckmann, Thomas, 2–3

Maschler, Yael, 6
maximization, 86–89
 in behavioral sciences literature, 86, 87
 overview and nature of, 86
Maynard, Douglas, 3
Mazerolle, Paul, 44
McNall, Karlyn, 86
McNeill, David, 275
meaning making, 6, 208, 275
members (membership categorization analysis), 159
membership categorization analysis (MCA), 158–60, 172, 173
membership categorization devices, 159
Méndez, Juan E., 60–61
metadiscourse, 251, 304. *See also* reflexive language
metadiscursive expressions, 270
metalanguage, 6, 303–7
 definitions, meanings, and scope of the term, 6, 303–4
 examples of explicit, 309–23
 function of, 6
 transmodal sequences and, 308
 writing, 6
 See also metalinguistics
metalanguaging, 6
metalinguistic comments, 320, 321
metalinguistic legitimation, transmodal, 318. *See also* transmodal metalanguage: as legitimation
metalinguistics, 291, 304–6, 310–12, 314–17
 defined, 304
 See also metalanguage
metaphoric gestures ("images of the abstract"), 275
metatalk, 306–7, 311
minimization
 in behavioral sciences literature, 85–87
 in interrogations, 71, 74, 77–81, 89, 101, 106, 107
 See also blame mitigation
Miranda rights
 understanding one's, 125, 229 (*see also* Miranda warning: and non-native speakers of English)
 waiving, 230, 240, 242, 243
Miranda v. Arizona, 115, 228
Miranda warning, 69–70, 81, 228
 elements that must be included in, 229
 in Jones case, 67, 68
 and non-native speakers of English, 228–29, 242–44
  cases, 230–43
 in Smith case, 68, 69
motivational interviewing, 43
multimodal analysis, 5, 270, 277, 278
multimodal cues, 5

multimodality, 5, 270, 280, 283, 288, 291, 292
multimodal transcription, 277, 278, 284, 292
murder cases, 130
  2012 attempted first-degree murder case in Tennessee, 239–42
  "AttMurder," 278, 279, 284–91
  Smith case, 67–69, 71–79
  Tennessee murder case (2000), 230–39
  See also Truong interrogation

narrative construction, 6, 156
  turn-taking and, 180–85
narrative-construction processes, 179, 180, 196–97
narrative-construction strategies, 197
narrative fore- and backgrounding of information by judges, 350–53, 361–62
narratives
  defined, 114, 127
  storytelling and, 114–16 (*see also* storytelling)
  See also confession narratives
narrative termination, 120
neighbors, disputes between, 300
Netherlands
  criminal trials in, 332, 349, 361 (*see also* fore- and backgrounding of information by judges; indirect perspectives; judges: tasks of)
    organization of, 354
  interrogations in, 331, 337
  police record styles in, 329–30, 332–34 (*see also* police record styles)
neutrality, 30–34, 136, 331. *See also under* judges
Newfield, Denise, 307–8
noncooperation, PEACE-fully overcoming, 50–51
Norfolk Four, 130

objects, doing things with. *See under* gestures
Olson, David, 6
opening approaches, 210
opening engage-and-explain phase. *See* engage-and-explain phase
opening phase of interview, 161, 201, 252, 333. *See also* engage-and-explain phase; transmodal metalanguage: as framing
opening sequence, 161
open-mindedness, 44, 46, 48
open questions/open-ended questions, 44, 49, 51, 142, 146, 329
oral proficiency interview (OPI), 239
ownership, story, 117, 124, 128–30, 250
"own words," suspect's
  allowing or instructing suspect to tell story in, 250, 291
  confession narratives made in, 126
  in-your-own-words requirement, 245
  police records written down in, 12, 361
  retelling the negotiated story in, 128
  suspect writing down what happened in, 130
  See also first-person viewpoint/first-person perspective; free narrative; reflexive language

participation frameworks, 115, 179, 201, 252
  defined, 115
patience, 51, 52
PEACE model (of police interviewing), 25, 26f, 31, 34, 58–61, 65–66, 140, 153
  effectiveness, 49–51
  effectiveness of rapport in PEACE interviews, 49–50
  a major change in interviewer behavior, 46
  overcoming denials and noncooperation PEACE-fully, 50–51
  overview, 26f, 46–47, 136
  phases
    Account, Clarification, and Challenge, 25, 26f, 31, 34, 141, 145–47
    Closure, 141, 147
    Engage and Explain, 50, 142–45, 143f
    Preparation and Planning, 26f, 137, 145
  Reid and, 82, 118
  studies of, 48–49
Pennycook, Alastair, 307–8
Police and Criminal Evidence Act 1984 (PACE), 21, 45, 276
police caution, 332, 333, 337. *See also* Miranda warning

police-detainee interview, using identities in a, 161–72
  deploying categories to support competing versions of events, 162, 172–73
    accusing and denying using category-implicative predicates, 169–70
    deploying categories in accounts and denials, 162–64
    invoking a category as an account, 167–69
    invoking an institutional identity to reject an account and support an accusation, 170–72
    projecting and claiming positive moral categories to elicit a confession, 156–57, 164–67
police interrogation. *See* interrogation, police
police interview records. *See* police record(s)
police interviews. *See* interview(s), police; police-detainee interview
police record(s), 329
  in judicial context, 276–77
  from police interrogation to, 330–34
  writing up, 329–30
police record styles, 334–35
  constructing stories in different styles, 337–46
    monologue style, 335, 337–40
    question-and-answer style, 336–37, 344–46
    recontextualized style, 335–36, 340–43
  verbatim transcript, 337
police reports, 5–7
  institutional implications, 5–7
  nature of, 6
Pomerantz, Anita, 123
practice codes. *See* codes of practice
pre-opening (phase of interview), 202
preparation (gestures), 275
Preparation and Planning. *See under* PEACE model: phases
preparatory stage of interrogation, 71
preservation (of selected aspects of work), formulation and, 274
presumption of guilt. *See* guilt-presumptive strategies
production media, 273
proof, constructing, 2
protective order application interviews, 301
provocation, 98, 99
  the accumulative construction of, 90
provoked actions, 89, 90

question-and-answer style (police records), 336–37, 344–46
Question-Answer-Typing (QAT) structure, 301–2
Question-Answer-Writing (QAW) structure, 302
questioning, empathic vs. forensic, 31–38
questioning strategies, 185–88
questions
  confirmation-seeking, 256
  See also clarifying questions; closed questions/closed-ended questions; open questions/open-ended questions

rape, 250, 256, 261, 264
  "appropriate" resistance and "utmost resistance" standard for convicting of, 261
  See also rape cases: Jones; sexual violence
rape cases, 30, 35–38, 257–60, 263
  Jones, 67–69, 75–80
rape-supportive culture, 250–51
rape victims, 252, 257
  cross-examination, 265
  See also under inconsistencies
rapport, 48, 61
  definitions, 53–55
  effectiveness in PEACE interviews, 49–50
  nature of, 53–55
rapport building, 39, 50, 52, 60
  vs. being impartial, 27–31
  missed opportunities for, 49
  reasons for, 28
reactance, psychological, 44
reconstruction of narrative events. *See* narrative construction
recontextualization phrase, 336
recontextualized style, 335–36, 340–43
recording(s) of interrogations, 45
  absence/lack of, 331, 337
  audio-recorded interviews, 269, 270, 276–77

recording(s) of interrogations (*continued*)
audio recording, 45, 67, 68, 152–53, 276, 293, 293n1, 294n4, 331, 337
transcription of, 269, 276–77, 337
video-recorded interviews, 249, 251, 270, 276–77
video recording, 47, 117, 118, 270, 276–78, 293, 293n1, 294n4, 331, 337
Record of Taped Interview (ROTI), 276, 292
recycling of information, 180
reflexive language, 263–64, 303–7
participation frameworks and, 251–54
and threats to authorship, 258–63
See also metadiscourse
Reid, John E., 90
Reid technique, 76, 80, 107, 127
appeals to self-interest with and without a time-limited offer, 71, 74–77
and confessions, 71, 74, 80, 86
as guilt-presumptive, 8, 107
origin, 66
steps in, 70–71
strategies and techniques used in, 66–68, 71, 74, 80, 81, 86–88, 105
reliances, 270
replaying prior interaction, 5, 273
reported speech (RS), 5
resistance strategies
contest, 193–96
correction, 192–93
"Rights sheet," 240, 241
Russell, Sonia, 180

Sacks, Harvey, 158, 159
Sanford, Davontae, 130
self-interest. *See* appeals-to-self-interest strategy
separateness
vs. connectedness, 72, 74
defined, 72
between suspect and police, 81
between suspects and law-abiding individuals, 72, 77
sex, illegal solicitation of, 157, 159
cases of, 160–72
sex crimes, 33–34
provocation and, 90
sex offenders
interviews of, 44, 57–58
patterns of cooperation between interviewers and suspected, 139–42
account, clarify, and challenge phase, 145–47
closure phase, 147
engage-and-explain phase, 142–45
passing the floor, 151–53
role of second interviewer, 148–50
sexual abuse
of children, 57–58
of elderly, 126
sexual assault of a minor, 34–35, 148–50
sexual assault victims
with intellectual disabilities, 22, 36, 38
See also rape victims
"sexual deviant," accusing suspect of being a, 126–27, 159, 160
sexual violence
attitudes toward, 250–51, 262
norms of discourse around, 264
See also rape
Shuy, Roger, 107, 119
social-interrogation phase, 333, 335, 343
social phase of interrogation, 330–35, 343, 346
social talk (phase of interrogation), 332–34
specialist interviews, 48, 147
speech acts, 69, 70
spontaneous actions, 89–90
storytelling, 114, 115, 122–23, 125–28
activating mechanisms and initiation of the process of, 121
as central to the law, 115–16
collaboration and contamination in, 6, 114, 115, 117, 120, 122–23, 125–27, 132
completion of, 120
confessions and, 113–17, 126, 128, 131, 132
interrogations as invitations for, 117
overview and nature of, 115
police reports as type of police-directed, 6
summarized versions of interview records, 270, 331–32, 334, 340, 346
material omitted from, 339–40
See also Record of Taped Interview
summarizing
by judges, 349, 350, 354–59, 362
See also closure phase; formulations

summary statements, 238–39, 252–53
sympathy (used in interrogations), 77–82
  and confessions, 78, 81
  vs. empathy, 30–31, 58

Tebble, Helen, 203–5
"tell me in your own words," 250, 291. *See also* "own words," suspect's
Tennessee, 2012 attempted first-degree murder case in, 239–42
Tennessee murder case (2000), 230–39
Terrorism Act 2000, 293n1
theme development
  defined, 89
  minimization and, 89
"third degree," 66
Thornborrow, Joanna, 3
time-limited offers, 71, 74–77
transcription, 269, 276, 277, 337
  politics of, 276–77
  of recordings of interrogations, 269, 276–77, 337
  See also multimodal transcription
transformation, formulation and, 274
transforming texts in legal context, 300–303
transmodality, 307–8, 324
  defined, 307
transmodal metalanguage, 324
  as elicitation, 311–16
  as framing, 309–11
  functions, 324, 325t
  as legitimation, 316–23
transmodal remaking, 308
transmodal representational practices, 307
transmodal sequences, 307–8
Trinch, Shonna, 306
Truong interrogation, 87–89, 106–7
  the discourse structure of blame mitigation, 89–90, 106–7
    the accumulative construction of provocation, 90
    the accumulative construction of responsibility, 101–6
    the accumulative construction of spontaneity, 97–101
    assembling the accumulated provoking factors leading to victim's death, 95–97
    establishing inevitability and accident, 97–100
    establishing the burden of responsibility for child care, 91–92
    examining Truong's reactions to unfair treatment, 92–95
    positing loss of control as cause for the accident, 100–101
    proposing a dysfunctional homelife, 102–3
    proposing a dysfunctional mother-daughter relationship, 101–2
    securing a progressive admission of responsibility, 103–6
  maximization techniques employed in, 88
  minimization techniques employed in, 88–89
turn-taking, 143–44, 180–85, 197, 209f

van Charldrop, Tessa (T. C.), 301–2
Vanderhallen, Miet, 55
verbum dicendi, 357
Vervaeke, Geert, 55
video, witnesses giving their evidence on, 276
video-recorded interviews. *See* recording(s) of interrogations

Walsh, Dave, 49–51
Warren, Earl, 115
"why didn't you do that?," 37–38
Williamson, Tom, 43, 46
witnesses
  giving their evidence on video, 276
  interviews with, 301 (*see also specific topics*)
words, doing things with. *See under* gestures
wrongful convictions, 85. *See also* confessions: false